Origins of American Political Parties, 1789–1803

Origins of AMERICAN POLITICAL PARTIES 1789-1803

John F. Hoadley

THE UNIVERSITY PRESS OF KENTUCKY

Copyright © 1986 by The University Press of Kentucky

Scholarly publisher for the Commonwealth, serving Bellarmine College, Berea College, Centre College of Kentucky, Eastern Kentucky University, The Filson Club, Georgetown College, Kentucky Historical Society, Kentucky State University, Morehead State University, Murray State University, Northern Kentucky University, Transylvania University, University of Kentucky, University of Louisville, and Western Kentucky University.

Editorial and Sales Offices: Lexington, Kentucky 40506-0024

Library of Congress Cataloging-in-Publication Data
Hoadley, John F., 1951–
   Origins of American political parties, 1789–1803.

   Bibliography: p.
   Includes index.
   1. Political parties—United States—History.
2. United States—Politics and government—Constitutional period, 1789–1809. 3. United States. Congress—History.
I. Title.
JK2260.H63   1986   324.273′09   85-15787

ISBN: 978-0-8131-5320-9

Contents

List of Tables   vii

List of Figures   ix

Acknowledgments   xi

Introduction   3

1. The Concept of Party   8
2. The Historical Tradition   20
3. The Development of Electoral Institutions   32
4. Party Institutions in Congress   47
5. Spatial Analysis of Party Development   60
6. Factionalism in the Early Years, 1789-1793   86
7. Polarization and Party Politics, 1793-1797   118
8. Partisan Competition in Congress, 1797-1803   141
9. Political Parties in Eighteenth-Century America   171

Appendix A. Party Affiliation of Members of Congress   192

Appendix B. Representing Individual Roll Calls in Spatial Configurations   220

Notes   235

Bibliography   244

Index   253

Tables

1. Quality of Fit between Agreement Scores and Spatial Configurations   76
2. Cluster Analysis—Two-Cluster Solutions   81
3. Cluster Analysis—Size of Clusters   84
4. Classification of Roll Calls, House of Representatives   88
5. Issue Scales in the First Congress   89
6. Key Votes—First Congress (1789-1791)   97
7. Regional Voting on Locating the Capital   105
8. Factions in the First House   106
9. Key Votes—Second Congress (1791-1793)   114
10. Geographical Distribution of Party Voting Blocs, Third and Fourth Houses   126
11. Key Votes—Third Congress (1793-1795)   132
12. Key Votes—Fourth Congress (1795-1797)   134
13. Regional Distribution of Electoral Votes, 1796   142
14. Partisan and Regional Distribution of Voting Blocs   145
15. Classification of Issues, Fifth House   148
16. Dissent from Party Voting Blocs, Fifth House   149
17. Regional Distribution of Electoral Votes, 1800   162
18. Partisan and Regional Distribution of Voting Blocs, Seventh House   168
19. Distribution of Congressmen in the MDS Space: An Analysis of Variance   179
20. Party Labels in the *Biographical Directory*   193
21. Party Labels in the ICPSR File   194
22. Comparisons of Party Labels   196
23. Partisan Composition of Congress   198
24. Party Affiliations of House Members, 1789-1803   199
25. Party Affiliations of Senators, 1789-1803   215
26. Results of Regression Analysis   228
27. Results of Discriminant Analysis   232
28. Comparisons among Analytic Methods   233

Figures

1. Spatial Configuration, First Congress, House, 1789-1791 62
2. Spatial Configuration, First Congress, Senate, 1789-1791 63
3. Spatial Configuration, Second Congress, House, 1791-1793 64
4. Spatial Configuration, Second Congress, Senate, 1791-1793 65
5. Spatial Configuration, Third Congress, House, 1793-1795 66
6. Spatial Configuration, Third Congress, Senate, 1793-1795 67
7. Spatial Configuration, Fourth Congress, House, 1795-1797 68
8. Spatial Configuration, Fourth Congress, Senate, 1795-1797 69
9. Spatial Configuration, Fifth Congress, House, 1797-1799 70
10. Spatial Configuration, Fifth Congress, Senate, 1797-1799 71
11. Spatial Configuration, Sixth Congress, House, 1799-1801 72
12. Spatial Configuration, Sixth Congress, Senate, 1799-1801 73
13. Spatial Configuration, Seventh Congress, House, 1801-1803 74
14. Spatial Configuration, Seventh Congress, Senate, 1801-1803 75
15. Declining Levels of Stress 78
16. Indices of Partisanship, House and Senate, 1789-1803 82
17. Spatial Configuration, First Congress, House, 1789-1791 90
18. Spatial Configuration, First Congress, Senate, 1789-1791 92
19. Spatial Configuration, First Congress, Senate, 1789-1791 (Two Dimensions) 94
20. Spatial Configuration, First Congress, House, 1789-1791—All Issue Areas 95
21. Spatial Configuration, First Congress, House, 1789-1791—National Authority 100
22. Spatial Configuration, First Congress, House, 1789-1791—Domestic Economics 102
23. Spatial Configuration, First Congress, House, 1789-1791—Location of the Capital 104
24. Spatial Configuration, Second Congress, Senate, 1791-1793 110
25. Spatial Configuration, Second Congress, House, 1791-1793 111
26. Spatial Configuration, Second Congress, House, 1791-1793—All Issue Areas 112
27. Spatial Configuration, Third Congress, House, 1793-1795 120
28. Spatial Configuration, Third Congress, Senate, 1793-1795 121

29. Spatial Configuration, Fourth Congress, House, 1795-1797   122
30. Spatial Configuration, Fourth Congress, Senate, 1795-1797   123
31. Spatial Configuration, Third Congress, House, 1793-1795—
    All Issue Areas   128
32. Spatial Configuration, Fourth Congress, House, 1795-1797—
    All Issue Areas   129
33. Spatial Configuration, Fifth Congress, House, 1797-1799   146
34. Spatial Configuration, Sixth Congress, House, 1799-1801   147
35. Spatial Configuration, Fifth Congress, Senate, 1797-1799   150
36. Spatial Configuration, Sixth Congress, Senate, 1799-1801   151
37. Spatial Configuration, Seventh Congress, House,
    1801-1803   166
38. Spatial Configuration, Seventh Congress, Senate,
    1801-1803   167
39. Vectors in a Multidimensional Scaling Space   222
40. Regression with a Dichotomous Dependent Variable   223
41. Primary Method for Ties   224
42. Discriminant Analysis with Different Priors   226
43. Discriminant Analysis with Equal and Unequal
    Covariance Matrices   226
44. Spatial Configuration, First Congress, House, 1789-1791—
    Party Variable   229
45. Spatial Configuration, First Congress, House, 1789-1791—
    Assumption Roll Call   230
46. Spatial Configuration, First Congress, House, 1789-1791—
    National Bank Roll Call   231

Acknowledgments

No book, even though it is the end product of solitary research and writing on the part of the author, is ever completed without the substantial help of many good friends and colleagues. I owe a large debt of gratitude to many people, without whose help this project might never have appeared between covers.

For their valuable advice and counsel, in official and unofficial capacities, I would like to offer my sincere appreciation to my graduate advisers: Bill Keech, Duncan MacRae, George Rabinowitz, Dick Richardson, and the late Frank Munger.

For their assistance, advice, and friendship, I would like to thank several colleagues: Whit Ayres, Ed Crowe, Nelson Dometrius, Robin Dorff, Peter Galderisi, Jim Gogan, Bill Gormley, Scott Keeter, Arlon Kemple, Allan Kornberg, Peter Lange, Don Searing, David Whiteman, Harry Wray, and Forrest Young.

Certain portions of this book have been adapted from my article "The Emergence of Political Parties in Congress, 1789-1803," *American Political Science Review*, 74, no. 3 (September 1980): 757-79. I appreciate the permission of the American Political Science Association to reprint this material.

For their help with computer programs, data acquisition, and related matters, I wish to express thanks to Sue Dodd, Ken Hardy, and the staff of the Institute of Research in Social Science at the University of North Carolina, Chapel Hill.

In addition, I want to acknowledge the necessary help of the Historical Archive of the Inter-University Consortium for Political and Social Research, for the use of roll call data. They bear no responsibility for the analyses or interpretations presented here.

For institutional support, financial and otherwise, I want to thank the Departments of Political Science at the University of North Carolina and at Duke University. In particular, the University Research Council at Duke provided financial support that was valuable in producing the figures used in this book.

Finally, several people must be singled out for very special thanks:

Mike Kalt and Brenda Cannon Kalt provided substantive assistance, computer help, and social support above and beyond the call of duty. To them, I offer my sincere appreciation.

George Rabinowitz introduced me to dimensional analysis, gave me vital help with computer programs, and provided needed criticism at the crucial early stages of the project. To him, I offer special thanks.

My wife, Beth Fuchs, provided inspiration and criticism and many hours of eitorial and substantive help, as well as love, patience, and support from the beginning to the end. To Beth, I offer my love and appreciation.

Last, my parents—Frank and Margaret Hoadley—inspired in me a dedication to learning and an appreciation for good writing. To them, I offer a special and heartfelt thanks.

Origins of American
Political Parties, 1789–1803

Introduction

In this book I explore the fundamental question of when and why political parties first appeared in the United States. The development of parties is examined for the period between 1789, the first year of the new government under the Constitution, and 1803, the year directly following the first transition of government from one party to another. This period, traditionally considered to be the time of the first party system, is of particular interest, because a process of party development was triggered by the actions of individuals who themselves did not believe parties could be a positive force in a governmental system. It was also a critical period of national development, when the United States was trying to establish itself as a newly independent nation under a democratic form of government, a form generally untested at that time.

Research on Party Development

Historians have differed considerably in their assessment of the development of American political parties during the final decade of the eighteenth century. The date of the emergence of parties has been placed anywhere from the first years of the new government to a time in the 1830s when the Whigs and the Jacksonian Democrats were competing for power.

According to one traditional interpretation of American party development, political parties existed from the beginning of the national government. Beard (1915) has found clear evidence of partisan behavior beginning in the First Congress, based on the economic interests of members. He also argues that these parties represented the same groups that had divided over the Constitution. Yet, as Risjord (1978, pp. 519-21) makes clear, Beard's thesis has lost favor among historians. At best, Risjord argues, there is only partial continuity between the constitutional factions and the parties that dominated the later years of the decade.

Ryan (1971) uses a different approach (cluster analysis of congressional votes) to conclude that there is evidence of parties as early as the First Congress. She relates this early partisanship to the divisions caused by Hamilton's fiscal programs. Henderson (1973), in critiquing Ryan's paper, suggests that alignments in the First Congress could better be described as sectional groups. He places the emergence of parties at about the time of the Third Congress.

Several scholars have cited the Jay Treaty as the issue that led to the open appearance of parties, thus placing the date at about 1795. Charles (1961) looks at simple measures of party voting in Congress to reach this conclusion, while Bell (1973) uses a more complex type of roll call analysis to reach a similar conclusion. Cunningham (1957) has searched contemporary newspapers and correspondence for evidence of party leadership and organization in the Republican party. Chambers (1963b) considers a variety of evidence in asserting that the Federalists were a party as early as 1792, while the Republicans could be seen as a party by about 1794. McCormick (1966), while assessing the same crucial time period, emphasizes political institutions and divisions among political leaders, rather than issues, as the key elements in party formation.

Some have pointed to events and issues during the Adams administration as crucial in the emergence of parties. Libby (1912) cites the Alien and Sedition Acts as the first clear sign of the existence of parties. His survey of legislative records for earlier years leads him to conclude that voting was not sufficiently polarized before 1797 to be labeled as party voting. Dauer (1953) has investigated the economic and cultural background of the partisan divisions from 1794 to 1802, focusing mainly on the Adams wing of the Federalist party. He seems to place the date of party emergence at 1797-98, with the passage of the Alien and Sedition Acts.

Other party historians have made an argument that true parties did not exist in this early period and have placed the date of party emergence after 1830. Hofstadter (1969), while not speaking directly about the dates of party development, shows that the idea of party was not readily accepted until the Jacksonian era. Nichols (1967), after tracing the roots of party back as far as the Middle Ages, claims that no parties existed until the emergence of the Whigs. In a critical review of the literature on early political parties, Formisano (1974, 1981) denies that the groups of the 1790s were parties or at least claims that no "party system" existed. The partylike voting patterns in Congress were not sufficiently accompanied by party organization and a party electorate to meet his definitional criteria. According to Formisano (1981, pp. 34-35), historians "have been misled by the bitter partisan invective of the time and have confused partisan emotion—passionate to be sure—with party structure."

Formisano's case is a strong one, yet it appears to contradict the central thesis of this book. While differences exist between the two studies, I propose that they are mostly in emphasis and interpretation. In fact, my position is probably close to the argument (Formisano, 1981) that parties existed but that a party system did not. The case is something like the metaphor of the half-full or half-empty glass. Formisano wants to remind us of the lack of full development of parties. I prefer to point to the antiparty attitudes and the underdeveloped political institutions and to emphasize the remarkable level of partisan development achieved in only a few years.

Some studies of American party development (Bell, 1973; Ryan, 1971) have looked exclusively at patterns of voting in the Congress or at the emergence of party competition in elections for president. Others (Cunningham, 1957, 1978*b*; Formisano, 1974, 1981) have chosen to consider different aspects of party, such as the development of party leadership and organization, the emergence of state and local parties, and the penetration of partisanship to the level of the general voting public. Some differences in the conclusions reached in these studies have resulted from varying definitions of the idea of party. Others have resulted from contrasting evaluations of the available empirical evidence. By attempting to establish a clear conceptual view of party and by employing a new methodological approach, I hope to provide some conclusions regarding party development that will help to remove the confusion in the literature.

At a broader level, the importance of this study of political party development can be demonstrated from the perspective of democratic theory. Dahl (1966), among others, has delineated three essential characteristics of any democratic polity: (1) the right of public participation in the determination of public policy, (2) the right of representation, and (3) the right of organized opposition to those who govern. Political parties have often played an essential role in the evolution of each of these characteristics.

In the United States, the principle of participation in elections was established in the Constitution, although in a rather limited form. The appearance of parties had the effect of broadening that right, in part by providing a means to circumvent the antidemocratic nature of the Electoral College. The importance of party development to an emerging democracy is even more evident with regard to the rights of representation and organized opposition. Without parties, the linkage between the public and those who govern was tenuous at best. Parties gradually provided a means for making that linkage much stronger. People could elect their representatives as members of a particular party with some assurance that their interests would be represented in the decision-making process.

Finally, the right of organized opposition is of special importance, because most early political leaders shared an antiparty tradition rooted in a norm favoring unanimity. The emergence of parties led by those same individuals was essential to the growing acceptance of the idea of legitimate opposition within the American political system. In particular, the presence of a strong and independent opposition party in Congress provided a means for acceptable dissent from programs initiated by the executive branch.

An Overview

A number of different background elements must be considered before a detailed analysis is made of the events surrounding the appearance of an opposition party in the United States Congress. These discussions are informative on their own, but they are particularly helpful in establishing the context in which early parties emerged. First, in chapter 1, I consider uses of the term *party* both in history and in modern political science. It is important to understand what is meant by this concept and to make clear distinctions between *party* and competing terms such as *faction*. From these considerations emerge a conceptualization of party and a view of party development that guide the research in this book. In addition, the antiparty tradition that dominated the thinking of America's first generation of political leaders provides a vital backdrop to their partisan activities.

The historical tradition is dealt with in chapter 2; specifically, I place the development of American parties in the context of events in both England and colonial America prior to 1789. It is critical to know what historical precedents were available to the political leaders of the 1790s, for these examples guided them in their actions and their attitudes toward parties. The absence of an extended history of parties made the quick appearance of partisan voting patterns even more remarkable.

Further historical background is provided in chapters 3 and 4, where I explore the nature of political institutions by the end of the eighteenth century. Since events do not take place in a vacuum, it is crucial to understand the manner in which elections were held as well as the state of development of the national legislature. The operation of these institutions has obvious implications for the manner and pace of party development; in fact, the question of whether parties actually appeared by 1800 must be answered within the context of how developed the political institutions of that era were. Only with this knowledge can we proceed to an informed discussion of events in the 1790s.

An overview of this period of party development is presented in chapter 5, with the central empirical analysis of partisan voting in Congress. Here I use a variety of methods—multidimensional scaling, cluster analysis, and indices of party voting—to demonstrate the process of polarization that was taking place in the Congress. In addition, a brief discussion of the use and interpretation of the various analytical methods is provided.

This general picture of party emergence is highlighted in substantial detail in the three chapters that follow. In chapter 6, I examine the early factional patterns that were prevalent in the First Congress, with special attention to the sectionalism that provided a basis for these factions. Sectionalism was then and continued to be one of the most salient political divisions. In chapter 7, I explore the transition from factions to parties so clearly evident in the patterns of congressional voting from 1793 to 1797. During these years, culminating with the Jay Treaty debate, the factions became polarized into voting blocs that are best described as parties. In chapter 8, I discuss Congress in the more partisan years from 1797 to 1803, with special concern for the broadening electoral base of the new parties.

For each period, attention is directed to the elections where members were chosen for each new Congress, to the agenda of issues that helped to shape the emerging parties, to the regional variations in the process of party development, and to the behavior of certain key members of Congress whose behavior symbolized the events of this period and whose leadership helped to shape these events.

Finally, in the concluding chapter, I return to the fundamental question that underlies this research: when and why parties appeared in the United States. Various explanations for the emerging partisanship are considered, as is the possibility that the polarization of voting could be better explained by common ties of region or boardinghouse.

In the end, the conclusion is unequivocal. The period from 1789 to 1803 witnessed dramatic events that can only be adequately described as a process of party development, a process that was remarkable for its swift appearance during an era when the idea of parties was greatly feared.

1. The Concept of Party

The concept of party is central to the goals of the present research. In order to trace the development of American political parties, it is first necessary to reach a satisfactory definition of a political party. Otherwise, the question of when parties first appeared becomes lost in a plethora of differing definitions. In this regard, it is important to distinguish carefully between the concepts of party and faction.

In this chapter, there are several principal goals. First, I establish the meaning of party and faction at the time of the Constitution. This is important for an understanding of party development in the face of the antiparty philosophical tradition that prevailed at the time. This tradition, which had a great effect on the course of party development, is explored with special attention to its roots in the philosophical thinking of eighteenth-century Europe. Second, I examine several attempts by political scientists and historians to establish reasonable definitions of *party* and *faction*. The lack of consensus in this regard helps to explain the disagreements concerning the course of American party development. Finally, I present a view of the concepts of party and faction that serves to guide the research and conclusions about party development.

The Concept of Party before 1789

The word *faction* has a longer history (at least in a political context) than does the word *party*. The etymology of the two words is the first step in understanding the differences between the concepts. *Faction* comes from Latin roots conveying the idea of "excessive, ruthless, and thereby harmful behavior." *Party*, on the other hand, has historically shared at least two different ideas; these are reflected in the English words *partition* and *partaking*. In any case, *party* would seem to have a "less negative connotation" while sharing a fairly similar usage by the seventeenth and eighteenth centuries.[1]

The eighteenth-century understanding of these words is illustrated by their definitions in Samuel Johnson's well-known *Dictionary of the English Language*, published in 1755:

Party: (1) A number of persons confederated by similarity of designs or opinions in opposition to others; a faction.
Faction: (1) A party in a state. (2) Tumult, discord, dissention. [quoted in Olson, 1973, p. v]

It is clear from these definitions that the words were synonyms, but that *faction* had a more negative connotation.

At the time of the Constitutional Convention, a clear distinction between the two terms had not yet been realized. According to eighteenth-century usage, *faction* (for which the word *party* was often substituted) usually referred to a group involved in the political arena but working toward private ends. *Party*, on the other hand, was "a new name for a new thing" (Sartori, 1976, p. 64). During its evolution in the seventeenth and eighteenth centuries, the word *party* had gradually acquired a more distinct and positive meaning than *faction*. That this distinction was not commonly recognized in 1789 is illustrated by the writings of James Madison in *The Federalist*, where he cautioned against both the "violence of faction" and the "rage of party." Although he was explicit about using these terms interchangeably, he clearly had in mind the old idea of faction and not the new idea of party.[2] Even those writers who attempted to distinguish the two terms failed to establish any clear difference (Hofstadter, 1969; Sartori, 1976).

The Philosophical Tradition

The Anglo-American tradition from which the Founding Fathers could draw at the close of the eighteenth century found little favorable to say about political parties.[3] These antiparty feelings on the part of most political thinkers reflected a concern that parties would become the instruments of special interests, thus preventing the national consensus they considered necessary for good government.

Hofstadter (1969, pp. 16-39), in his survey of the development of the idea of party in early American thinking, has isolated three different schools of thought or "archetypal views of party" represented in British political thought in the eighteenth century.[4] These three traditions then became the dominant themes as American political leaders developed their thoughts on party. The philosophers whose work has defined these three traditions are Henry St. John Bolingbroke, an English politician and writer of pamphlets; David Hume, the Scottish philosopher and essayist; and Edmund Burke, Irish philosopher and leading member of Parliament.

The first school of thought holds that "parties are evils that can be avoided or abolished or suppressed, even if this must be done, paradoxically, through the temporary agency of a party of national unification" (Hofstadter, 1969, pp. 16-17). Such views originated in England with Bolingbroke, a Tory who wrote two important pamphlets on politics between 1733 and 1738. There was some attempt in his writing to distinguish between party and faction, something rarely done at that time. "Governing by party . . . must always end in the government of a faction. . . . Party is a political evil, and faction is the worst of all parties" (quoted in Sartori, 1976, p. 6). Clearly, the difference was simply a matter of degree, for neither idea represented a desirable phenomenon.

The only favorable role Bolingbroke could see for a party was suggested by the country party in Britain, the group that claimed to represent the interests of the whole country in opposition to the monarch. When a court faction (the supporters of the Crown) became too powerful and threatened constitutional rule, a country party could protect the state and restore stability. In so doing it would remove the root of its own existence, restoring the nonpartisan consensus considered ideal at that time.

The next stage in the intellectual history of the political party is depicted in the archetypal view "that though parties are indeed evil, their existence is an unavoidable by-product of a free state, and that they must therefore be endured with patience by all men who esteem liberty" (Hofstadter, 1969, p. 24). Hume is perhaps best known as a philosopher and epistemologist, but he also made significant contributions (in essays written between 1742 and 1752) to the development of attitudes toward party as represented by this view. Compared to Bolingbroke, he saw a more important distinction between party and faction, with this difference including a view of party that is somewhat more positive.

The distinction between party and faction is not entirely explicit in Hume's writing, but he does condemn faction in no uncertain terms: "Factions subvert government, render laws impotent, and beget the fiercest animosities among men of the same nation" (quoted in Sartori, 1976, p. 7). Parties, on the other hand, were viewed as an inevitable consequence of free government. But things are even more complex, for Hume presented a typology of party and faction. Here he distinguished among parties based on interests (factions), those based on principles, and those based on affections. It is those based on principles that can be expected to appear in any free state and that are not so evil as to be abolished.

The third archetypal view represented in eighteenth-century British political thought states that "parties are not only inevitable but necessary and, on balance, good" (Hofstadter, 1969, p. 29). Its principal spokesman, perhaps the only one at that time, was Burke. His thoughts concerning political parties were written in 1770, at which time he had served four years in Parliament affiliated with the Whigs, who had been both in government and in opposition during these years.[5]

Burke left no doubt that he saw faction and party as different entities. Factions were characterized by a "mean and interested struggle for place and emolument" (quoted in Sartori, 1976, p. 9), while his famous definition of *party* denoted a very different thing: "Party is a body of men united, for promoting by their joint endeavours the national interest, upon some particular principle in which they are all agreed" (quoted in Sartori, 1976, p. 9). One can see the link here between Hume and Burke, but this statement is a far more sophisticated and clearer justification for the political party. Parties were far more than a necessary evil; they could become a constructive force in the government, for "groups of men openly linked to each other by conviction and loyalty, and openly subject to judgment by the people, were those most likely to bring good government" (Hofstadter, 1969, p. 31).

Although Burke's view was articulated in 1770, just prior to the establishment of a new nation in America, his favorable opinion of party seemed to have little or no impact on American political thought at that time. In fact, one point of agreement among those who would come to be identified as Federalists or Antifederalists or Republicans was a condemnation of party or faction. Their agreement, however, was not total, for some preferred the strong antiparty position of Bolingbroke while others came from the more moderate tradition of Hume.

Among the former group were two individuals, Hamilton and Ames, who were to become extremely partisan Federalists. Their position, very much like that of Bolingbroke, expressed the fear that factions would destroy the efforts toward creating a strong national government. "Faction in this government will always seek reenforcements from State factions, and these will try, by planting their men here, to make this a State government" (Ames, quoted in Bernhard, 1965, pp. 188-89). This was the reaction of Ames to the increasing importance of Madison's Republicans in the House. Efforts by Hamilton, Ames, and other Federalists to operate in the manner of a party were more justified. Just as Bolingbroke could defend the country party in its attempt to reestablish constitutional rule, the Federalists could defend their actions as attempts to establish national authority prior to a return to nonpartisan unanimity.

From the school of thought represented by Hume came what Hofstadter (1969, p. 29) has called "the dominant philosophical conception of party in early American thought and the central problem of the Jeffersonians as anti-party party-builders." The most forceful spokesman for this point of view was James Madison. Writing in *The Federalist*, No. 10, he makes his negative opinion of party or faction very clear: "By a faction [party] I understand a number of citizens, whether amounting to a majority or a minority of the whole, who are united and activated by some common impulse of passion, or of interest, adverse to the rights of other citizens, or to the permanent and aggregate interests of the community" (Hamilton, Madison, Jay, 1961, p. 78). Yet he admits that parties are the inevitable result of the natural human tendency to differ, and that any attempt to change this would sacrifice liberty, an unacceptable course of events. Thus, in Madison's phrases, the task of "curing the mischiefs of faction" (p. 78) must be "sought in the means of controlling its effects" (p. 80). The chief concern here is the ability of a majority faction, which is not seeking the best interests of an entire nation, to oppress the minority. In a pure democracy (with a small population), the effects of faction may be impossible to control.

But Madison saw a solution within the American Constitution. The principle of representation embodied in the republican form of government, the various levels of government established in a federal system, and the large society made possible in this system all "make it less probable that a majority of the whole will have a common motive to invade the rights of other citizens" or at least "to discover their own strength and to act in unison with each other" (Hamilton, Madison, Jay, 1961, p. 83).

Over the decade that followed the writings of *The Federalist*, Madison's views were modified somewhat as he observed the actual workings of parties. Writing in 1792, he still clung to the view of parties as a necessary evil, but he suggested some hope that parties in competition could work in the public interest. This hint of a positive role for parties may have been partially motivated by a desire to justify his own role as a party leader. His own experience also caused a softening of his earlier view that a majority faction was the most dangerous. Feeling that the Republicans represented a majority, his fears had shifted to the dangers of an ascendant minority faction—the Federalists (Hofstadter, 1969, pp. 80-84).

Even when partisanship became a dominant fact of politics in the years just before the election of 1800, few people made any attempt to adopt Burke's position that parties could be a positive force in government. Robert Goodloe Harper, a South Carolina Federalist, one of the few exceptions, argued that the effects of party were on balance beneficial (Cunningham, 1965, pp. 23-25). But more often the partisan behavior of those years was confirmation of the fears raised by the spirit of party.

The Concept of Opposition

One of the most distinctive characteristics of democratic government is the existence of a legitimate political opposition. Hofstadter has expressed this basic principle as follows: "Free opposition, working through party organization, whether concentrated in a single party or shared by several, is regarded today in most of the Western world to be essential to a representative democracy" (Hofstadter, 1969, pp. 5-6). In a similar way, Dahl (1966) has included the right of organized opposition among the three essential characteristics of any democratic polity.

The concept of opposition is ultimately rooted in very basic human tendencies. The instinct to disagree is one that is not easily repressed. But institutionalized political opposition did not appear until the end of the eighteenth century. While there were some rudimentary attempts at establishing a formal opposition in the Roman world, it was not until the influences of Christianity, of medieval feudalism, and of royal absolutism had subsided that opposition could truly begin to emerge. These institutions were accompanied by absolutist perspectives on the world, where only one interpretation of events was legitimate. Any attempt to introduce alternatives would be suppressed by those in power.

The first form of opposition to enter into the European political systems came in the form of opposition to the Crown by the parliament as a united body. Once the monarch's absolute power was removed, whether by force as in France or by peaceful means as in England, the role of opposition could move to groups within Parliament (Ionescu and de Madariaga, 1968).

Several elements have been posited as being essential to the development of an institutionalized political opposition (Ionescu and de Madariaga, 1968, p. 69). The first is the emergence of an articulate public opinion. It was only with the breakdown of the feudal system and the rise of an independent middle class that it became possible to speak of independent opinion. Then, as increased literacy, communication, and printing expanded the availability of information and as people gained a sense of national identity, public opinion became a viable force. Governments were forced to recognize its importance during the eighteenth century. The second relevant factor is a system of representation based on individuals rather than property. As long as each class (estate) had its own mandated representatives, Parliament could not become the true forum for opposition.

Third, the development of opposition was facilitated by particular parliamentary procedures. The most important of these were the principles of majority rule and minority rights. As long as unanimity was the decision-making rule in a parliamentary body, dissent was eliminated by persuasion or coercion. With the institution of majority rule, "dissent was disassociated from treason or disobedience" (Ionescu and de Madariaga, 1968, p. 51). The final element was the formation of groupings (parties) that were loyal to constitutional rule. As long as one feared that the opposition might overthrow the regime or otherwise threaten constitutional rule, it was only natural to regard such opponents with fear and to attempt to prevent their accession to power. But once a consensus was obtained on a constitution, opposition was clearly restricted to specific policies. With such a consensus, the recognition of legitimate opposition was made far easier.

In certain ways, the development of opposition in the United States differed from its evolution in Europe. In the absence of a monarch, early opposition in the colonies was embedded in the assemblies that had to resist the power of the royal governor. The Revolution easily eliminated this obstacle, placing the people in the role of sovereign. Thus, opposition was regarded as seditious rather than treasonable (Ionescu and de Madariaga, 1968). Madison's views, as expressed in *The Federalist*, are more sympathetic to the idea of opposition than to party. Opposition was inevitable and linked directly to liberty, whereas party was a danger because a unified party in power could abuse its position and neglect the rights of others (Hofstadter, 1969). Opposition rose through the actions of Madison and Jefferson, but it was rarely regarded as legitimate until the peaceful transition of power in 1801 helped to prove the acceptance of constitutional rule.

The Concept of Party in Modern Political Science

At the present time, the distinction between party and faction is much clearer, although more complex, than it was at the time of Madison. The word *faction* now tends to be used in several different contexts. In one, it retains the negative connotations of the old concept. This is illustrated by two definitions found in the 1967 edition of *Webster's Seventh New Collegiate Dictionary* that are not very different from those in Johnson's 1755 dictionary: "(1) a usu. selfish or contentious group: clique; (2) party spirit esp. when marked by dissension." This use of the term has been discussed by Sartori (1976, p. 25), who comments that "faction is always, at least in common parlance, a bad name." While admitting that American political science uses the word differently, he suggests that a negative meaning is firmly attached to use of the word by those in the practice of politics.

To an American political scientist, however, *faction* is used in two different contexts. One is in systems of one-party politics, especially the American South. Those groups that characterize politics inside the Democratic party are traditionally labeled factions. To avoid the confusion caused by this usage, Sartori (1976, pp. 71-75) has suggested substitution of the word *fraction* for such intra-party groups. While this idea has merit, it is not possible to dictate a change in language usage so quickly.

The final context for factions is in a period of politics without parties: the preparty politics of colonial America, nonpartisan local politics, or the politics of other units unaffected by partisanship (e.g., the United Nations or the Confederate States). In such a setting, *faction* might denote a group that forms around a single issue or personality, but with limited durability and minimal organization. "Faction [is] . . . a portion of an electorate, political elite, or legislature, whose adherents were engaged in parallel action or co-ordination of some consistency but of limited durability, in conflict with other portions" (Chambers, 1963a, p. 97). While the first meaning (a selfish or contentious group) is important in tracing the developing use of the word, most of the literature on party development is concerned exclusively with use of the word in no-party politics. The factions that preceded parties in America were often regarded by contemporaries as contentious or self-seeking, so the meanings have been linked. Whether these factions indeed deserved a negative rating is an open question. For present purposes, *faction* is used to denote the limited groups that may appear in the absence of parties, and any presumption that factions are necessarily "contentious" or "selfish" should be avoided.

Finding a satisfactory definition of *party* presents a significant challenge. It has been said that "it is perhaps easier to say what a party is not than to say what it is" (Commager, 1950, p. 309). Clearly, there is consensus that a party is more durable than a faction, is more extensive than a legislative voting bloc, and has different goals than an interest group. Beyond this point, various approaches have been employed by both political scientists and historians seeking a reasonable definition.

Some have provided only very loose definitions; examples include Binkley's (1966) characterization of parties as broad combinations of interest groups and Beard's (1915) use of the term to describe any group of people who generally share a set of beliefs. But such weak definitions lead to ambiguous conclusions about party development: "They encourage evasion of distinctions between party and non-party politics, and leave unexposed questions which are basic to a theory of modern party politics" (Chambers, 1963a, p. 93). Fortunately, there are other definitions that more clearly differentiate parties from factions, voting blocs, or interest groups. To this end, parties have been characterized by the agreement of partisans on policy questions (ideology), or by the functions or roles they fill in the political system, or by the type of structures or elements incorporated within them.

Edmund Burke's classic definition, quoted earlier, attempted to characterize parties in terms of the agreement of members on "some particular principle." Such definitions, however, have generally lost favor among modern political scientists, although MacIver (1964, p. 396) has provided one very similar to Burke's: "an association organized in support of some principle or policy which by constitutional means it endeavors to make the determinant of government." While it is reasonable to expect members of a party to agree frequently on policy issues, one should be wary of making this the sole defining factor. Many interest groups would be accurately described by MacIver's definition. Policy agreement is, however, an important factor in our search for political parties in the eighteenth century.

People such as Schattschneider (1941) and Schumpeter (1950) have criticized the narrow scope of definitions in the tradition of Burke and have suggested an emphasis on the key functions performed by parties. Schattschneider, in his classic treatise on political parties (1941, p. 35), has defined the party as "first of all an organized attempt to get power," meaning control of government. A more elaborate definition along the same lines is provided by Ranney and Kendall (1956, p. 85): "Political parties are autonomous organized groups that make nominations and contest elections in the hope of eventually gaining and exercising control of the personnel and policies of the government." Along with specifying the functions of a party, both of these definitions require an organization.

Epstein (1967, p. 9) has argued that this requirement of an organization raises an unnecessary restriction, and his definition substitutes the requirement of a party label: "[Party is] a group, however loosely organized, that seeks to win elections under a given label." Finally, Sartori (1976, p. 63) has drawn upon much of the earlier work to propose a concise definition of his own: "A party is any political group identified by an official label that presents at elections, and is capable of placing through elections (free or nonfree), candidates for public office."[6] In sum, each of these definitions focuses on the function of seeking power through the electoral process, with an additional requirement of an organization or a label.

It is evident from these definitions that involvement in the electoral process is clearly one function that distinguishes parties from other types of groups. In fulfilling this function, parties may help to recruit and screen candidates, supply symbols and names to help identify candidates to voters, and provide victorious candidates a mechanism for working toward policy goals once in office.

There is, however, at least one other major role of parties, although it is less useful in making distinctions. This is what Sartori (1976, p. 27) calls "channels of expression." The party is one of several institutions that can help people communicate their demands to the government. Furthermore, because a party can simultaneously channel the demands of a number of people and because it possesses the potential to control policy-making mechanisms, it adds a degree of pressure that aids popular control of public policy.

Recently, students of party politics have looked away from functional definitions and have sought to understand party in terms of structural features. The first appearance of such a definition is attributed to the late V.O. Key, Jr. (1964, pp. 163-65), although he provides no brief statement of his definition. The first quotable definition is one that actually combines structural and functional approaches (Sorauf, 1964, p. 13): "The political party may be defined as an agency for the organization of political power characterized by exclusively political functions, by a stable structure and inclusive membership, and by the ability to dominate the contesting of elections." Sorauf (1967, p. 37) later moves to defining party from a more purely structural perspective, borrowing heavily here from Key's ideas: "The political party can be thought of as a tripartite organization or structure. It is composed of three elements. 1. The organization proper. . . . 2. The party in office. . . . 3. The party-in-the-electorate."

Drawing in part on Sorauf's ideas and in part on his own study of the origins and history of American political parties, Chambers (1967, p. 5) has written a very detailed definition: "A political party in the modern sense may be thought of as a relatively durable social formation which seeks office or power in government, exhibits a structure or organization which links leaders at the centers of government to a significant popular following in the political arena and its local enclaves, and generates in-group perspectives or at least symbols of identification or loyalty." Finally, Formisano (1974, p. 475) has incorporated the key features of the definitions by Chambers and Sorauf into a far more concise statement: "Party exists when activists, officials, and voters interact and when they consciously identify with a common name and symbols." These structural definitions are particularly useful in looking for the existence of parties, because they emphasize the variety of elements that are included within a party. It is, of course, important to recognize the overlap between the various definitions. Chambers, in particular, has managed to use both structural and functional approaches.

Formisano (1981) has more recently emphasized the distinction between a party and a party system. In particular, he argues that a party system normally includes such components as a formal nominating process, political platforms, and other institutions. Further, he asserts that a party system must include full competition between two or more parties.

It is difficult to provide an effective summary of the variety of definitions offered for the term *party*, and it proves even more difficult to settle on a single definition that best represents the concept. One of the few scholars who has considered these conceptual questions at length is Chambers (1963a), whose extended discussion offers a "concept or analytical-historical model of party in terms of structure, function, and ideology." The definition by Chambers presented above comes from a later, more concise statement of this discussion. A party is "a social structure . . . [in] the political arena . . . directed toward exercising the power, filling the available offices, and shaping the general policies of government" (p. 108). This structure then has four defining characteristics and a fifth, contingent characteristic: (1) "comparatively stable or durable leader-follower relationship" (p. 108); (2) "communication and co-ordination . . . between central leaders . . . and . . . local actives" (p. 109); (3) "regular procedures for performing functions linking the public or electorate and the governmental decision-making process" (p. 109); (4) "a set of in-group perspectives . . . which constitute an ideology" (p. 109-10); and (5) "attached to the party structure [is] a comparatively durable combination of interests" (p. 110).

Together, these characteristics include aspects of party structure, performance of party functions, and existence of an ideology; yet they fall short of requiring an elaborate organization or a highly consistent ideology. Chambers has designed his definition such that a group fulfilling all five conditions can be classed as a party, whereas factions fail to show most of the characteristics. This design, however, followed a conclusion that parties existed in the United States only after 1790; thus, there may be problems in using this model for a study of American party development.[7]

Theories of Party Development

There is one additional approach to the problem of finding a suitable definition of a political party, one that considers the process through which a party comes into existence. Implicitly, at least, a theory of party development must contain within it a definition of *party*. Furthermore, such a definition by its nature presents party not as an object that does or does not exist, but as a continuum along which a group may be placed—a conceptualization that proves to be especially useful, since it avoids many of the weaknesses of the definitions discussed above.

The classic statement on party development comes from Duverger (1959), who distinguishes between two different patterns of party origins: parliamentary and extraparliamentary. The latter pattern occurs only after the extension of suffrage in a nation and thus is not relevant to the American case. In many European nations, parties have emerged as a result of activities in churches, trade unions, or philosophical societies. Such parties are representative of the pattern of external origins. The more relevant pattern to this study, although less common in the course of history, is marked first by the creation of parliamentary groups based on any grounds.[8] Eventually electoral committees appear in such a system, and finally linkages are formed between parliamentary groups and electoral committees.

Several political scientists have attempted to elaborate on Duverger's statement of party origins (Chambers, 1966; Huntington, 1968; LaPalombara and Weiner, 1966). Integrating these considerations leads to the view that party development is a process taking place in four stages.[9] In the first stage, *factionalism*, groups form in the legislature over a variety of issues and personalities. These factions are rarely organized and last for only a short time. At this point, none of the characteristics of party (relationship between leaders and followers, in-group perspectives, etc.) are present. But since the emergence of factionalism is a logical precursor of parties, it is reasonable to characterize this stage as one of preparty politics.

In the second stage, *polarization*, these factions are stabilized into more permanent legislative groups that oppose each other over a broad range of issues. This coalescence into polar groups is frequently set off by a single issue of overriding importance or by the cumulation of several cleavages. Some would unquestionably characterize groups in this stage as parties, but the lack of any mass component or involvement in the electoral process would prevent most from using that label. More important than a simple designation as party is to see this stage as a crucial step (although not a necessary or inevitable one) along the continuum of party. Here the members of these polarizing blocs should begin to develop an in-group perspective or a characteristic set of beliefs. From this point, an identification with party symbols or a party label should arise naturally, as members begin to think in partisan terms.

In the third stage, *expansion*, the public is drawn into the process of party development, usually after the extension of suffrage. Electoral committees may arise at the local level to influence decision makers, or they may be created by officeholders to strengthen their own positions. With this involvement in the electoral process, the group is more clearly acquiring the characteristics of party and becoming worthy of that label. By this stage, regular procedures are likely to be developed for the operation of elections, and party affiliations are becoming significant factors in the electoral process. Additionally, at least some degree of coordination is implied between national and local elites, although no firm and permanent linkage has appeared.

In the fourth and final stage, *institutionalization*, a permanent linkage is created between the parliamentary group and its corresponding electoral committees. At this point, some type of national organization should begin to direct and coordinate the party's activities. With the achievement of this stage, a group has moved to the end of the party continuum and is clearly deserving of that designation. Regular means for operating in the electoral process are developed (e.g., nominations), and a party ideology exists, together with accepted party symbols and a name.

The party continuum can extend to include highly institutionalized parties with rigid belief systems, highly cohesive behavior, and a powerful organizational structure. It is clear, however, that no one wants to restrict the use of the term to such parties, for that restriction would contradict the empirical realities of modern usage, especially in the United States. The problem comes in designating the level of organization or the degree of ideological consistency that would constitute minimal requirements for parties. It is this problem, however, that illustrates the advantages of a conceptualization that views party as a continuum rather than as a dichotomy.

A Theoretical Framework

It is this conceptualization of party as a continuum that guides the research presented in this book. The four stages designated in the previous section can be used to highlight key points along the continuum from preparty politics to highly developed partisanship. Additionally, attention is directed at those key features of party noted by most definitions: (1) a group of public officials; (2) a group of supporters in the public; (3) involvement in the electoral process; (4) an organization, however minimal; and (5) some form of symbols or labels. All of these features have already been identified within one of the four stages along the party continuum, but they are listed again here to highlight their significance.

While this conceptualization should apply in any case where parties are originating out of a parliament, certain features of the American political scene of the 1790s may have influenced the attainment of these criteria. The first is the impact of the philosophical and historical background of this period. Because most American leaders had inherited a tradition that denied the value of parties, certain aspects of party development were met with unusual obstacles. In particular, the adoption of party symbols or labels was resisted by those unfriendly to the idea of party. Similarly, party caucuses and other party institutions were often rejected as inappropriate. While a process of party development is expected to overcome such obstacles, parties might remain anonymous for an overly long period.

The second feature that could potentially impede party development was the status of various political institutions in the eighteenth century. The electoral process was not characterized by the elaborate institutions present today. No formal nominating procedures existed; voice voting was still used in some states; and electioneering was not considered proper behavior for a candidate. These procedures changed as parties took their places in the political arena, but the existing norms and procedures surely affected partisan involvement in elections. Similarly, the institutions associated with congressional parties (formal leadership and caucuses) were unknown in the eighteenth century. Such institutions came as a result of party emergence, and their absence would be expected to slow the emergence of a party organization, as well as to make the nascent parties suspect in the eyes of a twentieth-century observer.

These topics receive full attention in the chapters that follow, for they are important to a proper understanding of the development of parties in the United States. Ultimately, any conclusion concerning the emergence of parties is dependent on how the term *party* is understood. In the end, many of the differences among party historians can be attributed to differing definitions. It is hoped that conceptualizing party as a continuum will help to avoid a game of semantics where authors offer different conclusions simply because of different definitions. Instead, the emphasis can be placed on the actual process of party development, with an assessment of a group's progress along the continuum.

2. The Historical Tradition

The Anglo-American philosophical tradition provided little support for the notion of party. Yet the idea of party was not totally without historical precedent. It is possible to look for examples of partisan behavior in several different settings. Outside of Great Britain, the states of eighteenth-century Europe were all governed as absolute monarchies. The parliament of France, for example, never even met from 1614 until the Revolution in 1789 (Loewenstein, 1967, p. 54). With only minor exceptions, there are no possible examples of the emergence of a party system before 1789 in continental Europe.[1] The ancient republics of Athens, Rome, and Venice were states with some semblance of factions or coalitions. But these, even if they were known in America, were hardly examples of party systems in any modern sense (Dahl, 1966). The Athenian political system could be described as a very primitive system of coalitions: "There were no parties in anything like the modern sense, either among the politicians or the general public. At one end of the scale there were groups or cliques among the politicians. But such alliances were probably based on personalities rather than principles, and seem to have been temporary" (A.H.M. Jones, cited in Dahl, 1966, p. xvii*n*). There was, nevertheless, an important historical precedent in Great Britain, the nation whose political history was best known to Americans. Because the early American political leaders were subjects of British rule, they were obviously familiar with British politics. The examples of partisan behavior and institutions in Great Britain were thus significant models for developments in the United States.

Political Parties in Great Britain

It is difficult to trace precisely the emergence of political parties in Britain; in fact, the state of parties as late as the mid-nineteenth century is a point of historical controversy. It is certainly not possible to unravel the complexities of British party history here. What is clear is that the process of party development in Great Britain began prior to the American Revolution; the following pages represent an attempt to assess briefly its progress.

The problem of party development in Britain, far more than in America, was clearly tied to the acceptance of legitimate opposition. The eventual acceptance of the idea of opposition was in turn linked to the development of

Parliament. It is these events, too, that distinguished Britain from the governments elsewhere in Europe.

Absolute monarchy left no room for opposition to the government (the monarch). But in Britain, as early as the signing of the Magna Charta in 1215, some limited opposition to the monarch became tolerated. The earliest suggestion of any party development comes in the sixteenth century: "Party, in the bare sense of a group of men of similar views and who act together in parliament for common purposes, appears at least as early as the reign of Elizabeth. The Puritans in her later parliaments consistently opposed her prerogative in matters of Church and State" (Mackenzie, 1951, p. 108). During this entire period, up to the early seventeenth century, the British system of government was evolving in two important regards. First, Parliament was gradually assuming a more important position relative to the Crown. The second and related development was increased legitimacy for opposition to the Crown. The combination of these developments allowed for the emergence of parliamentary parties, an event that can best be presented in several stages.

The first tentative beginnings of British party emergence occurred during the Long Parliament (1640-60) and the Puritan Revolution. The struggle of that period was essentially between supporters of Parliament, known as the Roundheads, and supporters of the Crown, the Royalists or Cavaliers (Loewenstein, 1967). Although it has been called the first party division (Jennings, 1961), its importance lies in the attempt to assert the power of Parliament against the king, an important step in the development of the idea of opposition. The groups existing then were primitive parliamentary factions responding to the issue of parliamentary prerogative, an issue resolved by revolution rather than by political action. Although they had a short-lived intensity, they involved neither the electoral base nor the organization characteristic of parties. Nevertheless, the party system that developed across the next two centuries had important roots in the differences between Roundheads and Cavaliers.

The next era of importance to British party history was the Restoration (1660-88), when the monarchy was returned to power. During this period, "a new feature was the emergence of two identifiable political groups or groupings, which came to be known as Whigs and Tories. . . . The groupings were nothing like political parties in the modern sense of the word; they were cliques or unorganized caucuses of the nobility and their hangers-on both in Parliament and outside" (Loewenstein, 1967, p. 64). These groupings were frequently known as "country" and "court" parties, a designation that emphasizes the fact that they were primarily groups formed around feelings toward the Crown. Jennings (1961) emphasizes that these were heavily based on family "connexions," more than on any set of issues or any basis of mass support. Yet they were of sufficient importance to be cited as the "origins of the two great parties of the eighteenth and nineteenth centuries" (Mackenzie, 1951, p. 109). Furthermore, they were sufficiently widespread that it became possible to speak meaningfully of one group or the other winning a majority in general elections in 1679 and 1681 (Loewenstein, 1967). The Whigs, the country party, were victorious in those elections. But because they favored limiting royal authority, they were driven out, through exile or execution, by Charles II in favor of the Tories, (the court party), who were more supportive of the Crown.[2]

The groups during this period are probably best described as parliamentary factions, continuing in the general tradition of the Cavaliers and Roundheads. Again the issue of parliamentary prerogative was predominant, but it was joined by divisive religious questions, especially after the accession to the throne of a Catholic, James II, in 1685. Still, partial resolution of these issues occurred not through the victory of one faction, but through the uniting of the factions against the king. There were tentative signs of potential polarization of the factions and expansion into the electoral arena, but intervention of the Glorious Revolution quickly rearranged the politics of that time.

The Glorious Revolution in 1688 was a key event in establishing the role of Parliament in the government. The Crown thereafter became more dependent upon Parliament and the balance of forces therein. In the years immediately following, parties seemed to play less of a role; governments were formed on an essentially bipartisan basis. Differences were suppressed temporarily, while the results of the Revolution were affirmed. Yet parties were becoming a fact of life in British politics, and an exclusively Tory ministry was formed in 1700, followed by a Whig ministry in 1708 and by another Tory ministry in 1710.[3] Loewenstein (1967, p. 80) claims that there was "firm establishment of the two-party system" by about 1710.

Any statement concerning party development at this time must, of course, be modified by a consideration of the various aspects of party. Scholars seem to agree generally that none of the modern institutional forms associated with parties existed at that time. There was no organization, nor was there any substantial electoral base. At a time when the electorate was still very small, elections continued to be won or lost mostly on the basis of "connexions." Whether the parliamentary factions seen in earlier years were beginning to polarize after the 1688 Revolution is a question that suffers from a lack of evidence. The statements of historians imply that a degree of polarization did take place, but that the parties (or factions) were still far from being cohesive (Hill, 1976).

With the accession of George I and the Hanovers in 1714, there were significant developments in the emergence of parliamentary government. Due in part to the king's inability to speak English, power shifted further from the Crown toward Parliament. Power did not, however, move to the parliamentary parties; rather, the power vacuum was filled by influential ministers such as Walpole (1721-42), sometimes regarded as the first prime minister. At the end of Walpole's tenure in office, it became clear that parliamentary leaders could force the appointment of their chosen prime minister (Loewenstein, 1967).

This period became, in fact, a time of declining importance for parties. For a combination of reasons, the Tories entered a period of hibernation, while the Whigs remained dominant. With this decline of two-party competition, factionalism within the Whig party became prevalent. The government did not need the entire group of Whigs to survive, and the opposition thus tended to include rebellious Whigs together with the remaining Tories. That the opposition did not come from a disciplined party is illustrated by a description of the opposition to Walpole: "Composed of a heterogeneous cluster of malcontents drawn from every segment of the political spectrum—from the far left, the inheritors of seventeenth-century libertarianism, as well as from the far right, ex-Jacobites and ex-Tories now undistinguishable from the centrist Whigs—it only rarely approached substantial voting strength in Parliament, and only once . . . in effect defeated the government" (Bailyn, 1968, p. 35). Nevertheless, while some historians hold that the period marked the disappearance of the Tories (Blake, 1970), others contend that the party maintained its existence (and a high degree of cohesion) through these times of misfortune (Hill, 1976). The Whigs clearly remained alive, but it was an existence noted more for its factions than for its unity as a party.

When George III became king in 1760, there was renewed activism for the Crown and a change in the course of party development. The long term in power for the Whigs came to an end in 1770, when they were replaced by the Tories. In this revitalization, however, the Tories resembled a royal or court faction more than a true party. This ascent of the Tories forced the Whigs into opposition, providing them the opportunity "to transform themselves into a national party in the true sense of the word" (Loewenstein, 1967, p. 92). It also marked the first time that "formally organized parliamentary political parties were formed in 'opposition'" (Ionescu and de Madariaga, 1968, p. 57). At this time, too, Burke, a leader of the Whigs, was articulating his view of the legitimacy of opposition parties. During this period, the Whigs were successful in drawing upon the forces of public opinion, as well as organizing themselves in Parliament: "The Whigs were the first to form a parliamentary party, combining for common action inside the House, but with a headquarters and organization outside the House and in the country at large" (Loewenstein, 1967, p. 92).

The election of 1784 can be marked as an important turning point for the British party system. The Tory landslide for William Pitt as prime minister served to end the Crown's right to appoint ministers, thus establishing the relationship between government, Parliament, and the electorate, as well as consolidating the two-party system. Pitt for the Tories and Fox for the Whigs can be regarded as the first party leaders. Yet even then party unity was limited, and many voters and legislators remained independent of any party ties (Blake, 1970; Jennings, 1961; Loewenstein, 1967).

By the end of the eighteenth century, the British party system was far more developed than it had been two centuries earlier. But although many of the characteristics of modern parties were beginning to emerge, it is important not to overstate the maturity of that party system.

> In this Old Whig system, however, we are still far from finding political formations like the Conservatives and Liberals of Victorian times, not to mention the parties of today. In contrast with Old Tory thought and practice [before 1700], it was legitimate for Members of Parliament, acting in concert, to struggle for office and to initiate legislation or policy proposals on broad matters of national concern. To this extent some

progress had been made in legitimizing party in the Victorian and modern meanings of the word. But that such bodies, united on differing principles, should be normal and durable features of political life was in general not accepted and certainly not thought desirable. (Beer, 1969, p. 22)

The chief basis for such skepticism concerning the development of British parties at this time is found in the evidence presented by Namier (1955, 1957). Concentrating on the years from 1760 to about 1790, he builds a strong case that there was "no trace of a two-party system, or at all of party in the modern sense" (Namier, 1955, p. 34).

Two of his specific findings deserve mention. First is an analysis of the election of 1761 (Namier, 1957, pp. 158-72). In that election, there were actual contests in only 48 of the 315 constituencies (15%). It is true that potential contests elsewhere were averted by the withdrawal of candidates, but this is partly the result of the small size of the electorate. The average number of eligible voters in a constituency was fewer than 500. Many members won their seats solely on family ties and the power of their purses. The nature of elections did not change until the 1832 Reform Act, and until then it is difficult to speak of any mass basis for parties.

Namier also brings into question the degree of polarization (1955, pp. 21-32). Rather than the polarizing two-party system suggested by others, he argues that "three broad divisions, based on type and not on party, can be distinguished in the eighteenth-century House of Commons" (p. 21). These were the followers of the Crown, a court faction whose loyalty was based mostly on patronage; the independent country gentlemen, who avoided any alliance with factions; and the political factions in contention for power, including the well-known leaders and their followings. A 1788 circular analyzed the House along these lines and placed only a third of all members into the parties of Pitt and Fox, usually identified as the two major parties.

Historians have differed considerably in their assessments of British party development, a fact made clear in the preceding discussion. Some have argued strongly that parties were a visible and important factor in Britain at least as early as 1700 (Hill, 1976; Trevelyan, 1949). Others have claimed that these eighteenth-century political arrangements cannot be called parties at all (Jennings, 1961; Namier, 1955). In particular, they point out the lack of any mass electorate to support the emerging parliamentary factions. Regardless of their positions, most scholars at least agree that the next major turning point in British party development was the Reform Act of 1832, which expanded the electorate, allowing a greater popular basis for the parties.[4] It is neither possible nor necessary to resolve here the question of when political parties, in a modern sense of the word, did exist in Great Britain. What is important is the general state of British party development at the time when the American leaders were experimenting with their own new political system.

It is certainly true that the British political system provided many of the historical precedents for the newly developing political institutions as the United States tried to implement the new Constitution. As has been illustrated, factions and even embryonic parties were characteristic of British politics in the seventeenth and eighteenth centuries. Nevertheless, at least prior to 1770, this factionalism in Britain was very uneven and not considered legitimate by many participants. In retrospect, it is easy to see this early factionalism as a logical and natural forerunner of the modern party system. But to the observer of that time, factionalism could easily appear as an undesirable characteristic of the political system. By the end of the eighteenth century, there were clear signs in Britain of a more vigorous and better-accepted party system. But by that time the Americans were less attentive to the examples of their British counterparts; furthermore, by that time they had an extensive experience of their own from colonial politics.

Political Parties in Colonial America

The vast majority of the American settlers came from Great Britain, and it is natural that Britain was the source of so many American political characteristics. This tendency is accentuated by the fact that many of the settlers came to America as a direct result of the factional divisions in Britain. Also, because the Americans were under British rule, the divisions that affected British politics also came to affect American politics.

Factionalism was a part of American politics from the beginning. Indeed, factional disputes arose even on the ships that crossed the Atlantic in 1606-07 to begin the Jamestown settlement. The first factional disputes, which were present in every one of the new settlements, were generally over questions of religion and personality (Nichols, 1967). These were the same kinds of issues that were producing conflict in Britain at that time. As the years passed, governmental institutions in the colonies became more structured, and the colonists became more American and less British. The colonial governments generally consisted of an assembly composed of colonials and a royal governor, either sent from Britain or appointed by the Crown. This structure led to frequent disputes between assemblies and governors, and this form of factionalism became the rule in nearly every colony (Bailyn, 1968).

There were, of course, variations in the factionalism of different colonies. The southern colonies were generally more homogeneous and more dominated by elites, and thus they had less severe factionalism. In New England, a tradition of strong legislatures made the disputes with the royal governors most severe, resembling the "country party" and "court party" of seventeenth-century Britain. The middle colonies housed a more flexible and complex political system, and in New York the factionalism was closer to a modern party system than elsewhere (Nichols, 1967).

In the period preceding the Declaration of Independence and the war of independence, the issue of self-government served as the primary catalyst for factionalism in the colonies. The two underlying sources from about 1740 to 1776 were, first, the ongoing struggle between royal governors and popular colonial assemblies, and, second, the economic and religious differences that existed within many colonies (Main, 1973). During this period, however, protests gradually began to arise against various actions of the British

Parliament, such as the Stamp Act. Those protests frequently grew out of the court-country factionalism that had become important.

As events unfolded, a new political cleavage had begun to appear by 1764. On one side were the more radical groups (known as Whigs or Patriots), sympathetic to the use of force and violence against British actions; on the opposite side were the conservatives (known as Tories or Loyalists), including many of the more wealthy and well-established colonials, who favored "law and order." When the Continental Congress was called into session in 1774 and again in 1775, the radical-conservative split was an important factor in the deliberations. The Whigs (radicals) were chiefly responsible for calling the sessions and were numerically in control of the Congress (Nichols, 1967). However, it has been estimated that, while the Whigs were the only group with any political organization, the Loyalists (conservatives) were the larger group in the colonies, at least outside of New England and Virginia (Libby, 1912).

In 1775, events at Lexington and Concord moved the disputes from the arena of debate to the arena of war. In effect, the factionalism of Patriot against Loyalist became a civil war. As a result of the fighting, the Patriots gained control of the government in each of the colonies and generally were able to exclude the Loyalists from the government altogether. By the time of the Second Continental Congress, convening later that same year, the Tories were no longer welcome to participate, although they were in effect one of the major causes for deliberation. Without the old factionalism, new divisions arose among the Patriot delegates at the Congress. One group favored conciliation of some sort with the British. A group of radicals, especially from Massachusetts and Virginia, favored immediate independence. The remaining delegates, a majority of the Congress, stood somewhere in the middle. The deliberations of the Congress were, then, essentially a battle over which course the middle group would take. In the end, of course, independence was declared (Nichols, 1967).

In the years following the Declaration of Independence, there was only minimal significant activity by the central governments. In fact, it was a period of questioning what sort of central government to have. The important arenas of government during these years were the several state governments, and these developed their own factionalism. Main's (1973) study of these state legislatures has revealed that consistent alignments of legislators were evident in most states. Slightly over two-thirds of the legislators can be classified into one of the two "parties," with the remainder "neutrals." The two so-called parties were the Localists, consisting especially of agrarian interests, and the Cosmopolitans, dominated by the commercial interests. The two factions disagreed on many of the important issues, but most often on the various economic issues: spending and taxes, salaries for governors and legislators, and debtor/creditor questions. On some of the more purely political issues that had been more dominant in earlier years, such as loyalty to Britain and the power of the executive in the new state constitutions, these particular factions generally did not form.

In terms of the type of individuals found in the two parties, three factors seem to divide them: type of constituency, occupation, and wealth. Cosmopolitans tended generally to be well-to-do landowners or professional people from urban, coastal, commercial centers. Localists were more often farmers with moderate property holdings from the rural interior. It is, of course, difficult to say whether these groupings should be denoted as parties in any sense of the word, especially since they formed mostly on one kind of issue. Yet the consistency of these groupings across state boundaries provides an argument that they were not merely temporary factions. Furthermore, it appears that the people in the states recognized the similarities of attitudes and did perceive the existence of legislative blocs or parties. This evidence speaks strongly for regarding these groups as at least the beginnings of a party system.

Divisions in the Continental Congress

The Articles of Confederation were ratified in 1781, thus establishing a central government for the new nation. This event also coincided with the surrender of Cornwallis and thus the end of the war for independence. The new national Congress was not very powerful because of various provisions in the Articles, but, like its predecessor before 1781, it succeeded in determining policy for the new nation. Of course, many of the issues divided the members of the Congress along various lines. The most consistent divisions were regional. New England, the Middle states, and the South had different cultural and economic traditions, thereby leading to different positions on political issues. Since no one region was able to dominate and win for its own positions, alliances between regions were necessary. By the end of the government under the Articles, factionalism had become "increasingly polarized along a North-South fault that had been implicit in the partisan politics of the Congress from the outset of the Revolution" (Henderson, 1974, p. 6).

Again, the labeling of the groups presents difficulties. Henderson (1974, pp. 5, 6) describes "a rudimentary legislative party politics" and both "preparty" and "postfactional" politics. Party labels, party platforms, and mass-based party organizations were not, however, part of the system at this time. In fact, antiparty sentiment on the part of the political leaders deterred developments of this sort. Yet the consistency of voting blocs in the Congress across time and across a variety of issues suggests very close links to the partisan politics of the years to follow.

By 1786, factionalism in the Continental Congress had become strongly polarized along North-South lines (dividing between Pennsylvania and Maryland). This factionalism, accentuated by the weakness of the Articles of Confederation and emphasized in the attempt to negotiate a treaty with Spain, led some people to fear a permanent separation of northern and southern states. This fear and the concern over Shays's Rebellion were important factors in the convening of the Constitutional Convention in 1787 (Henderson, 1974). It is frequently suggested that the question of stronger central government (particularly, a stronger national executive) was the main source of partisan division during the years prior to the Constitution. This party system of Federalists, favoring a stronger national executive, and Antifederalists, favoring a more limited national government, tended to cut across many of the old factional divisions, including the regional division. The Federalists, smaller but better organized, tended to come from the commercial and trading centers, while the Antifederalists were concentrated in the interior regions (Libby, 1912).

Divisions in the Constitutional Convention

The divisions that occurred throughout the proceedings of the Constitutional Convention have been the object of frequent attention from historians. The two conflicts most frequently cited are the representation issue and the slavery issue. The former placed small states against large states on the choice between equal representation for states and representation by population. The latter divided North and South over the slave trade itself as well as the counting of slaves for tax and representation purposes. Both of these issues were ultimately settled by means of compromise.

A very different interpretation of the dynamics of the Constitutional Convention is suggested in an analysis by Beard (1913). His thesis essentially states that economic factors were of prime significance in the writing of the Constitution. More specifically, he argues that the economic interests and property holdings of the delegates tend to explain why various delegates behaved as they did at the Convention. He classifies the delegates roughly into two groups, those whose chief interests were in real property (small farmers, wealthy manor lords, and slaveholding planters) and those whose chief interests were in personal property (money, public securities, manufacturing and shipping, and unsettled lands held for speculation). Because the latter interests were more numerous at the Convention, the resulting document tended to protect those economic interests.

Beard's thesis has been frequently challenged in the decades since its publication. One of its chief critics is McDonald (1958), who has published a complete replication of Beard's book for the purpose of refuting its premises. In his study, he has the advantage of more plentiful information than Beard had forty-five years earlier. McDonald considers the economic interests of the various delegates, concluding that interests were diverse and no consolidated economic interest group was present. Furthermore, by classifying each delegate and thus each state delegation as dominated by realty (real property) or personalty (personal property), he tests whether the votes cast at the Convention corresponded to these two economic interests. The results fail to reveal any evidence for the significance of these economic groupings.

The hypothesis that differences between small and large states provided the key dividing point in the Convention was actually first suggested by Madison in his journal of the Convention. However, McDonald (1965) points out that the division that dominated the Convention, while identifiable as a small-state bloc and a large-state bloc, can be better described as North against South, or best described as landed states (those that, by charter or otherwise, held claim to unoccupied lands) against landless states. These latter descriptions coincide reasonably well with the findings of Henderson (1974), who argues that the divisions at the Convention were chiefly a continuation of the factionalism of the Continental Congress. Virginia led a bloc that was "nationalist" and southern in character, opposed by a bloc composed chiefly of the small northern states. Henderson further confirms the significance of the issue of western lands, an issue partially resolved by the passage in Congress of the Northwest Ordinance during the Convention itself.

The descriptions of factionalism at the Constitutional Convention are complex and at times contradictory. Ulmer (1966) has attempted to use two techniques of bloc analysis on the recorded votes of state delegations to identify any consistent voting coalitions. He concludes that bloc voting did exist, but was not concentrated on any specific issues. In general, the blocs were made up of contiguous states, and economic issues appear to be connected with the bloc formation. However, neither the realty-personalty groupings, nor the small state-large state groupings, nor a North-South division are directly reflected by the results of the analysis.

My own attempt to replicate Ulmer's analysis using the spatial analysis technique (described in chapter 5) reveals some of the reasons why there is so little agreement on the nature of factionalism in the Constitutional Convention. The analysis produces a configuration of the twelve participating states, based on the frequency with which they voted in agreement on all the issues of the Convention.[5] The structure of factionalism was not highly developed, especially in comparison to the party structures that developed a few years later. Furthermore, the structure revealed is not one of a well-defined set of voting blocs. The clustering identified by Ulmer is not fully contradicted by my analysis, but Ulmer seems to imply a more coherent pattern of voting than my analysis reveals.

A recent analysis by Jillson (1981) adds a temporal dimension to the study of voting coalitions at the Convention. By looking at coalitions for a limited series of votes, he was able to demonstrate three different shifts in the coalition structure, each coinciding with one of the major compromises during the deliberations. Thus, Jillson argues that a critical realignment process characterized the Convention. In a later analysis, Jillson and Eubanks (1984) provide some theoretical bases for these shifting coalitions, linking them to the differences between debating great constitutional choices and arguing over relative advantages for different regions and interests.

Regardless of which analysis best describes the dynamics or decisions of the Convention itself, it appears clear that no solid foundations for a party system were established. At most, there existed a set of shifting factions, but they certainly did not exhibit the strength, depth, or stability of parties.

The contest over ratification of the Constitution was in many ways a simple extension of the conflicts in the Convention. But for a variety of reasons, the lines of conflict over ratification developed rather differently. Main (1961) has considered the importance of several factors in explaining the divisions between Federalists, who supported ratification, and Antifederalists, who were opposed to ratification. His conclusion is that merchants and all other individuals whose livelihood was directly dependent on trade were far more frequently aligned with the Federalists: "The mercantile interest, understood in this broad sense, is the key to the political history of this period. Its counterpart is the non-commercial interest of the subsistence farmer. This is a socioeconomic division based on a geographic location and sustains a class as well as a sectional interpretation of the struggle over the Constitution" (Main, 1961, p. 271). Nevertheless, there is considerable doubt as to whether the conflict over ratification produced any truly national alignments. The unique conditions of each state complicated the contest to a great degree.

> Adoption of the national Constitution thus emerged from a diversity of local forces, divisions, and decisions. Though "Federalists" from state to state co-operated to some degree, they did not constitute a national party. The so-called "Anti-Federalists," far from being a single national formation, can be thought of only as a conglomeration of more or less like-minded elements from state to state. Nor was the contest a clear, two-way battle between conservative, investing, or "business" groups on the one side and radical, agrarian, or "populist" masses on the other: the actual group foundations of interest and opinion on both sides varied in different areas and were often contradictory as between states. The issue was dualistic, to adopt or not to adopt; but the lines of forces involved were pluralistic and loose. (Chambers, 1963b, p. 29)

Summary

From the earliest colonial assemblies to the writing and approving of the Constitution, American political history is filled with accounts of divisions and factionalism. The nature of these divisions was varied, and the cleavages over one set of issues generally did not correspond with those over the next set. Clearly, none of the factions during this period was a party in the modern sense of the word. "American politics in the 1770's and 1780's, with the exception of Pennsylvania politics, remained a swirling confusion of interests, issues, leaders, opinions, shifting factions or factionlike formations, and loose alignments, marked by extremes of particularism and localism" (Chambers, 1963b, pp. 20-21). Nevertheless, the factionalism of these years did provide some early indication of the kinds of divisions that might be expected to have some importance in the new government: "Even more ironic is the fact that party development of the 1790s began as a remarkable continuation of the factionalism in the Continental Congress. The Southern and Eastern nuclei of the Republican and Federalist parties as well as the divisions in the Middle states were replications of the structure of congressional parties. The struggles over the location of the national capital, Hamilton's fiscal program, and Jay's diplomacy were re-enactments of the partisan battles of the Confederation era" (Henderson, 1974, p. 420).

Some of the old issues were essentially resolved before the new government went into effect. The fact of ratification made it pointless to continue debating the desirability of the Constitution, for it was now the law of the land. Even the recalcitrant states of North Carolina and Rhode Island had ratified by the end of 1790, since they had been placed in the untenable position of being excluded from the new government. On the other hand, there were still differences in perspective between North and South and between commercial interests and agrarian interests, and these differences seemed likely to continue to cause division on political issues. Thus, it is not surprising that factionalism did develop under the new government. Whether this factional system would develop into a party system was, of course, impossible to know.

Neither the Anglo-American philosophical tradition nor the political history of Britain, the colonies, or elsewhere provided much support for the idea of a party system. "Wherever the Americans looked, whether to the politics of Georgian England, their own provincial capitals, or the republics of the historical past, they thought they saw in parties only a distracting and divisive force representing the claims of unbridled, selfish, special interests" (Hofstadter, 1969, p. 40). Thus, it is not at all surprising that the Constitution made no mention at all of political parties and, in fact, the Electoral College was constructed on the assumption that parties would not exist. Neither is it surprising that Madison and other leaders should have spoken in such severe terms about the dangers of party.

Nevertheless, in spite of the absence of clear historical precedents or the existence of philosophical support for the idea of party, the process of party development was soon underway. Within a decade of the new nation's beginning, partisan conflict had become quite substantial.

3. The Development of Electoral Institutions

Historical developments do not take place in a vacuum; rather, a specific historical and political context surrounds events. The historical and philosophical environment for the new nation was discussed in earlier chapters, where we saw the absence of either historical precedent or philosophical support for the idea of party. There is, however, more to the picture; the party emergence, which provides the focus for this book, also belongs in a specific political context.

The eighteenth-century political world bore little resemblance to the twentieth-century surroundings to which we are so accustomed. Many of the institutional settings and structures we now take for granted were absent. The secret ballot, universal suffrage, and active campaigns for office were just appearing on the scene. The institutionalized Congress, with its complex network of committees and leadership ranks, was nearly inconceivable.

The purpose of the next two chapters is to describe both electoral and congressional institutions as they existed near the end of the eighteenth century. Additionally, attention is given to some of the many transitions underway at that time. With this background, the significance of various signs of party development should be much clearer and we can avoid the trap of interpreting events out of their proper historical context.

Electoral practices in the latter part of the eighteenth century differed considerably from the procedures followed nearly two centuries later. Political scientists (Duverger, 1959; Key, 1964) have suggested the impact of election laws on the outcome of elections and the fates of political parties. In this chapter, several aspects of the administration of elections are discussed, including restrictions on suffrage, selection of candidates, forms of balloting, and norms for electioneering.

Like many of the political customs in the United States, most electoral practices can be traced to roots in the British tradition. These British models, however, had been adapted and modified by some 150 years of experience in the American colonies. This development was distinctly different in the various colonies; at the time of the Constitutional Convention, no consensus existed on a proper system of suffrage or suitable electoral laws. In order to avoid a difficult division at the Convention, most such decisions were left to the individual states. Senators were to be chosen by the state legislatures, so that suffrage and electoral regulations were not relevant. There were two constitutional provisions with respect to elections for the House of Representatives: first, "the Electors in each State shall have the Qualifications requisite for Electors of the most numerous Branch of the State Legislature" (Article I, Section 2); and second, "The Times, Places and Manner of holding Elections for Senators and Representatives, shall be prescribed in each State by the Legislatures thereof; but the Congress may at any time by Law make or alter such Regulations, except as to the Place of Choosing Senators" (Article I, Section 4). Most of the power for establishing procedures was thus left to the states. Generally, states had electoral laws to deal with the selection of state assemblies and other offices. While these laws were often simply applied to the new federal elections, new laws sometimes had to be written; in addition, electoral procedures could be as much the result of customs and traditions as of laws. Norms for electioneering and the manner of elections were generally well established during the colonial period.

Because they came from a variety of political cultures, the states had different traditions for elections. Furthermore, the last years of the eighteenth century marked a period of change in several ways. The spirit that led to the Declaration of Independence and the American Revolution frequently brought demands for wider suffrage and more democratic elections. At the same time, the emergence of a new level of government, first the Continental Congress and later the national Congress, opened up new political arenas. Some states had in the past held few elections at other than the local level; the need to select presidential electors and members of Congress was sometimes the impetus for new electoral laws. Clearly, this was a transitional period, and any discussion of electoral procedures can only be illustrative and not exhaustive of the systems used in the various states.

The development of electoral procedures had direct relevance to the appearance of political parties in the eighteenth century for a variety of reasons. In particular, historical evidence that parties influenced the outcomes of elections may have been affected by the manner in which elections were held. Traditional styles of nominating candidates and campaigning for office often made it difficult for organized groups to play a direct role in the electoral process. Thus, it is vital to see both the kinds of procedures that existed at the time and the way in which these procedures changed as partisan politics grew in importance.

Size of the Electorate

The eighteenth-century electorate was a relatively small and select group by any modern standard. Determining its size with any degree of precision is, however, not any easy task. Several historians have attempted to make such an estimate, but their results have been rather inconsistent. No such effort is made here; rather, the factors affecting the size of the electorate are examined: first, the legal restrictions on suffrage; and second, the reasons why some eligible voters might not have cast their votes.

Laws concerning suffrage were fairly specific in most states, although enforcement of the laws was not always consistent. Certain restrictions, limiting the franchise to free white males, over twenty-one years of age, were common to all states and in fact hardly needed stating. Blacks were occasionally permitted to vote in some northern states, but this was not the norm. At some earlier times, there had also been religious qualifications for voting, but these had generally been removed by 1789. In some states, residency requirements were added (Porter, 1918; Williamson, 1960).

Beyond these basic restrictions, the most important restriction on suffrage was a requirement for property ownership. It was generally believed in those days that only those individuals whose attachment to the community was strong and permanent should be permitted to vote. This would help to ensure stability in the state and check the actions of the poor, unskilled masses. The best available measure of stake in the community (at least in the eighteenth century) was the holding of property (Williamson, 1960). In contrast to the situation in England, it was relatively easy to own property, since land was plentiful. Thus, the use of property as a suffrage qualification was less restrictive in America.

Each of the colonies had such a property qualification, some measuring real estate by acreage, some by value, and others allowing personal property or the payment of taxes as an alternative to holding real estate (Porter, 1918). An example of the property qualifications is found in Virginia (1685-1800), where one qualified as a freeholder, thus being eligible to vote, by one of three criteria: (1) holding of twenty-five acres of land with an occupied house; (2) holding of fifty acres of unoccupied land; (3) holding of a house and lot in town. It has been estimated that between one-third and one-half of the adult white males were eligible to vote by these criteria. Those excluded were tenant farmers, plantation overseers, common laborers, as well as many artisans, merchants, and professional men. The latter groups, small in number in Virginia, were often able to vote by means of alternatives to property qualifications in other states. Property restrictions had the additional effect of generally excluding free blacks, foreigners, and "other undesirables" who might not have been explicitly excluded by law (Sydnor, 1952).

The American Revolution created an environment for the liberalization of suffrage, although changes did not occur immediately in every state. Intermediate restrictions were introduced in several states. In some cases, a personal property requirement replaced the old real estate rules, whereas other states permitted anyone who was a taxpayer to vote. By 1800, four states had established universal manhood suffrage, and only five states (including Virginia) retained real estate property qualifications. While the last property requirement was not removed until 1856, the trend was clearly against such requirements by 1800. In many cases, the removal of property requirements did lead to other restrictions that were previously redundant, such as qualifications based on residence, race, and citizenship (Porter, 1918).

As indicated earlier, the actual size of the electorate in the late eighteenth century is difficult to estimate. It is generally agreed that roughly one-fifth of the population consisted of free adult males. One historian (Williamson, 1960, p. 38) has suggested that, before the decline of property qualifications, between 50% and 75% of that group were freeholders eligible to vote. Naturally, as restrictions were removed, the size of the eligible electorate increased. Another historian (Dinkin, 1982) has estimated that from 60% to 90% of all adult males were eligible by 1789. In considering how many people actually participated in any given election, two factors are important: the enforcement of suffrage laws and the extent of nonvoting.

Like most things associated with elections in this era, enforcement of suffrage laws was inconsistent. In Virginia, the evidence suggests that application of the laws was principally dependent on the way the laws would affect the various candidates. Frequently, in a close election, both sides would appeal to ineligible voters to increase their totals. This practice could then result in the loser challenging the election (Pole, 1972). Elsewhere, enforcement was equally arbitrary, either deliberately overlooking election fraud or permitting an implicit liberalization of suffrage (McCormick, 1953).

The frequency of nonvoting was as variable in the eighteenth century as in the twentieth. Turnout could be very high (90%) in a closely contested election, or it could be very low (5%) at other times. Dinkin (1982, ch. 7) has estimated average turnout in the late 1780s to be 20% to 30% of adult white males, with turnout in the first congressional elections ranging from 12% to 44%. The reasons cited have not changed over two centuries. People stayed home due to lack of interest, bad weather, unavailability of suitable alternatives, or distance from the polls. The latter reason was, of course, far more common in the days when transportation was slow. As discussed later, polling places were often at great distances from some voters (Sydnor, 1952; Williamson, 1960).

Districting

There is one aspect of electoral laws that relates specifically to congressional elections. That was the determination of whether members of Congress should be selected by individual districts or on an at-large basis by means of a general ticket. This decision could affect the conduct of elections, especially the system of nominations, and thus it is an important prior consideration. The importance of districting is readily apparent from the fact that it frequently became a political issue in itself. It is clear that as the level of partisanship rose, this districting could have a significant impact on the fortunes of the emerging parties.

Once the Constitution was ratified in 1789, it became necessary to hold elections for members of Congress. Five states chose their congressmen by districts, and five states by the general ticket method. Two states were allotted only one representative each, and Maryland combined features of the two systems. Of the largest states, Virginia and Massachusetts adopted the district system, while Pennsylvania opted for a general ticket (Paullin, 1904). In the six elections that followed through 1800, there were few changes, although these are significant. Pennsylvania changed its system three times, finally settling on a district system. In 1792, Maryland adopted a district plan to replace its hybrid system. New Jersey also experimented with district elections once, in 1798. Events in these three states should help to illustrate the importance of the choice between districts and the general ticket for the development of parties.

It was not until 1794 that Pennsylvania settled on the district system as the permanent method for selecting its delegation to the House of Representatives. Federalists in the General Assembly of 1788 had attempted to assure the selection of a united Federalist delegation to the first Congress by establishing a general ticket system. In 1791, the Assembly changed by a single vote to the district system for the Second Congress. This change was due to the influence of those from the western part of the state, an area that would benefit numerically by the new system and would ultimately become the center of Republican power. A year later, the same issue was reargued, with sectionalism again an important factor. But the outcome changed. A return to the general ticket system was enacted, a move encouraged by the fact that no one knew yet how many seats the state would have in the new Congress. The issue was resolved permanently in 1794, when the Assembly voted to adopt the district system. This time there was no evidence of any factional divisions; rather there was agreement that the general ticket system was impractical in a state as large as Pennsylvania (Tinkcom, 1950).

In the first elections for Congress, Maryland attempted to solve the districting question by creating a mixed plan. The state was divided into districts, and the candidates were required to live in the districts they hoped to represent. But, because the Federalists wanted to avoid the possibility of selecting any Antifederalists, all the representatives were to be elected by general ticket (one from each district). Political divisions in the state were heavily sectional, and this plan successfully averted the election of any Antifederalists. In 1790, political alignments were somewhat different, and the ticket associated with the Federalists was defeated. In response to this outcome, the law was changed and a district election system was adopted. This, together with the realignment of districts, helped the Federalist interests to regain political superiority in Maryland, although partisan alignments were still very unclear (Renzulli, 1972).

New Jersey established a general ticket method of electing members of Congress in 1789, an election that proved to be very controversial. Antifederalist factions within the state argued unsuccessfully for the change to district elections over the next several years. Then, in 1798, a split within the Federalist party was the impetus for implementing a district plan. A reunited Federalist party returned to the old system in 1800; however, the Federalist ticket was defeated, a fact that demonstrates the risk of such strategies. Just as in Pennsylvania and Maryland, the main determinant in choosing between district elections and a general ticket was partisan advantage (McCormick, 1953).

Among states that had established district elections for members of the House, one problem remained: the establishment of the actual districts. This, too, had the potential of becoming a partisan question. The art of gerrymandering probably dates to the first time districts were ever used in elections, although the name awaited the famous Massachusetts district of 1812 when Elbridge Gerry was governor. The first obvious example of the partisan drawing of a congressional district was the work of Patrick Henry, governor of Virginia in 1788. What one historian has labeled a "Henrymander" (Brant, 1950, p. 238) occurred when the Antifederalist Henry was determined to keep James Madison, a leading Federalist, out of the federal Congress. Having already blocked Madison's route to the Senate, Henry designed a district with a strong opponent (James Monroe) and a hostile majority. Madison, however, was able to overcome this strategy, winning the election with 57% of the votes cast (Beeman, 1972; Brant, 1950). Other instances of districting for partisan advantage have been documented for New York, but again such efforts were not always successful (Young, 1967, pp. 132, 332, 564).

Nominations

In the era before political parties were the dominating force in politics and before the advent of the Australian (secret) ballot, nominations were not usually made by any formal process. A citizen would cast his vote for any individual for any office. Of course, if candidacies were not announced in advance, elections could become rather haphazard affairs with a scattering of votes for an assortment of individuals. When elections were held on only a local basis, nominations could be made simply as a matter of course at the town or county meetings. By 1789, with the larger constituencies of congressional elections, some kind of nominating procedure had become necessary. Otherwise, the election might be reduced to a contest among several local candidates. In many states, any voter could place a candidate in nomination. This was accomplished in a few states by submitting names to an official who posted the list of nominees before the elections. But in other places there was no official system of nominations. Candidates could simply make known their own candidacies, or they could be nominated by their friends through letters printed in the newspapers (Dallinger, 1897; Dinkin, 1982, ch. 4).

Initially, these informal nominating systems were adequate, although surprises emerged on occasion. In Virginia, it was even possible for a person to be elected to office without advance warning or any intention of being a candidate. Such was the fate of John Marshall in 1795, who was supporting a different candidate (Sydnor, 1952). Gradually, as factional and party politics became more important, ways were found to make nominations in a more effective manner. In New York, groups of electors gathered in various towns and nominated the candidates previously selected by their party, even while avoiding any designation as a party (Young, 1967, p. 137). Elsewhere nominations were the responsibility of meetings of freemen or state legislatures, or they were still left to informal procedures.

Where congressional candidates were competing in a general ticket system, a coordinated plan of nominations was vital if a party or faction hoped to have its people elected. Thus, in these states more elaborate systems evolved. In Maryland's first congressional election, party tickets were assembled and announced in the newspapers. Yet there was considerable confusion, as the competing factions tried to win votes by tampering with the tickets and publishing incorrect listings of the opposition candidates. With the change to a district system in 1792, the need for statewide tickets was removed and nominations became less formal (Renzulli, 1972). In New Jersey, where nominations were submitted to county officials, various groups endeavored to assemble slates of candidates. In 1789, one group's greater effectiveness in agreeing on a common slate led to its victory, although in a disputed election (McCormick, 1953).

The most elaborate nominating systems at an early date were in Pennsylvania, which had the most developed party system prior to the Constitution. In preparing for the 1789 elections, both the Federalists and the Antifederalists held conventions for the purpose of selecting candidates for Congress and presidential electors. These have been cited as the first known nominating conventions, and their effectiveness was registered in the election results. The change to district elections in 1791 removed the incentive for conventions. The result was a confusing situation where incumbents were unwillingly placed in opposition to each other. The return to a general ticket in 1792 brought back the need for a nominating system. In fact, the precise manner of making nominations served as an issue that separated the two factions. What started as a single convention evolved into a series of meetings and the naming of two competing slates, although with seven (of thirteen) names appearing in common on both tickets. The election results were equally indecisive, with some victories for both tickets. The chief result of these attempts at devising nominating procedures was a return to district elections (Cunningham, 1957; Luetscher, 1903; Tinkcom, 1950).

As the party system developed, nominating procedures evolved quickly. By 1800, nominations were being made by the newly organized parties in the various states. Whether a state had an official nominating procedure or names were simply put forth in the newspapers, the parties usually agreed on appropriate candidates and gave adequate publicity to these slates. An individual voter could still put a name into competition, but his lone voice would be scarcely heard over the increasingly powerful party committees (Cunningham, 1957; Dinkin, 1982, ch. 4).

Electioneering

In the seventeenth and eighteenth centuries, electioneering was not considered appropriate behavior for a prospective candidate for office. While it was fit and proper for a gentleman to serve if elected, it was certainly not proper for him to seek office. One should be "surprised into office by the overwhelming insistence of friends" (Welch, 1965, p. 66). Such a system was fine in the old days when elections were held on a local level and the franchise was restricted. A responsible freeholder was expected to be able to choose someone based on his personal knowledge of the character of the various men being suggested for selection. As election districts were enlarged, suffrage was broadened, and substantial issues complicated the selection process, the norms against electioneering began to be strained by the desire of candidates to publicize their views and broaden their electoral basis of support (Dinkin, 1982, ch. 5).

In colonial Virginia, it was said that "in the days before the election the candidate maintained a dignified aloofness from the voters; however, this rule was broken perhaps as often as it was observed" (Sydnor, 1952, p. 46). Even if a candidate were to mingle with the voters, campaign promises were definitely not considered proper. One candidate, who had made numerous promises, disavowed all such pledges in a statement to the assembled voters on the day of the election. One acceptable custom that developed during this period was "treating," where a candidate kept an open house, serving food and drink to all who came. This practice required drawing a very thin line, since one should not offer food and drink to influence a voter. Yet everyone found ways of resolving this ethical dilemma, and much food and drink was consumed (Sydnor, 1952, ch. 4).

The norms concerning electioneering were already being strained by the time of the first federal elections in 1789. Candidates were no longer "surprised" into an election without their knowledge, but appearances were still important. To many, this meant leaving all electioneering to friends, even while playing a key role behind the scenes. To Theodore Sedgwick, elected as a Federalist in western Massachusetts, it meant concealing his political ambitions even from his wife (Welch, 1965).

James Madison's fight to win election to the House despite the concerted efforts of Patrick Henry sheds additional light on styles of electioneering in the eighteenth century. Madison was attending to the business of the Continental Congress in New York prior to the election, allowing his friends to make limited efforts on his behalf. The effort, however, was not going well, and he was urged to return and make some personal appearances. Although Madison did not want to be involved in personal electioneering, he was convinced to return to Virginia to refute some charges against him by Henry. The opponent was James Monroe, who, despite their political differences, remained a good friend of Madison. Once Madison had decided to travel around the district, he and Monroe chose to make joint appearances in debates throughout the district during the final two weeks before the election. Madison won the election and managed to maintain his friendship with Monroe, who soon became a close political ally. At the same time Madison managed to resolve his feelings on electioneering with the demands of a congressional election (Beeman, 1972; Brant, 1950; Dinkin, 1982).

While personal electioneering was at best a questionable form of behavior in the first decade of the new government, use of the press was a far more common and accepted means of electioneering. The newspapers of that day generally had strong political identities, serving openly as advocates of a point of view. Even before elections became partisan affairs, the press was highly involved. Because a candidate could not appeal personally to the voters, his friends would make the case for his election in letters and articles, usually appearing under pseudonyms in the style of the time. This anonymity often led to a certain license with the truth, and campaigns were often reduced to charges concerning the character of the candidates, in some ways a situation not unlike that of today (Bernhard, 1965).

As partisanship increased and electoral contests became more consequential, the norms against electioneering received less and less attention.

Incumbent congressmen were being challenged on the basis of their records in office; elections were no longer simply a selection of the better man. The old norms, however, did not die easily. In the presidential election of 1796, Jefferson was the choice of the Republicans around the country and the object of some serious electioneering. Yet he kept himself out of the campaign, maintaining what appears to have been a sincere indifference with regard to the results (Cunningham, 1957).

In 1794, a Virginia congressman, John Page, addressed his constituents on the subject of electioneering: "Courting popularity as it is called, and attempting to gain the affections or *votes* of the people, is so nearly connected with an officious attention to them, and an unwearied effort to gratify their curiosity or their wishes, that any one of the citizens of these United States who is acquainted with the history of mankind and the frailty of human nature, will agree with me, that the more attention I pay to my business in Congress, and the less to my constituents, the greater must be my respect for them, their dignity and permanent interests" (John Page, *An Address to the Citizens of the District of York*, June 20, 1794, in Cunningham, 1965, p. 134). His comments, curiously similar to Edmund Burke's classic remarks, are a strong statement in favor of the traditional type of election. He concludes that the best man should be chosen, "whether he should offer himself as a candidate or not" (Cunningham, 1965, p. 136). His ideas, however, were becoming less popular, perhaps the reason he felt he must defend his lack of personal campaigning.

The changing norms are more apparent in the 1798 reelection campaign of Maryland's Samuel Smith, a campaign full of charges and countercharges in the heated political atmosphere. Smith was publicly involved, writing letters to the press and speaking out on his own behalf. His most effective campaigning in this successful contest was among the militia, where he was a general. Smith spent over six hundred dollars of his own money in a revival of the Virginia tradition of "treating." His behavior, while condemned by the opposition, was far more acceptable in the political world of 1798 than it would have been a decade earlier (Cassell, 1971).

Just as personal campaigning had limited importance in the eighteenth century, party organizations were all but nonexistent in the first years of the new nation and thus played almost no role in the earliest campaigns. By 1792, however, party organizations began to be at least somewhat visible in some state elections. This was particularly true in nominations in both New York and Pennsylvania, as described earlier. But even in these states, where parties were more developed than elsewhere, the role was very limited. At the national level, Republican leaders in New York, Pennsylvania, and Virginia consulted with each other on the selection of a vice-presidential candidate. This beginning of national cooperation among Republicans was an important first step in the development of a national party organization (Cunningham, 1957, pp. 45-49).

In the following year (1793), popular associations began to arise around the country, particularly in response to the events in France. These associations, known as Democratic or Republican societies, emerged in every part of the country and were the subjects of great controversy during their brief existence. Their greatest fame came as a result of a speech to Congress by Washington late in 1794, in which he denounced the groups as "self-created societies," blaming them for the Whiskey Rebellion. This charge, coinciding with a worsening situation in France, led to the disappearance of most of the societies by 1796 (Cunningham, 1957, pp. 62-67; Link, 1942).

While they existed, the societies did exert a degree of political influence on the election of 1794, always on the side of the Republican candidate. In particular, their role in New York and Philadelphia has been cited as instrumental in Republican victories over Federalist incumbents. In Philadelphia, a rich merchant who was sympathetic to Republican positions (Swanwick) was able to defeat by only a small margin a three-term incumbent (Fitzsimons) who spoke out strongly against the "self-centered societies" (Luetscher, 1903; Tinkcom, 1950). In New York City, an intense contest was waged in the newspapers by supporters of Republican Edward Livingston and incumbent Federalist John Watts. Livingston won narrowly, with 53% of the vote. While there was no doubt that the New York Democratic Society was outspoken in Livingston's support, he himself apparently did not acknowledge any partisan support (Luetscher, 1903; Miller, 1939; Young, 1967, pp. 420-421).

In spite of these electoral successes, it is not entirely clear how extensive an impact the Democratic societies had on the politics of 1794. Miller (1939, p. 141) has argued, "Without a doubt it was the activity of the Democratic Societies that dominated the elections of 1794," referring not just to the New York and Philadelphia contests. It is clear that the narrow margins of victory in the latter two cities could well have been attributable to the work of the societies there, but whether their impact was as extensive as claimed by Miller is questionable. Cunningham (1957, p. 65) suggests that the societies "can best be described as pressure groups." Perhaps the relevant point is that these groups did have an influence on election outcomes, but that this influence should not be categorized as the effect of party organization. In a Republican "party" that still lacked much of an institutionalized existence, the societies were precursors of a party organization and helped to demonstrate a potential for success that existed with the "republican interest."

Vast increases in the level of party organization occurred between the elections of 1794 and 1796. Several events (including Washington's retirement and the contest over the Jay Treaty) crucial to the emergence of parties made the 1796 election more partisan and spurred on the development of party organizations. On the Federalist side, Hamilton had created a moderately extensive organization, and local campaigns were being run more frequently by party organizations.

After 1794, encouraged by the chance to elect a Republican president, leading Republicans were increasingly consulting with each other to coordinate electoral efforts within and across state lines. Their level of sophistication is illustrated by the campaign waged in Pennsylvania on behalf of Jefferson. John Beckley, clerk of the U.S. House, took on the role of state campaign manager, providing lists of electors, coordinating the work of influential citizens, and distributing large numbers of handbills. The campaign was a successful one, with fourteen of fifteen electoral votes going to Jefferson (Cunningham, 1956; Fay, 1936).

By 1796, party organizations had reached a level where they played a major role in both state and national elections. While norms against electioneering persisted, thus limiting and modifying the role that parties might play, party organizations continued to be important in elections held between 1796 and 1801.

Electoral Procedures

Election day in the eighteenth century did not much resemble its twentieth-century counterpart. The local elections of colonial days for the most part lacked formal procedures. On a designated town meeting day (in the North) or county court day (in the South), a time was reserved for selecting new officers. In most cases, a simple show of hands or voice vote was adequate to determine the results. But the increasing complexity that led to more formalized nominations also led to changes in the conduct of elections. Controversy sometimes arose, as electoral regulations could affect the fates of various candidates or interests. These conflicts centered on such matters as the use of ballots or viva voce voting, the time and place of elections, and the requirement of a majority for election. In general, the years surrounding the Revolution marked a significant transformation of electoral procedures in most states to a system that was more orderly and democratic than that of earlier years (Dinkin, 1982, ch. 6).

When a simple voice vote or show of hands proved to be inadequate, more elaborate procedures of voice voting (viva voce) were developed. Virginia, which did not abandon this method of elections until the Civil War, followed very specific procedures.

> To open proceedings in the court house the sheriff, after reading aloud the writ, took his place behind the long table, at each end of which sat the candidates. If, as usually happened, a poll was required because the result could not be decided by shout, the electors filed up, one by one, announced their votes and were then, as a rule, entitled to be thanked by the gentleman of their choice. "Sir, I shall treasure that vote as long as I live"; "Sir, may you live a thousand years," were acceptable epithets from a grateful recipient. The elections often lasted all day, and might go on for two or three, but when the sheriff was satisfied that all the votes had been taken he might close the poll at his own discretion. [Pole, 1972, p. 33]

Elections occurred on the regular county court day, when people came to town to carry on their business. It was always a lively day; when elections were held, the excitement increased, generally helped by a free flow of liquor. This form of voice voting was very dramatic, adding to the excitement, because votes were cast openly and one could see at any time who was leading. Of course, the lack of secrecy could put a great deal of pressure on a voter who had to announce his choice to the world (Pole, 1972; Sydnor, 1952).

As suffrage was granted to more people, the problems with voice voting became greater. The enfranchisement of those who were not financially independent provided the potential for vote fraud, as a landlord could exert an undue influence on the votes of his tenants. Such conditions helped to create a movement toward the secret ballot. While English precedent favored the use of voice voting, the secret ballot had its origins as early as ancient Athens. The written ballot was the most common form, but for a time Massachusetts used the corn and bean system, where the voter deposited into a container a corn for a yes vote and a bean for a no vote. Many colonies experimented with paper ballots; by 1789, it appears that only New Jersey and several southern states were still using voice voting. By 1800, only Kentucky and Virginia had not adopted the written ballot (Albright, 1942; Harris, 1934; Williamson, 1960).

Some of the reasons why adoption of the secret ballot was controversial are revealed by the actions of New Jersey between 1774 and 1797. During the Revolution, viva voce voting was sometimes used to limit the influence of Tories, who might be unwilling to show their preference in public. On the other hand, there were common fears that voice voting would allow the influence of the wealthy to be increased. As of 1789, ballots were required for congressional elections, but some counties were allowed to continue use of voice voting for local elections. By 1797, the ballot was being used in all elections (McCormick, 1953).

The ballot used in those days was not the Australian ballot printed by the state, a reform that arrived only late in the nineteenth century. Typically, a voter was required to write the names of his selections on a slip of paper and bring it to the poll. Printed ballots were not allowed at that time in many states and did not become common until after 1800. Like many electoral procedures, the printed ballot was the result of partisan activity. A precursor of the printed ballot appeared in the 1796 presidential election in Pennsylvania, and it was indeed the result of the developing partisan machinery there. That state had adopted a general ticket system for selecting its fifteen electors, and it was feared that voters would fail to write all the names on their ballots. John Beckley, who ran the Pennsylvania campaign that year, urged party supporters to write out as many tickets as they could for distribution to potential voters. This effort was successful: the Republicans won fourteen of fifteen votes for Jefferson (Cunningham, 1956).

When most elections were local affairs, there needed to be only a single polling place, normally the site of the county court or town meeting. While this might require a lengthy journey for some, such a trip might be necessary anyway for business reasons. The incentive to come was often increased by the festival atmosphere. In Virginia, it was often the custom for people to remain overnight for the election, often staying at the home of a candidate. This helped to boost turnout, although it also swelled the flow of liquor. Of course, distances also had the effect of preventing some from voting. If someone could not be spared from the farm that day, he simply lost his vote. As mentioned previously, polls in Virginia were generally held open until the sheriff was convinced that everyone had been given a chance to vote. This system was not uncommon in other colonies, despite the discretion it afforded a sheriff to place his personal stamp on the election outcomes (Sydnor, 1952).

As various states made provisions for electing a governor and congressional districts were formed incorporating several towns or counties, some standardization of the time and place of voting was needed. By 1789, New York electoral law was representative of the evolving practices. Elections were held annually at a fixed date, lasting for as many as five days. Each town was given a polling place, which was an improvement over earlier laws. Yet, even with this law, voting still required a major effort, particularly for those in the western part of the state (Young, 1967).

The impact of these provisions of electoral law is demonstrated most clearly by New Jersey's disputed election in 1789. Many revisions were made in the New Jersey election law between 1774 and 1797. By 1789, the number of polling places had been increased from one per county to an average of four in each county, giving convenient access to the polls for many more voters. The first congressional election, held on a general ticket system, was scheduled to begin on February 11, 1789, with the closing date to be determined by local election officials. This election was being contested by one slate of four candidates, the Junto ticket of West Jersey, and a partial slate of two from East Jersey. The election was characterized "by attacks on personalities and appeals to sectional jealousy" (McCormick, 1973, p. 68) and became very heated. Election fraud was widespread. Most of the polls in East Jersey had closed by February 23, twelve days after opening. After seeing these results, West Jersey leaders recirculated their ballot boxes to round up more votes, putting their ticket ahead. By March 18, only one county remained open (Essex in East Jersey). The governor's council decided it could not wait for the Essex results to certify the winners, and the Junto ticket was deemed victorious. The Essex polls were not closed until April 27, over ten weeks after opening, but too late to be counted. The election machinery had proved highly susceptible to manipulation, and changes were made before the next election (McCormick, 1953, 1973).

Several other issues were occasionally raised in the search for fair and reasonable election laws. One question was that of appropriate election officials. In some cases, election judges were selected on election day, but this made their choice unnecessarily influenced by the ensuing contest. In other places (such as Virginia), the county sheriff was responsible for conducting elections, although he was sometimes a close ally of one candidate. Eventually, with the rise of partisanship, it sometimes became necessary to appoint a bipartisan group of election officials.

One electoral provision was apparently unique to the state of Massachusetts at the time. This was the rule requiring that a congressional candidate receive a majority of votes cast to be elected. This provision often necessitated a series of runoff elections, especially in the earliest years before parties dominated the political scene and before there were any powerful incumbents. In 1788 and 1789, four of the eight districts required more than one election, with five elections necessary in one district before the winning candidate received a slim majority. By 1790, six districts picked their candidates in single elections. One district, however, required nine elections over a period of nineteen months (Hall, 1972).

A technicality in Delaware's election law led to a disputed election in 1792. The law stated that each voter should return a ballot with two names, one of which must be from outside his home county—although Delaware had only one seat in Congress. Confusion over the enforcement of this law led to a challenge of the results. Patten, a Republican, had been elected by a plurality of thirty votes, but Latimer, his Federalist opponent, claimed that ballots should not be counted if they contained only a single name. On this basis, enough votes were thrown out to make Latimer the winner. After an investigation by the House, Patten was expelled and Latimer was seated (Munroe, 1954, pp. 204-5).

Regulation of elections was initially the responsibility of local election officials. State officials were then normally required to certify the results. Once the results were certified, any further challenges were the responsibility of the House of Representatives. The Constitution (Article I, Section 5) provides that "each House shall be the Judge of the Elections, Returns and Qualifications of its own Members. . . ." Every session brought some charge of an improper election. These were sent to a Committee on Elections and investigated. In many, lack of clear evidence or the desire to avoid controversy led the House simply to approve the certified results, as in the New Jersey case of 1789. Often, however, the desire for partisan advantage caused one side to be favored, a factor that may have prevailed in the 1792 Delaware case.

Several other electoral disputes occurred during the first seven Congresses. One of particular importance was the 1791 contest between Wayne and Jackson in Georgia (Rose, 1968, pp. 60-68). Wayne, identified as a Federalist, was the apparent winner, but the result was challenged by Jackson, an ardent opponent of the administration. The House eventually declared the seat vacant on a partisan vote, a decision analyzed further in chapter 6.

While specific procedures existed to resolve controversies over the results of congressional elections, it seems that the pursuit of partisan advantage generally exceeded any desire for a fair resolution. In nearly every case, the dominant party in Congress resolved disputes in favor of the contestant who was most likely to side with it in the political debates.

Conclusion: Elections in the 1790s

Many traditional electoral institutions had the potential to place severe restrictions on the pace of party development. In particular, the informal system for nominating candidates and the norms that limited active campaigns would have prevented any extensive involvement of parties in the electoral process. Other aspects of traditional electoral institutions were less likely to inhibit the emergence of parties directly, but they could be expected to affect the forms these new parties might take.

If strict limitations on suffrage and the use of voice voting had been maintained for a longer time, it is unlikely that any form of mass-based party could have developed. In its place, a system of elite factions, like the networks of court and country followers, would have been a more likely development. To the extent, then, that these traditions were maintained, the transition to mass involvement in partisan politics was deterred.

In other ways, the underdeveloped state of electoral institutions was a boon to the emerging parties. Where forms and procedures were neither well developed nor generally accepted, there was little cost to those who would manipulate the system for partisan advantage. Thus, those in the majority could change suffrage restrictions, switch between district and at-large systems for congressional elections, adjust the timing of elections, or otherwise change the rules. In these actions, it became obvious that decision makers often did see things in wider partisan terms.

The important theme here, however, is not the specific rules for elections or the means of manipulation. Rather, it is the fact that the electoral institutions had a very different form in the eighteenth century than they do in the twentieth. As the development of modern electoral institutions progressed, the climate for parties gradually improved. Nevertheless, it should not be surprising that, as parties made their appearance, their forms did not always match twentieth-century expectations of how parties should look.

4. Party Institutions in Congress

The empirical research presented in this book consists chiefly of an analysis of voting patterns within the Congress. On this basis, we should be able to draw certain conclusions about levels of party voting at various times. Yet, as discussed in chapter 1, the existence of party depends on more than the presence of cohesive voting blocs. It also depends on the appearance of institutions of party leadership and formal party structures. Thus, in this chapter we examine available evidence on the organizational aspects of parties in Congress. Such organizations, if they are present, either can be the product of a unified voting bloc trying to increase its power or can represent the efforts of a president or others to build majorities around their legislative programs.

While a good deal of attention has been given to questions of party leadership in the twentieth century, little has been written about leadership in the eighteenth century. Historical documents and records seemingly do not provide much help on these questions. As a result, the literature is dependent upon limited facts and much speculation, meaning that it is sometimes contradictory. What follows is an attempt to draw together what is available and to evaluate this information with a skeptical eye.

The focus in this chapter and throughout the book is primarily on the House of Representatives, rather than on the Senate. The "upper" chamber was generally viewed in these early years as less significant than the House. Its work load was lighter, since most legislation originated in the House; in fact, the Senate sometimes tried to adjourn early enough to attend the more lively House sessions. In addition, the Senate normally met behind closed doors until 1795, further shielding it from the public eye. Finally, the selection of senators by state legislatures insulated the Senate from direct public pressures (Wormser, 1982). Because of these differences, the House is the chamber more suited to a study of emerging partisanship.

The Speaker of the House

The Constitution provides that the House should choose for itself a Speaker, the only House officer specifically authorized. Precedents existed both in the British House of Commons and in colonial assemblies for such an office. It was the custom in legislatures that the Speaker be the leader of the dominant party or faction, in addition to fulfilling his chief duty of controlling debate and applying the rules when the legislature was meeting. Other than the custom that the Speaker be a member of the House, there are no formal qualifications for the office in the House of Representatives (Follett, 1896).

In modern Congresses, the election of the Speaker occurs on a roll call vote, and it is the one vote during each Congress that is virtually guaranteed to be a party vote. In the eighteenth century, the election was held by ballot, and the winner had to receive a majority of all votes. For most of the elections from 1789 to 1801, little is known beyond the identity of the victor, although there has been some informed speculation concerning the nature of these contests.[1]

The initial order of business for the First Congress in 1789, once a quorum was achieved (which took nearly a month), was the selection of the first Speaker. The choice was Frederick A.C. Muhlenberg, who had previously presided over legislative bodies in Pennsylvania. It has been suggested that his election was due to his moderate position on the issues of the day, to his experience as a presiding officer, and to his residence in the Middle states. Sectional concerns were foremost at that time, and Muhlenberg profited from the fact that the president hailed from Virginia and the vice-president from Massachusetts. His chief opponent was apparently Jonathan Trumbull (Conn.), a stronger Federalist who was a New Englander; Muhlenberg won by a "considerable" majority.[2]

Trumbull and Muhlenberg were again the main persons considered for the speakership of the Second Congress in 1791, but this time Trumbull was selected. A principle of rotation in office seems to have been a key factor; some believed that different persons from other regions should have a turn at leadership. Concerns of partisanship may have had an additional effect. "Muhlenberg had shown signs of a leaning away from administration measures, and Trumbull may have been more trusted" (Follett, 1896, p. 65). The intense legislative battles of the First Congress apparently had an impact on the subsequent choice of leadership in the next Congress.

In the Third Congress, Muhlenberg was returned to the office of Speaker after a one-term absence. The circumstances of his selection in 1793, however, differed from those in 1789, although his moderate views were again a key factor. He had become in effect the candidate of those in opposition to the administration, which had an apparent majority in the House. Some administration supporters preferred Theodore Sedgwick (Mass.), a strong Federalist partisan. But Muhlenberg won by ten votes on the third ballot (Lientz, 1978; Welch, 1965, p. 155n); his victory probably reflected the preference of the House for a Speaker who was not a strong partisan. The Republicans supported him rather than their own leading men, although he was probably closer to being a Federalist. The weakness of the office kept the Speaker from being a key factor in the business of the House and therefore provided an incentive for selecting a man of moderate views.

The dynamics of the speakership election in the Fourth Congress were much like those of the 1793 contest. Again, a moderate man who was at least nominally a Federalist became Speaker in 1795 through the support of both

Federalists and Republicans. Sedgwick was to have been the Federalist candidate (Welch, 1965, p. 155), but upon recognizing that his views were too extreme for him to be elected, his supporters shifted their votes to Jonathan Dayton (N.J.), whose views were moderate enough to win Republican support. Whether the more partisan Republicans supported their own candidate is unknown, but the vote has been given as forty-six to thirty-one (Follett, 1896, p. 66).

Little is known about the election for Speaker of the Fifth Congress in 1797 beyond the fact that Dayton won a second term by a vote of seventy-eight to two (Lientz, 1978). It seems that, in a closely divided Congress like this one, a moderate Federalist made a reasonable compromise candidate. The preference for nonpartisan Speakers is further demonstrated by the selection of a Speaker pro tempore on two occasions during the second session of the Fifth Congress. The man selected was George Dent (Md.), whose record in Congress showed little attachment to either party. On the first occasion Dent received forty out of seventy-three votes, with the remaining votes mostly divided between a more extreme Federalist and a partisan Republican, while the vote was more one-sided on the second date (*Annals*, 5th Cong., 2nd sess., pp. 1475, 1835). Even Dayton's moderation was not received favorably by everyone, however. On the traditional vote of thanks to the Speaker, normally passed without opposition at the end of the session, twenty-two votes (of sixty-two) were cast against the resolution.

For the first time, the election of a Speaker became a clearly partisan contest in 1799. The two principal candidates in the Sixth Congress were Sedgwick, an extreme Federalist, and Nathaniel Macon (N.C.), a solid Republican. The election required two ballots, and on the first, thirteen votes (of eighty-five) went to the candidate who represented moderation, Dent. Since Dent had no chance of success, most of his votes went to the other candidates on the second ballot. Sedgwick led the first ballot, forty-two to twenty-seven, over Macon and was left one vote short of the necessary majority. On the second ballot he won a narrow victory, forty-four to thirty-eight with four votes for other candidates.[3] This contest demonstrated the increasing partisanship involved in congressional matters, and Sedgwick's actions as Speaker showed that he viewed himself as a party leader (Lientz, 1978; Welch, 1965, pp. 205-6; *Annals*, 6th Cong., 1st sess., p. 186).[4]

The losing candidate in 1799, Macon, was elected Speaker of the Seventh Congress in 1801 after the Republicans had gained a clear majority in Congress. The Federalists offered a candidate, James Bayard of Delaware, but the vote was decisive, fifty-three to twenty-six (Lientz, 1978). Macon served four terms as Speaker, being generally regarded as an able party leader.

The evidence across seven Congresses clearly suggests increasing involvement of parties in the selection of a Speaker. The earliest Speakers, especially Muhlenberg and Dayton, were men of moderate views, who generally served as presiding officers relatively uninvolved in the partisan contests that were becoming more frequent. Sedgwick and Macon, on the other hand, represent the changing of the office to one that was an active part of the party leadership.

A contrary conclusion is suggested by Young (1966), who argues that speakership elections were evidence of a general lack of party organization in Congress. Based on an analysis of elections from 1798 to 1859, he draws this conclusion concerning the elections during the Jeffersonian era: "The erratic performance on speakership elections . . . suggests either a minimal degree of party involvement in the selection of an officer whose role would clearly have been of great usefulness to a legislative party, or a conspicuous failure to achieve consensus and cohesion in performing this elementary function of a legislative party" (Young, 1966, p. 123). It is difficult to reconcile this statement with the evidence for the years immediately preceding the Jeffersonian era. One possibility is that Young is being overly cautious in his search for evidence of party organization. Alternatively, the level of partisanship apparent in 1799 and 1801 was simply greater than that of the three decades that followed. I shall return to Young's conclusions later with regard to other aspects of party organization.

Formal Leadership in Congress

The leadership positions of majority leader and minority leader were not formally established until late in the nineteenth century. The only formal positions of leadership in the early Congresses were the chairmanships of several committees. Alexander (1916) indicates that the chairman of the Ways and Means Committee was generally regarded as the floor leader; however, other historians seem to assign less importance to that position.

In general, the committee system was not very important between 1789 and 1803, for most committees were established only for a fixed time to deal with a specific bill (Harlow, 1917). Cooper (1970), in his study of the origins of the committee system, asserts that committees clearly were viewed as creations of the House and considered legislation only after the House had resolved its general position on the issue. As the committees thus dealt chiefly with the details of legislation, committee chairmen were mostly moderators of discussion, not significant political leaders. While partisanship had become a factor in committee appointments and decision making by the late 1790s, committees were not a major source of party leadership.

While no House members held significant positions of formal leadership, other than the Speaker, one important position was the clerk of the House. Not a member of the House, the position of clerk did gain importance in these early years due chiefly to the first incumbent, John Beckley. He was a close ally of Jefferson and Madison and served the emerging Republican party in numerous capacities. For example, in the 1796 presidential campaign, Beckley served as the Republican campaign manager in Pennsylvania. As a result of this successful partisan effort, he lost his job by a single vote at the beginning of the subsequent Congress. Only when the Jeffersonians achieved full control of the government in 1801 did Beckley regain his position.[5]

Informal Party Leadership

Some system of informal leadership can be expected to develop in any group activity, and there is no reason to expect anything different in the United States Congress. Furthermore, if conflict in the Congress is being organized on the basis of parties, then these informal leaders are likely to be considered as party leaders. "That there were leaders on Capitol Hill, in the sense of activists striving to win support for their views, cannot be doubted. That party partisanship had some degree of relevance for these efforts is to be presumed. . . . The question is whether there were leadership roles looking specifically to the achievement of party solidarity and providing that persistence of effort which, in the absence of party caucuses or other formal organization, was presumably required to maintain any semblance of party cohesion" (Young, 1966, pp. 127-128). For the Jeffersonian era between 1800 and 1828, Young answers his question in the negative. What he found was a large number of people who provided leadership on specific issues, but no individuals whose leadership was either long-lasting or oriented toward party cohesion. In this section, this same question is considered for the period from 1789 to 1801.

In the earliest Congresses, nearly every observer would agree that the principal legislative leader on the Federalist side was not a member of Congress. Rather he was the controversial secretary of the treasury, Alexander Hamilton. Many of the major legislative initiatives in the First Congress came directly from Hamilton. In fact, his leadership was so pervasive that it earned him the bitter criticism of his opponents. William Maclay, the Pennsylvania senator who often observed the House and recorded his thoughts in a journal, referred frequently to Hamilton's involvement as a legislative leader. He said in one context, "Mr. Hamilton is all-powerful, and fails in nothing he attempts" (Maclay, 1927, p. 376). At least from the evidence of Maclay, Hamilton was involved much in the manner of a modern floor leader, caucusing with members, trying to round up votes, and helping to schedule legislation.

Of course, because Hamilton was not allowed to speak in debate or introduce bills, he had to depend on members for further leadership. On the first few issues, he worked closely with Madison, but this alliance lasted for only a few months (Brant, 1950). For the remainder of the First Congress, he turned to two staunch Federalists from Massachusetts, Fisher Ames and Theodore Sedgwick, and a South Carolinian, William L. Smith. Even at the young age of thirty-two, Ames was becoming a leading spokesman for Hamilton in the First Congress. He was a brilliant orator whose speeches were highly regarded even by his enemies, and it was said that his speech was the final decisive factor in the approval of funds for the Jay Treaty. It was Ames who often took responsibility for defending Federalist programs (Bernhard, 1965).

Sedgwick, a close ally of Ames, also played a key role in many of the early legislative battles. While Ames retired after the Jay Treaty session, Sedgwick continued to provide leadership in the Adams years, first serving in the Senate and then returning to the House as Speaker. Sedgwick was generally associated with the extreme (High) Federalists, who attacked Adams on some issues. Other prominent leaders among the High Federalists were Smith (S.C.), Harper (S.C.), and Cabot (Mass.). Smith and Harper were both prolific writers of pamphlets, in addition to their legislative roles. Adams did continue to command the loyalty of a few Federalist leaders, men such as Marshall (Va.), Otis (Mass.), and Murray (Md.) (Dauer, 1953; Kurtz, 1957; Welch, 1965).

The Republican leadership appeared on the scene nearly as soon as that of the Federalists. While Madison worked briefly as an ally of Hamilton in the first session of the First Congress, he soon took exception to several parts of the administration program. He very quickly became active in leading the opposition to this program. Yet most would concede that his role at that time was not that of a party leader; instead, he was taking a personal stand on an issue and trying to win supporters to his side. It was not long, however, before Madison was regarded as the foremost leader of the Republican interest in Congress. By the time of the contest over the Jay Treaty in 1796, Madison was acting in a role that did not much differ from that of a modern party leader (Brant, 1950; Cunningham, 1957).

Madison was not alone, however, in his efforts. Like the Federalists, the Republicans could at times count on an ally in the Cabinet. While Jefferson was secretary of state, he became directly opposed to most of Hamilton's programs. In respect for his position in Washington's Cabinet, he tried to avoid any public leadership role, but he did play an important role in planning strategy with his friend Madison. In 1793, his retirement from the Cabinet marked a complete withdrawal from politics, and he did not resume a leadership role until becoming vice-president in 1797, a date that coincides with Madison's retirement from Congress (Cunningham, 1957).

Upon Madison's temporary retirement, there was a leadership vacuum in the Republican congressional delegation. Madison had played such a dominant role that his shoes were difficult to fill. In 1797, three men who had aided Madison extensively picked up the reins of leadership. Gallatin (Pa.), Giles (Va.), and Nicholas (Va.) were all active leaders, working closely with Jefferson, now in the position of vice-president. Sedgwick described his opponent as "under the *controul* of the Genevese [Gallatin], . . . a well organized and disciplined Corps, never going astray" (Sedgwick to King, April 9, 1798, quoted in Cunningham, 1957, p. 123). Although an exaggeration, this description illustrates the recognition of Gallatin as a party leader (Cunningham, 1957; Walters, 1957).

When the Republicans became the majority party in 1801, there was an even keener need for leadership, especially with Gallatin joining the Cabinet. Although Giles had returned to Congress, leadership roles were taken up by Macon (N.C.), Randolph (Va.), and Nicholson (Md.). Macon was elected Speaker, Randolph served as chairman of the Ways and Means Committee, and Giles continued to be an important congressional ally of Jefferson; consequently, there was a lack of consensus on where the real leadership rested (Cunningham, 1963).

Young (1966) has raised the general question of whether leadership in the early Congress was directed at party solidarity rather than the achievement of personal goals. It is difficult to answer this question without a more extensive examination of the thoughts and deeds of those who provided leadership. Little is in fact known about the motivations of these leaders.

For the Federalists in the early years, Hamilton and his congressional allies did provide strong policy leadership. While Hamilton may have been pursuing personal goals, it does appear that the various leaders were truly seeking unity behind the package of proposals initiated by the administration, ranging from the fiscal programs in the First Congress to the Jay Treaty in the Fourth.

In the Adams years, however, divisions among the Federalists led to a more confused picture. Hamilton and Adams were pursuing different paths, and congressional leaders were forced to choose sides. But even then the sides were never clearly drawn. It is evident, therefore, that no set network of Federalist *party* leadership existed in these later years.

Whereas Federalist leadership was on the decline almost as soon as it was established, Republican leadership was more stable in the 1790s, perhaps due to the role played by Jefferson, Madison, and Gallatin, three men who made a significant mark on history. Or perhaps it was their opposition status that produced a greater need for organization and unity. Whatever the reason, it does seem that the Republicans were blessed with good, strong party leadership during this era. Even Young (1966, p. 279*n*) acknowledges this point: "The impression is, moreover, that the Republican party leadership was rather more closely knit during the 1790s, where their party was an opposition party in Congress, than it was after the Republicans acquired the status of majority party." This point is accentuated by the lack of agreement on leadership for the Seventh Congress, when the Republicans had finally reached majority status.

Thus, we see a rather mixed picture of party leadership. There were times when leadership played a substantial role and other times when there was an absence of effective leadership. We must next consider the role played by the party caucus, a potentially key arm of an organized party.

The Party Caucus

The congressional party caucus has had a varied history, with periods of prime importance and times of disuse. In the 1790s, there was no formal institution known as the caucus. Nevertheless, it is clear that members of Congress belonging to one party did meet on several occasions. Two different party functions provided the incentive for caucus meetings during this period. One was the need to unite on candidates for presidential elections. The other was the need for the party to provide a degree of coordination in its legislative strategy.

The evolving system of nominations within the various states was discussed in the previous chapter; the presidential election, however, provided special problems. The Constitution provided for an Electoral College whose members would simply vote for the best available person, regardless of any party loyalties. This system worked as long as everyone agreed on the choice of George Washington. In his absence, or at the vice-presidential level, some coordination of effort was needed between states if a party was to be successful. The only institution that regularly provided such contacts among the states was Congress, so a party's congressional members would meet to consider nominees.

Most historians believe that the formal congressional nominating caucus did not appear until 1800 or 1804 (Dallinger, 1897; Young, 1966). It is clear that, in 1792, no caucus met to agree upon an opponent for John Adams, the incumbent vice-president. An informal meeting of several party leaders was held, finally settling on George Clinton. Their effort proved to be reasonably successful, with fifty of the fifty-five Republican votes going to Clinton (Chambers, 1963b; McCormick, 1982).

Washington's retirement in 1796 opened up the political system to party maneuvering. There was little doubt about the identities of the two presidential candidates: Jefferson and Adams. More open to question was the choice of vice-presidential candidates. The Republican congressmen held a caucus, but they were unable to agree on a choice. Burr received only thirty electoral votes, compared to fifty-nine for Jefferson, a sign that there was little coordinated effort by Republicans for Burr or anyone else (Cunningham, 1957; McCormick, 1982). One reason may have been that the electoral system did not provide for separate vice-presidential balloting. The Federalists held what one historian has labeled a "quasi caucus" to nominate Adams and Thomas Pinckney of South Carolina as their candidates (Nichols, 1967). Some Federalist leaders, including Hamilton, apparently were hoping that southern votes would put Pinckney ahead of Adams.

By 1800, the nominating process had become relatively formalized, as both parties apparently held congressional caucuses. Records of these secret meetings do not exist, so information is sketchy. The Republicans had agreed on Jefferson as their presidential candidate without any disagreement. For vice-president, Aaron Burr was nominated unanimously at a meeting of about forty-five congressmen at Marache's boardinghouse, the residence of several Republican leaders. It appears, however, that this caucus was simply ratifying the work done by key Republican leaders in consultation with the potential candidates (Cunningham, 1957; Dallinger, 1897; McCormick, 1982).

The Federalists also used a caucus to nominate their candidates, or at least to ratify the choices being urged by Hamilton. The candidates so named were Adams and Charles C. Pinckney (S.C.). As in 1796, it was Hamilton's not-so-secret hope that some southern states would possibly vote for Pinckney and not Adams, thus electing Pinckney as president and leaving John Adams with no more than the second spot. This strategy, of course, proved to be unsuccessful. One irony is apparent in the meeting of the Federalist caucus. Several propagandists for the party were strongly chastising the Republicans for the use of a secret caucus, even while they were doing the very same thing (Cunningham, 1957; Dallinger, 1897; McCormick, 1982).

The congressional caucus was to become the principal method of nominating presidential candidates over the next two decades, only to be replaced later by national conventions. It has been argued that congressional caucuses never represented even the whole membership of congressional parties and thus were not evidence of party organization in Congress (Young, 1966). But in the elections of 1792, 1796, and 1800, the roots of the nominating caucus were evident, and even this is a minimal indication of self-conscious political parties. Still, information on these caucuses is so lacking that conclusions cannot easily be drawn.

In contrast, evidence of congressional party caucuses with the goal of formulating legislative strategy on policy issues or encouraging party loyalty is found as early as the First Congress. As noted earlier, Hamilton was the leader of the Federalists at this early date, and it appears that the party caucus was one of his tools of leadership. Senator Maclay, whose low opinion of Hamilton is clearly reflected in his journal, referred at one point to "the rendezvousing of the crew of the Hamiltonian galley" (Maclay, 1927, pp. 202-3). A month later he entered another reference: "the Speaker told me there had been a call of the Secretary's party last night" (Maclay, 1927, p. 230). Certainly these comments, coming from a member of the opposition, are only fragmentary evidence of the use of the party caucus. But there is further evidence that the Federalists continued to meet as a caucus. Harlow (1917, pp. 184-85) has uncovered at least three contemporary references to caucuses between 1797 and 1801, the last of these occurring during the attempt to resolve the deadlocked presidential election in 1801.

The Republicans seemed to be slower to use the party caucus, but their use of it may have had a more significant impact on congressional policy making than for the Federalists. Apparently, no caucuses were held prior to 1796, and only two between that date and 1801. Gallatin, one of the Republican leaders, recalled that "there were but two of those party meetings called for the purpose of deliberating upon the measures proper to be adopted" (Cunningham, 1957, p. 82). The second of these was in 1798 on the question of policy toward France, and little is known about it. The former meeting was held in 1796 on the subject of the Jay Treaty. Called by James Madison, it marked an attempt to agree upon strategy and to obtain unanimous support for the Republican position. The caucus was unable to obtain perfect loyalty for its position, and the issue finally lost by a single vote. Nevertheless, this effort did mark a significant use of the party caucus as a means of party leadership and organization.

Whether the caucus became a regular tool of party leadership after the Republicans had achieved a position of power in 1801 remains problematic. According to Harlow (1917, p. 187), "The Republicans certainly became familiar with the caucus before the election of 1800, and from the seventh Congress on they made regular use of it." Most of his evidence for this statement is drawn from the comments of Federalist congressmen or statements appearing in Federalist newspapers. The lack of confirmatory statements by Republican participants has led Young (1966, p. 126) to conclude that policy caucuses were neither a regular nor an important part of congressional activity in the Jeffersonian era. Unfortunately, the secrecy that would have surrounded any meetings that might have been held makes it difficult to resolve this question. For the years prior to 1803, it is clear that the caucus had been discovered as a tool of party leadership, but it seems reasonable to conclude that its use was infrequent.

The Boardinghouse

The importance of the boardinghouse as a center of political activity once the government had been moved to Washington has been convincingly demonstrated by Young (1966). His thesis states further that these congressional messes were more than simply places where politics was a frequent topic of discussion. In an analysis of voting on roll calls taken between 1807 and 1829, Young has shown that the cohesion of the boardinghouse groups was very high: "The official record of roll call votes . . . offers evidence which persuasively argues that the after-dinner 'parlor assemblages' in the congressional boardinghouses were 'caucuses' in fact if they were not so in name, and which explains why legislators occasionally applied the term 'party' to their boardinghouse fraternity" (Young, 1966, p. 102). Whether the observation that "the members who lived together . . . voted together" (p. 102) can be correctly interpreted as a causal statement must remain an open question, although it has been challenged by Bogue and Marlaire (1975) for the 1821-1842 period. An analysis of the Washington years is mostly outside the scope of this study, since the capital moved there in 1800 after twelve years in New York and Philadelphia. But the obvious importance of the boardinghouse in Washington opens the question of whether boardinghouses had any impact on congressional life in New York and Philadelphia.

Clearly Philadelphia and New York did not have the isolated and desolate character of the early Washington community. By the standards of that day, they were large, cosmopolitan centers of trade, culture, and politics. It is true, however, that many congressmen took up residence in hotels or boardinghouses much in the manner described in the Washington community.[6] Copies of extant congressional directories for those years give addresses for the members, showing an obvious tendency to live with those from the same state or region (Goldman and Young, 1973). Likewise, the biographies of several early congressional leaders have noted the boardinghouse residences of their subjects.[7] One suspects that boardinghouse groups were reasonably cohesive in their voting, a conclusion that appears valid from a cursory examination of the directories.

Little information is available concerning the role the boardinghouses served in the Philadelphia community. There is evidence that congressmen were concerned with having congenial companions in their residences. Sedgwick, a supporter of Hamilton from Massachusetts, moved from his initial First Congress residence in 1791: "Sedgwick's first lodgings in Philadelphia were with five other congressmen in a rooming house near Federal Hall, but as three of these fellow lodgers were enemies of the fiscal measures of Hamilton and two, Gilman of New Hampshire and Williamson of North Carolina, not 'even gentlemen,' Sedgwick found the situation impossible" (Welch, 1965, p. 104). His Massachusetts colleague, Fisher Ames, also faced the problem of uncongenial fellow lodgers in two consecutive sessions. While he did not move from his quarters, his association with five North Carolina congressmen is described in the following manner: "Ames wryly regarded his own position as that of a peaceable man living socially with the southerners, but he speculated that their political creeds had better not be compared. In conversations around the fireside, he had begun proselyting, and it seemed as though he were gaining ground. At least he found that they began 'to lick molasses''' (Bernhard, 1965, pp. 185-86). In these early years, it is obvious that congressmen were desirous of congenial surroundings. But this congeniality was as often defined by cultural patterns as by partisan ties. In those days, contact between the regions was limited. Ames, for example, had never been as far away as New York and referred to his future in the First Congress (in a letter shortly before his departure from Dedham) as "a state of terror and uncertainty" (Bernhard, 1965, p. 74).

Because Philadelphia and New York were thriving cities, congressmen did not segregate themselves so fully into boardinghouse fraternities as they would in Washington. There were alternative social centers available. Whereas Washington had no population other than those with some connection to government, Philadelphia was an important city years before any federal government was even imagined. The image of a college fraternity may have been appropriate for the Washington community, but a more useful image for the Philadelphia community would be the college dormitory.

Of course, the boardinghouse could serve in political roles, and there are examples of this possibility in the Fifth and Sixth Congresses (Cunningham, 1957, pp. 161-62). Francis' Hotel was the residence of Thomas Jefferson in 1797 and 1798, and William L. Smith, the Federalist leader, wrote to a colleague that a "knot of Jacobins" was in residence there (Phillips, 1909, p. 787). Jefferson himself referred to his lodging in a letter to one whose name had arisen in conversation there: "The circumstances took place in a familiar conversation with gentlemen, who with myself mess together every day at our lodgings, and was therefore the less guarded. . . . " (Thorpe, 1898, p. 489). The real political significance is shown in further comments by Smith, in which he noted that Senator John Henry (Md.) was particularly susceptible to the partisan influences of this group of Republicans.[8] A word of caution is, however, in order here. Examination of congressional directories for the Fifth Congress shows that Francis' Hotel housed a rather diverse set of people, both northerners and southerners, including some (in addition to Henry) whose Republican credentials were not at all strong. Jefferson's influence in this group may have been substantial, but evidence on that point is unavailable.

Of more undisputed political importance was Marache's boardinghouse in the first session of the Sixth Congress, the last session held in Philadelphia. Several important leaders in the Republican party found lodging there, including John Nicholas and John Randolph of Virginia, Nathaniel Macon of North Carolina, and several others. Only Gallatin of the congressional party leadership was missing, having chosen to take a small house with his family. But he had lodged at Marache's during three previous sessions along with Nicholas and several other Republicans. In contrast to the boardinghouse groups discussed by Young (1966), Marache's seems to have been a center for party activity rather than a competing power center. Although direct evidence is scarce, it seems that Marache's was regarded as "a sort of unofficial headquarters for Republican party leaders" (Cunningham, 1957, p. 162).

Congress moved to Washington from Philadelphia for the second session of the Sixth Congress in 1800, arriving in a city that was little better than a wilderness. Distractions for the membership were few, and one result was an increased role for the boardinghouse as a center of social activity. More congressmen were sharing each residence than in Philadelphia, and there appear to have been fewer loners.

Yet, is it possible that these residential patterns had substantial political implications? As we shall see in the analysis of voting patterns, cohesive party blocs were in existence prior to the move to Washington. So even the discovery that messmates voted together does not provide proof that this agreement resulted from their associations in the boardinghouse.

Young's study of the Washington community is primarily focused on the years after 1803, the end point of the current study, and thus it is unfair to criticize Young's conclusions. It may be that, for these later years, the boardinghouse filled a void left when the Federalist party was reduced to a shadow of its earlier strength. But it seems likely that, for the first years in Washington, community patterns were a *result* of political alliances, not a *cause*.[9]

Congress as an Institution in the 1790s

The Congress of the eighteenth century bore little resemblance to its modern counterpart, and some of the differences affected the potential for political parties to make their appearance. The most obvious difference was that the early Congress was a small, part-time legislature. The First Congress had fewer than 100 members (26 senators, 65 representatives), and it met for less than six months a year, including a special session to set up the new constitutional government. By 1800, the House had grown to 105 members, and Senate membership had hit 32, but rarely did a session last for longer than half the year.

Nor did the job of serving in Congress bring much prestige in those days. Turnover was high, because few chose to stay in office for long. In fact, no member of the First House served continuously through the Seventh House, and only seven members served for six of the seven terms. On average, 50% of the members of each new House were serving their first term.[10] Representatives apparently found a lack of rewards in office and often returned to positions in state offices. Travel to the capital was difficult, and life there brought long absences from family, little public recognition, and insufficient salaries. Young (1966) has shown that the move from Philadelphia to Washington made things even worse, and thus it is clear that this job brought little status to its incumbents.

The early Congress was also marked by minimal levels of organization. As described above, the only formal leadership role was the position of Speaker mandated by the Constitution. A few committees existed, mostly for short terms and for specified tasks. A network of leadership arose naturally, but there were frequent changes with turnover of membership and the shifting fortunes of individual leaders. Caucuses of the new party groups were important on occasion, but they had almost no formal, regularized function. Finally, there were no clear patterns for the selection of leadership. Seniority could hardly have played much role in those early years, so the few leadership contests were a mixture of personality and the search for partisan advantage.

Polsby (1968) has written of the institutionalization that has characterized the House of Representatives since about 1900. In the modern House, service is a career, decision making is highly structured, there are set procedures for leadership selection, and so forth. It is quite clear that Congress did not have these features in the 1790s, and in fact the contrast is most striking.

The significance of these observations is that one cannot expect to find dramatic signs of party leadership or organization in those early years of the Congress. But the absence of these features should hardly be cause to reject any theory of party development. Just as the appearance of parties was affected by the electoral institutions of that era, so, too, were the early parties shaped by the nature of the eighteenth-century Congress. The development of modern parties was to occur along with the evolution of a modern Congress and electoral procedures.

5. Spatial Analysis of Party Development

In previous chapters, I have considered the political context in which the new Congress operated in 1789. It was a political world that, in many respects, was not very hospitable to the development of political parties. Yet, within a few years, highly partisan competition had appeared in national elections and in the halls of Congress. It is this latter arena that provides the principal setting for the search for party emergence. Beginning in this chapter, I look closely at the voting records of congressmen to determine when voting coalitions appeared in a form that might be labeled parties.

The chief weapon in this search for parties is a set of maps of the voting alliances appearing in each new Congress from 1789 to 1803. These maps, or spatial configurations, are derived by means of multidimensional scaling (MDS) of the roll call agreement for all pairs of legislators. With these spatial maps, it is possible to consider various aspects of emerging partisanship. The increase of partisan voting between 1789 and 1803 is made very clear by any of several methods. Visual inspection of the configurations provides dramatic evidence of this trend, as does the increasing level of fit for these configurations. Cluster analysis helps to confirm the results of the multidimensional scaling analysis and to demonstrate more clearly the historical processes that were taking place at this time. Alternatively, several traditional indices of partisanship also provide strong evidence of the changes.

After having established that party voting did increase dramatically between 1789 and 1803, I can then provide (in chapters 6 to 8) a more detailed examination of this idea of party development. Use of the spatial maps to consider the patterns of voting in each individual Congress can demonstrate something of the nature of the developing party system. But first I must consider the available evidence. In this chapter I look at party development using a variety of methods, both to give an overview of the historical developments and to help justify dependence on the spatial configurations in the following chapters.

The Methodology

The principal data for this investigation are the records of how members of Congress voted on roll calls taken between 1789 and 1803. While there are inherent limitations in using roll calls, the official nature of these votes makes them a valuable source of information.[1] The chief analytic method is multidimensional scaling of measures of agreement between legislators. Since this method has been fully discussed elsewhere, I give only a brief summary of the approach.[2] Multidimensional scaling employs a matrix of agreement scores, defined simply as the proportion of times two legislators agree in their votes, out of the total number of bills on which both vote. These agreement scores are transformed into distances in a geometric space of some given dimensionality. The legislators are then represented as points in this multidimensional space in such a way that those who *agree* most often in voting are *closest* to each other in the resulting configuration of points, while those who *disagree* most are *farthest* away in the space.

Interpretation of a multidimensional scaling configuration is perhaps the most important and most difficult part of the analysis. First, the quality of a solution, or the fit between the data (agreement scores) and the configuration, is indicated by a statistic called *stress*, which measures the degree to which the configuration fails to reproduce accurately the relationships present in the data. Stress can range theoretically from 0.0, for a perfect fit, to 1.0, for a total lack of fit. Second, the appropriate dimensionality of a solution must be determined with respect to its stress. A solution can be derived in any number of dimensions, and the stress will always be lower when a higher dimensionality is allowed. Thus, the analyst must determine the most appropriate number of dimensions, according to the conflicting standards of good fit (low stress) and parsimony (a small number of dimensions). Finally, the interpretation of a configuration involves a search for meaningful dimensions, clusters, or other structural patterns. It must be emphasized that a two-dimensional solution should *not* automatically be discussed in terms of two linear dimensions, such as a factor analysis would be. The analyst must be attentive in searching for the structural interpretation that best represents the information contained in the scaling solution.

The Spatial Configurations

Spatial maps, or configurations, have been obtained for each Congress between 1789 and 1803 (First through Seventh), for both the House and the Senate. These configurations, which form the central core of the analysis that follows, were derived according to the procedures discussed above.

For each Congress, a complete matrix of voting agreement between legislators was computed, with all roll calls included and weighted equally.[3] All members of a particular Congress were included except for those who were absent on a large proportion of roll calls.[4] These agreement matrices then formed the basis for generating the multidimensional scaling configurations.[5] In each case, configurations were generated in one, two, and three dimensions. To consider more than three dimensions would lead to difficulty

text continues on page 76

62 Origins of American Political Parties

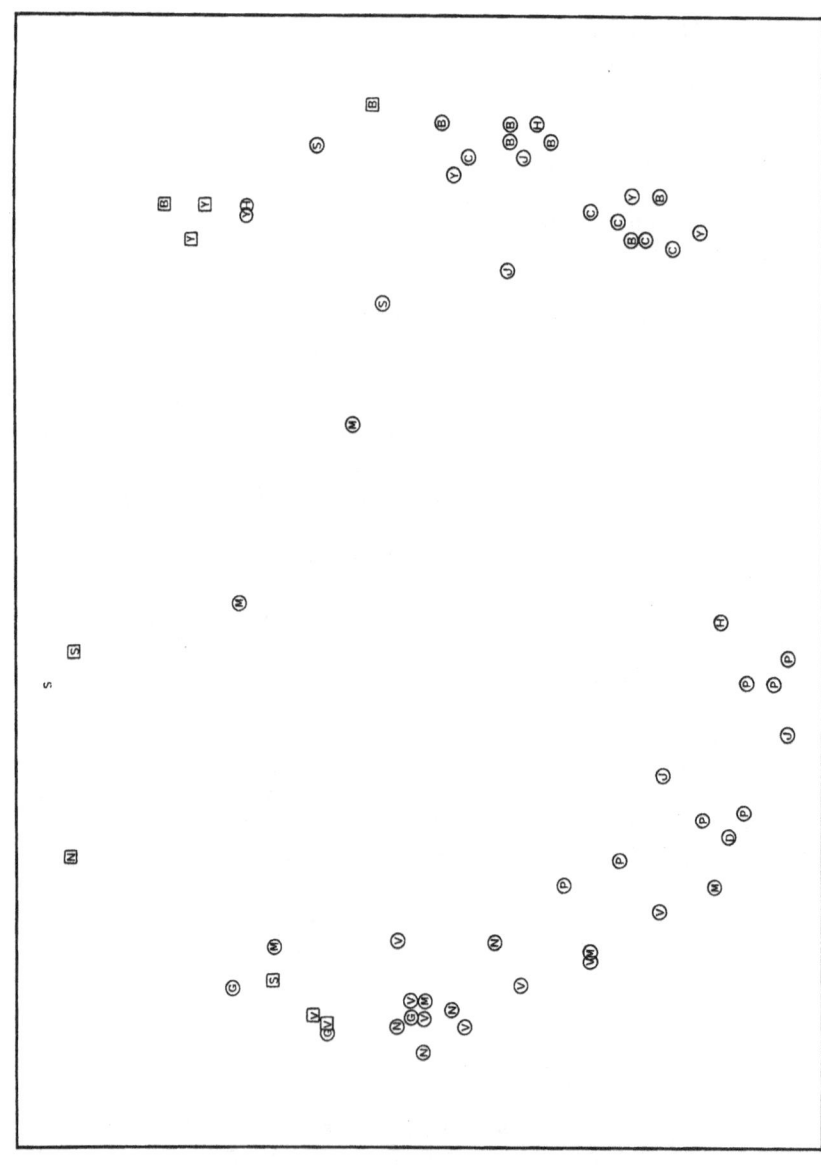

Fig. 1. Spatial Configuration, First Congress, House, 1789-1791

KEY

B – Mass. M – Md.
C – Conn. N – N.C.
D – Del.   P – Penn.
E – Vt.   R – R.I.
G – Ga.   S – S.C.
H – N.H.   T – Tenn.
J – N.J.   V – Vir.
K – Ky.   Y – N.Y.

ⓧ – Federalist
☒ – Republican
X – No party/Unknown

Letter = state
Circle/square = party

Spatial Analysis of Party Development 63

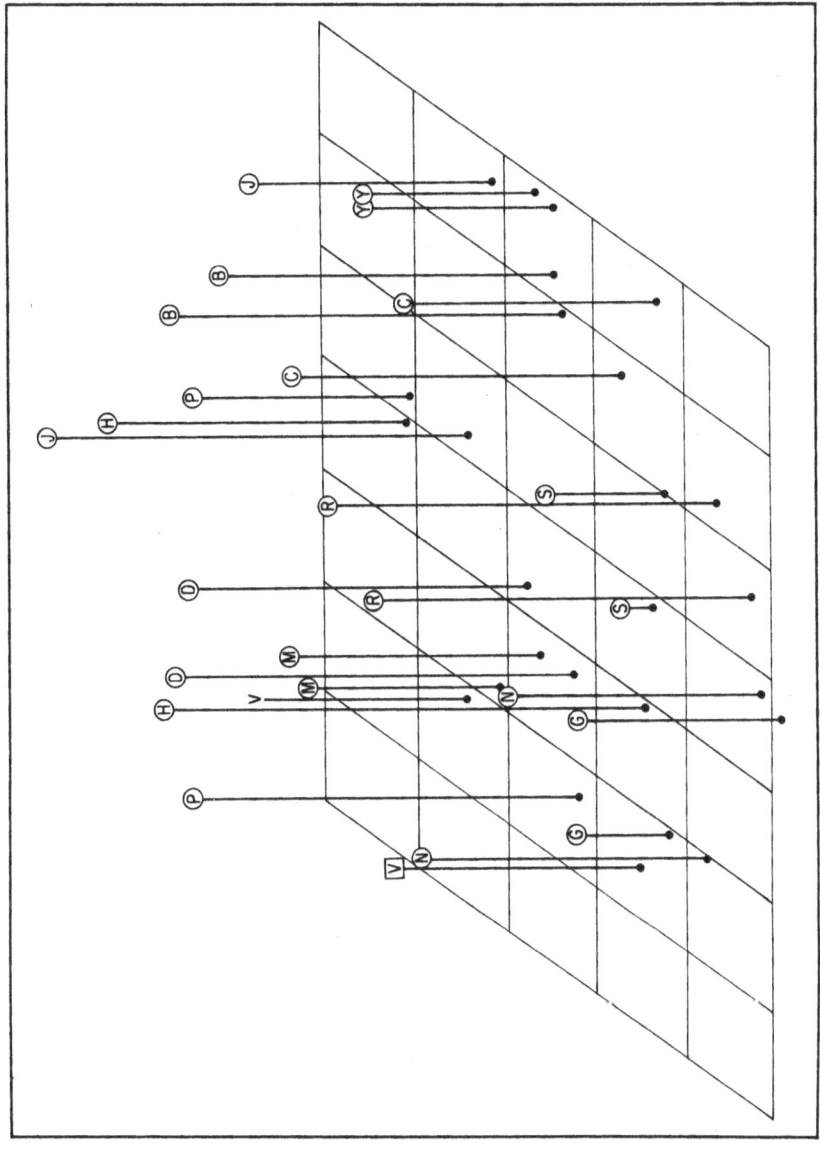

Fig. 2. Spatial Configuration, First Congress, Senate, 1789-1791

KEY

B – Mass.   M – Md.
C – Conn.   N – N.C.
D – Del.   P – Penn.
E – Vt.   R – R.I.
G – Ga.   S – S.C.
H – N.H.   T – Tenn.
J – N.J.   V – Vir.
K – Ky.   Y – N.Y.

⊗ – Federalist
⊠ – Antifederalist
X – No party/Unknown

Letter = state
Circle/square = party

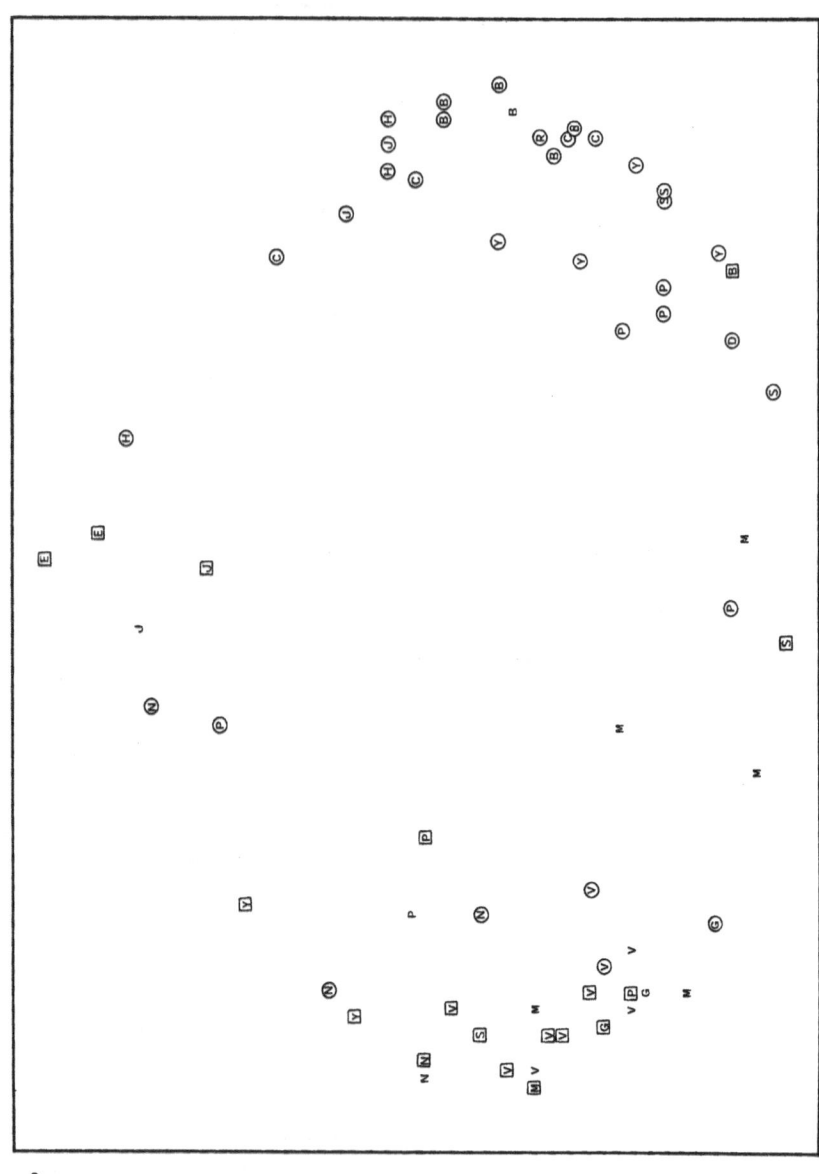

Fig. 3. Spatial Configuration, Second Congress, House, 1791-1793

KEY

B — Mass. M — Md.
C — Conn. N — N.C.
D — Del.   P — Penn.
E — Vt.   R — R.I.
G — Ga.   S — S.C.
H — N.H.   T — Tenn.
J — N.J.   V — Vir.
K — Ky.   Y — N.Y.

Ⓧ — Federalist
☒ — Republican
X — No party/Unknown

Letter = state
Circle/square = party

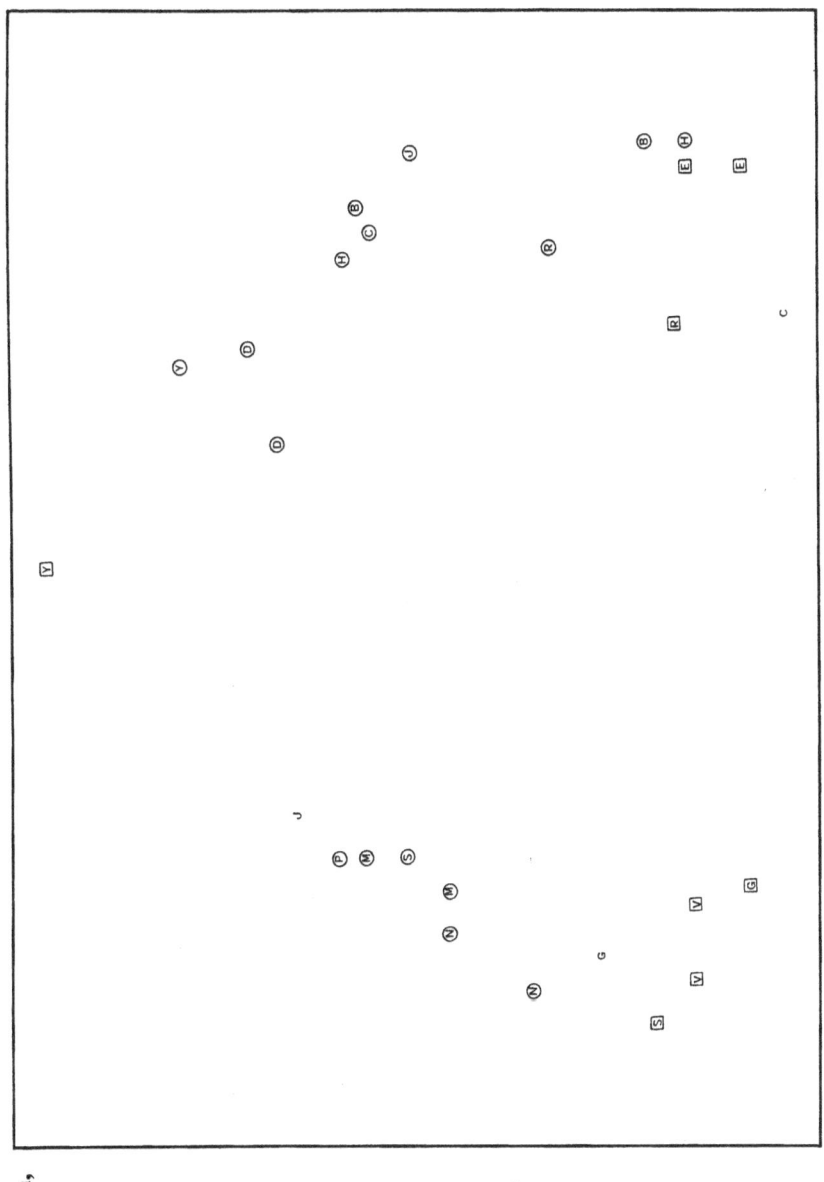

Fig. 4. Spatial Configuration, Second Congress, Senate, 1791-1793

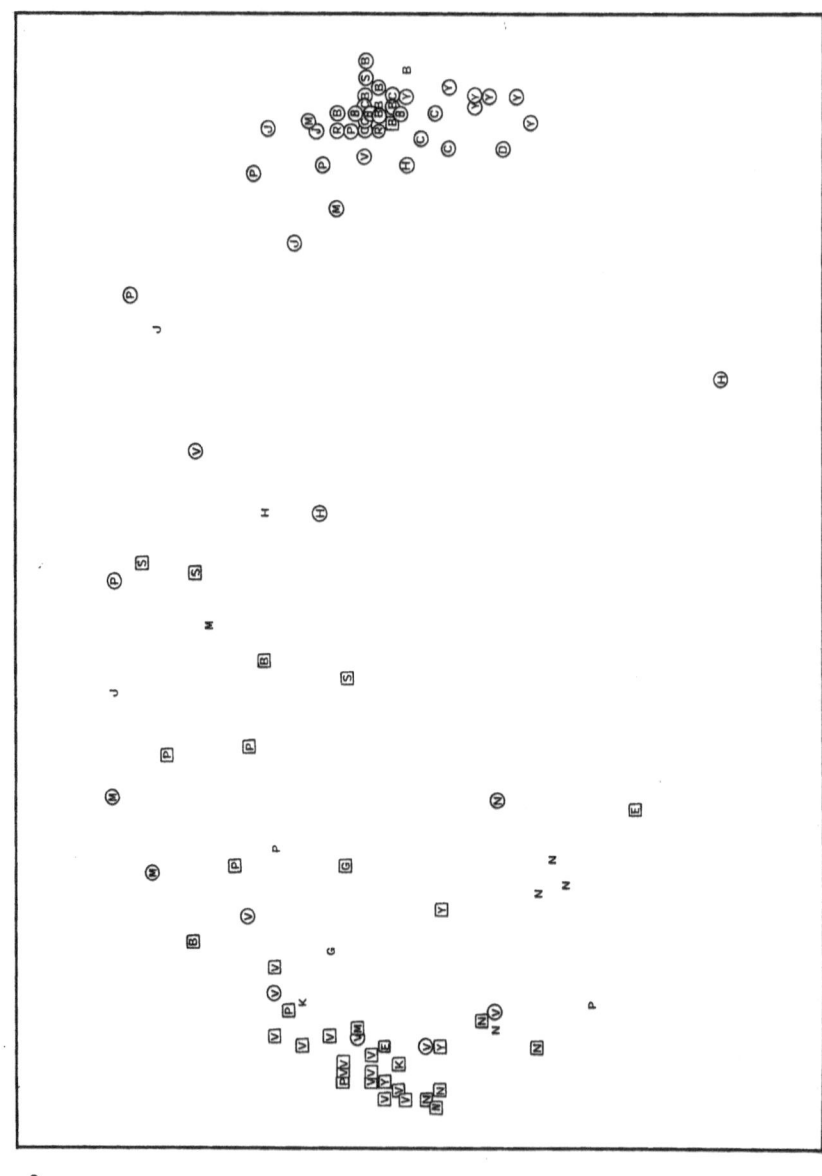

Fig. 5. Spatial Configuration, Third Congress, House, 1793-1795

KEY

B – Mass. M – Md.
C – Conn. N – N.C.
D – Del.   P – Penn.
E – Vt.   R – R.I.
G – Ga.   S – S.C.
H – N.H.   T – Tenn.
J – N.J.   V – Vir.
K – Ky.   Y – N.Y.

⊗ – Federalist
☒ – Republican
X – No party/Unknown

Letter = state
Circle/square = party

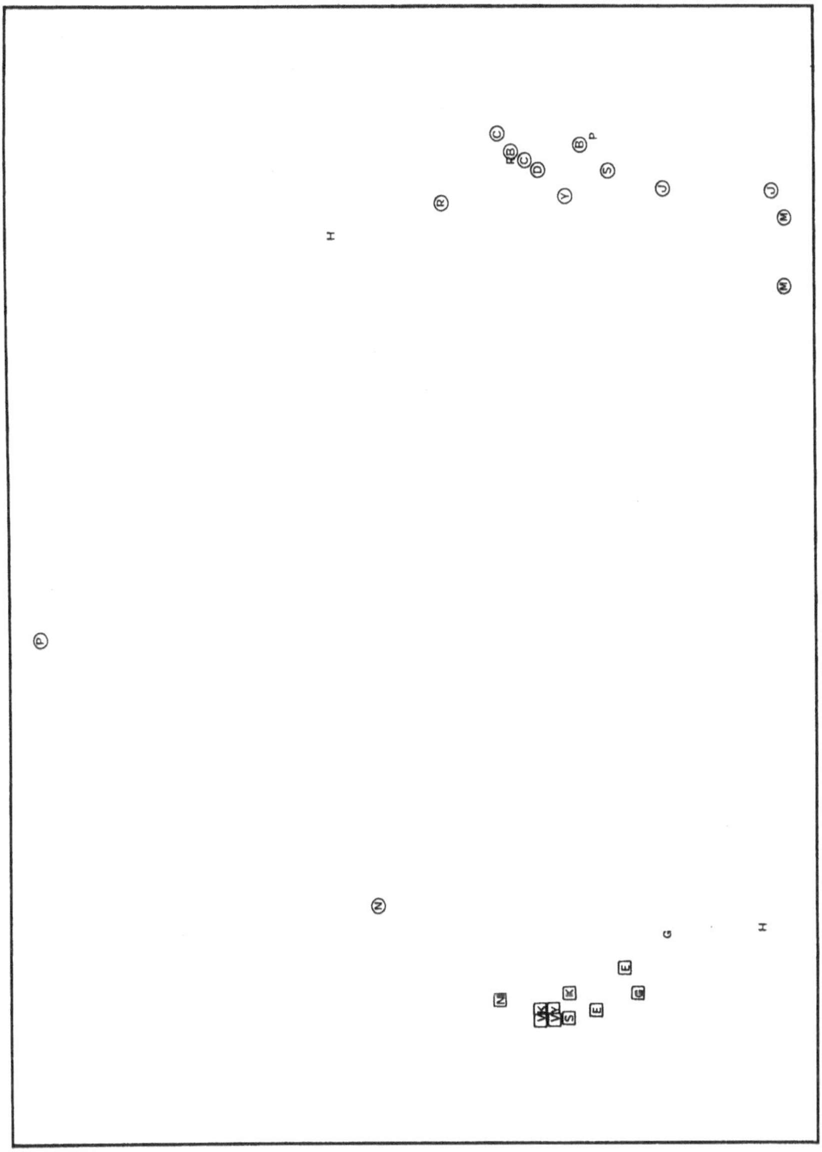

Spatial Analysis of Party Development 67

Fig. 6. Spatial Configuration, Third Congress, Senate, 1793-1795

KEY

B – Mass. M – Md.
C – Conn. N – N.C.
D – Del.   P – Penn.
E – Vt.   R – R.I.
G – Ga.   S – S.C.
H – N.H.   T – Tenn.
J – N.J.   V – Vir.
K – Ky.   Y – N.Y.

⊗ – Federalist
☒ – Republican
X – No party/Unknown

Letter = state
Circle/square = party

68 Origins of American Political Parties

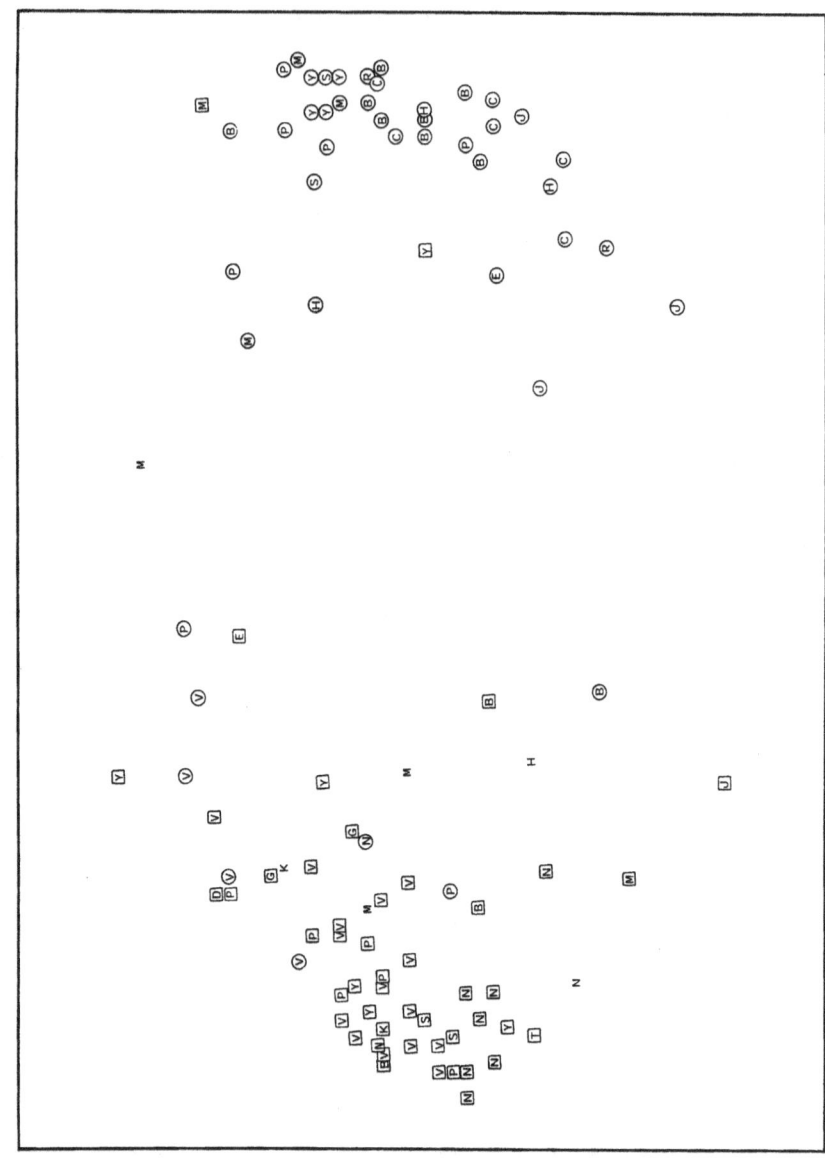

Fig. 7. Spatial Configuration, Fourth Congress, House, 1795-1797

KEY

B – Mass. M – Md.
C – Conn. N – N.C.
D – Del.   P – Penn.
E – Vt.   R – R.I.
G – Ga.   S – S.C.
H – N.H.   T – Tenn.
J – N.J.   V – Vir.
K – Ky.   Y – N.Y.

⊗ – Federalist
⊠ – Republican
X – No party/Unknown

Letter = state
Circle/square = party

Spatial Analysis of Party Development 69

Fig. 8. Spatial Configuration, Fourth Congress, Senate, 1795-1797

KEY

B – Mass. M – Md.
C – Conn. N – N.C.
D – Del.   P – Penn.
E – Vt.   R – R.I.
G – Ga.   S – S.C.
H – N.H.   T – Tenn.
J – N.J.   V – Vir.
K – Ky.   Y – N.Y.

Ⓧ – Federalist
☒ – Republican
X – No party/Unknown

Letter = state
Circle/square = party

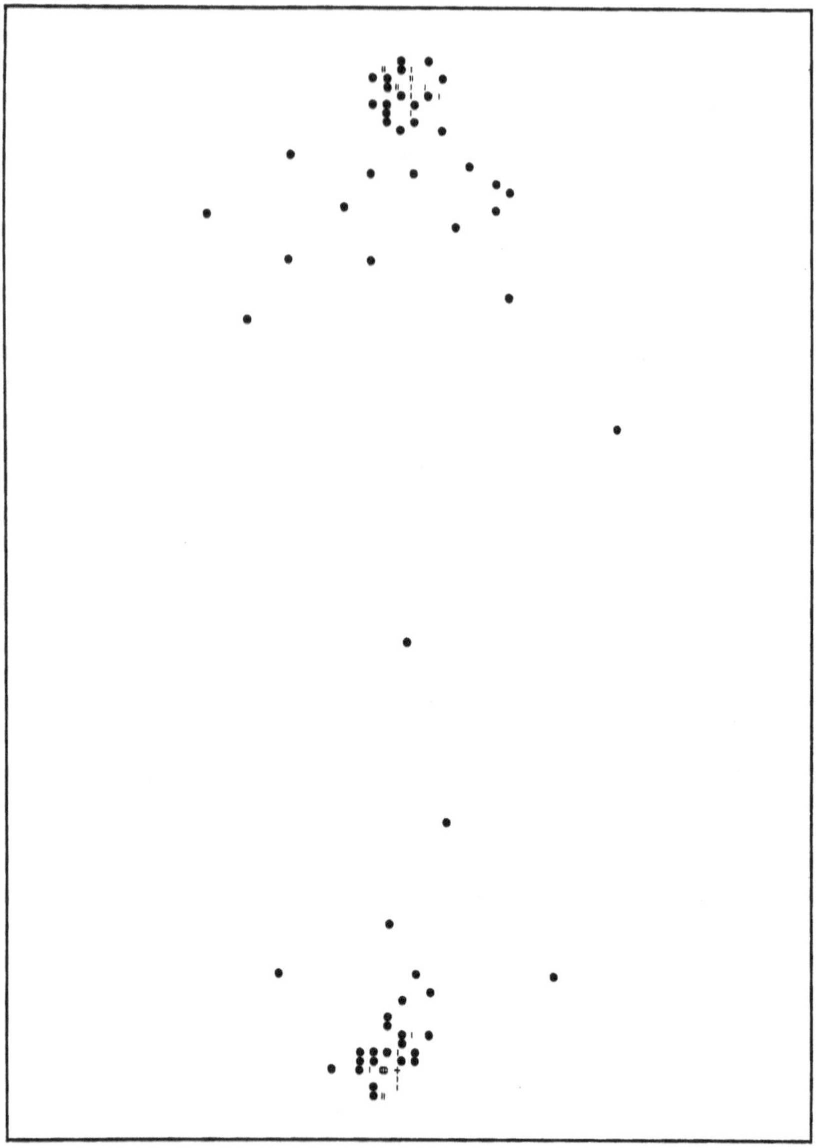

70   Origins of American Political Parties

Fig. 9. Spatial Configuration, House, Fifth Congress, 1797-1799

KEY

Symbol	Number of Members
●	1
=	2
"	3
+	4
⊕	6

Each symbol represents the number of congressmen at a particular point in the space.

Spatial Analysis of Party Development 71

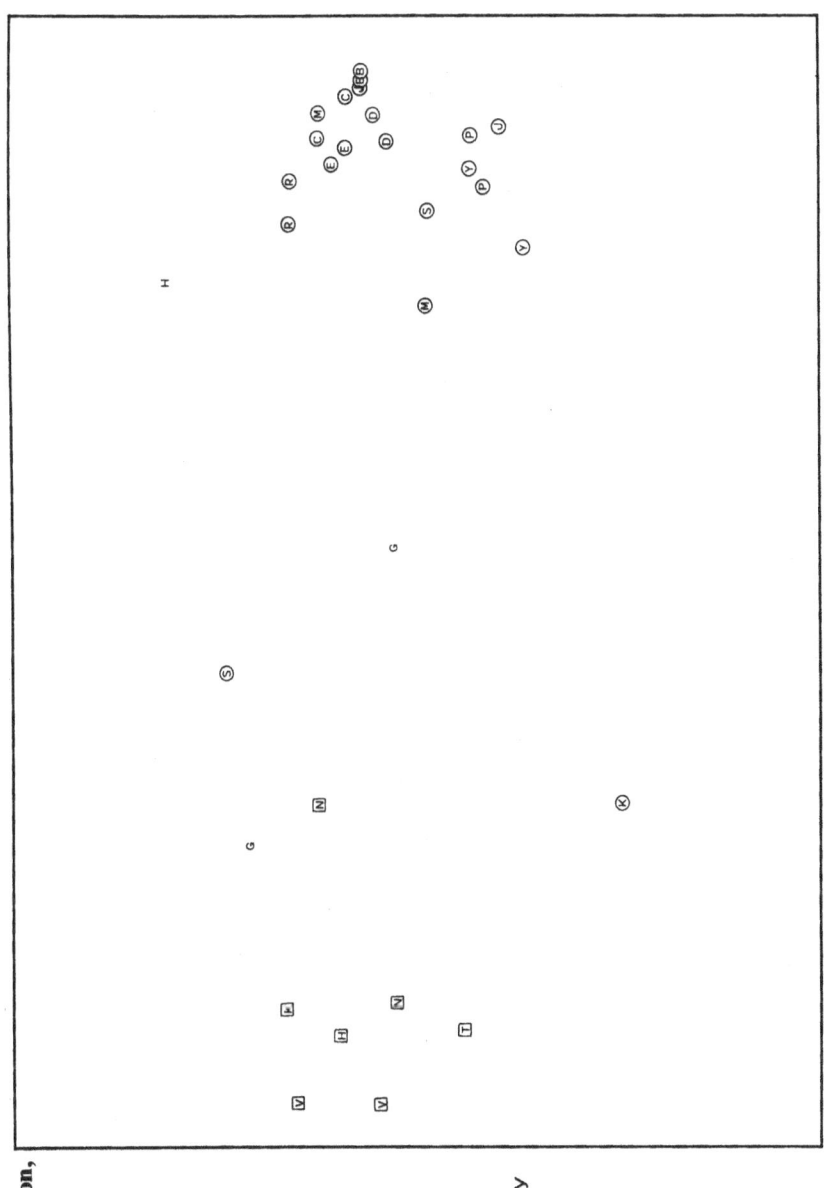

Fig. 10. Spatial Configuration, Senate, Fifth Congress, 1797-1799

KEY

B – Mass.   M – Md.
C – Conn.   N – N.C.
D – Del.   P – Penn.
E – Vt.   R – R.I.
G – Ga.   S – S.C.
H – N.H.   T – Tenn.
J – N.J.   V – Vir.
K – Ky.   Y – N.Y.

◯ – Federalist
▣ – Republican
X – No party/Unknown

Letter = state
Circle/square = party

72 Origins of American Political Parties

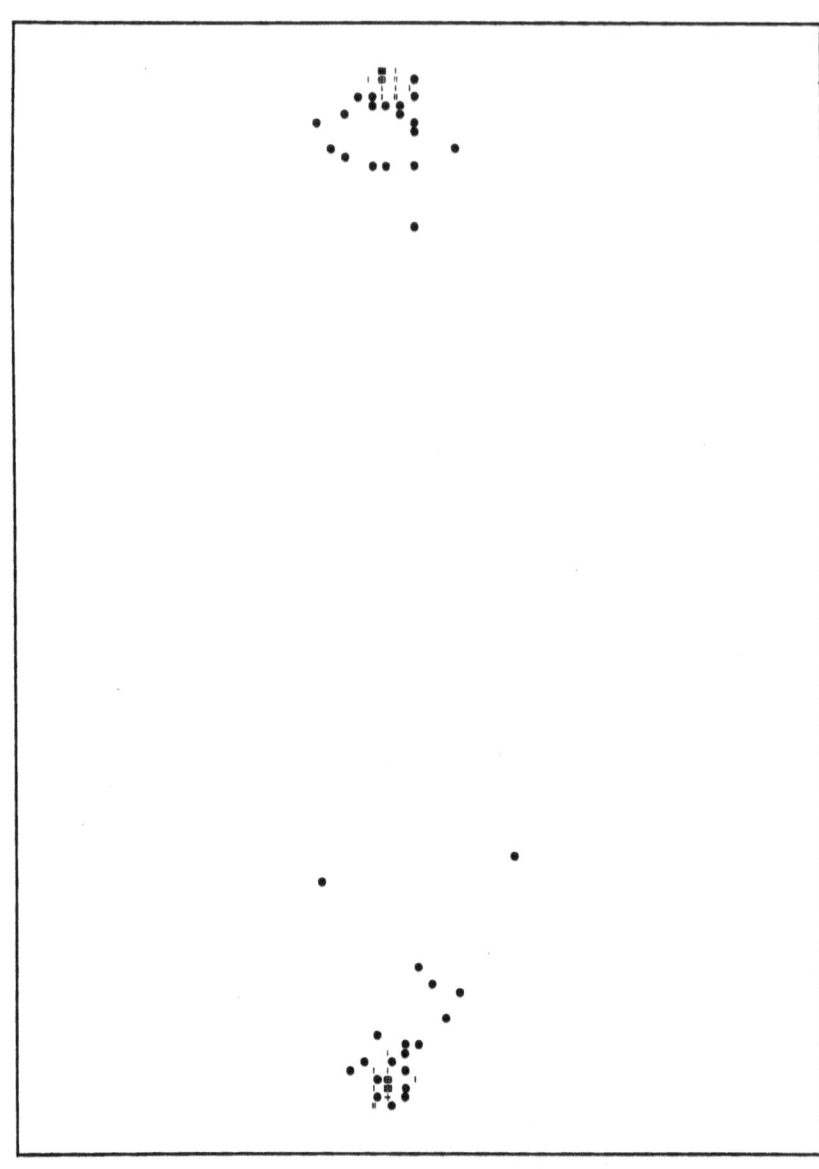

Fig. 11. Spatial Configuration, Sixth Congress, House, 1799-1801

KEY

Symbol	Number of Members
●	1
I	2
=	3
+	4
⊕	6
⊗	7
■	8

Each symbol represents the number of congressmen at a particular point in the space.

Spatial Analysis of Party Development 73

Fig. 12. Spatial Configuration, Sixth Congress, Senate, 1799-1801

KEY

B – Mass. M – Md.
C – Conn. N – N.C.
D – Del. P – Penn.
E – Vt. R – R.I.
G – Ga. S – S.C.
H – N.H. T – Tenn.
J – N.J. V – Vir.
K – Ky. Y – N.Y.

Ⓧ – Federalist
☒ – Republican
X – No party/Unknown

Letter = state
Circle/square = party

Fig. 13. Spatial Configuration, Seventh Congress, House, 1801-1803

KEY

Symbol	Number of Members
●	1
ı	2
ıı	3
+	4
⊕	6
⊗	10
■	14-15

Each symbol represents the number of congressmen at a particular point in the space.

Fig. 14. Spatial Configuration, Seventh Congress, Senate, 1801-1803

KEY

B – Mass. M – Md.
C – Conn. N – N.C.
D – Del.   P – Penn.
E – Vt.   R – R.I.
G – Ga.   S – S.C.
H – N.H.   T – Tenn.
J – N.J.   V – Vir.
K – Ky.   Y – N.Y.

Ⓧ – Federalist
☒ – Republican
X – No party/Unknown

Letter = state
Circle/square = party

Table 1. Quality of Fit between Agreement Scores and Spatial Configurations

Congress	Level of Stress			Number of Members	Number of Roll Calls
	1 Dim.	2 Dim.	3 Dim.		
House of Representatives					
First (1789-1791)	.468	.337	.263	62	109
Second (1791-1793)	.438	.304	.249	65	102
Third (1793-1795)	.278	.237	.201	100	69
Fourth (1795-1797)	.282	.233	.213	100	83
Fifth (1797-1799)	.084	.070	.066	100	155
Sixth (1799-1801)	.059	.055	.053	100	96
Seventh (1801-1803)	.041	.040	.040	100	141
Senate					
First (1789-1791)	.711	.489	.275	26	100
Second (1791-1793)	.420	.275	.185	27	52
Third (1793-1795)	.278	.191	.159	29	79
Fourth (1795-1797)	.179	.161	.142	30	86
Fifth (1797-1799)	.202	.162	.150	31	202
Sixth (1799-1801)	.207	.173	.151	36	120
Seventh (1801-1803)	.107	.097	.091	33	88

Note: Stress measures quality of fit, as defined in text.

in interpretation, and it turns out that an adequate fit is always possible in three or fewer dimensions. The level of stress for each configuration (in one, two, and three dimensions) is described in table 1, along with the number of members and roll calls for each one.

With the sole exception of the First Senate, the two-dimensional configuration has been selected as the best representation of voting patterns in each Congress. In several cases, three-dimensional solutions yield a distinct improvement in stress, yet this added accuracy is counteracted by increased difficulty in visualizing the resulting configurations. In the case of the First Senate, however, a two-dimensional configuration does not adequately represent the patterns of voting agreement, and a three-dimensional representation is preferable. One-dimensional configurations would be adequate in most of the later Congresses on the basis of stress, but there is no reason to restrict the figures to a single dimension. On the basis of the traditional guidelines, the only "poor" fit comes in the First Senate. Most of the other stress values indicate a "good" to "excellent" fit.[6]

Thus, the subsequent discussions center upon a consideration of two-dimensional spatial representations of the patterns of roll call voting in a particular Congress (with a three-dimensional configuration for the First Senate). These configurations are included with this chapter as figures 1 through 14. In each figure, the congressmen are represented by letters that indicate their home states (a key is provided). In addition, a circle or square is drawn around these letter symbols to indicate the party affiliation of that member. As the following discussions make clear, the party alignment during the First Congress was Federalist and Antifederalist, while Federalists and Republicans were the relevant groups in the later years. Ideally, these party labels should represent actual affiliations at the beginning of a particular session. Such precise information, however, is unavailable, although a current project connected with *The Historical Atlas of United States Congressional Districts, 1789-1983* (Martis, 1982) will help alleviate this gap in the future. For this study, the best available information from a variety of sources has been used. (See Appendix A for a listing of party labels and a discussion of the problems associated with these labels.) A special problem arises with House configurations of the Fifth, Sixth, and Seventh Congresses. The clustering in these years is so polarized that it becomes impossible to label each congressman, so density plots have been substituted. As we shall see, it turns out that this methodological dilemma actually symbolizes the ongoing process of party development.

The Polarization of Congressional Voting

There are several types of evidence showing that polarization took place. While the clearest and most dramatic evidence is found in the spatial configurations, other types of roll call analysis help to confirm these findings. Thus, it becomes clear that our conclusions are not dependent upon any particular methodology.

The single clearest finding that emerges from the examination of the spatial configurations is a pattern of increasingly polarized voting from the First Congress to the Seventh Congress. This overall trend is equally clear for the House of Representatives and for the Senate. In the First Congress, voting was not at all polarized, particularly in the Senate, and the clustering that does exist turns out to be restricted to certain issues. Over the eight years when Washington was president (1789-1797), the voting coalitions shifted considerably, according to various issues and electoral concerns. Out of these fluctuations, however, emerged a distinctly polarized Congress. By the Fourth Congress, one can delineate two clusters—which can best be identified as the Republican and Federalist parties (although this conclusion should await the evidence to be considered over the pages that follow). These two clusters still had not attained a high level of cohesion, and certain individuals remained in positions unaffiliated with the dominant voting blocs.

In the six years that marked the end of the era of Federalist domination and the beginning of the Jeffersonian era (1797-1803), voting in Congress remained highly polarized. Throughout these years, there were two very distinct voting blocs, corresponding to the two emergent parties, with only a few individuals maintaining independent positions. In the spatial configurations, it becomes impossible even to distinguish the positions of individual legislators because of the high degree of cohesion.

One way of measuring this increasing cohesion is to consider the stress, or degree of fit, for the spatial configurations. Stress, technically a measure

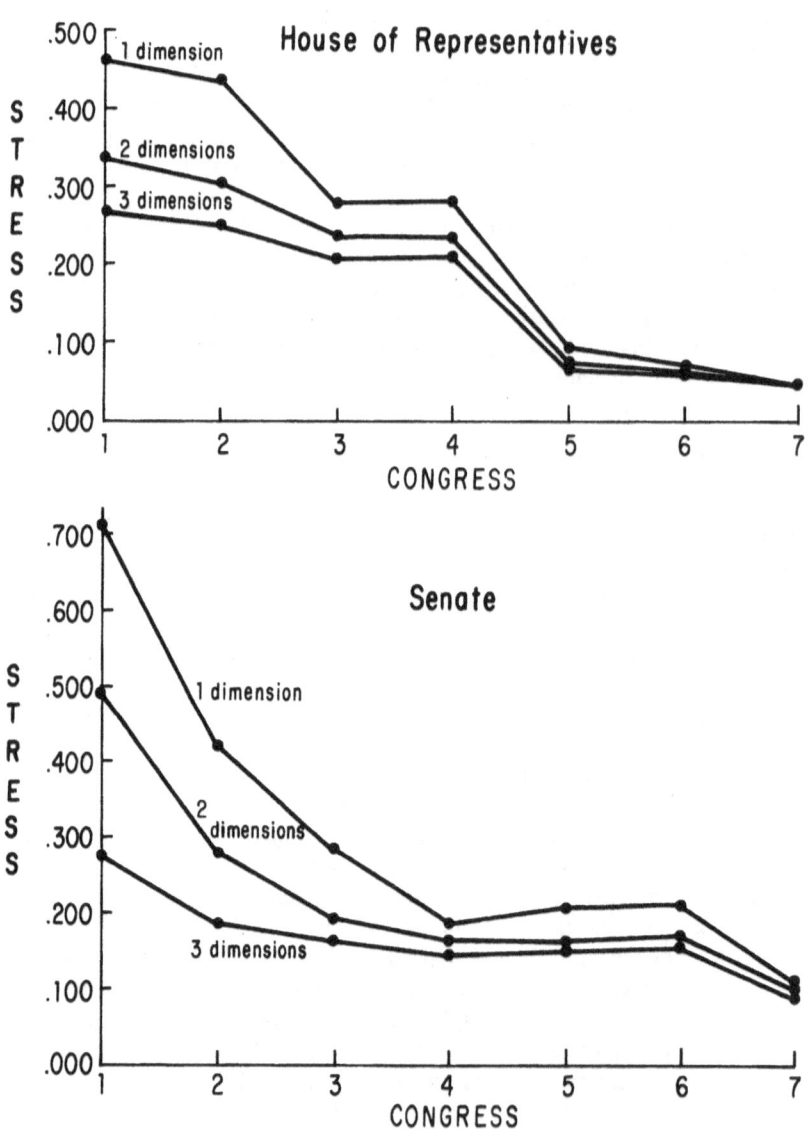

Fig. 15. Declining Levels of Stress

of how much the configuration fails to reproduce the ordinal information in the data, can also be viewed as a measure of the degree of inconsistency in voting patterns. Stress can reflect the idiosyncratic record of particular individuals, complex patterns that do not fit in the given number of dimensions, or scattered votes that simply fit no patterns (resulting from vote trading, carelessness, or whatever). The latter, more random factors should remain roughly constant; thus, variations in the levels of stress should generally reflect the first two factors.

Levels of stress for the seven Congresses from 1789 to 1803 are shown graphically in figure 15. Clearly, the overall trend is downward. With only a few small exceptions, stress has steadily declined over the entire period. Although it is far from a perfect indicator, this trend is quite consistent with the process of polarization observed in the configurations themselves. It indicates that there are fewer idiosyncratic individuals and that the likelihood of hidden patterns, which are simply not revealed by the spatial analysis, is lessening. Furthermore, it is also clear in figure 15 that the lines representing different dimensionalities are converging. This means that the lower-dimensional solutions are becoming increasingly adequate as representations of the voting patterns. The process taking place over time, then, is more than polarization in a two-dimensional space; it is also a reduction in dimensionality to a point where one-dimensional solutions would lose very little of the patterns.

One warning must be taken into account, however, before too much faith is placed on the stress statistic. In certain "degenerate" MDS solutions, stress can become artificially low. Thus, in a two-cluster structure, all pairs within clusters may agree more often than all pairs between clusters. The stress then can actually approach zero even while there may be diversity or inconsistency within the clusters. Such a situation is distinctly possible by the Seventh Congress. Yet, while stress may reach a somewhat artificially low point, further consideration of voting in the latter Congress shows that these results do not reflect substantial, if any, distortion of reality.

One major alternative to multidimensional scaling for studying the coalitions of legislators is cluster analysis. Several important studies of legislative voting have followed this approach (for example, Truman [1959]). In recent years, however, this method of roll call analysis has generally fallen into disfavor, with the exception of one attempt to revitalize it by providing it with a "sound statistical base" (Willetts, 1972, p. 581). For the present effort, the use of cluster analysis serves to supplement the MDS results.

The principal goal of cluster analysis is to place objects (here, legislators) into groups based on their scores on a number of variables (here, roll calls). We are interested in locating groups of legislators from their frequency of agreement with other members on a series of roll call votes, using the same matrix of agreement scores as in the MDS analysis.

While it is easy to define the basic procedure for clustering, it is difficult in practice to derive an efficient means of finding the best set of clusters. One can search for clusters by attempting to find directly the best division of legislators into two (or more) groups—but this approach is almost prohibitive for a large legislature. Alternatively, one can build up from small clusters to larger ones. The traditional tactic is to start with the closest pair and add to it until the resulting cluster fails to meet some criterion of cohesiveness, and then to continue with the unclustered individuals. But establishing the cutoff criterion proves to be quite problematic. In the third approach, known as hierarchical clustering, one begins with each individual defining a separate cluster, successively reducing the number of clusters by combining old ones until there is a single cluster containing all individuals. From the resulting tree diagram one can attempt to interpret the clustering patterns (Wallace, 1968).

No matter what approach is taken, clustering suffers from several limitations. One is designating the minimum level of homogeneity that may characterize a cluster, a problem only partially solved by hierarchical methods. Another is the fact that there may be no unique clustering solution, even after designating minimum levels of agreement. Different algorithms may lead to different sets of clusters, some preferring small, compact clusters, and others preferring more "snakelike" clusters. Third, cluster analysis is ineffective in analyzing even relatively simple structures that are not unidimensional, and it rarely can demonstrate relationships between the derived clusters.[7]

In spite of its many limitations, cluster analysis can be useful in conjunction with multidimensional scaling, because the results of clustering can help to highlight the features of a spatial configuration. Furthermore, cluster analysis of the same agreement matrices used for MDS may help to verify the results of that approach. This is especially important for situations where MDS configurations may tend to degenerate artificially into two very tight groupings.

Two types of clustering are used in this analysis: hierarchical clustering and the traditional form of clustering where the first cluster is made as large as possible before proceeding to a second.[8] Detailed results of this analysis are not presented here, since they do generally duplicate the spatial configurations and because the results of hierarchical clustering are difficult to display for a large legislature. Instead, certain summary results are shown, while the detailed results have been used in trying to understand the patterns found in the spatial configurations.

Because hierarchical clustering produces a fairly complex map of clusters at a variety of agreement levels, a measure of the quality of the clustering is needed. One such statistic is the ratio of lines within to total lines, very roughly analogous to the R^2 measure for regression analysis ("explained" pairs to total pairs). For a particular clustering level, it indicates what proportion of the agreements above that level represent links between individuals in the same cluster (agreements "explained" by the clustering). The appearance of very distinct clusters is indicated by a high ratio.[9] This ratio statistic, along with the minimum agreement for a particular level of clustering, can provide a rough guideline for interpreting cluster results.

One conclusion suggested by an overview of the MDS analysis is the movement of the congressmen into two groups, to be labeled parties, during the fourteen years covered by this study. The viability of this conclusion can be tested by cluster analysis by considering two-cluster solutions for the seven

Table 2. Cluster Analysis—Two-Cluster Solutions

	Ratio	Minimum Agreement	Prob (Agreement)
First	.522	26.6%	.548
Second	.543	21.2	.553
Third	.566	21.4	.545
Fourth	.648	33.3	.565
Fifth	.747	27.1	.545
Sixth	.990	53.3	.546
Seventh	.998	50.6	.573

Notes: Ratio = "Explained" agreement to total agreement (see text); Minimum Agreement = Minimum agreement to produce two clusters; Prob (Agreement) = Level of agreement expected by chance.

Congresses. Values for the ratio statistic and the minimum agreement level, as well as the level of agreement expected by chance, are shown in table 2. The latter figure is calculated as the mean value, over all roll calls, of the quantity, $p^2 + q^2$, where p is the proportion voting yes and q is the proportion voting no (MacRae, 1970, p. 220; Willetts, 1972). The regular increase for values of the ratio statistic is a clear indication that a two-cluster structure is becoming a more appropriate representation of activity in the Congress.

By 1799, the members had coalesced to an extent that, with few exceptions, they agreed more often with every other member of their own bloc (party) than with anyone in the opposing cluster. While the minimum within-cluster agreement level is just over 50% (even less than expected by chance), the average agreement score for two members in the same bloc is well over 80% during the last two Congresses. Between members of opposing clusters, the average agreement is close to 25%. Thus, the results of clustering clearly support the conclusion that two distinct voting blocs had emerged by the end of the century.

In the decade from 1789 to 1799, the cluster analysis is less conclusive. While the ratio statistic indicates that a two-cluster solution becomes a relatively more appropriate representation of voting patterns over these years, it is clear that more accurate representations are desirable. The minimum agreement level required for the delineation of two clusters is rather low (see table 2); as such, it is obvious that these clusters contain some rather divergent individuals.

In seeking to identify more appropriate sets of clusters for these early Congresses, the complete hierarchical clustering was examined. In each case, the ratio statistic reaches high values when there are nearly as many clusters as individuals—but such clustering is rather uninteresting. Otherwise, there is only one case where there is a better solution than the one with two clusters. In the Fifth Congress, a three-cluster solution (with two large clusters and a third of six individuals) is characterized by a ratio of .861 and a minimum agreement level equal to 51.7%. As such, this set of clusters compares favorably to the two-cluster solutions in the following Congresses. Further-

82 Origins of American Political Parties

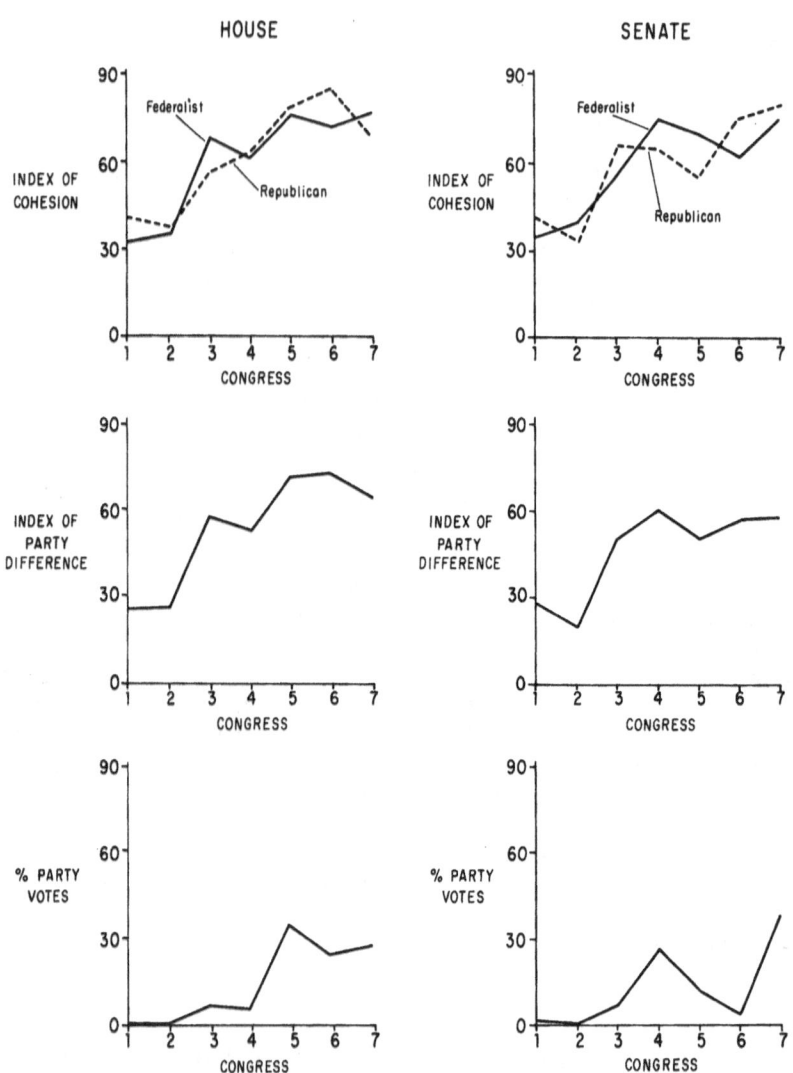

Fig. 16. Indices of Partisanship, House and Senate, 1790-1803

more, this result is generally consistent with the spatial configuration (see figure 9), which shows several congressmen in positions intermediate to the two dominant groups.

Thus far, clustering has been approached from one perspective, namely, designating the number of clusters and evaluating the quality of the results. Another angle on the problem is to select a minimum level of agreement, find the number of clusters, and evaluate the results. But, as noted before, selecting a minimum agreement score is no easy task. Many researchers seem to have selected a level on grounds of convenience or perhaps with regard to the results. In evaluating uses of cluster analysis, MacRae (1970, p. 220) discusses use of the expected proportion of agreement among legislators by chance, a figure used earlier in this chapter. Willetts (1972) has pursued this line a step further, suggesting that expected proportions of agreements can be calculated for various levels of statistical significance.[10] Thus, by designating a significance level, it is possible to search for "statistically significant" clusters. While this procedure is not strictly followed for this analysis, it does provide a way to set a baseline for the cluster analysis. For the Congresses included in this study, agreement at least as often as 65% should occur by chance no more often than once in 100 times, while 60% agreement is expected by chance about 5 times in 100.[11]

If we set 60% as the minimum level of agreement, the clusterings in table 3 are obtained. The data in this table are not difficult to interpret and are quite consistent with earlier findings. Again, the main differences come between the first four and the last three Congresses. Prior to 1797, there were a relatively large number of clusters, and about half the members were not in the two largest clusters.[12] There were no clearly defined patterns in these years; in particular, any claim that there were two dominant groups is simply not supported by the cluster analysis. After 1797, a two-cluster pattern is far more evident. Although members do not fall exclusively into two voting blocs at the level of 60% agreement, the proportion excluded from the two major blocs at this level is rather small. It is readily apparent that the cluster analysis results generally confirm the features of the multidimensional scaling configurations. If we were to present more complete clustering results, we would see that other features of the MDS configurations, such as regional groupings, can be highlighted. In the discussions that follow, the cluster analysis results frequently contribute to understanding the voting patterns. While specific results are generally not shown in detail, this perspective has aided the analysis of voting data and the subsequent presentation of results.

A more traditional type of roll call analysis, in addition to cluster analysis, may help to amplify further the multidimensional scaling results. Three indices of party voting are employed here—Rice's index of cohesion, Rice's index of difference, and Lowell's concept of the party vote.[13] The utility of these indices for studying partisanship across time has been demonstrated by MacRae (1970, pp. 200-207), who showed that the degree of partisanship in Congress (as measured by party votes) rose to its highest levels immediately following party realignments. Because the emergence of

Table 3. Cluster Analysis—Size of Clusters

Congress	Number of Clusters	% in Largest Cluster	% in Second Cluster	% in Other Clusters
First	9	27	23	50
Second	10	23	15	62
Third	12	39	18	43
Fourth	10	28	21	51
Fifth	6	44	42	14
Sixth	3	51	45	4
Seventh	5	54	37	9

Note: Cluster analysis, based on 60% minimum agreement for any pair of legislators within a cluster.

new parties might be regarded as a special case of partisan realignment, a similar pattern might be expected between 1789 and 1803.

The values of the index of cohesion, the index of difference, and the percentage of party votes are presented for the House and Senate from 1789 to 1803 in figure 16. It is readily evident from these data that cohesion in both legislative parties increased dramatically during this period, while party differences grew simultaneously. Levels of party cohesion and difference rose constantly during the first five Congresses, leveling off after 1797. The timing of these changes corresponds rather closely with the polarization observed in the MDS configurations. Parties developed steadily from 1789 until 1796, the year of the Jay Treaty controversy. By the Fifth Congress, they had reached a high level of development on any measure of congressional voting, a level sustained through 1803.

In order to make a better assessment of party development in these early years, comparisons can be made between the cohesion of the early parties and parties of the twentieth century. During the entire period from 1921 to 1969, the average index of cohesion of the two congressional parties was about 66, ranging from 55 to 77.[14] Using this standard of comparison, 1795 seems to mark the year when early parties reached the level of unity found in the twentieth century. Furthermore, beginning in the Fifth Congress, the level of party cohesion exceeded that in nearly any modern Congress. Similarly, the average index of party difference for the twentieth-century Congresses was about 41, a figure surpassed by the time of the Third Congress. The number of party votes averaged about 10% of all votes between 1921 and 1969; again, the early parties generally matched these levels. In fact, the proportion of party votes after 1797 reached a level obtained at few times in American history.

Conclusion

Regardless of the methodology employed, the finding is the same. There was a clear movement from 1789 to 1803 in the direction of polarized voting in Congress. What began as a rather disorganized and inconsistent set of alliances developed into a system of two cohesive and opposed voting blocs. Whether these blocs are properly called parties is a conclusion that awaits further evidence. In the next three chapters, we consider in depth this period of polarization, with the aim of shedding light on this crucial question.

6. Factionalism in the Early Years, 1789-1793

Having demonstrated that a dramatic surge in party voting did take place from 1789 to 1803, I can now examine in depth the patterns of voting within each individual Congress, so as to highlight the process of party development. Throughout this consideration, I give close attention to several different themes: (1) the declining influence of sectionalism relative to partisanship; (2) the individual careers of congressmen whose partisan ties emerged over several years; and (3) the changing issue basis of the voting patterns.

While sectionalism had been the dominant influence on congressional voting in the First Congress, its importance waned over the years that followed. By the time of Jefferson's administration, a significant degree of partisan diversity had emerged in each region. Both parties showed early strength in the Middle states, but New England was initially dominated by Federalists and the South by Republicans. Nevertheless, during this decade of party development, the minority parties in these regions made significant gains, leading to a more competitive political system. These trends should become evident through examination of the spatial maps of congressional voting.

Within the context of these basic aggregate trends, the individual careers of several members of Congress help to demonstrate the developments of these years. Certain congressmen shifted in their alliances over time, moving generally toward positions consistent with their party colleagues and away from regional alliances. Other congressmen are notable for leadership roles in their parties; thus, their positions should be relatively central to the voting blocs identified with those parties. Observing where such people are located in the spatial configurations should help us to reach conclusions about party development.

Finally, it is crucial to take into consideration the issue basis of the voting patterns in each Congress. In the less cohesive patterns of the early years, we can ask whether the diversity represented different responses to a variety of issues—or whether voting seems to have responded to some other set of cues. We should also ask whether the agenda of issues was changing as party cohesion increased. If so, the search for causes of party development must consider those who set the legislative agenda. Finally, for the latter years of the period, we should like to learn whether there were votes and issues on which the parties were not cohesive, a finding that could affect our conclusions about the nature of party development.

The final answers to some of the questions about partisan development, particularly those about the sectional and issue bases of the new parties, must be deferred to the last chapter. There we can draw together the pieces of evidence toward some general conclusions about the nature of party development during this period. But before examining the evidence, some preliminary observations must be made concerning the analysis of issues.

The Issues

The consideration of issues in the context of congressional voting is never easy. The dependency upon recorded roll calls is a major problem, as is the basic task of categorizing issues or selecting key votes. The latter task is particularly difficult in a historical period, where many judgments must rely upon the opinions of historians, some of whom saw the world from distinctive ideological perspectives.

The categorization of issues used here draws heavily on the work of Bell (1973), who has proposed a classification of roll calls of this period into ten groups: government authority, foreign policy, army, navy, frontier, location of the capital, domestic economics, slavery, partisan politicking, and miscellaneous and personal. His set of categories seems reasonable, although he himself warns against "too rigid an acceptance of the classification of votes" (p. 20). For this analysis, certain categories have been combined. Slavery, only a minor issue in the 1790s, is grouped with the miscellaneous category. Roll calls concerning the navy are grouped with foreign policy, since the navy was generally an instrument of foreign policy. Roll calls dealing with the army, on the other hand, had different meanings at different times. In general, those taken before 1796 were tied to the question of protecting the frontier; after 1796, the work of the army became more a foreign policy question. After this regrouping, there are six major categories of roll calls (plus a miscellaneous group): government authority, foreign policy, protection of the frontier, domestic economics, partisan politics, and (only in the First Congress) location of the capital. The proportion of votes within categories for each Congress is reported in table 4.

In order to test the validity of this set of categories, an attempt was made to replicate Bell's classification for the First Congress. Since Bell never gives a complete listing of roll calls by issue area, it is not possible to know precisely whether this replication was successful. But I was able to reproduce the category totals with deviations of only two or three roll calls. Only one major problem emerged, involving the classification of votes on import duties. These duties were part of the means for raising revenues and as such could be classified with domestic economics. Alternatively, they had implications for relations with other nations and thus were tools of foreign policy. For the First Congress, Bell has apparently classed these votes with domestic economics, except for a vote on whether to discriminate against British goods.

Table 4. Classification of Roll Calls, House of Representatives

Category	First	Second	Third	Fourth	Fifth	Sixth
Government authority	18%	29%	9%	10%	21%	12%
Foreign policy	4	4	26	30	36	11
Frontier protection	3	13	23	20	12	17
Domestic economics	32	35	32	18	16	15
Location of the capital	33	0	0	0	0	0
Partisan politics	0	0	0	0	0	37
Miscellaneous	10	19	10	22	15	8
N	109	102	69	83	155	96

Source: Bell (1973, p. 20).

While this is an acceptable resolution, it is important to recognize that there are distinct subgroups within each major category.

In research on congressional voting in the twentieth century, there have been various attempts at classifying roll calls, not based simply on the contents of the bill but also with regard to the similarity of voting patterns. In one such approach, Clausen (1973; Clausen and Cheney, 1970) has derived a set of policy dimensions.[1] He defines these in this manner: "The policy dimension is based on a consensus among legislators that a subset of roll calls is concerned with a common policy concept. The existence of consensus is induced from an objective measurement procedure, which compares the vote of every legislator with every other legislator on each roll call; it also compares the alignment of legislators on each roll call with their alignment on every other roll call" (Clausen, 1973, p. 22). Such a technique is not particularly appropriate for the purposes of this chapter, since we are concerned explicitly with whether different roll calls in a particular issue area fit the spatial map of congressmen in similar ways. Consequently, if votes that did not belong to a policy dimension were eliminated at this point, the chance to match them to the spatial configurations would, in effect, be lost.

Nevertheless, Clausen's technique has been tested for the largest issue areas of the First Congress, as shown in Table 5: national authority, domestic economics, and location of the capital. These results compare favorably with modern scales, and thus we can be more confident that this categorization is a workable one.

Even though the roll calls have been grouped into a reasonable set of categories, it is, of course, impossible to consider spatially every individual roll call. For this reason, it is necessary to select from the universe of roll calls a smaller group for consideration. One approach would be to choose a random sample of votes. But, as long as we have no desire to draw specific conclusions about the set of roll calls, there is nothing to be gained by this approach. A more useful angle is to choose key votes within each issue area. Important roll calls can be identified in various ways; here, votes have been selected for those issues that have received prominent mention by historians studying this period.[2]

Table 5. Issue Scales in the First Congress

	Number of Votes	Major Scale	Minor Scale	Other Votes	% in Major Scale
Economics	37	15	6	16	40.5
National Authority	20	10	6	4	50.0
Capital	37	22	13	2	59.5

Note: Analysis is based on Clausen's scaling technique, as described in text.

The role of issues can be studied in several ways. First, we can try to understand the historical context of each successive Congress—what issues were considered and their meaning and salience at that time. Second, we can represent each individual roll call spatially in the MDS configuration of legislators, as a line separating yes votes from no votes. The method used and its associated problems are discussed at length in Appendix B. Finally, particularly for the later years of this period, cross-tabulation may also prove to be informative.

In the discussions of individual Congresses that follow, two strategies are pursued simultaneously. One comes from the realm of traditional historical scholarship. Depending mostly on secondary sources, I attempt to provide a general description of the events during a particular time period. Then, building from this base, I use the results of dimensional analysis to amplify our understanding of these historical events. The latter approach is highly dependent upon the set of figures first presented in chapter 5 and repeated in various forms in this chapter, and the reader is advised to consider them carefully. The methodology for representing individual votes in a configuration of legislators—a key part of the analysis to follow—is fully explained in Appendix B. But in order for the presentations in this chapter to be fully clear, a fairly detailed explication of the technique is needed, as well as an indication of how the figures should be read and interpreted. Certain descriptions of the methodology are included in the discussion of patterns in the First Congress.

Factionalism, 1789-1791

Once the new Constitution was proposed at the Philadelphia Convention in 1787, it needed ratification by at least nine states to become effective. The ensuing decision-making process involved considerable disagreement and very close votes in several states (see chapter 2). This conflict between supporters (Federalists) and opponents (Antifederalists) on the Constitution became the major issue affecting elections for the First Congress in 1788 and 1789. While personality and local issues were often the decisive factors in these elections, nearly every state experienced contests between Federalists and Antifederalists.

In the eyes of some historians (Beard, 1915; Risjord, 1973), the importance of this conflict continued well beyond the constitutional battle

90 Origins of American Political Parties

Fig. 17. Spatial Configuration, First Congress, House, 1789-1791

KEY

B – Mass. M – Md.
C – Conn. N – N.C.
D – Del.   P – Penn.
E – Vt.   R – R.I.
G – Ga.   S – S.C.
H – N.H.   T – Tenn.
J – N.J.   V – Vir.
K – Ky.   Y – N.Y.

Ⓧ – Federalist
☒ – Antifederalist
X – No party/Unknown

Letter = state
Circle/square = party

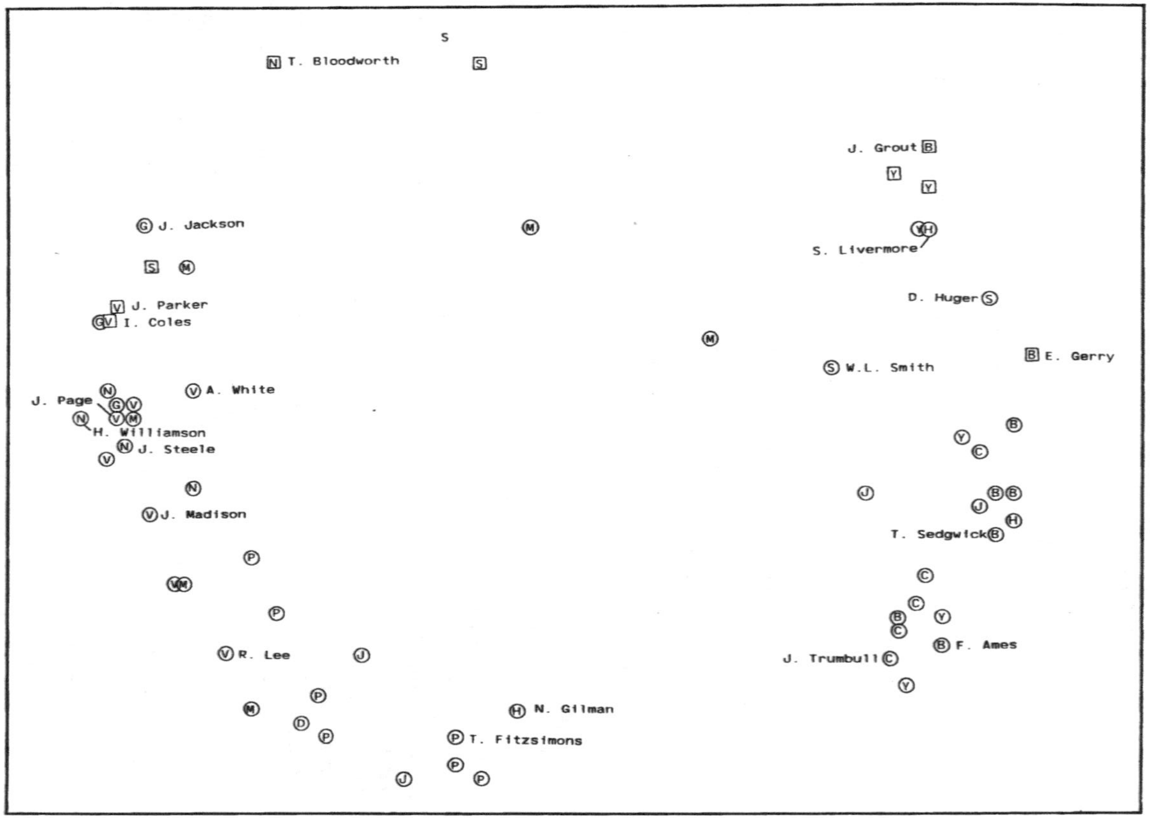

itself. According to this view, the roots of the first party system are found in these differences over the Constitution. While this perspective has lost favor among historians, it is nevertheless one that should be considered.

The Federalists, who had more incentive to become involved in the new government since they had greater stake in its success, were victorious in most contests. In fact, only ten (of sixty-five) seats in the House and only two (of twenty-six) seats in the Senate were won by Antifederalists (Paullin, 1904). But despite the importance of these divisions over the Constitution, this issue did not dominate voting in the First Congress. A look at the MDS configuration (figure 17) helps to illustrate what was happening. Those identified as Antifederalists are separated roughly at the top of the voting configuration; a line across the plot would divide the two groups with only a few exceptions. But the dominant cleavages were evidently not based on this constitutional issue, since the most obvious clustering in the figure is along other lines. (The identity of these other cleavages is discussed later in the chapter.) This fact is further illustrated by noting that the average agreement on roll call votes between Federalists and Antifederalists (49.3%) was not much below the average agreement within either group (Federalists, 55.1%; Antifederalists, 57.9%).[3]

The nature of the election contests is illustrated by those taking place in Massachusetts and Virginia. Two interesting electoral matches involved men who were destined to become party leaders within a few years. Fisher Ames, a young Federalist leader from Massachusetts, had been eloquent in his defense of the Constitution. He was matched against Sam Adams, a man with strong credentials as a patriot who believed that the Constitution did not adequately protect the rights of the people. In spite of his youth and lack of political experience, Ames was chosen by a narrow majority of the voters (Bernhard, 1965; Goodman, 1964). Two Antifederalists (Gerry and Grout) were elected in Massachusetts, but in neither case did the contest represent a simple choice between the two alternative groups (Goodman, 1964; Hall, 1972).

An examination of the configuration (figure 17) shows that there was at least some connection between election labels and positions on recorded votes. Grout and Gerry, the two Antifederalists from Massachusetts, are found in positions distinct from Ames and his Federalist colleagues.

Antifederalist strength was greater in Virginia, where the governor (Patrick Henry) was an outspoken opponent of the Constitution. Through his influence, the state legislature chose two Antifederalists for the Senate, defeating James Madison in the process. Madison, one of the chief architects of the Constitution, was at this time regarded exclusively as a Federalist. He then chose to be considered for a seat in the House of Representatives. While Henry did his best to block Madison, putting up James Monroe (an Antifederalist) as an opponent, Madison won the election, as described in chapter 3 (Beeman, 1972; Brant, 1950). Out of a delegation of ten members, Virginia did send three Antifederalists (Bland, Coles, and Parker) to the House. But, as in Massachusetts, local factions were at least as important as party.

Again, we see in the configuration (figure 17) some distinction between

92 Origins of American Political Parties

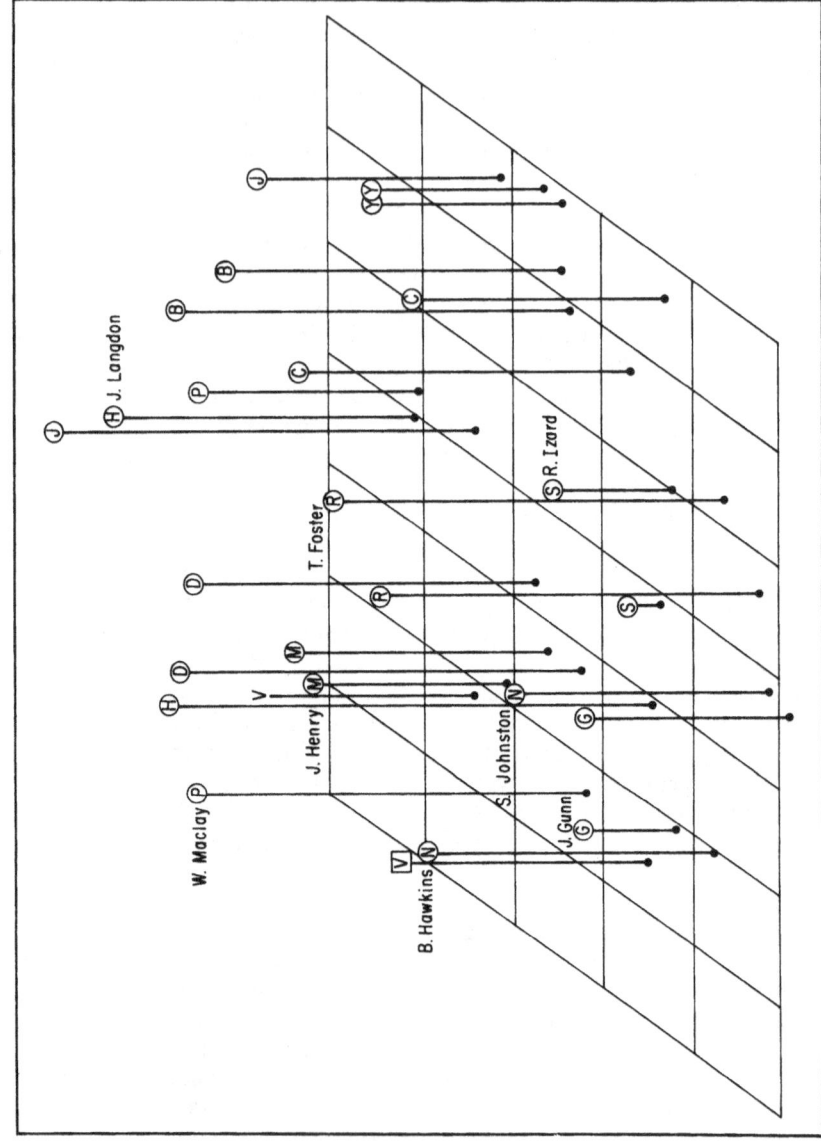

Fig. 18. Spatial Configuration,
First Congress, Senate,
1789-1791

KEY

B — Mass. M — Md.
C — Conn. N — N.C.
D — Del.   P — Penn.
E — Vt.   R — R.I.
G — Ga.   S — S.C.
H — N.H.   T — Tenn.
J — N.J.   V — Vir.
K — Ky.   Y — N.Y.

⊗ — Federalist
⊠ — Antifederalist
X — No party/Unknown

Letter = state
Circle/square = party

the voting records of Virginia's two Antifederalists (Bland died shortly after the session opened) and seven Federalist representatives (led by Madison). Overall, these differences are hardly dramatic, but they were important on some issues. More noteworthy, however, is the fact that all the Virginians, regardless of their opinions on the Constitution, are closer to each other than to any of the representatives from Massachusetts. Regional ties seem to have outweighed differences over the Constitution, an observation considered later in the chapter.

In general, few clearly defined patterns are evident in the spatial maps for the First Congress. This is especially true in the First Senate, where the lack of pattern seems to represent a completely undeveloped system of voting. This situation was noted by contemporary observers: "The mariner's compass has thirty-two points; the political one, perhaps as many hundreds" (William Maclay, quoted in Chambers, 1963b, p. 39). In effect, the minimal patterns that do exist in the First Senate are so weak that three dimensions are required to obtain a spatial representation with stress as low as that obtained in two dimensions for other years (see table 1).

A closer look at this configuration (figure 18) does reveal that there was some geographical clustering of the senators, with a rough division between North and South. This was recognized by Samuel Johnston, a senator from North Carolina, remarking (early in 1790) that "the sentiments of the Northern or Eastern, and Southern members constantly clash, even when local interest[s] are out of the question. This is a thing I cannot account for. . . ." (letter to James Iredell, March 11, 1790, quoted in Cunningham, 1957, p. 7). Even some of the exceptions might be used to argue that signs of future trends are evident here. William Maclay, of Pennsylvania, an outspoken critic of Hamilton, was aligned rather closely with those from the South, an alignment consistent with his sympathies for the future Jeffersonian Republican party.

If we overlook a high level of stress and examine the two-dimensional configuration (figure 19), we can try to get a clearer idea of the emerging partisan divisions. While the regional division is still evident, there is a definite line dividing the senators into two blocs. No ready explanation exists for this division, although both regional and partisan factors supply partial answers. The complete answer probably lies in the dominant issues considered by the Senate. In the end, the most significant characteristic of voting in the First Senate is its lack of clear pattern.

While it is difficult to find obvious explanations for voting in the First Senate, voting in the House of Representatives was far more structured (figure 17). Although the stress in two dimensions is not perfect, it is far better than the stress for a two-dimensional representation of the Senate. Three principal voting blocs, which are best described as sectional groupings, are evident from either multidimensional scaling or cluster analysis. One bloc includes mostly members from New England and New York. The second consists almost exclusively of southern congressmen, and the third is dominated by members from Pennsylvania and several neighboring states. The principal exceptions to this clustering come from New Jersey, Maryland, and South Carolina. The four New Jersey congressmen are divided between the New England/New York and Pennsylvania blocs, according to their proximity to

94   Origins of American Political Parties

Fig. 19. Spatial Configuration, First Congress, Senate, 1789-1791 (Two Dimensions)

KEY

B – Mass.   M – Md.
C – Conn.   N – N.C.
D – Del.   P – Penn.
E – Vt.   R – R.I.
G – Ga.   S – S.C.
H – N.H.   T – Tenn.
J – N.J.   V – Vir.
K – Ky.   Y – N.Y.

Ⓧ – Federalist
☒ – Antifederalist
X – No party/Unknown

Letter = state
Circle/square = party

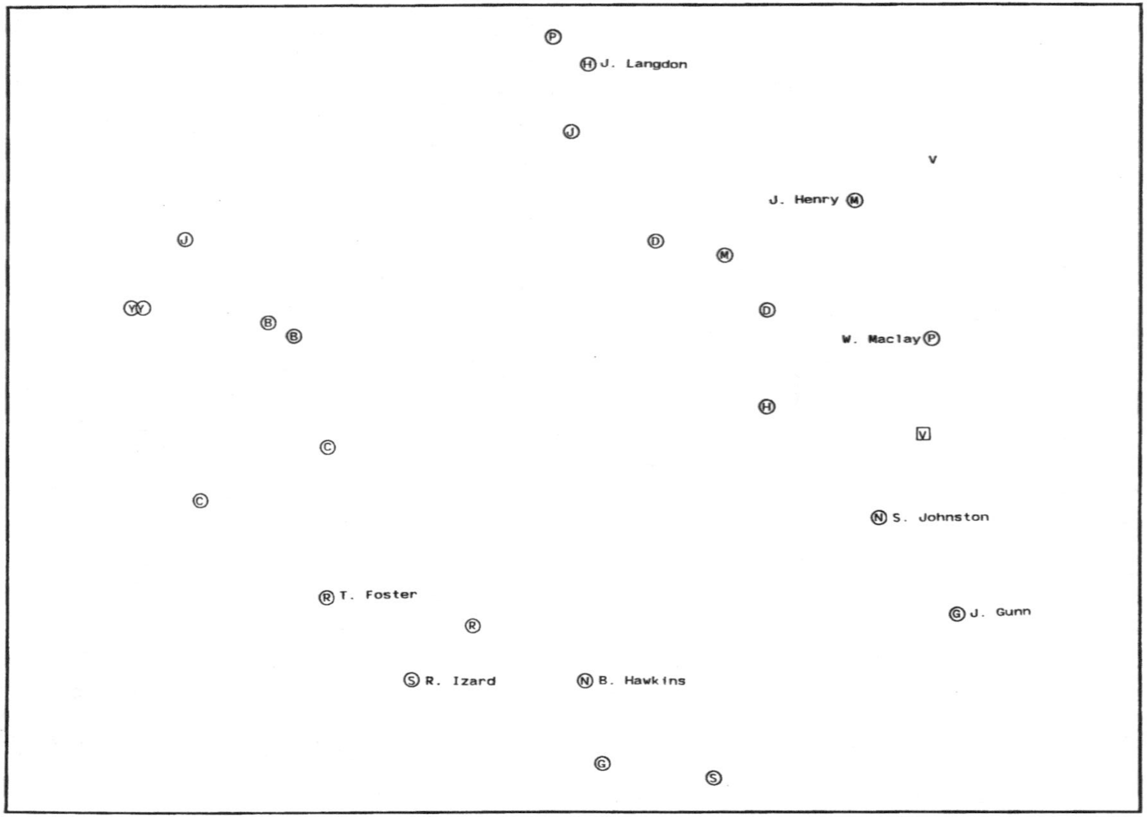

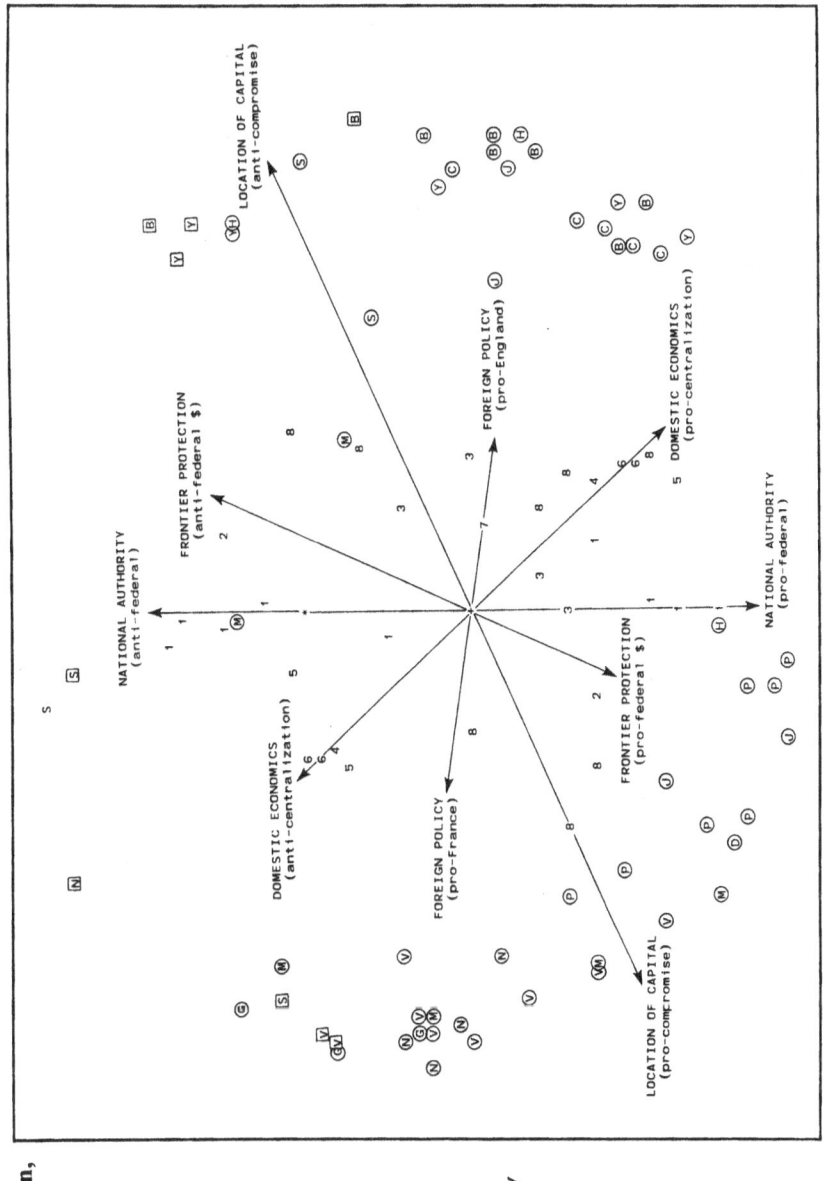

Fig. 20. Spatial Configuration, First Congress, House, 1789-1791—All Issue Areas

the cities of New York and Philadelphia—a sectional division that was important in factionalism in that state (Prince, 1967). Maryland's congressmen are placed with or near each of the three voting blocs, perhaps in accordance with that state's location between North and South. Finally, the South Carolina delegation contains two members (W.L. Smith and Huger, representing the coastal towns of Charleston and Georgetown) who voted in agreement with the New England bloc. Throughout the early years, South Carolina had the strongest Federalist party of any southern state, a fact best explained by trading interests centered in the port of Charleston (Rogers, 1962).

While this grouping into sectional blocs is very evident, it is hardly the entire picture. Within each sectional bloc there is considerable diversity that cannot be explained by geographic alliances. Furthermore, we would like to know what produced the regional groupings and the limited pattern of divisions between Federalists and Antifederalists.

To this end, we embark upon an examination of specific issues, using some of the techniques discussed in Appendix B. Of the 109 roll calls taken in the House of Representatives during the First Congress, about 30 have been selected for closer consideration.[4] This subset of votes was chosen to include the most important ones during this period, as designated by several historians (Bell, 1973; Bernhard, 1965; Brant, 1950; Cunningham, 1957).

Although the subset is not a random sample of votes, this strategy seemed preferable, because we are interested in the effect of the more salient issues of the day. Several steps were taken to ensure that they were reasonably representative. A cluster analysis technique for identifying scalable subsets of votes (MacRae, 1970) was applied to the universe of votes taken in the First Congress (using a cutoff of Yule's $Q = 0.8$). Based on the results of this clustering, at least one vote was included among the key votes for every cluster containing three or more votes. While this does not ensure that every interesting vote is included, it does help to provide for the inclusion of the more common patterns. Of course, one unavoidable problem lies in the fact that issues on which roll calls are taken are not always representative of all matters considered by the Congress. But while we must not lose sight of this limitation, there is little we can do about it.

For each key issue, a vector was placed in the space of congressmen in such a way that its direction indicates who provided the greatest support and opposition to that particular piece of legislation. The method for projecting these vectors and its justification are presented in Appendix B. It suffices to say here that a regression model provides the location of the vector. An overview of the key issues is provided in figure 20, and the degree of fit for these issues is reported in table 6.[5] In this figure, the members of Congress are represented by letters identical to those in figure 17. Roll calls are represented by numbers corresponding to the eight major issue areas. (The key to these numbers is found in table 6.) More precisely, the vector for a particular roll call is determined by connecting the center of the space to the point indicated for that roll call. The degree of fit for each key vote, as shown in table 6, is the squared multiple correlation from the regression model. It is a very imperfect statistic for measuring the fit of a roll call to the space, but the

Table 6. Key Votes—First Congress (1789-1791)

Vote	Date	Description	b1	b2	R^2
National Authority (#1)					
V14	06-22-89	Give president power to remove appointees	−.063	.231	.061
V19	08-18-89	Consider all constitutional amendments	−.046	.651	.474
V20	08-21-89	Amendment to limit national authority to "expressly" delegated powers	−.022	.726	.601
V21	08-21-89	Amendment to prohibit Congress from interfering with local authority over elections	−.086	.782	.633
V22	08-22-89	Amendment to prohibit direct taxes by federal government	.025	.529	.477
V36	09-11-89	Congressional salaries	.003	−.520	.270
V39	09-24-89	Amendment concerning speedy and public trial by jury	.012	−.624	.506
V45	09-28-89	Presidential authority over the militia	.167	−.320	.195
V55	05-27-90	Presidential authority over salaries of foreign service officers	.027	−.463	.243
Protection of the Frontier (#2)					
V18	08-12-89	Money for negotiating Indian treaties	−.206	−.299	.228
V72	06-22-90	Eliminate money to trade with and bribe the Indians	.194	.622	.415
Domestic Economics—Funding of Debts (#3)					
V53	05-26-90	Fund old money at 100:1	.388	.017	.472
V54	05-26-90	Pay back interest on old money	.252	.171	.288
V92	07-29-90	Amendment on funding debts	.004	−.243	.057
V93	07-29-90	Amendment on funding debts	.082	−.180	.051
Domestic Economics—Assumption of State Debts (#4)					
V88	07-24-90	Reject assumption of state debts	−.328	.360	.456
V91	07-26-90	Accept assumption of state debts	.314	−.318	.401

Table 6. (continued)

Vote	Date	Description	b1	b2	R^2
Domestic Economics—Revenue Bills (#5)					
V96	08-06-90	Lower salt duty from 12¢ to 9¢	−.139	.458	.262
V98	01-17-91	Eliminate tax on spirits	−.373	.332	.607
V102	01-27-91	Passage of revenue bill	.313	−.507	.586
Domestic Economics—National Bank (#6)					
V103	02-01-91	Recommit national bank bill	−.357	.455	.596
V104	02-03-91	Recommit national bank bill	−.352	.403	.558
V105	02-08-91	To vote on national bank bill	.370	−.389	.621
V106	02-08-91	Passage of national bank bill	.365	−.403	.616
Foreign Policy (#7)					
V16	07-01-89	Discriminatory duties against England	.215	−.011	.142
Location of the Capital (#8)					
V33	09-07-89	Permanent capital on Susquehanna	.347	−.248	.396
V38	09-22-89	Permanent capital on Susquehanna	.251	−.155	.226
V43	09-28-89	Permanent capital in Philadelphia	.392	−.431	.624
V62	05-31-90	Temporary capital in Philadelphia	−.387	−.312	.599
V66	06-11-90	Temporary capital in Baltimore	.448	.446	.811
V85	07-09-90	Temporary capital in Philadelphia; permanent capital in Washington	−.529	−.227	.891
V95	08-05-90	Temporary capital in Philadelphia	.406	.295	.612
V115	03-01-91	Temporary capital in Philadelphia; permanent capital in Washington	−.297	−.009	.305
Party					
		Party codes (Paullin, 1904)	.001	.452	.353

Note: Vote numbers are taken from the ICPSR data file, with vote descriptions based on Bell (1973); $b1$ and $b2$ provide coordinates for the vote vectors; R^2 is the fit between the vote and the configuration.

alternatives are equally inadequate or prohibitively difficult to compute (see Appendix B). Accordingly, the R^2 measure should be used only as a rough indication of fit.

Summary vectors have been drawn in figure 20 for the various issue areas. These are nonsystematic attempts to indicate the general direction of support for major issue areas. In the absence of these summary vectors, we would look at the clustering of votes in an issue area (represented on the plot by a common number) as an indication of the general pattern for that issue. It is readily apparent that the diversity of voting patterns is at least partially attributable to the variety of issues considered in the First Congress and the differing responses to these issues.

About three of every four votes taken in the First Congress came in the domains of domestic economics, location of the national capital, or authority of the new national government (see table 4). It is evident in figure 20 that great diversity existed in these areas alone. The vectors representing votes on national authority (#1 on plot) generally run vertically on the page, a direction consistent with a vector representing the Federalist-Antifederalist distinction. The major regional blocs are generally split by these issues, with North-South differences being relatively unimportant.

In contrast, most of the vectors for the general area of domestic economics (#3, #4, #5, #6) run from upper left to lower right. This orientation emphasizes the differences between the major regional blocs, with the Pennsylvania cluster falling in a position intermediate to the other groups. Votes taken on the possible location of the capital (#8 on plot) vary more among themselves than do those in other issue domains, and these differences (as we shall see below) are related to the variety of options being considered. If we focus on the vote that represents the final compromise for a capital site (as shown in figure 20), we see an alignment different from those just discussed. Here the regional blocs representing the South and the area around Pennsylvania are generally united in opposition to the New England representatives. By expanding the analysis to include issues involving protection of the frontier (#2) and foreign policy (#7), neither of which saw many roll call votes, we find alignments that differ from any of the above issue areas.[6]

The several key votes in the area of national authority are quite consistent with each other, as illustrated in figure 21 (where vectors are drawn for just these votes). Four votes concerned the adoption of the Bill of Rights, three were over the authority of the president, and one reflected levels of congressional salaries. Only the vote taken on presidential authority over the militia (V45) deviated to any significant extent from the other votes. It involved concerns over the role of the army and protection of the frontier, and these competing cues may have caused some different alignments. All of the other votes fell very close together.

The roll call votes taken on national authority issues were more likely than those in any other category to show the differences between Federalists and Antifederalists. The average value of the index of party difference for national authority votes was 53.3, while the average for all the other votes was 22.2. Another distinctive feature of votes in this issue area is that nearly all took place during the first session of the First Congress. It was the business

100 Origins of American Political Parties

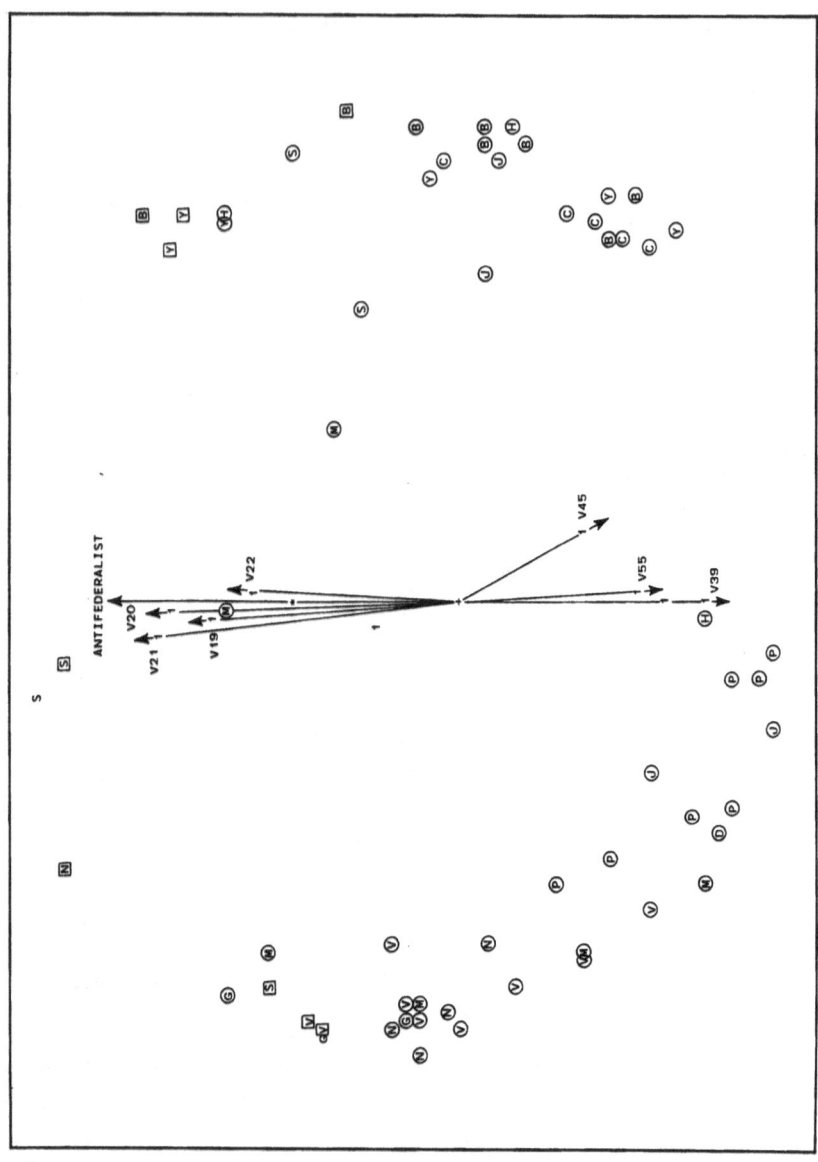

Fig. 21. Spatial Configuration, First Congress, House, 1789-1791—National Authority

KEY

B — Mass. M — Md.
C — Conn. N — N.C.
D — Del.   P — Penn.
E — Vt.   R — R.I.
G — Ga.   S — S.C.
H — N.H.   T — Tenn.
J — N.J.   V — Vir.
K — Ky.   Y — N.Y.

⊗ — Federalist
⊠ — Antifederalist
X — No party/Unknown

Letter = state
Circle/square = party
Number = issue area

of that first session to complete, in effect, the work of the Constitutional Convention. Adoption of the Bill of Rights was nearly made a condition of ratification by several states, and attention was also directed at working arrangements for the new government.

In these matters, the same Federalist leaders who had supported the Constitution were active advocates of establishing the authority of the national government. Madison, soon to become a leader of the opposition, operated during this first session as a close aide and floor leader for Washington. He was a strong legislative leader and even earned reluctant praise from Ames, who was not overly quick to compliment a southerner (Bernhard, 1965; Brant, 1950). Nevertheless, this political marriage was not destined for a long life. Once these initial measures had passed, thus providing a more solid foundation for the new government, new issues arose and produced some very different political alignments.

In addition to setting the wheels of government in motion, the First Congress was faced with a need to bring order to the economy of the new nation. Vast debts had been incurred during the Revolution, and the Continental Congress had not done much to establish a sound financial basis for the government. Thus, domestic economics was an area of vital importance for the new Congress. The key issues in this area, portrayed in figure 22, encompass votes on proposals to fund the national debt (#3 on plot) and assume state debts (#4), votes on several revenue bills (#5), and votes on the creation of the national bank (#6). All of these bills were part of a general economic program proposed by Hamilton for the purpose of putting the nation on a sound fiscal basis.

Some historians (Beard, 1915; Chambers, 1963b; Ryan, 1971) have credited this set of programs as being the impetus for the first signs of organized (even partisan) opposition in Congress. Whether or not this is true, the fact that these matters caused a split between Hamilton and Madison for the first time is of immediate relevance. These men, who had recently collaborated in writing *The Federalist*, were both anxious to establish a viable national government, and they agreed on the national authority measures considered during the first session. But they differed on some key details of the economic program (Brant, 1950; Cunningham, 1957; Ferguson, 1961).

Of the major components of Hamilton's program, funding was the first to be considered. There was consensus on the basic need for funding the national debt, and no roll call was recorded on the final vote. Similarly, there was no recorded vote on the major amendment introduced by Madison, aimed at preventing speculators from making substantial profits from the funding process. Of the four amendments to the funding bill on which votes were recorded (#3 on plot), none fits the House configuration very well. Bell (1973, pp. 116-21), whose analysis also shows that these votes are unlike most of the others, speculates that people were voting on these amendments from different motives. Without statements by those involved, it is impossible to evaluate such an explanation, but it is consistent with the spatial analysis.

On the question of assumption of state debts, direct votes were recorded—although in the form of amendments to the funding bill (#4 on plot). These roll calls fall within the general pattern of domestic economics votes,

102 Origins of American Political Parties

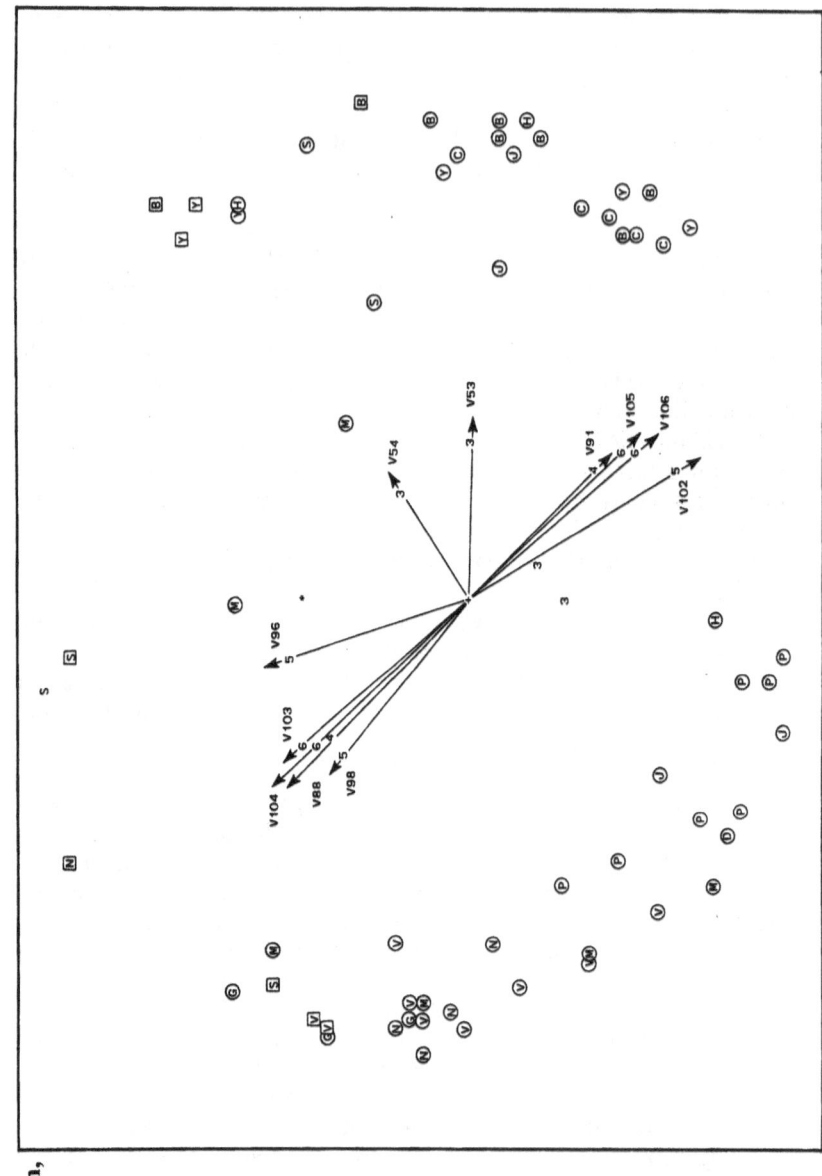

Fig. 22. Spatial Configuration, First Congress, House, 1789-1791—Domestic Economics

KEY

B – Mass.   M – Md.
C – Conn.   N – N.C.
D – Del.   P – Penn.
E – Vt.   R – R.I.
G – Ga.   S – S.C.
H – N.H.   T – Tenn.
J – N.J.   V – Vir.
K – Ky.   Y – N.Y.

Ⓧ – Federalist
☒ – Antifederalist
X – No party/Unknown

Letter = state
Circle/square = party
Number = issue area

although the fit is not high (as measured by R^2). The direction fits the observation of historians (Ferguson, 1961, ch. 14) that attitudes toward assumption were largely based on the fiscal status of the various states. States with large unpaid debts (Massachusetts and South Carolina) were anxious to have the national government assume this burden. The greatest opposition came from southern states (especially Maryland, Virginia, North Carolina, and Georgia) that had cleared their debts and saw assumption as unfair to them. The ultimate passage of assumption rested on a compromise involving the location of the capital, which is discussed below.[7]

The final elements of the Hamiltonian program were the revenue measures (#5 on plot) and establishment of the national bank (#6). Roll calls on these bills, coming during the third session, all produced the same general alignment of votes, as illustrated in figure 22.[8] By this time, the factions had at least somewhat solidified. Jefferson, from his Cabinet post, had split with Hamilton; Madison had finally moved away from the side of the administration, taking on a leadership role in opposition (Brant, 1950; Cunningham, 1957). The support for Hamilton on these issues came from New England and from the Middle states (except Maryland), while the South provided nearly unanimous opposition.

Some have suggested that the alignments on Hamiltonian economics had causes other than those suggested above. Beard (1915) argues that an explanation can be found in the personal financial interest of members of Congress, a hypothesis that cannot easily be tested here. While some of the earliest votes (those on the funding amendments) do not fit the pattern well, the spatial analysis shows that the dominant pattern in the area of domestic economics is a regional one, separating the North from the South. Unless personal wealth was concentrated in the North, this finding is inconsistent with Beard's thesis.

While economic issues would remain important for years, one issue was a unique part of the First Congress—the location of the capital (#8 on plot). Figure 23 shows the alignment of several diverse votes on the capital. The history of this issue was rather complex, and its resolution was spread over nearly two years. In the first year, votes were taken on several different locations. The House initially settled on a site along the Susquehanna River. But after the Senate rejected that option, both houses agreed to place the capital in Philadelphia. Both of these options led to similar, although not identical, coalitions of support (see figure 23). The New England group was strongly in favor of any site not in the South, so they supported both proposed locations. Similarly, the Pennsylvania bloc was pleased with both sites—since either would place the capital within their boundaries. The southerners, on the other hand, were united in opposition, holding out for a more proximate site (Bernhard, 1965; Brant, 1950).

These decisions did not, however, settle the matter. Although it appeared that the issue had been resolved in the first session, each regional bloc continued to agitate for its location. New Englanders actually preferred the capital to be in New York, the southerners were lobbying for a site on the Potomac, and Pennsylvania continued to work for a location within its borders.

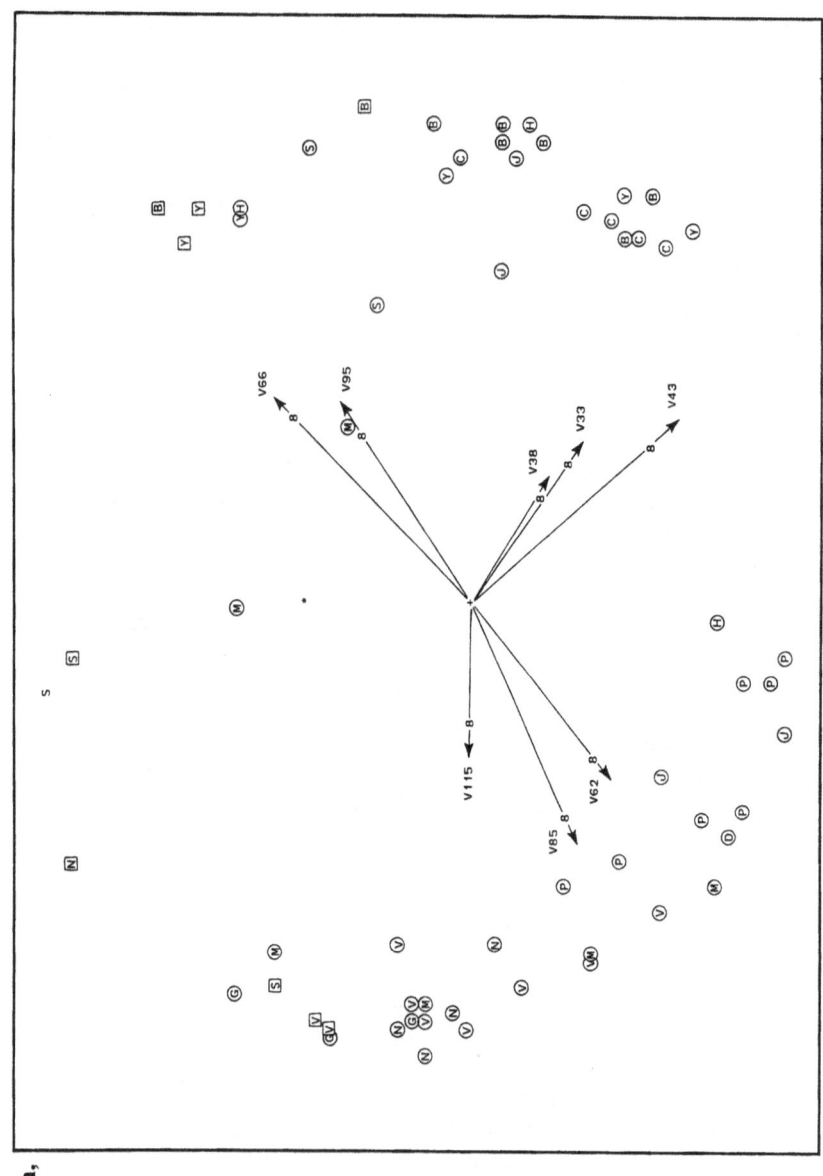

Fig. 23. Spatial Configuration, First Congress, House, 1789-1791—Location of the Capital

Table 7. Regional Voting on Locating the Capital

	Vote 38 Susquehanna	Vote 85 Compromise
New England	12- 0	0-16
New York	6- 0	0- 6
New Jersey	0- 3	2- 2
Pennsylvania	6- 0	7- 0
Delaware	0- 1	1- 0
Maryland	5- 1	4- 2
South	2-12	18- 3
Total	31-17	32-29

The final settlement was to locate a permanent capital on the Potomac, along with a temporary capital in Philadelphia. But the decision came only after complex bargaining that linked it to Hamilton's proposal for the assumption of state debts. In an early example of congressional logrolling, Hamilton won two key votes on the assumption bill from White and Lee of Virginia. In exchange, he convinced the Pennsylvania delegation to accept a capital site on the Potomac (along with a temporary home, for ten years, in Philadelphia). While many were not thrilled with this compromise, it did provide a resolution to two difficult problems (Bernhard, 1965; Cunningham, 1957).

The spatial representation of several of these key votes (shown in figure 23) demonstrates the dramatic shift between the votes taken in the first session and those taken later as the compromise emerged. The vectors representing the latter votes are nearly at right angles to the earlier votes. This is primarily a reflection of the movement by the Pennsylvania bloc. In the first votes, they were in an intermediate position (most agreeing with the New Englanders), whereas in the vote to accept the compromise, the Pennsylvania bloc aligned itself with the South (see table 7). One additional vote on the capital site was taken during the third session, which confirmed the previous compromise. While some votes had shifted and the result does not fit as well into the configuration, the orientation of this vote was very similar to previous votes on the compromise decision.

In summary, over the course of the First Congress, there existed a variety of coalitions and alignments, with changes occurring as issues moved on and off the congressional agenda. This situation clearly fits the model of factionalism (presented in chapter 1). Each of the three major issue domains was dominated by a different set of factions.

The Federalist and Antifederalist factions first arose over the ratification of the Constitution and continued to be important during the first session of the Congress, particularly on votes that focused on the authority of the national government. Yet these factions were not destined for long life. Their importance declined during the third session.[9] This change reflected in part a shift in the agenda, but the fact that these groups were not at all relevant to

Table 8. Factions in the First House

		Location of capital	
		Pro-compromise	Anti-compromise
National authority	Federalist	14	14
	Antifederalist	10	13

		Economics	
		Pro-bank	Anti-bank
National authority	Federalist	22	5
	Antifederalist	11	8

		Economics	
		Pro-bank	Anti-bank
Location of capital	Pro-compromise	11	16
	Anti-compromise	26	3

Note: National authority factions based on vote V21; Location of capital factions based on vote V85; Economics factions based on vote V106. Further descriptions are found in table 6.

later issues is clear evidence that they were best described not as parties but as factions.

A second important set of factions in the First Congress comprised the three regional groups that arose over the choice of a site for the national capital. Based roughly on their proximity to the cities of New York, Philadelphia, and Washington (Potomac River), these groups joined in varying combinations on different proposals. The foundation for these factions was certainly the promotion of self-interest, with an eye toward the symbolic and economic benefits of having the capital in their part of the country.

Finally, there were factions that arose over the Hamiltonian economic program. These groupings were not very stable, for different bases of support existed on the various components of the program. But the basic similarity of the vectors suggests that distinct factions had arisen. Furthermore, it is clear that these factions were substantially different from those based on other issues.

Differences among the three sets of factions can be demonstrated by means of simple cross-tabulations. If we represent each faction by votes on a representative roll call, as shown in table 8, we can compare factional memberships. The lack of identity between the Federalist-Antifederalist factions and the blocs based on the choice of a capital site are the most evident.

The economic factions, on the other hand, drew their membership to some extent from the other factions. The supporters of Hamilton were more likely to have been supporters of broader national authority and opponents of the capital compromise. Of course, there is far from a direct match. Opponents of Hamilton, generally from the South, nearly all voted for the accepted capital site and were slightly more likely to have been Antifederalists. Madison, as both a Federalist and an opponent of Hamilton, was one of a small band (including two other Virginians and two from Maryland). But it should be noted that the North Carolina delegation (four out of five being Federalists) was not included in the national authority votes, since the state had not yet ratified the Constitution. Because this opposition group became the core of the Republican party, it is important to see that it was not a simple extension of the Antifederalist faction. Rather, it included several who were "federalists only in support of the Constitution and not federalists in upholding all of the centralizing measures of the new government" (Gilpatrick, 1931, p. 45).

It should hardly need restatement that there were no parties by the time the First Congress adjourned. There is even some doubt as to the existence of identifiable factions in the Senate. But factionalism clearly characterized voting in the House of Representatives. In fact, the Hamiltonian faction had acquired a degree of sophistication; Maclay (an opponent) claimed that he had seen evidence of active leadership by Hamilton, including convening at least one informal caucus (Maclay, 1927). Chambers (1963*b*, p. 39) has suggested that "the debt and bank issues, with the prestige of Washington's 'name,' had produced a 'court faction.'" As we examine subsequent Congresses, it will become evident that the economic factions provided the foundations for future party development. But for the period of 1789 to 1791, the only correct characterization of the political patterns is factionalism.

A Period of Transition, 1791-1793

By the Second Congress, voting patterns were still best described as factional, but sectionalism was beginning to give way to partisanship. There was not yet, however, a clear movement toward polarization of legislators into two cohesive groups. Nor was there much evidence of partisanship in elections for this Congress.

The elections for Congress in 1790 and 1791 witnessed nearly a total absence of partisan contests in most states, especially in New England and the South. Although there were a few seats contested in a manner best described as partisan, these were clearly exceptions to the rule. Local issues and personalities were more frequently the controlling influences.

Typical of the dominance of local factors were the congressional elections in Maryland. Under Maryland's general ticket system, the 1788-89 elections had provided voters a reasonably clear choice between a slate of Federalists and one of Antifederalists. In contrast, by 1790, these groups had realigned into two geographic factions. A Chesapeake ticket proved to be victorious over a Potomac ticket, although the latter was generally the descendant of the Federalist faction and included four of the six incumbent congressmen (Renzulli, 1972, pp. 149-53; Risjord, 1978, pp. 396-400).

There was somewhat greater evidence of partisanship in the elections held in both Pennsylvania and New York, but even there the contests were hardly examples of party domination. In New York, the political leanings of most candidates were well known, although it was not always easy to predict how they would respond to the new national issues being considered in Congress. In the end, it appears that the county of residence was probably a better predictor of electoral success than any political factors (Young, 1967, pp. 161-65, 590).[10] In Pennsylvania, where party groups had played a significant role in 1789 under the general ticket system, the change to district elections reduced the level of partisanship to only marginal importance (Tinkcom, 1950, pp.45-48).

In two southern congressional districts, it appears that elections were strongly influenced by partisan forces. But even here, the real story may lie in localism. North Carolina's Fayetteville district matched William Barry Grove, an advocate of the Constitution, against Timothy Bloodworth, the incumbent and an outspoken opponent of the Constitution and administration policies. Their campaign was accented by a series of advertisements in local newspapers. But in spite of an apparently heated contest in which Grove won 65% of the 3,166 votes cast, the election was very one-sided at the county level. In only two of the twelve counties in the district did the leading candidate get less than 90% of the vote. Each candidate won the counties that were nearest to his home county. This "friends and neighbors" voting pattern belied the apparent partisanship in the contest (Gilpatrick, 1931; *North Carolina Chronicle or Fayetteville Gazette*, February 7, 1791).[11]

In Georgia, James Jackson, a leader of the opposition to the national administration, was being challenged by Anthony Wayne, a war hero and friend of the government. The unusual prominence of national issues in this district was triggered by concerns over whether the federal government should be responsible for dealings with the Indians and the Yazoo land in the western part of the state. Wayne won the election, but the result was later challenged by Jackson, with the House eventually declaring the seat vacant (see chapter 3). This election was certainly the most partisan contest in the South and perhaps in the nation, but the special circumstances confirm its place as the exception that helps to prove the rule (Rose, 1968, pp. 59-68).

The evidence, then, is clear that partisan factors were not of great importance in elections for the Second Congress. But the question that remains is whether the voting records of those elected were equally independent of the effect of party.

In the Senate of the Second Congress, the configuration (figure 24) takes on a roughly circular shape, representing a transitional stage in the development of party voting. In fact, this circle is better described as a sequence of four distinct blocs plus one isolated individual (Aaron Burr). The clearest fact about these blocs is their regional basis. In the lower-right bloc, all senators are from the New England states, while everyone in the lower-left sector of the configuration comes from the South. The two upper blocs are dominated by senators from the Middle states, with the remaining New Englanders to the right, and the last southerners to the left. This regional grouping is even more distinctive than the similar pattern for the First House. Thus, sectional alliances that were important in prior years were still the dominant influence at this time.

Regional patterns, however, are not the only distinctive feature of this configuration. Those few senators who can be identified historically as Republicans are grouped near the bottom of the configuration, while those in the remainder of the plot (except Burr) are Federalists. Thus, among the southern senators, those who were maintaining ties to the Federalists (Izard, Johnston, Hawkins, Gunn) must have voted differently from their fellow southerners on at least some issues. While one could hardly claim that this was evidence of clear partisanship, it does indicate that the forces that would eventually distinguish the parties had begun to take effect.

Aaron Burr's isolated position is particularly intriguing, given his special role in early American politics. His point in the spatial configuration is even more isolated than it appears in figure 24. In a three-dimensional configuration, Burr alone defines the third dimension, showing his individualized voting in this Congress. Chosen as a senator from New York because of a "reputation for independence which fascinated substantial men of both parties" (Young, 1967, p. 189), Burr was truly independent of partisanship in the Second Congress. Only in later years did he become a confirmed Republican, both in his congressional voting and in his political ambitions.

The configuration that depicts voting in the Second House (figure 25) bears many similarities to that of the previous House (figure 17). The principal feature is again the importance of regional blocs. The New England and southern groups remain significant, but there is no longer a distinct Pennsylvania bloc. There is, in addition, a peculiar split among the southern congressmen. Something has separated the North Carolina delegation from the other southerners, although the split is not a major one. As before, South Carolina provides the main exception to this regional alignment, with those from coastal districts continuing to be allied with northern congressmen. A second exception of note is the two-member delegation from the newly admitted state of Vermont, the first state that had no direct access to the coast. Vermont's congressmen, like its senators, claimed an identification with the Republican party. Their votes, however, place them neither with the New England Federalists nor with the southern Republicans.

Delegations that changed the most from the First to the Second Congress were those from the Middle states. No longer was each state delegation a cohesive voting bloc. The representatives from New York and Pennsylvania had become internally divided, with three Pennsylvanians in both the southern and northern blocs, and two others between the two blocs. In New York's delegation, two members aligned themselves with the South, and the other four voted with New England. These locations tend to match the historical record of party labels. But one suspects (on the basis of knowledge about the 1790-91 elections) that their labels were acquired *because of* these voting alignments, rather than serving as preexisting voting cues.

The New Jersey delegation remained divided, but no longer along geographic lines. Aaron Kitchell, known a few years later as a founder of the state's Republican party (Prince, 1967), is among a small group at the top of the figure—a group that may represent a transitional voting bloc. Finally, the Maryland delegation was still much closer to the southern bloc, but only half of it could be considered part of that bloc.

110 Origins of American Political Parties

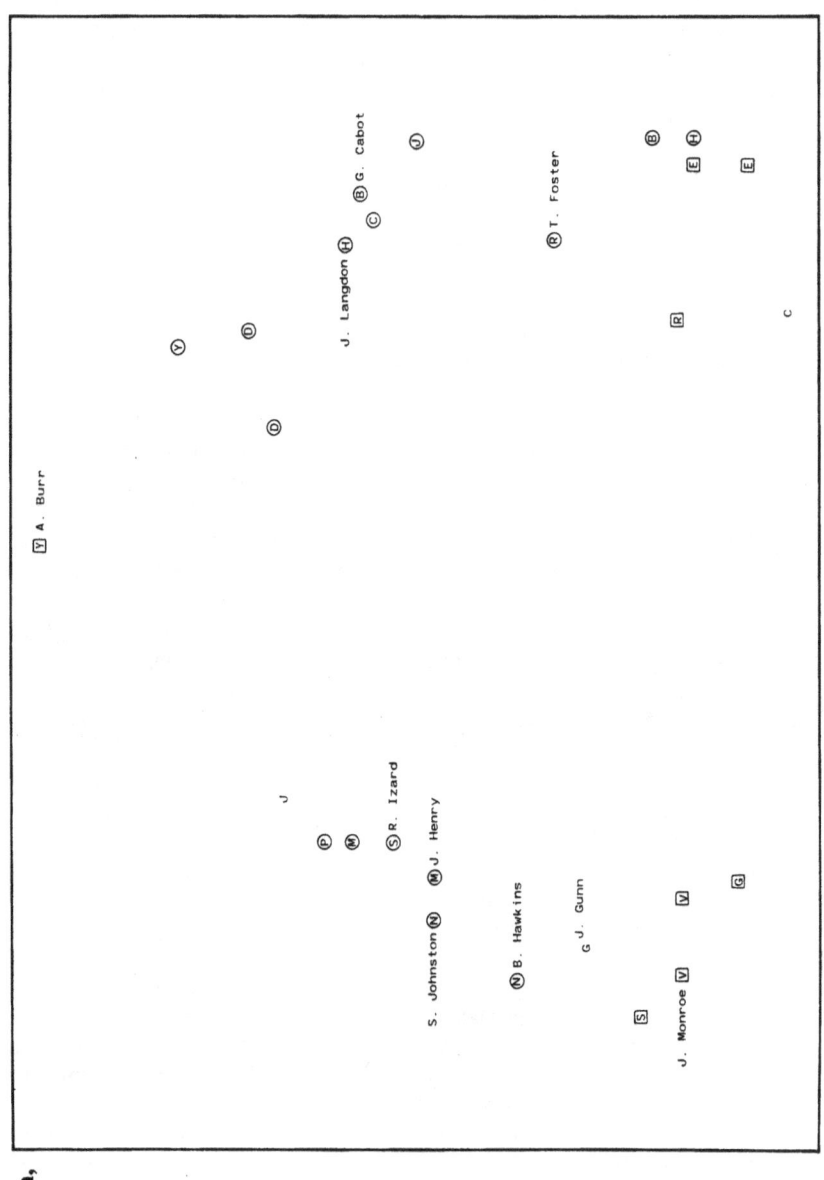

Fig. 24. Spatial Configuration, Second Congress, Senate, 1791-1793

KEY

B — Mass.   M — Md.
C — Conn.   N — N.C.
D — Del.   P — Penn.
E — Vt.   R — R.I.
G — Ga.   S — S.C.
H — N.H.   T — Tenn.
J — N.J.   V — Vir.
K — Ky.   Y — N.Y.

Ⓧ — Federalist
☒ — Republican
X — No party/Unknown

Letter = state
Circle/square = party

Factionalism in the Early Years 111

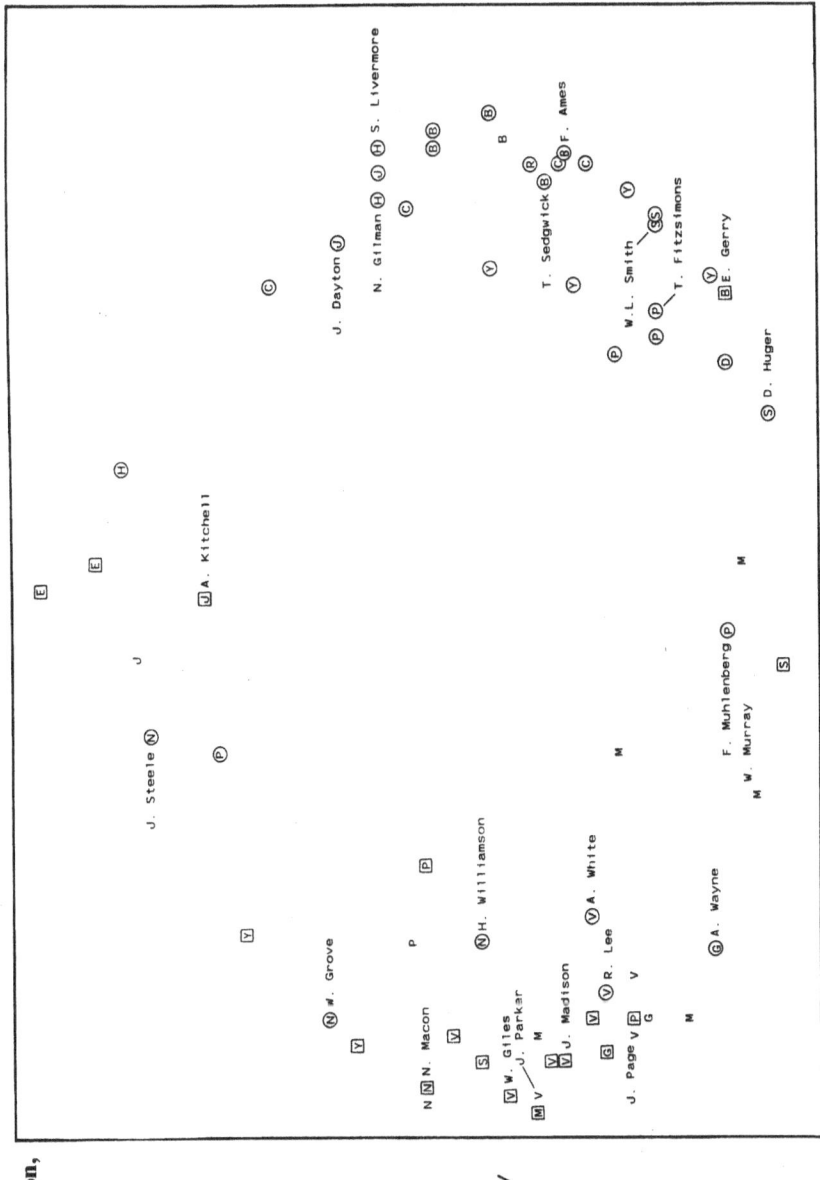

Fig. 25. Spatial Configuration, Second Congress, House, 1791-1793

KEY

B – Mass.   M – Md.
C – Conn.   N – N.C.
D – Del.   P – Penn.
E – Vt.   R – R.I.
G – Ga.   S – S.C.
H – N.H.   T – Tenn.
J – N.J.   V – Vir.
K – Ky.   Y – N.Y.

⊗ – Federalist
⊠ – Republican
X – No party/Unknown

Letter = state
Circle/square = party

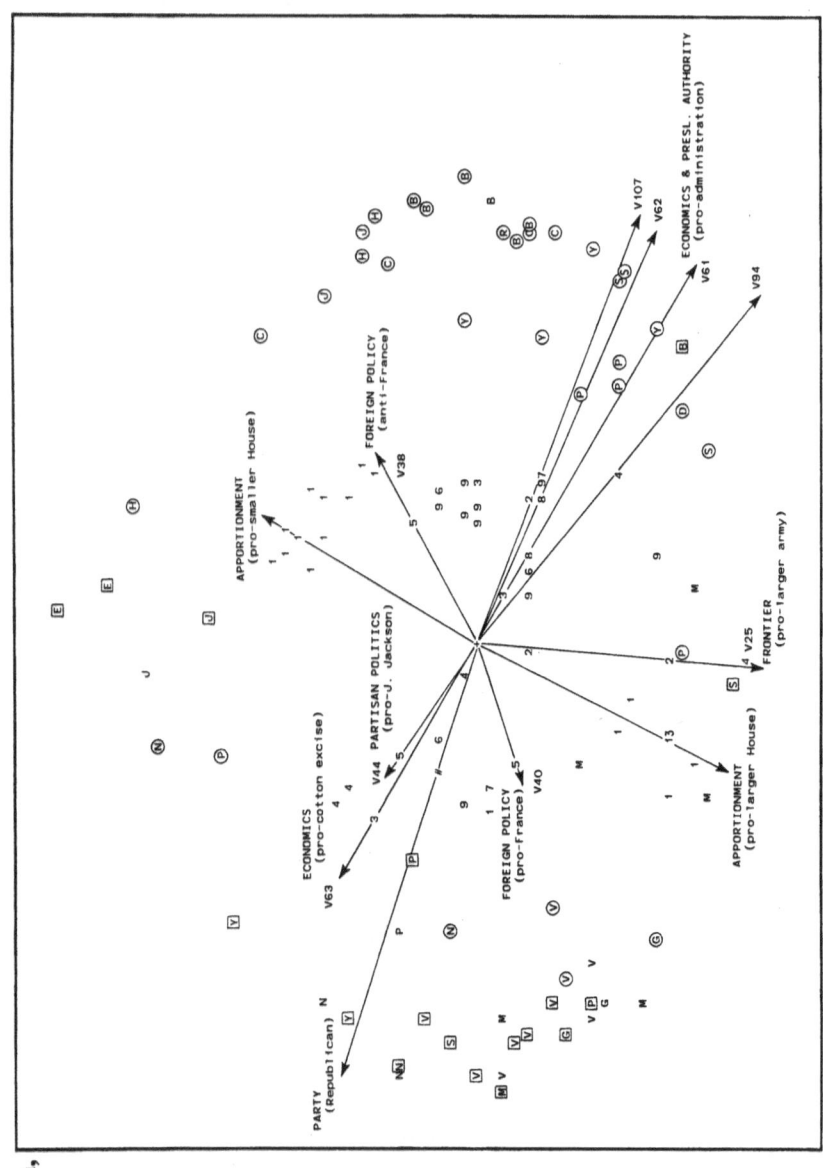

Fig. 26. Spatial Configuration, Second Congress, House, 1791-1793—All Issue Areas

Thus, sectionalism clearly remained the dominant cleavage in the Second Congress. Even those few individuals from the South or New England whose party affiliations (at least as labeled in later years) were atypical for their regions voted more closely with regional alliances than with their fellow partisans (see figure 25). The partisan groups are well defined, at least in retrospect, with the left (southern) bloc being dominated by Republicans and the right bloc mostly Federalists. Men such as Madison and Giles (on the Republican side) and Ames and Sedgwick (for the Federalists), who were becoming the chief spokesmen for partisan interests, are located at the centers of their respective voting blocs.

But it is the exceptions that tend to prove that these voting alignments are more clearly based on sectionalism than on party. For example, Elbridge Gerry, from the Middlesex district in Massachusetts, had been an Antifederalist in the Constitutional Convention, refusing even to sign the final document. He later became a leader in the Republican party, eventually serving as vice-president under James Madison. But in the Second Congress, Gerry was allied more often with the Federalist bloc than with his nominal Republican colleagues, an alliance that lasted for Gerry for another decade before his reemergence as a Republican leader after 1800 (Formisano, 1983, pp. 72-74).

In the South, there were several whose party attachments have been recorded for posterity as Federalists.[12] But, except for those from South Carolina, they voted most often with other southerners. Anthony Wayne, whose election was the subject of such a strong challenge by Republicans, nevertheless voted very much like a Republican. The other election that was contested on apparently partisan grounds sent Grove to Congress. In spite of his Federalist label, his voting record placed him at the edge of the cluster of southerners, most of whom became known as Republicans. These cases reinforce the thesis that patterns of voting in the Second Congress were not yet clearly determined by partisan affiliations.

An overview of the voting alignments in the Second House reveals a dominance of regional patterns, but with some signs of a transition toward partisan voting. Perhaps a consideration of the issues can help to show more clearly what sort of transition was taking place. One issue that was important in the First Congress, the location of the capital, had been resolved and thus was not on the agenda of the Second Congress. Otherwise, the agenda was not substantially different. National authority and domestic economics remained the most salient issue domains, although the nature of these issues had changed. The frequency of votes on the protection of the frontier was greater than in the previous Congress, but foreign policy was still not the subject of very many votes.

In contrast to the situation in the First Congress, voting on specific roll calls did not fall into very consistent patterns. Vectors representing the key votes (Bell, 1973; Bernhard, 1965; Brant, 1950) are shown in figure 26, and descriptions, coefficients, and degree of fit are given in table 9. Perhaps the less distinct patterns were a reflection of the generally lower salience of issues in the Second Congress. The Bill of Rights and a basic economic program having been approved, the questions were more likely to be on details of implementation rather than on fundamental principles. In addition, the mild

Table 9. Key Votes—Second Congress (1791-1793)

Vote	Date	Description	b1	b2	R^2
National Authority—Reapportionment (#1)					
V11	11-15-91	Ratio of 1:30,000 (larger House)	−.254	−.521	.462
V12	11-23-91	Ratio of 1:34,000 (smaller House)	.304	.527	.587
V17	12-19-91	Refuse Senate bill (1:34,000)	−.406	−.515	.753
V33	02-21-92	Ratio of 1:34,000 to 1797; 1:30,000 after 1797	−.244	−.378	.324
V45	03-23-92	Agree to Senate bill	.383	.372	.550
V58	04-09-92	Ratio of 1:33,000 for 1793	.464	.298	.755
National Authority—Other (#2)					
V20	01-05-92	State vs. federal authority over post roads	−.020	−.155	.028
V61	04-12-92	Presidential authority over militia	.229	−.142	.207
V62	04-12-92	Presidential authority over militia	.384	−.186	.528
Protection of the Frontier (#3)					
V25	02-01-92	Protection bill (larger army)	−.046	−.547	.287
V36	03-06-92	Uniform militia	.122	−.070	.054
V64	04-21-92	Defense of frontiers and aid to fisheries	.387	−.126	.556
V76	12-18-92	Offensive use of militia against Indians	−.250	−.516	.441
Foreign Policy (#4)					
V38	03-10-92	Recommit congratulatory note to France	.325	.197	.409
V40	03-10-92	Send congratulatory note to France	−.334	−.108	.417
Partisan Politics (#5)					
V44	03-21-92	Seat Jackson in place of Wayne	−.304	.227	.353
Domestic Economics (#6)					
V48	03-26-92	Establish national mint	.243	−.510	.437
V54	04-03-92	Extend assumption of state debts	.204	−.130	.145
V63	04-19-92	Duty on imported cotton	−.470	.283	.772
V65	04-30-92	Higher tax on whiskey	.423	−.006	.573
V73	11-21-92	Withdraw request for plan for redemption of debt	−.270	.123	.268
V94	01-28-93	General settlement of accounts	.454	−.375	.790

Table 9. (continued)

Vote	Date	Description	$b1$	$b2$	R^2
V107	03-01-93	Anti-Hamilton resolution	.428	−.176	.696
Party		Party codes (author's estimates)	−.355	.100	.457

Note: Vote numbers are taken from the ICPSR data file, with vote descriptions based on Bell (1973); $b1$ and $b2$ provide coordinates for the vote vectors; R^2 is the fit between the vote and the configuration.

amount of polarization that had taken place meant less shifting of large voting blocs. The variation from one vote to the next may be due simply to individuals who crossed bloc lines for relatively idiosyncratic reasons. But before accepting such a conclusion, let us look at the key votes.

The authority of the central government remained a major issue domain in the Second Congress, but the votes generally did not deal with fundamental questions of the power of national government. Over half of these votes related to the size of the House and apportionment of seats to the states (#1 on plot). Such concerns were only indirectly related to the authority of the national government. A few votes dealt with states' rights and others with the authority of the president (#2 on plot). But here again they were connected to specific applications rather than to basic principles.

Of those votes involving national authority that were not on the question of reapportionment, one (V20) is not well represented in the configuration. It was concerned with whether state or federal government would have certain power in regard to post roads. For whatever reason, it was not highly related to the factions generally present in this Congress. The two votes on presidential authority over the militia (V61 and V62), which involved the power of both the president and the federal government, were more clearly related to general voting patterns. They triggered a basic division between the two major voting blocs.

In all, seventeen different votes were taken on the reapportionment of the House during the Second Congress. The fundamental issue was how large the membership would be. While the debate at times invoked serious questions of representation, for most members it was a simple question of which plan would work to the advantage of their home state or region (Bernhard, 1965, pp. 106-8; Brant, 1950, p. 345). The various votes all divided the House along similar lines based on region. These alignments, as represented by the vectors (see figure 26), are at right angles to those on national authority. In either case the Virginia (or southern) bloc was directly opposed to the New England bloc. The main difference came in those members from the Middle states who fell in the center of the reapportionment axis, regardless of their alignment with the "party" blocs.

Four key votes have been identified in the area of frontier protection (#3 on plot). In general, however, these votes represented a mixture of concerns.

Attitudes toward use of the militia on the frontier may have involved thoughts about presidential and federal authority, sectional biases (coastal against interior regions), and, potentially, foreign policy considerations.[13] As a result, it is not surprising that the four key votes did not follow any one pattern. The earliest vote (V25), on a move to a larger army, may provide the purest consideration of frontier issues. But, in the end, the only safe conclusion is that the frontier issue was generating no clearly defined factional pattern.

Foreign policy concerns had received little formal attention in the First Congress, and the single key vote did not fit the general patterns found in the spatial configuration (see figure 20). In the Second Congress, there was still little clear attention to this issue domain. The only key votes (#4 in figure 26) were on a congratulatory message being sent to France. While this has the appearance of being a rather minor matter, it apparently generated a conflict suggestive of future divisions (Bell, 1973, pp. 139-40). These two votes, in addition, seem to have divided the House along lines at least marginally different from those for the other issue areas. There was a core of anti-French congressmen in New England. Only later developments, however, would suggest whether these votes were forming the basis for foreign policy factions.

The last general issue area to be considered is domestic economics (#6 on plot). Congress did not address the type of broad proposals such as funding and the national bank that dominated the previous years. Rather, the representatives were concerned with following up on the major initiatives passed earlier, with such measures as the settlement of accounts between the states and the federal government. Certain economic measures such as the tax on whiskey and the establishment of a national mint seem to have involved somewhat specialized coalitions, although the major voting blocs were still opposed. In two other key votes on the national debt, the alignments differed substantially from the patterns in the configuration (as measured by R^2).

Three of the votes on economic legislation are particularly interesting. One imposed a duty on imported cotton (V63); the second was on the final settlement of accounts with the states (V94); and the third was a resolution of censure directed at Alexander Hamilton (V107). Each of these votes fits the configuration well, and each divided the House along roughly the same axis. The anti-Hamilton vote and that on settling accounts were in effect measures of evaluation for the administration in the economic domain, while the cotton duty had a strong regional bias, one consistent with the attitudes toward Hamilton.

A strong argument can be made that the voting alignment defined by these three economic votes was one that represented the emerging partisan alignment. Because Hamilton was regarded as the nation's leading Federalist to the extent that such terms were meaningful, these votes were comparable to votes of confidence for the governing party. The fact that the two votes on presidential authority over the militia coincided with this axis seems to reinforce such a conclusion.

Further support for the idea that a party axis has been identified comes from the vote on whether to seat Jackson in place of Wayne from the Georgia congressional district (#5 on plot). Rose (1968, p. 68) labels this vote as "Prior to Jay's Treaty . . . the most important popular test in the South of emerging partisan strength on both sides." In fact, its vector falls along the same general axis as the key vote on Hamilton and the others mentioned above, as does the vector representing the party identification of the members. While this axis is not completely well defined, it does provide a strong indication of the progress of party development.

In the end, it becomes difficult to state with assurance the extent to which voting in the Second Congress had a partisan basis. Because the parties that did emerge in this decade had such a distinctive regional flavor, it is problematic to separate regional and partisan patterns. While the party vector fits well along the same axis identified by a number of key votes, the exceptions noted above tend to block any firm conclusions. The behavior of New England Republicans such as Gerry and southern Federalists such as Grove, who voted by region more than by party, suggests that it was still a transitional period of party development. Nevertheless, the signs of partisan voting patterns on different issues suggest movement beyond simple factionalism. In the final chapter, after the events of later years have been inspected, I shall attempt to draw stronger conclusions.

We can gain further confidence in the thesis that party development was in progress and that voting patterns were not simply the result of regional factions by observing certain events that were taking place around this time. Jefferson had split with Hamilton by the end of 1791, and he and Madison became regular allies in political matters. They took a journey to New York state together for the alleged purpose of studying botany. Whether this was their sole motivation is a question for debate among historians, but it seems unlikely that they would have avoided political topics during the entire trip. In a more open venture, they encouraged Philip Freneau to establish a newspaper, the *National Gazette*, which was to become the chief Republican journal in the nation. Assistance for Freneau came in the form of a clerkship in Jefferson's State Department and the publication of official notices in his paper—an arrangement that would hardly survive in the modern political world (Brant, 1950; Cunningham, 1957).

It was also during the years of the Second Congress that people began to speak of the existence of parties in Congress. This is evident in the writings of many of the leaders of that period, including Jefferson and Hamilton (Cunningham, 1957, pp. 20-22). By January, 1793, Ames was moved to write (letter to Dwight, quoted in Bernhard, 1965, p. 213), "Virginia moves in a solid column, and the discipline of the party is as severe as the Prussian. Madison is become a desperate party leader." While his observations are surely exaggerated, the fact that he conceived of disputes in partisan terms is significant.

With the evidence considered here, it would be hard not to conclude that the political system was at least beginning a transition from factional to partisan politics. Whereas there was really no evidence of any consistent patterns of conflict in the First Congress, we see the beginnings of such patterns in the Second Congress. We know from later developments that these signs did indeed have significance for future events.

7. Polarization and Party Politics, 1793-1797

The polarization of congressmen into two cohesive voting blocs primarily occurred during Washington's second administration, from 1793 to 1797. Whether these blocs can be designated as parties is ambiguous, for, as discussed in chapter 1, the concept of party involves more than cohesive voting in Congress. Polarization in Congress is, however, quite clear and is illustrated by the configurations for the Third Congress (figures 27 and 28) and the Fourth Congress (figures 29 and 30). In the Second Congress, the members grouped themselves into a set of clusters, reflecting the state of transition from factional to partisan politics. By the Fourth Congress, there is a clear bipolar structure, with two voting blocs corresponding to the emerging Federalist and Republican parties. The stress statistic (see table 1) is substantially lower for the Third and Fourth Congresses than for the earlier two, which provides further confirmation of the trend.

Elections from 1792 to 1795

Before a more complete consideration of this polarization process, a look at the congressional elections may shed light on the extent of party development in these four years. Consistent hard evidence is lacking, but it does appear that party was more and more becoming a factor in the elections of 1792-93 and 1794-95. As noted for the previous elections, partisanship was taking hold more quickly in the Middle states, but there were also signs of awakening party activity in the other regions.

The Middle states (New York, New Jersey, Pennsylvania, Delaware, and Maryland) were distinctive for several reasons. Their economies were generally more diverse than those of either New England or the South. They included major ports at New York, Philadelphia, and Baltimore, as well as farm land and an undeveloped frontier. The population of these states was relatively cosmopolitan, perhaps because of their patterns of colonial settlement. But most important was the greater political diversity—certainly in part a result of these other differences. Even in the colonial period, these states had more sophisticated patterns of party competition (see chapters 2 and 3), and this tradition influenced events after the 1787 Constitution.

The quickest emergence of parties as a factor in congressional elections took place in Pennsylvania, with real party activity even in 1789. A switch was made in 1792 to a general ticket system of elections. With thirteen seats to fill on an at-large basis, the incentive was great for those with similar interests to draw up tickets. The process turned out to be rather chaotic, but eventually two tickets were drawn up. Seven men, however, found themselves on both tickets—surely a stroke of luck for them, for all were easy winners. For the other six seats, three victors came from each ticket. Thus, while this process had some signs of partisanship, it was hardly an election dominated by strong parties (Cunningham, 1957; Tinkcom, 1950).

By the 1794 election, Pennsylvania had reverted to the district system and had witnessed a corresponding waning of partisanship. There was hardly any statewide coordination. While the partisan press followed events in various districts, "in no instance was specific mention made of political parties" (Tinkcom, 1950, p. 140).

In New York, gubernatorial politics produced a heated contest between Clinton and Jay in 1792. The two groups of supporters were to provide nuclei for the emerging parties, but they were still better characterized as personal followings. In the congressional elections later that same year, nearly every one of the ten districts had a contest that could be described as a two-party affair. Young (1967, p. 325) has suggested that party labels—in particular, the term *Republican*—were coming into "common usage." By the elections of 1794, it had become even easier to treat the various races as occurring between Federalists and Republicans (Cunningham, 1957; Young, 1967).

A new force in electoral politics during this same period was the emergence of the "Democratic societies" around the country (Link, 1942). These were groups consisting of supporters of the Republican party and its goals. Their role was much like that of a pressure group, providing a forum for political discussion and an outlet for activism. Their part in elections was never very great, but they are generally credited with providing crucial margins of victory for two Republican candidates in 1794, Livingston of New York City and Swanwick of Philadelphia (see chapter 3 for further discussion of these contests). But Livingston would not even admit to being a Republican or acknowledge the support of the Democratic societies (Luetscher, 1903; Young, 1967).

While electoral contests in New York and Pennsylvania may not have been partisan in the modern sense of candidates competing openly as representatives of their parties, they did offer real alternatives to the voters. The polarization of the Congress, in terms of roll call voting, did include those from New York and Pennsylvania in each of the major blocs. With only a few exceptions, the members voted in accordance with the labels placed on them at the time of election (see figures 27 and 29). At least one of these exceptions has an explanation. John Williams was elected from western New York as a Republican, but he eventually abandoned that party on foreign policy grounds, notably the Jay Treaty (Young, 1967). Otherwise, the perceptions of party attachment generally seem to have matched the reality.

In Delaware, partisanship was sufficiently heated by 1792 to result in a disputed election. Patten managed to be the first Republican sent to Congress

120 Origins of American Political Parties

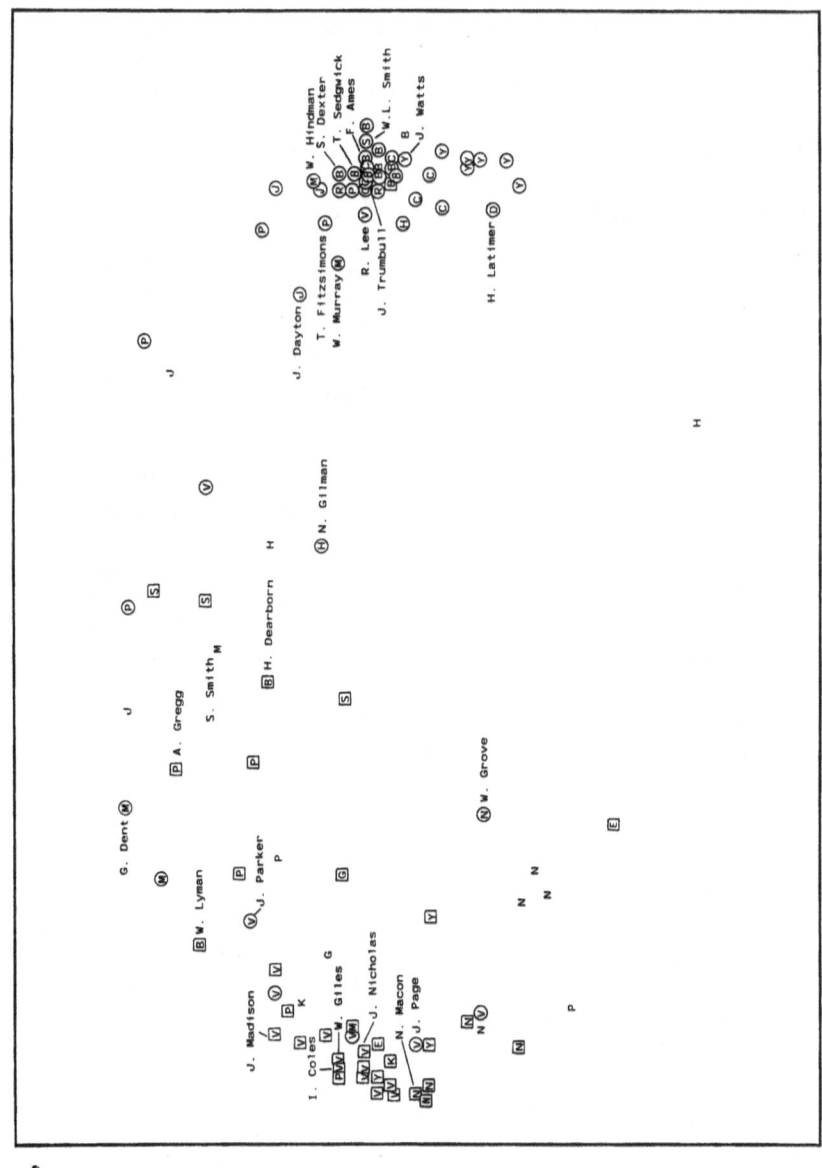

Fig. 27. Spatial Configuration, House, Third Congress, 1793-1795

KEY

B — Mass.   M — Md.
C — Conn.   N — N.C.
D — Del.   P — Penn.
E — Vt.   R — R.I.
G — Ga.   S — S.C.
H — N.H.   T — Tenn.
J — N.J.   V — Vir.
K — Ky.   Y — N.Y.

Ⓧ — Federalist
☒ — Republican
X — No party/Unknown

Letter = state
Circle/square = party

Polarization and Party Politics 121

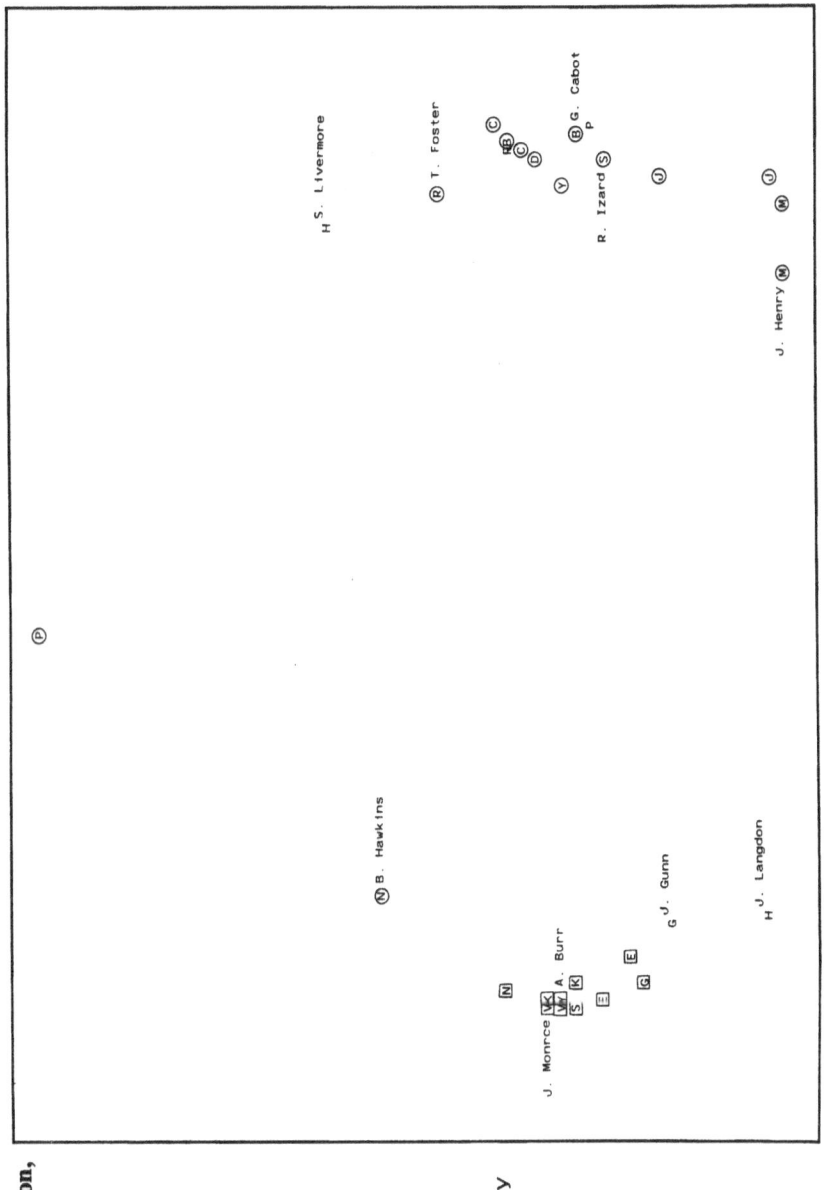

Fig. 28. Spatial Configuration, Third Congress, Senate, 1793-1795

KEY

B – Mass.   M – Md.
C – Conn.   N – N.C.
D – Del.   P – Penn.
E – Vt.   R – R.I.
G – Ga.   S – S.C.
H – N.H.   T – Tenn.
J – N.J.   V – Vir.
K – Ky.   Y – N.Y.

⊗ – Federalist
⊠ – Republican
X – No party/Unknown

Letter = state
Circle/square = party

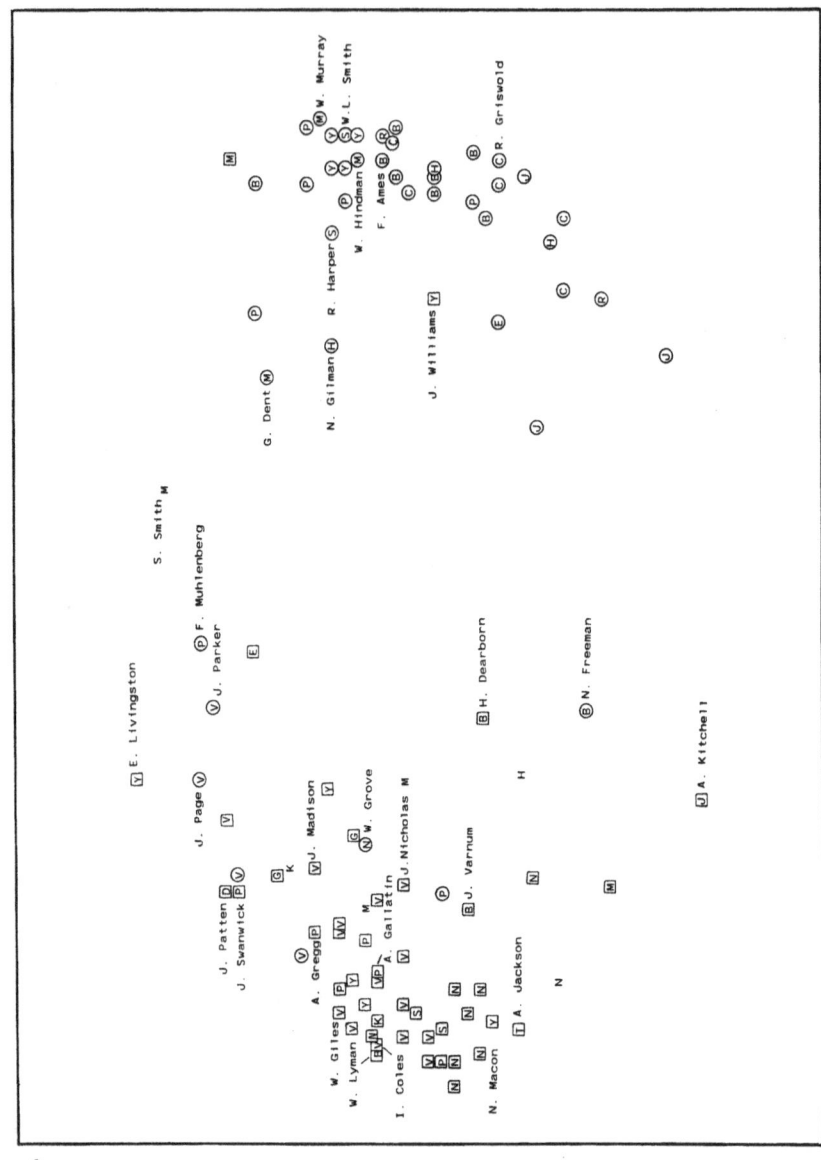

Fig. 29. Spatial Configuration, Fourth Congress, House, 1795-1797

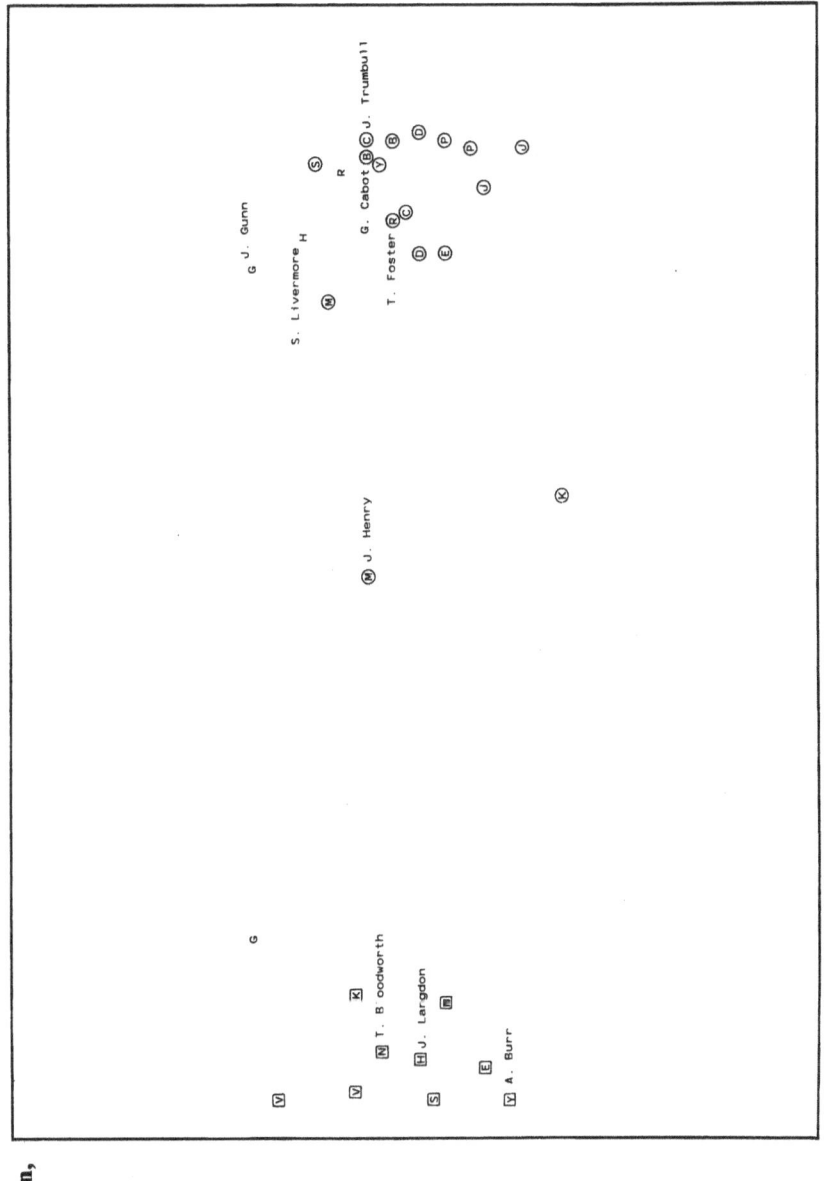

Fig. 30. Spatial Configuration, Fourth Congress, Senate, 1795-1797

KEY

B – Mass. M – Md.
C – Conn. N – N.C.
D – Del.   P – Penn.
E – Vt.   R – R.I.
G – Ga.   S – S.C.
H – N.H.   T – Tenn.
J – N.J.   V – Vir.
K – Ky.   Y – N.Y.

Ⓧ – Federalist
☒ – Republican
X – No party/Unknown

Letter = state
Circle/square = party

from Delaware, but the Federalist Latimer convinced a majority of Congress to overturn the result on the basis of electoral irregularities (see chapter 3) and give him the seat. In the next election (1794) Patten won the uncontested right to the seat (Munroe, 1954, pp. 202-6). That the contest was a choice between policy stands and not simply personalities is illustrated by the contrast between Latimer's point in figure 27 and Patten's in figure 29.

In the remaining Middle states (New Jersey and Maryland), the involvement of party in congressional elections did not develop so quickly. For them, party lines did not harden until a later time.

The states of New England and the South proved to be far more resistant to the inroads of partisanship in congressional elections. In part, this was a result of generally slower party development. Both regions had political traditions based on a strongly individualist style of electioneering; candidates "relied upon the support of their friends rather than a party organization to advance their interest" (Cunningham, 1957, pp. 33).

Additionally, development was hindered by the homogeneity of political interests. Without the stimulus of real competition, there was little incentive for people to organize into parties or to use party labels. In the South, the Federalist interest was represented in only a few places. The coastal region of South Carolina was still the most important Federalist stronghold in the South. But there were also significant pockets in Virginia (Ammon, 1953; Risjord, 1973) and in North Carolina. Except for South Carolina, the electoral contests were not clear tests of partisan strength. And, as we shall see shortly, even the few southern Federalists who got to Congress did not generally vote with their northern allies. While these men subsequently became the vanguard of a larger group that emerged between 1796 and 1800, they hardly represented an organized party at that time (Rose, 1968).

The situation was similar in New England, where the Republican interest was minimal. Vermont, with its Republican delegation to Congress, remained an anomaly in the region. But elsewhere the Republicans had little impact. The signs of their emergence in the region came first in Massachusetts in 1794. Earlier elections were quiet affairs dominated by personalities and local issues. But in 1794 (with the help of local Democratic societies), intense campaigns were waged in four districts by the Republicans in support of two incumbents (Dearborn and W. Lyman) and against two Federalist incumbents (Ames and Dexter). The outspoken Ames was given a good fight, but he managed to survive. Elsewhere Republicans won, giving them three of the state's fourteen seats (Bernhard, 1965; Goodman, 1964).

A modern observer of the 1792 or 1794 elections for Congress would not find the involvement of parties very substantial. Yet some definite beginnings could be seen by this time. "It was evident that the divisions in Congress were coming to have considerable effect in the campaigns of representatives seeking re-election. . . . In the election campaigns the candidates tended to impart to the voters something of the partisan spirit, something of the cleavage, that had shown itself in Congress, and in seeking a public following, they were helping, wittingly or unwittingly, to speed the formation of political parties in the United States" (Cunningham, 1957, p. 31). Indeed, this conclusion should quicken our interest in the cleavages in the House and

Senate. We have noted a general trend toward polarization; now we consider the nature of that polarization more carefully.

Voting in the Third and Fourth Congresses

In the Senate from 1793 to 1797, the configurations have a clearly bipolar structure (figures 28 and 30), with two voting blocs corresponding to the emerging Federalist and Republican parties. The parties generally retained a highly sectional character, for the Republican bloc consisted almost entirely of southern senators, while the Federalist bloc included mostly senators from New England and the Middle states. Because of this overlap of party and region, there is some difficulty in determining whether these voting blocs formed because of partisan or regional affiliation. Nevertheless, for most cases where a senator's party ties and sectional loyalties were in conflict, he voted according to his party ties.

There was only one clear case where a senator was allied on the basis of region rather than party. Hawkins of North Carolina was a Federalist of the old school, having been chosen for the Senate in 1789. Like his former colleague, Johnston, he was a rather loyal supporter of the southern interest that was becoming linked to the Republicans. Yet both men were sufficiently identified with the policies of the administration to have no chance of being returned for second terms. Candidates facing the North Carolina state legislature vied for the honor of being the most outspoken opponent of the Federalist administration (Gilpatrick, 1931).

Otherwise, senators who represented the minority interest in their regions did indeed cast their votes as loyal partisans. One Republican, Langdon of New Hampshire, was a convert to that party from a position of strong Federalism. Historical sources have noted his conversion, but it is frequently attributed to the debates over the Jay Treaty (Charles, 1961, p. 116). Yet his movement between the Second and the Third Congresses suggests that a different explanation is needed. Mayo (1937) has argued that his shift was a decision of conviction, based heavily on foreign policy considerations. This explanation seems reasonable, although an analysis based on roll call votes alone cannot help us to attribute motivations for such a shift.

The configurations for the House of Representatives, like those for the Senate, show a clear movement toward a pattern of polarization (figures 27 and 29). In each Congress, two distinct polar groups formed the cores of two emerging parties. In addition, there were several individuals who did not clearly belong to either group. While this basic pattern appeared for both the Third and Fourth Congresses, voting in the latter was more polarized. Instead of a large number of individuals who voted with neither cluster, nearly everyone in the Fourth Congress could be placed in one group or the other, although the groups were still not highly cohesive.

In the previous years, prior to this polarization, the dominant feature of the configurations was a set of regional voting blocs. I argue in this section that these regional blocs were being transformed into partisan blocs that differed from those of earlier years. Yet it is clear that the new parties retained

Table 10. Geographical Distribution of Party Voting Blocs, Third and Fourth Houses

	New England	Middle	South
Third Congress, House			
Federalist bloc	22	16	2
Intermediate	6	11	7
Republican bloc	1	7	28
Fourth Congress, House			
Federalist bloc	20	18	2
Republican bloc	6	18	36

Note: Based on spatial configurations, figures 27 and 29.

a distinctive sectional character. As shown in table 10, a majority of those in the Federalist cluster came from New England, and a majority of the Republican bloc were southerners. Admittedly, the actual delineation of blocs is arbitrary; but it is clear that any reasonable delineation produces similar results. Given the great cultural and economic differences between regions, it should not be surprising that the emerging parties were so distinctively regional.

Yet, in spite of the dominance of regionalism, partisan diversity had clearly emerged within several states. This was particularly true in the larger Middle states: New York, Pennsylvania, and Maryland. In each, elections were revolving around partisan concerns, and they were sending to Congress delegations that included partisans from both emerging groups. For the other regions at this time, partisan diversity was present, even if far more limited. New Hampshire, Vermont, and even Massachusetts had elected a few men who voted with the Republicans. Massachusetts, for example, had two representatives (W. Lyman and Dearborn) allied with the intermediate group in the Third Congress. But after increased partisan activity in the 1794 elections, these two men, together with Varnum and Nathaniel Freeman, voted more frequently with other Republicans.[1] The South Carolina coastal area continued to provide virtually the only exceptions (W. L. Smith and Harper) to Republican solidarity in the South. The sole remaining southerner to vote with the Federalist bloc (in the Third Congress) was Richard Bland Lee, of Virginia, who was rewarded for his Federalist leanings with defeat in the election of 1795 (Cunningham, 1957). Most who identified themselves as Federalists in Virginia or North Carolina still voted more frequently with their Republican neighbors.

Much can be learned about the polarization process by a careful look at those congressmen who were not clustered with either polar group. In the Third Congress (figure 27), about 24 of the 100 house members were in this intermediate position. Among these individuals, two particular categories were represented. The first type is the northern Republican (such as Gregg of Pennsylvania or W. Lyman of Massachusetts) who was moving toward his partisan allies from a position of regional loyalty. The Third Congress catches them in midstream. The second type is the southern Federalist (Parker of Virginia or Grove of North Carolina) moving in the opposite direction, but again toward a position of partisan consistency. By the Fourth Congress (figure 29), most northern Republicans had reached at least the fringe of the Republican bloc. The small group of southern Federalists, on the other hand, remained loosely aligned with the Republicans, showing that partisanship was developing more slowly in the South.

An additional observation can be made about the progress of party development by the end of the Fourth Congress. The Federalists had developed quickly into a unified voting bloc, while cohesive voting emerged more slowly for the Republicans. This conclusion, supported by the spatial configurations, is further confirmed by comparing the average agreement among Federalists (83.3%, Third Congress; 77.0%, Fourth) and Republicans (73.5%, Third; 72.7%, Fourth). This difference might be partially attributed to the advantages of being in power. Because much of the agenda was set by the Federalist administration (with Hamilton in an active role), the Republicans in opposition had more difficulty reaching any kind of unity. Also, the Federalists found leadership from men in the administration (such as Hamilton) and had the popular figure of Washington associated with their side, although he tried to maintain a nonpartisan stance. The opposition leadership drew upon strong individuals such as Madison, Jefferson, Giles, and Gallatin. But they tended to suffer from a lack of coordination and the lingering bias against the concept of opposition to the government.

In sum, by the end of the fourth Congress, the American party system had reached a level of development best labeled polarization. Nearly every member of Congress could be classified with one party or the other, either by the political leaders of the time or on the basis of this analysis of voting agreement. Party organization and party discipline were growing, although still with limited effectiveness.

The question, therefore, is what made the difference. What changed from 1792 to 1796, from sectional factions to polarized parties? Once again we turn to a consideration of the issues. Had the agenda of issues changed or had legislators begun to behave differently on the same old issues? Did cohesive voting come earlier on some issues than on others? While these questions certainly do not have simple answers, they must nevertheless be addressed.

The agenda of issues did change gradually across the first four Congresses (see table 4). Foreign policy began to consume a higher proportion of the session as the years passed. Protection of the frontier also grew in importance. Together these two areas incorporated half of the recorded votes in the Third and Fourth Congresses (up from 7% in the First). In this same period, questions involving the authority of the national government became correspondingly less important.

Key votes have again been selected for the Third and Fourth Congresses (Bell, 1973; Bernhard, 1965; Combs, 1970). For the former Congress, a listing of the votes, with the coordinates for their vectors and the degree of fit, is provided in table 11; in table 12, the same information is included for the Fourth Congress. In figures 31 and 32, spatial representations of the key votes are shown—with the numbers corresponding to the votes, as noted in

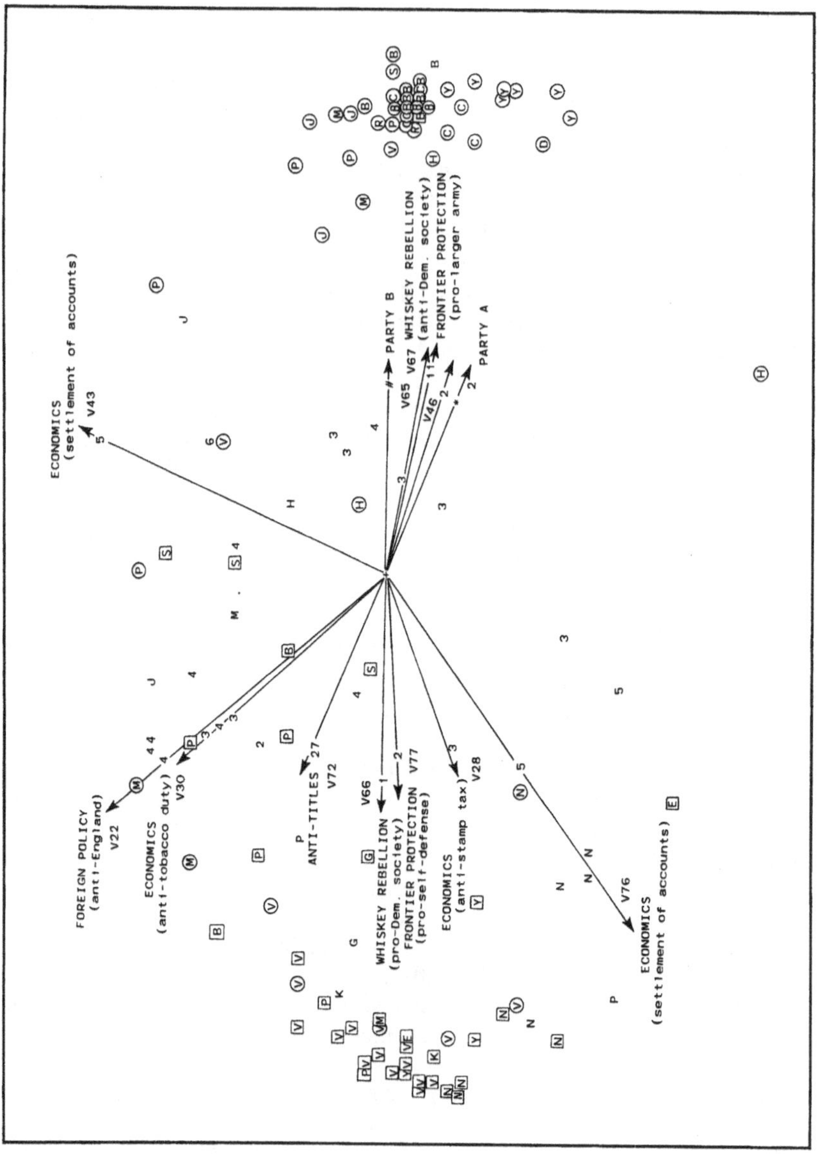

128 Origins of American Political Parties

Fig. 31. Spatial Configuration, House, Third Congress, 1793-1795—All Issue Areas

KEY

B — Mass.   M — Md.
C — Conn.   N — N.C.
D — Del.   P — Penn.
E — Vt.   R — R.I.
G — Ga.   S — S.C.
H — N.H.   T — Tenn.
J — N.J.   V — Vir.
K — Ky.   Y — N.Y.

○ — Federalist
□ — Republican
X — No party/Unknown

Letter = state
Circle/square = party
Number = issue area

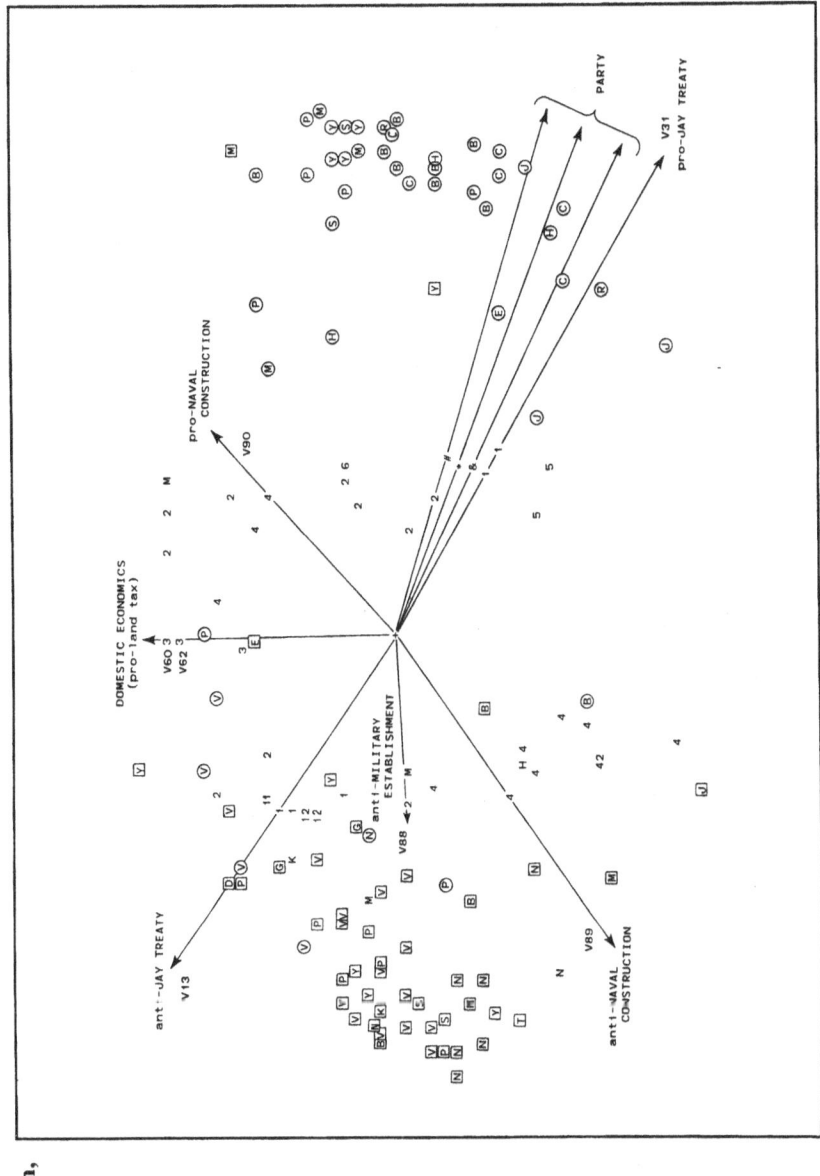

Fig. 32. Spatial Configuration, Fourth Congress, House, 1795-1797—All Issue Areas

130 Origins of American Political Parties

Table 11. Key Votes—Third Congress (1793–1795)

Vote	Date	Description	b1	b2	R^2
National Authority (#1)					
V65	11-27-94	Condemn self-created societies for role in Whiskey Rebellion	.473	−.097	.857
V66	11-27-94	Condemn societies only in western Pa.	−.481	.021	.884
V67	11-27-94	State that insurrection was countenanced by societies elsewhere	.480	−.093	.889
Protection of the Frontier (#2)					
V46	05-19-94	Raise additional provisional military force	.431	−.106	.748
V54	05-30-94	Reject increase in military establishment	−.421	.183	.698
V63	06-06-94	Establish standing army in Southwest	.441	−.195	.787
V77	02-27-95	Reject bill to prevent depredations on Indians	−.435	−.016	.738
V78	02-28-95	Allow armed pursuit of Indians on Indian land	−.413	.302	.674
Domestic Economics—Revenue Bills (#3)					
V27	05-07-94	Eliminate proposed carriage tax	−.346	.379	.518
V28	05-08-94	Eliminate proposed stamp tax	−.403	−.141	.653
V30	05-08-94	Eliminate proposed duty on tobacco	−.386	.429	.618
V31	05-09-94	Eliminate proposed duty on U.S. trading ships	.223	−.016	.192
V44	05-16-94	Increase duty on American tonnage	−.145	−.432	.131
V52	05-27-94	Passage of stamp tax	.274	.124	.313
V55	05-31-94	Passage of retail wine and liquor tax	.167	−.107	.132
V57	05-31-94	Passage of duty on property sold at auction	.326	.130	.455
Foreign Policy (#4)					
V22	04-15-94	Consider prohibition of all trade with Great Britain	−.444	.539	.847
V23	04-18-94	Consider embargo despite Jay's mission	−.433	.570	.815
V24	04-21-94	Prohibit all trade with Great Britain after 11-01-94	−.420	.577	.809
V33	05-10-94	Double proposed duty for British tonnage only	−.291	.081	.411

Table 11. (continued)

Vote	Date	Description	b1	b2	R^2
V35	05-12-94	Continue embargo only for ships bound for West Indies, Bermuda, Nova Scotia	−.242	.478	.289
V36	05-12-94	Continue embargo only on British trade	.057	.380	.106
V56	05-31-94	Pay debts owed to the French Republic	−.364	.410	.655
V61	06-04-94	Allow president to purchase 10 galleys for naval service	.342	.033	.441
Domestic Economics—Settlement of Accounts (#5)					
V21	04-08-94	Investigate procedures used in general settlement	−.268	−.548	.374
V43	05-16-94	Pay interest on balance due to states	.292	.704	.492
V76	02-21-95	Eliminate stringent repayment provisions from public credit bill	−.451	−.313	.819
Partisan Politics (#6)					
V16	02-14-94	Assign seat denied to Patten to Latimer	.303	.440	.432
Titles—Naturalization Bill (#7)					
V72	01-02-95	Require immigrants to renounce foreign titles	−.401	.170	.663
Party					
A		Party codes (Bell, 1973)	.400	−.147	.598
B		Party codes (author's estimates)	.443	.021	.769

Note: Vote numbers are taken from the ICPSR data file, with vote descriptions based on Bell (1973); $b1$ and $b2$ provide coordinates for the vote vectors; R^2 is the fit between the vote and the configuration.

Table 12. Key Votes—Fourth Congress (1795–1797)

Vote	Date	Description	b1	b2	R^2
National Authority/Foreign Policy (#1)					
V13	03-24-96	Livingston Resolution calling for Jay Treaty papers	−.466	.315	.897
V16	03-30-96	Consider Washington's refusal to furnish Jay Treaty papers	−.478	.234	.927
V20	04-06-96	Meet on Washington's response to Livingston Resolution	−.469	.287	.911
V21	04-07-96	Consider House right to consider Jay Treaty	−.480	.262	.933
V22	04-07-96	Pass House right to consider Jay Treaty	−.456	.346	.900
V23	04-07-96	House need not give reason for request for papers	−.456	.346	.900
V28	04-14-96	Commit resolution against Jay Treaty	.478	−.264	.945
V30	04-30-96	Approve Jay Treaty but call it "highly objectionable"	−.429	.158	.701
V31	04-30-96	Approve Jay Treaty	.422	−.238	.692
Protection of the Frontier (#2)					
V18	04-05-96	Subdivide northwest land into 320-acre lots	.270	−.037	.266
V19	04-05-96	Subdivide northwest land into 160-acre lots	−.319	.356	.424
V32	05-06-96	Admit Tennessee as a state	−.423	.482	.811
V37	05-21-96	Retain light dragoons currently in army	.333	.118	.546
V38	05-21-96	Retain post of major general	.360	.464	.575
V40	05-23-96	Reconsider V37	.363	−.093	.619
V41	05-23-96	Reconsider V38	.393	.130	.617
V47	05-28-96	Admit Tennessee without a census	−.469	.261	.959
V49	05-28-96	Assign Tennessee one representative	−.468	.240	.958
V63	01-24-97	Reduce army from 4 regiments to 3	−.331	−.554	.522
V64	01-24-97	Restore the dragoons	.206	.641	.415
V71	02-07-97	Reduce army from 4 regiments to 3	.322	.631	.518
V88	03-01-97	Override Washington's veto of bill reducing military establishment	−.447	−.033	.782

Table 12. (continued)

Vote	Date	Description	b1	b2	R^2
Domestic Economics—Revenue Bills (#3)					
V60	01-20-97	Impose a land tax	−.040	1.238	.503
V61	01-20-97	Impose a tax on slaves	−.112	.848	.376
V62	01-20-97	Agree to land tax and slave tax	−.041	1.186	.459
Foreign Policy (#4)					
V24	04-08-96	Increase number of frigates	−.371	−.380	.544
V25	04-08-96	Outfit 2 frigates instead of 3	−.236	−.528	.317
V26	04-09-96	Outfit 3 frigates	.270	.399	.361
V73	02-11-97	Repeal prior acts about frigates	−.349	−.562	.660
V74	02-11-97	Build 3 frigates	−.217	−.465	.359
V75	02-11-97	Reject use of live-oak or red-cedar for frigates	−.281	−.760	.555
V76	02-11-97	Build 3 frigates	−.418	−.106	.682
V77	02-13-97	Build 3 frigates	.074	.493	.127
V79	02-18-97	Add appropriations for 3 frigates	−.297	−.353	.430
V89	03-02-97	Finish only hulls of 3 frigates	−.437	−.306	.760
V90	03-02-97	Finish the whole of 3 frigates	.355	.351	.576
Partisan Politics (#5)					
V52	05-31-96	Unseat Smith in favor of Lyon	.430	−.407	.837
V65	01-25-97	Reject petition against Varnum's election	.313	−.370	.432
National Authority (Executive Power) (#6)					
V93	03-03-97	Increase executive flexibility in expending appropriations	.441	.152	.770
Party					
A		Party codes (Bell, 1973)	.443	−.192	.731
B		Party codes (Dauer, 1953)	.452	−.145	.758
C		Party codes (author's estimates)	.441	−.196	.775

Note: Vote numbers are taken from the ICPSR data file, with vote descriptions based on Bell (1973); b1 and b2 provide coordinates for the vote vectors; R^2 is the fit between the vote and the configuration.

tables 11 and 12. One is initially struck, when studying these figures, not by the expected tendency of votes to be represented by vectors that run horizontally on the figure (from one bloc to the other), but by the failure to do so consistently. There appears to be little difference in the degree of pattern in these later Congresses compared to the earlier ones. In some ways, this speaks more eloquently about the methodology than about the state of party development. For these vectors to provide meaningful representations of individual votes, there should be a relatively uniform distribution of legislators in the voting space. Therefore, as voting becomes more polarized and the distribution of legislators is less uniform—as occurs by the Fourth Congress—these vector representations become less useful. Nevertheless, we need not abandon this methodology; it is adequate if the result is read only for general patterns.[2] Detailed considerations depend more heavily upon tabular analysis.[3]

Previously I have argued that the major voting blocs in these years were the result of partisan forces. Where the actual party vector is drawn depends, of course, on the extant party labels. As discussed in Appendix A, there are major problems in categorizing people into parties. Party vector A (in figure 31) is based on the work of Bell (1973), who has attempted to place everyone in a party based on past or future actions. If we try to eliminate those whose party labels are derived from future alliances, we can produce instead the party vector B. The difference lies mainly in the intermediate group, the majority of whom were to be called Republicans, although they did not yet acknowledge such a label.

Regardless of which party axis is adopted as the "correct" one, it is a simple task to identify a number of key issues that divide the congressmen in a partisan manner. One of these is a series of votes taken in the aftermath of the Whiskey Rebellion. This little uprising took place in western Pennsylvania, where farmers took to arms to protest the tax on whiskey in 1794. The revolt was quickly quashed, however, when Washington sent troops to the scene. Federalists in Congress tried to place blame for the rebellion on what they called "self-created societies," which everyone recognized as the Democratic societies (Miller, 1938). Three votes on this matter (#1 on plot) split the two party blocs nearly without exception. Since the issue so directly involved a key component of the emerging Republican party, we gain confidence in our designation of the voting blocs as partisan.

The other issues in the Third Congress that were predominantly partisan in nature were a bill to forbid immigrants from retaining their foreign titles (#7 on plot) and several bills on the protection of the frontier and the size of the military establishment (#2 on plot).[4] The vote concerning titles is significant, because it illustrates the philosophical differences between the parties. A true believer in democracy (a Republican) would not stand for the retention of titles so symbolic of the European monarchy. Federalists, however, saw no harm; in fact, Adams had expended substantial energy during the First Congress in trying unsuccessfully to have adopted a "suitable" title for the president. The frontier issue has less obvious partisan connections, but it generally revolved around the question of whether the central government (with a large standing army) or the states (with their militias) would bear responsibility for protection against the Indians. From this perspective, the positions of the parties should be clear.

In the Fourth Congress (figure 32), the party axis is less ambiguous than in the Third. This fact alone is a sign of the growth of the parties, as is the increased correlation between the party variable and the spatial configuration (see R^2 in the tables). It is not surprising, moreover, that the party axis again divides the major voting blocs.[5] What is something of a surprise is the set of votes that appears most highly related to the party axis. In contrast to the Third Congress, where national authority (the Whiskey Rebellion) and frontier protection were highly partisan issues, the only distinctly partisan issue (according to the spatial analysis) was the Jay Treaty, which is best classified as foreign policy, although it has elements of all issue areas.

Foreign Policy and the Jay Treaty

The contest over ratification and appropriation of funds for the Jay Treaty was the dominant issue of the Fourth Congress. Furthermore, it is regarded by a number of historians (Bell, 1973; Charles, 1961; Kurtz, 1957) as crucial in the progress of party development. The treaty itself was preceded by other significant events in the foreign policy arena. Yet, curiously, votes taken in conjunction with foreign policy developments in the Third Congress do not appear to coincide with party lines.

War had broken out between Britain and France in 1793, in the aftermath of the French Revolution. American opinion, by this time, was sharply divided between those who felt close ties to England and those who preferred an alliance with France. Among the Federalists (especially Hamilton), there was generally a feeling that America's economic health was dependent on a close trade partnership with Great Britain—or at least the absence of a hostile stance. Jefferson, Madison, and their Republican colleagues saw little need for a close alliance with England and were accordingly anxious to resist hostile actions by the British. They saw, moreover, several reasons to maintain close ties with France. The French nation had been willing to support the American colonies during the Revolution when help was much needed. The Republicans also felt sympathetic toward the democratic ideals espoused in the French Revolution. These opposing viewpoints brought the leaders to odds, beginning with Madison's attempt in 1789 to impose discriminatory duties against England (V16 in the First House—#7 in figure 20) (Combs, 1970, pp. 47-85).

The American response to the war between Britain and France was a proclamation of neutrality by President Washington in 1793. But a question arose as to what constituted a neutral stance, and on this Hamilton and Jefferson disagreed. Their disagreement eventually came to a head over a series of proposals in Congress to restrict trade with Britain. Three votes (V22, V23, V24—#4 on plot) are represented in figure 31; while they do not coincide with the party axis for the Third Congress, they do fit the space well. The vector representation of these votes is at a considerable angle from the votes on the Whiskey Rebellion, which were highly partisan. The main difference, however, lies not in the core blocs of partisan congressmen who were united on both issues, but rather in the intermediate group. (In fact, only nine of eighty-seven who participated on both issues—10.3%—switched from one to the next.) The latter members were split on the Whiskey Rebellion, but were united with the Republicans on the trade embargo.

Two observations follow from the consideration of these foreign policy votes in the Third Congress. First, foreign policy was a rather partisan issue in 1794, although the vector analysis does not show this fact clearly.[6] Thus, the strong partisanship over the Jay Treaty is not such a departure from the past. Second, it is clear that the group being called the intermediate bloc was in fact a key swing bloc in the House. It held the balance of power and, being aligned with neither party bloc, could determine the outcome of an issue.[7]

The Federalists' strategy for dealing with England went beyond their attempt to defeat the trade embargo, an attempt that was successful in the Senate. They also proposed increasing the size of the navy, a measure where the intermediates provided support, and enlarging the army, also important as a frontier protection issue. But most important for later developments, they proposed sending a special ambassador to England to negotiate the points of conflict between the two nations. For this task, they selected John Jay, a loyal Federalist who, curiously, continued to serve as chief justice of the Supreme Court. Republican leaders saw this move as a means to resolve the question by treaty, thus removing it from the House to the Senate, where Federalists had a firmer majority. "A bolder party-stroke was never struck. For it certainly is an attempt of party, which finds they have lost their majority in one branch of the legislature, to make a law by the aid of the other branch and of the executive, under color of a treaty, which shall bind up the hands of the adverse branch from ever restraining the commerce of their patron nation" (Jefferson to Madison, September 21, 1795, quoted in Combs, 1970, p. 128). Clearly both in the perceptions of those involved and in a subsequent analysis of votes cast in the House, consideration of the various components of the foreign policy issue had taken on a substantial partisan character as early as the Third Congress (Combs, 1970, pp. 116-36).

The treaty itself was the outcome of negotiations over a number of concerns, including the neutrality of American shipping in the war between Britain and France, reparations for American ships seized by England, British activity on the western frontier, British seizure of slaves during the Revolution, American trade debts dating to before the war, and the general status of British-American trade. Once the terms of the treaty became known, there were many objections, primarily from the Republicans. They saw the treaty as the predictable product of a Federalist envoy and were particularly concerned about the favorable trade status granted to Britain at the expense of France and the failure to provide compensation for slaves abducted by Britain. Scholars differ on whether Jay was to blame for the provisions that seemed to be advantageous to Federalist interests (Bemis, 1962; Combs, 1970; DeConde, 1958). Yet the important fact is that the terms did stir up a heated partisan debate in the country and in the Congress (Charles, 1961; Combs, 1970; Varg, 1963).

Once negotiation of the treaty was complete, it was considered by the

Senate, meeting in secret session during the summer of 1795. This debate of a treaty whose contents had not been made public nonetheless took place in a heated political atmosphere. People had strong opinions as to the merits of the treaty, and the debate was not only spirited, but also partisan. In the end, the treaty was ratified by the vote of twenty to ten, precisely the needed two-thirds majority.

Technically, there was no role for the House with regard to the treaty, for the Constitution gives the Senate exclusive domain over treaties. But since funds had to be appropriated for executing the terms of the pact, the House found an opportunity to have its say on the substance. For nearly two months—March and April of 1796—the House debated the treaty and related matters.

This debate marked one of the first organized attempts by an opposition group to defeat an important administration proposal. Madison took a firm role in attempting to block the treaty's implementation.[8] Careful thought went into the determination of what vote would be the crucial one, and a party caucus was held—perhaps the first ever by the Republicans—to determine what strategy would be followed. In the end, Madison's party lost by a single vote, due in part to ineffective party control and discipline over treaty opponents. Nevertheless, this effort did mark a significant step in the development of the Republican party (Cunningham, 1957).

Nine recorded votes were taken during the course of the House debate on the Jay Treaty, and all of these (#1) are included among the key votes represented in figure 32. Each of the votes relates very strongly to the spatial patterns of the Fourth Congress (see R^2 in table 12), and each adheres very closely to a single axis, one nearly identical to the party axis. Regardless of which party variable is used, there were almost no defections on the first seven votes, which concerned the preliminary questions of the right of the House even to consider the treaty and to receive papers from the president about the negotiations (the Livingston resolution, an early congressional attack on executive privilege). With a strong Republican majority in Congress, the treaty opponents were easy winners on these votes, and the treaty appeared doomed. But on two final votes (V30 and V31), Republican unity broke down and the treaty won narrowly.

Fifteen men who generally voted with the Republican interest and opposed the administration on preliminary treaty votes supported the treaty on one or the other of the two final votes.[9] The first of these (V30) was a vote to approve the treaty but to call it "highly objectionable." This roll call followed an unrecorded vote the previous day in the Committee of the Whole, where the treaty failed on the vote of the chairman. Explanations are lacking for this vote, but it appears that several Republicans found the amendment too weak, while others may have found it an unsatisfactory means of showing opposition.

On the final vote to approve funds for the treaty, ten Republicans provided the key margin of victory for the administration. They are a diverse group, coming from six states and a variety of positions in the spatial configuration. If there is a common thread, it is that they are not from the classic mold of southern Republicans; otherwise, they have little in common. What, then, motivated these crucial defectors?

Historians have not reached any consensus on the reasons for the switch of these ten votes to the administration and support of the Jay Treaty. Some have suggested the importance of public opinion, for many petitions were being circulated on both sides.[10] Others have cited the importance of an eloquent and emotional speech by Ames prior to the vote (Bernhard, 1965, p. 268; Renzulli, 1972, p. 176). Finally, another theory suggests that some members, who disliked elements of the treaty and wanted to have a thorough debate on it, voted for it because they feared that its defeat would have dire consequences for the young nation. To them, it was better in the end for the House to avoid such a dramatic veto of administration policy and the possible consequences for relations with England (Cassell, 1971, pp. 62-70; Charles, 1961, pp. 110-15).

Regardless of what ultimately motivated each of these ten men, the key point is that this was an extraordinary issue, one on which we should expect other factors to overcome even the strongest partisan appeals.[11] The fact that the votes did fall substantially along partisan lines even on the final vote builds a strong case for the strength of the emerging party system.

Before completing this discussion of the Third and Fourth Congresses, we must look briefly at those issues where partisanship seemed to be less salient. In the Third Congress, the least partisan votes were those in the field of domestic economics. In particular, votes on settlement of accounts with the states (#5 in figure 31) and those on certain revenue measures (duty on tonnage, stamp tax, and others—#3 on plot) seem to cut across party lines. This is especially ironic in light of the fact that economics appeared to be the most partisan issue area in previous years. Again, however, the spatial analysis tends to exaggerate the differences between votes. Vectors representing V22 and V76 (figure 31) are nearly at right angles, although only twelve of seventy-nine (15.2%) people switched sides. Most of these were among the intermediate group in the spatial plot.

The explanation for the nonpartisan nature of at least one of these issues (V43), a measure to pay interest on balances due to the states, lies in the self-interest of particular states. Representatives voted on the basis of whether their state would benefit from such an action.

In the Fourth Congress, we can focus on two different issues whose vectors do not coincide with the party vectors (figure 32): a tax on land and slaves (#3 on plot) and naval construction (V89 and V90—#4 on plot). The latter issue was connected with the Jay Treaty conflict, but the specific votes in question took place almost a year after the treaty was settled.

The votes on construction of new frigates (V89 and V90) did cut across party lines, but only in a limited way. The Federalists kept their forces united, but division once again struck the Republican camp. As in the Jay Treaty conflict, enough Republican defectors joined the Federalists to win approval of the administration's request for a stronger navy, although there was only a partial overlap between the defectors on this and the Jay Treaty votes.

The remaining issue that does not appear to follow party lines was proposed taxation on land and slaves (V60, V61, V62). These taxes were advocated by a Republican, Gallatin, and marked a departure from Hamiltonian economic policy (Bell, 1973, pp. 112-14). The vectors representing these three votes, more than any others in either the Third or Fourth Congress, cut across the predominant party blocs, and this conclusion is confirmed by cross-tabular analysis. There was little evidence of party voting on this issue; as a result, there were some strange alliances.

Party Development from 1789 to 1797

The changes occurring in Congress by 1797 were nothing short of remarkable. While signs of partisanship were apparent in the Second Congress, there was nothing like the degree of polarization that emerged in the following years. One could generally forecast the division of votes on any given issue from the membership of the dominant voting blocs.

Still, party cohesion was far from perfect. On a key issue like the Jay Treaty or the construction of naval vessels, it was possible for the outcome to be reversed by defections from party. Additionally, members would sometimes desert their party when the interests of their own state or region were involved. But the key to the puzzle is that political conflict was starting to operate more regularly within a partisan framework. Party unity had become strong enough that it was usually the first factor to be considered on an issue before Congress.

To what can we attribute the increased polarization evident by the end of the Fourth Congress? Has this consideration of issues suggested any answers? With the exception of a few roll calls, votes were polarized within each of the four major issue domains. But there were key differences. Government authority issues were of special importance in the First Congress, where they produced a set of factions based on support for the central government. In subsequent Congresses, votes on the actual authority of the national government became rare. Instead, national authority votes concerned such issues as apportionment of the legislature and presidential authority. Thus, while it was generally a partisan issue area, it had become relatively unimportant.

Frontier protection grew substantially in importance over eight years, but within this area there were a variety of concerns, such as the role of the army and states' rights. Throughout, frontier issues remained distinctive, partly because of the different ideas involved and partly because members from districts near the frontier frequently had reason to depart from traditional alliances on these issues.

In the first two Congresses, the most important and most frequent roll calls were in the area of domestic economics. The economic factions in the First Congress seem to be the most obvious predecessors of the new parties, an idea generally confirmed in the next few years. The close involvement of the administration in the economic arena was a crucial factor in this development. Specific economic issues became less partisan in the Third and Fourth Congresses, mostly as a result of local self-interest, either the taxation of certain items or the ongoing settlement of accounts between the states and the federal government. In the early years, such issues were major policy questions that stimulated partisan divisions; in later years, the question became one of who would pay the costs and receive the benefits of these policies. In the latter question, localism was often predominant. Nevertheless, these developments were not a matter of members creating new factions, but rather one of defecting from their party loyalties on specific issues.

Finally, the issue that dominated the Fourth Congress was foreign policy, and its development as a partisan issue was discussed above. Foreign policy was largely a new item on the congressional agenda for the Third and Fourth Congresses (see table 4), but in some regards it was not new at all. The Jay Treaty debate brought in themes of presidential authority, economics, frontier protection, and even slavery; as such, it represented a culmination of developments in all issue domains.

Perhaps the most significant theme, however, was the stance of the administration. From the economic programs in the First Congress to the anti-Hamilton resolution in the Second to the Whiskey Rebellion in the Third and the Jay Treaty in the Fourth, the most highly partisan issues involved evaluations of actions by the administration (sometimes Washington himself, but more often associates like Jay and Hamilton). It should be no surprise, of course, that this theme dominated early partisan activity, for similar concerns underlay the nascent partisanship of eighteenth-century England and the colonies. But the nonpartisan stance taken by Washington often overshadowed the partisanship of his administration. And when his antiparty influence was removed upon his retirement, partisanship could only become stronger.

While evidence certainly shows that the polarization along party lines was not mere coincidence, it is not at all clear that the two groups can properly be called parties as of 1797. Elections prior to the Third and Fourth Congresses were not contested along party lines in most states, although popular perceptions were generally supported by the subsequent voting records of successful candidates. Nevertheless, congressional leaders were very aware of the partisan composition of the membership. Estimates were advanced, in letters by Ames, Madison, Jefferson, and others, soon after elections were concluded in most states.

The spotlight now turns to the elections in 1796 and 1797, for members of the Fifth Congress. The increased polarization of voting and the heightened salience of partisan conflict, due particularly to the debate over the Jay Treaty and related foreign policy matters, could be expected to lead to a substantially greater involvement of the emerging partisan blocs in the elections. To the extent that this was true and party members continued to vote in cohesive and opposing blocs, we would be much closer to meeting the criteria for a developed party system.

8. Partisan Competition in Congress, 1797-1803

Major changes occurred in the United States from 1789 to 1797. Certainly one of the most significant developments was the polarization of members of Congress into two reasonably cohesive voting blocs. Thus, John Adams, the new president taking office in 1797, faced a very different political situation than George Washington had to deal with in his administration. In this chapter, a closer look is taken at the role of parties between 1797 and 1803, encompassing the Adams years and the beginning of the Jeffersonian era.

Years of Partisan Controversy, 1797-1799

Elections held in 1796 and 1797 to select a new president and Congress took place in a very different political atmosphere than had existed in earlier years. The Jay Treaty conflict (with its final vote on April 30, 1796) had a significant impact on the subsequent congressional elections, which were characterized by a level of partisanship not previously seen. The retirement of Washington, who tried to keep politics on a nonpartisan plane, also tended to raise the level of partisanship.

The presidential campaign of 1796 not only showed the clear effects of increased partisanship, but also helped accelerate the emergence of parties. Even before the official announcement of Washington's retirement in September, 1796, key political leaders were speculating on the forthcoming contest and working to influence its outcome. It was soon evident that Adams and Jefferson would be the only serious candidates and that the choice would not be based only on personalities. That support for these two men came from within their own parties is clear from historical accounts of the elections (Chambers, 1963b; Cunningham, 1957).

There is no reason to describe the presidential election in detail, for it has been well documented by historians (Cunningham, 1957; Dauer, 1953; Kurtz, 1957; Malone, 1962; McCormick, 1982). Several points, however, deserve emphasis. First, Jefferson himself played almost no role in the campaign. His silence was in keeping with the old tradition, especially in Virginia, about the passive role of candidates (see chapter 3). But even more, it illustrates

Table 13. Regional Distribution of Electoral Votes, 1796

Region/State	Adams		Jefferson	
New England		39		0
Connecticut	9		0	
Massachusetts	16		0	
New Hampshire	6		0	
Rhode Island	4		0	
Vermont	4		0	
Middle States		30		18
Delaware	3		0	
Maryland	7		4	
New Jersey	7		0	
New York	12		0	
Pennsylvania	1		14	
South		2		50
Georgia	0		4	
Kentucky	0		4	
North Carolina	1		11	
South Carolina	0		8	
Tennessee	0		3	
Virginia	1		20	
Total Vote		71		68

Source: Dauer, (1953, p. 106).

Jefferson's sincere lack of interest in becoming president at that time (Cunningham, 1957, pp. 107-8).

A second observation is the active campaign waged by supporters of the two candidates. The best example of electioneering was the work done in Pennsylvania under the direction of John Beckley (Cunningham, 1956; Fay, 1936), discussed in chapter 3. The leaders in this election effort, including Beckley, were mostly from the newly emerging core of party loyalists, and the election effort helped to solidify these groups.

A third observation relates to the actual focus of the campaign. It seemed primarily to be one of personalities and not issues. There was nothing like a platform on either side, and pamphlets and letters published during the campaign mostly emphasized the personal qualifications of Adams and Jefferson. Of course, this hardly seems different from a modern election campaign, and the positions of candidates on the key issues of the day, such as the Jay Treaty, were obviously widely known.

Finally, we should take note of the actual distribution of votes for president in 1796. In line with the prevailing patterns of party division, votes fell substantially along regional lines (see table 13).[1] Electors in New England and the South were nearly unanimous in casting their votes for Adams and

Jefferson, respectively, while those in the Middle states were divided. In fact, the outcome in the Middle states was more divided even than it appears in the final votes. For example, electors were selected on a statewide basis in Pennsylvania, and the vote was nearly evenly divided between the two parties.

In the 1796 presidential election, then, we see signs of the strengths and weaknesses of the emerging parties. We also see a continuation of the strong regional basis of the party system. Of more direct relevance to our present concerns, however, are the elections for members of the Fifth Congress held at that time.

In 1794, there were few outward signs of partisanship in the congressional elections, although there were many contests between those sympathetic to the emerging parties. By 1796, it was far more common to see the explicit use of party designations, at least in some states. Evidence of such designation in the press is documented by Cunningham (1957, pp. 109-14) for contests in New York, Pennsylvania, Delaware, and Massachusetts. Elsewhere, however, partisanship had still not become an open part of congressional elections.

The fight over acceptance of the Jay Treaty, together with the other issues that helped to polarize the Fourth Congress, meant that party alliances were highly visible to anyone who followed the congressional debates. In this light, it would be hard for partisanship not to play a role in the elections. But the key question is whether contests posed a choice between the two party interests or whether a multitude of candidates entered the contests—in other words, whether the party groups were sufficiently organized and accepted to dominate the structuring of the electoral choice.[2]

In New York and Pennsylvania, where partisanship had gotten its earliest start, many contests were in fact two-candidate affairs. While candidates often avoided any direct use of party labels, reports in the press left little doubt as to the appropriate designations (Cunningham, 1957; Tinkcom, 1950; Young, 1967). In Maryland, matters were not nearly so clear, particularly because of two incumbents, Dent and Samuel Smith, whose loyalties were not strictly based on partisan cues. Yet, even here, the role of party was becoming increasingly important (Cassell, 1971; Renzulli, 1972).

The fact that both Republican and Federalist interests were represented in significant numbers in the Middle states was a strong incentive for parties to be actively involved in the campaigns for Congress. In contrast, the dominance by a single party in both New England and the South was undoubtedly a reason why active involvement of the parties came more slowly. It seems quite likely that the minority would have joined the fray in an active way had there been any serious chance for success.

In New England, this suspicion appears to be confirmed by the partisan activity in Boston, where competing groups presented the voters with slates of candidates. Yet, in other districts, multiple ballots were required to achieve the requisite majority—including one where a Republican sympathizer was finally selected. For whatever reasons, the involvement of Republicans in New England politics was still quite limited (Cunningham, 1957; Goodman, 1964; Welch, 1965).

Federalist activity in the South was not much stronger than Republicanism in New England, but there continued to be significant pockets of Federalist strength. In South Carolina, two Federalists were elected to Congress, plus a third (Rutledge) whose party ties were ambiguous at that time. Nevertheless, there is little evidence of party involvement in the state; in fact, the multitude of candidates in contests for the state legislature suggests a pattern of multifactionalism (Cunningham, 1957; Rogers, 1962; Rose, 1968). Elsewhere in the South, the pattern was very similar. Grove from North Carolina and several Virginians are labeled Federalists by historians, but it is not at all clear how widely such labels were recognized in 1796.

In conclusion, the route to partisan competition in elections was a slow one, especially in New England and the South. There were still few places where the new parties were openly involved in the selection or endorsement of candidates, but in the aftermath of the debates during the Fourth Congress, there was apparently a strong involvement of partisan forces beneath the surface. The informed voter of that day would have been well aware of the partisan record of most contestants or at least the partisan cues transmitted in the press or elsewhere.

Spatial analysis of voting in the subsequent Congresses (Fifth and Sixth) reveals a set of patterns that lend support to the idea that the 1796-97 elections began a new period of partisan politics. Voting in the House of Representatives had become highly polarized and extremely well defined, as seen in figure 33 (Fifth House) and figure 34 (Sixth House). The stress for these configurations is very low and supports an excellent fit even in a single dimension (see table 1). The actual configurations reveal two very tight clusters with only a few individuals outside of both blocs.

The configurations are presented in two dimensions rather than one, because a two-dimensional plot provides more information to the reader without any loss of clarity. There is, however, one change in the presentation of plots for these Congresses, in contrast to the earlier ones. Because the clustering of members is so dense, individual points cannot be labeled. So figures 33 and 34 take the form of density plots, where each symbol represents the number of individuals at a particular location. Because no labels are provided for the party and region of the membership, the partisan and regional distributions of the major blocs are provided in table 14. While this form of presentation is not as efficient for providing information about the Congress, the necessity for it is a dramatic indication of the increased polarization.

Cluster analysis of House members in these two Congresses helps to demonstrate the cohesiveness of the emerging parties. The average levels of agreement among Federalists were 82.7% (Fifth Congress) and 86.4% (Sixth); among the Republicans, 86.9% (Fifth) and 86.0% (Sixth). These levels of intra-group agreement are extremely high and are well above comparable levels in previous years (or, in fact, in modern times). The only real exceptions to the polarization into partisan voting blocs were in the Fifth Congress, where three individuals were noticeably unaligned: George Dent (Md.), Josiah Parker (Va.), and Samuel Smith (Md.). All three served in Congress for several terms and had a history of inconsistent partisan ties. Yet,

Table 14. Partisan and Regional Distribution of Voting Blocs

MDS Bloc	Total	Party			Region			
		Fed.	Rep.	None	New Eng.	Middle	South	West
Fifth House (1797–1799)								
Federalist	52	51	1	0	25	21	6	0
Republican	45	0	44	1	3	12	27	3
None	3	2	1	0	0	2	1	0
Total	100	53	46	1	28	35	34	3
Sixth House (1799–1801)								
Federalist	51	51	0	0	22	15	14	0
Republican	49	6	43	0	3	21	22	3
Total	100	57	43	0	25	36	36	3

Note: Party codes are based on Dauer (1953); MDS blocs are based on the spatial configurations, figures 33 and 34.

by the Sixth Congress, even these three men were clearly aligned with one of the party blocs.

The inevitable question concerning these voting blocs is whether they can appropriately be labeled parties. In describing the patterns of electoral activity, it was noted that the groupings had a distinctive regional character. This is especially true in the Fifth Congress, where representatives from New England and the South were highly united in their voting (see table 14). But the fact that there were defections from regional loyalty in favor of partisan loyalty helps to build a persuasive argument for designating these blocs as partisan aggregations. Furthermore, the swing in the South toward the Federalist side in the 1798 election (documented below) provides additional evidence that these developments were part of a process of party emergence, rather than a series of regional alignments.

If this evidence is not convincing, we can consider whether those elected under partisan labels (explicit or implicit) voted consistently with these designations. Of course, there is no authoritative listing of party labels (see Appendix A). But the designations listed by Dauer (1953) appear to be reasonably reliable. The cross-tabulation of this classification with the voting blocs for the Fifth and Sixth Congresses is given in table 14; the correspondence is quite good, with only one "error" in the Fifth. That one individual was Tillinghast (R.I.), whose electoral success and failure seem to be explained by his Republican label—even while his votes placed him with the Federalist bloc in the Fifth (and again in the Seventh) Congress (Robinson, 1916). The exceptions from the Sixth Congress are considered later in this section. But, the exceptions notwithstanding, the evidence seems to substantiate further the notion that voting blocs had a partisan basis. After a brief look at Senate voting, I shall turn to an examination of the issues during these years.

In the Senate, the membership was also polarized into two groups, although clusters were somewhat less well defined than in the House (see

146 Origins of American Political Parties

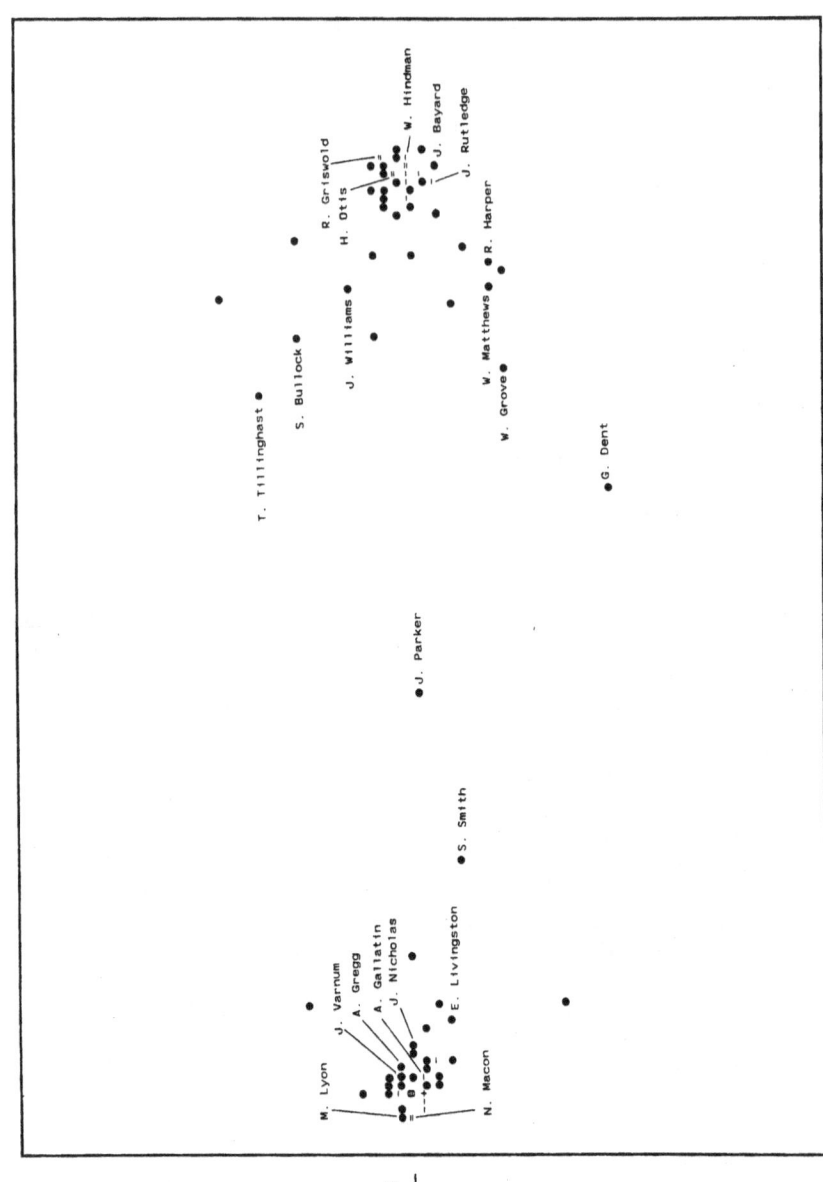

Fig. 33. Spatial Configuration, Fifth Congress, House, 1797-1799

KEY

Symbol	Number of Members
●	1
=	2
=	3
+	4
⊕	6

Each symbol represents the number of congressmen at a particular point in the space.

Partisan Competition in Congress 147

Fig. 34. Spatial Configuration, Sixth Congress, House, 1799-1801

KEY

Symbol	Number of Members
●	1
I	2
=	3
+	4
⊕	6
⊗	7
■	8

Each symbol represents the number of congressmen at a particular point in the space.

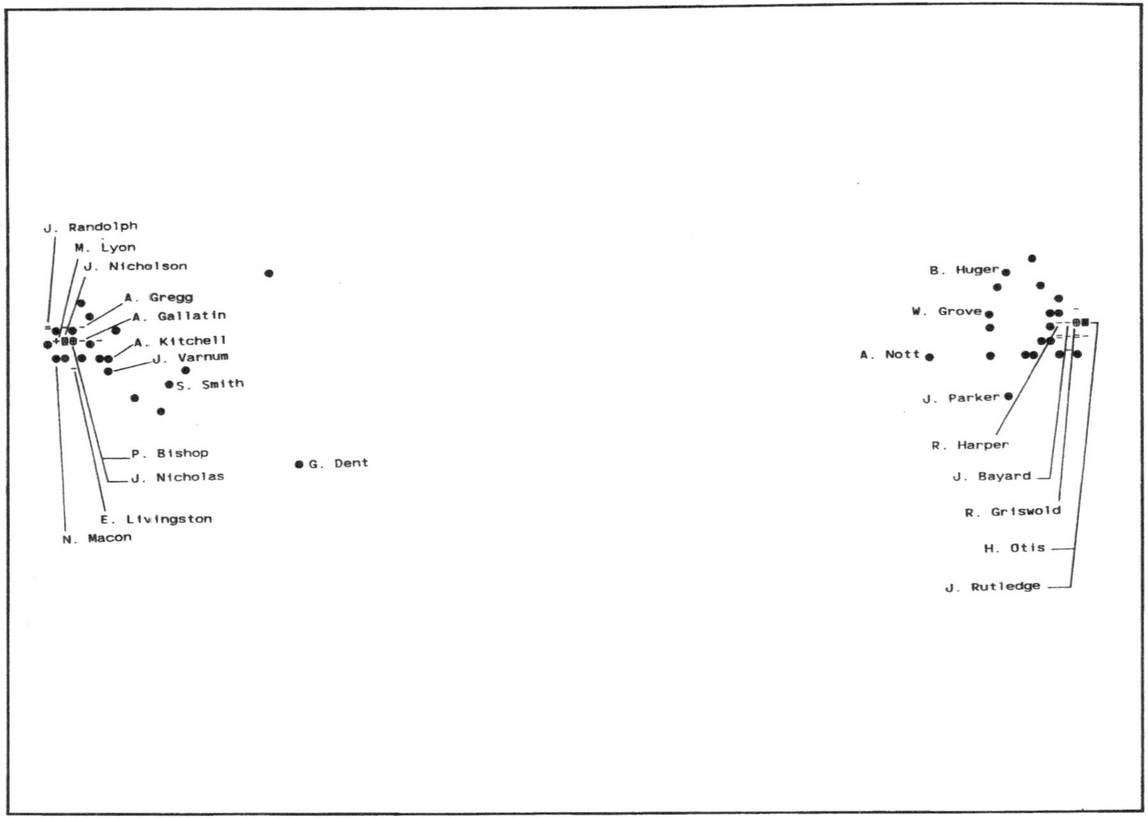

Table 15. Classification of Issues, Fifth House

Category	Number	Percentage
National Authority	6	3.9
Economics	26	16.8
Frontier	1	0.6
Foreign Policy—General	34	21.9
Foreign Policy—Army	21	13.5
Foreign Policy—Navy	20	12.9
Partisan Politics	31	20.0
Miscellaneous	16	10.3
Total	155	99.9

Note: Categories based in part on Bell (1973); percentages do not total 100.0% due to rounding error.

figures 35 and 36). The Federalist voting bloc continued to hold a working majority in the Senate, with only North Carolina and Virginia consistently on the Republican side. The clearest trend in Senate voting was the cleavage along sectional lines, yet enough senators split from the dominant party in their region to allow us to conclude that the voting blocs were following something more than sectional interests. Again, the patterns observed for the Senate help to confirm and reinforce conclusions reached about party development in the House.

Along with the arrival of a new president and Congress in 1797, there was a substantial change in the content of the congressional agenda. Even more than in the previous sessions, the Fifth Congress was dominated by foreign policy concerns. Our classification of issues—seen in table 15—for the Fifth Congress differs somewhat from Bell's, presented in table 4. The chief difference appears to come in the votes taken on the Alien and Sedition Acts and the Logan Act, which have been placed in the category of partisan politics, rather than national authority. In a sense, the best place for these measures would be the modern category of civil liberties. It seems, however, that the concern was not over any questions of constitutional law or the role of the central government, but over simple matters of friends and enemies.

In any case, nearly half of the votes were directly concerned with foreign and military policy. The role of the army, formerly a matter of frontier policy, was by now a major component of foreign policy. One could further claim that most of those votes classified within domestic economics or partisan politics were indirectly involved with foreign affairs. Most of the economic proposals were for taxes to support enlargement of the military establishment, and the Alien and Sedition Acts were in part a result of the crisis atmosphere. Only one vote was taken on frontier policy, and there were few matters that clearly dealt with national authority.

All this attention to foreign policy resulted from the worsening of relations with France; while the Jay Treaty helped to improve matters with Great Britain, the situation with regard to the French became very serious.

Table 16. Dissent from Party Voting Blocs, Fifth House

No. of dissenters	No. of votes	% of votes	Cumulative %
Republican Voting Bloc			
0	52	33.5	33.5
1	36	23.2	56.7
2	16	10.3	67.0
3	11	7.1	74.1
4–5	7	4.5	78.6
6–7	7	4.5	83.1
8–10	9	5.8	88.9
11–15	7	4.5	93.4
16–20	10	6.5	99.9
Federalist Voting Bloc			
0	42	27.1	27.1
1	19	12.3	39.4
2	16	10.3	49.7
3	9	5.8	55.5
4–5	18	11.6	67.1
6–7	11	7.1	74.2
8–10	10	6.5	80.7
11–15	16	10.3	91.0
16–23	14	9.0	100.0

Note: Voting blocs are based on the spatial configuration, figure 33; percentages do not total 100.0% due to rounding error.

Like the negotiations with Britain, the dealings with France divided the Congress along partisan lines.

The high degree of polarization, evident in congressional voting patterns beginning with the Fifth Congress, is a strong indication of party development. But at the same time it inhibits the detailed analysis of issues that was possible for earlier years. The appearance of two cohesive clusters in the MDS configuration renders the vector analysis of individual issues impossible.[3] As a result, we can proceed only with a cross-tabular analysis.

A detailed analysis of a large number of individual roll calls could be little more than a recounting of the depictions of historians and would serve little purpose. Thus, the analysis is restricted to general comments on each major issue area and some attention to those votes that cut across party lines.

If we use the two major voting blocs as a point of reference—excluding only Parker, Smith, and Dent, as not being contained within either group—we can demonstrate the depth of party unity with the figures in table 16.[4] This table shows how often various levels of dissent from party unity occurred on the roll calls of the Fifth Congress. The party voting blocs were undivided on a substantial portion of all votes taken, and a small number of dissenters were present on most votes. All of this is further evidence of the cohesiveness of these voting blocs. But was this unity present across different issue areas?

The major topic of concern was what has been labeled the quasi war with

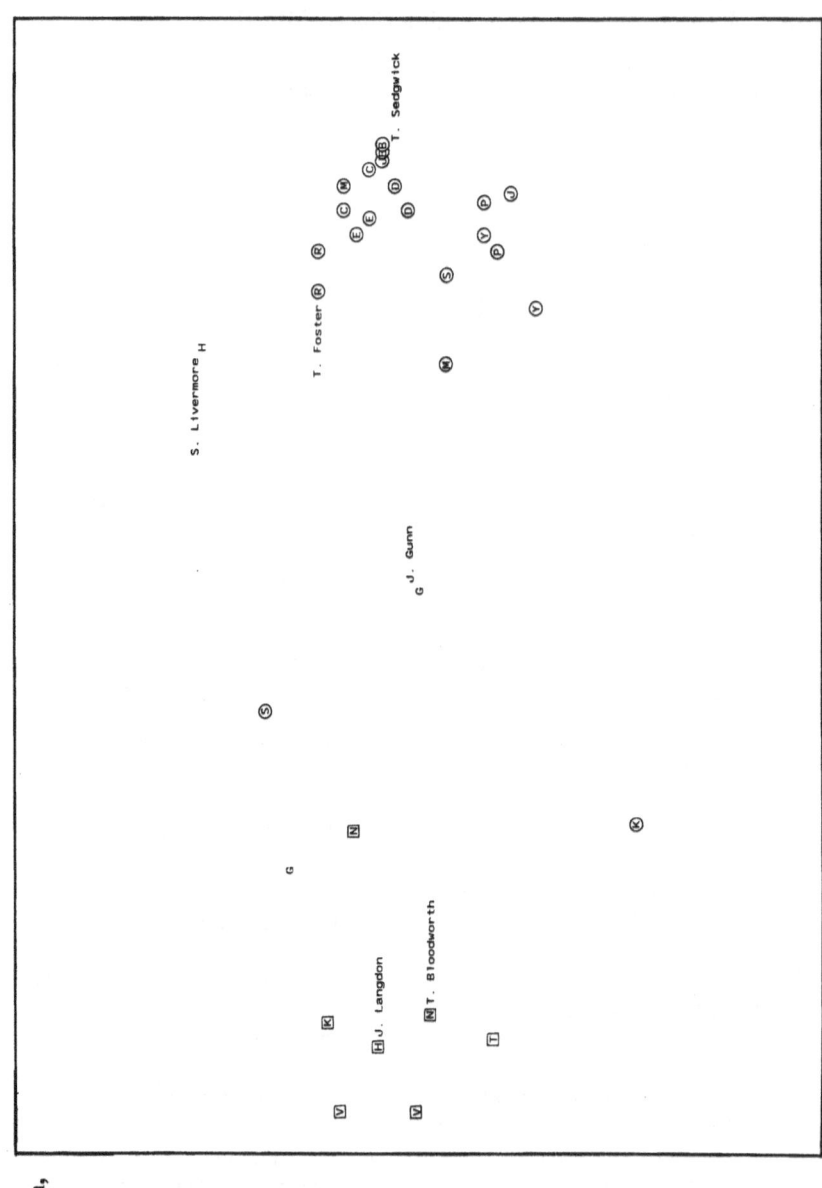

Fig. 35. Spatial Configuration, Fifth Congress, Senate, 1797-1799

KEY

B – Mass. M – Md.
C – Conn. N – N.C.
D – Del.   P – Penn.
E – Vt.   R – R.I.
G – Ga.   S – S.C.
H – N.H.   T – Tenn.
J – N.J.   V – Vir.
K – Ky.   Y – N.Y.

Ⓧ – Federalist
X̄ – Republican
X – No party/Unknown

Letter = state
Circle/square = party

Partisan Competition in Congress 151

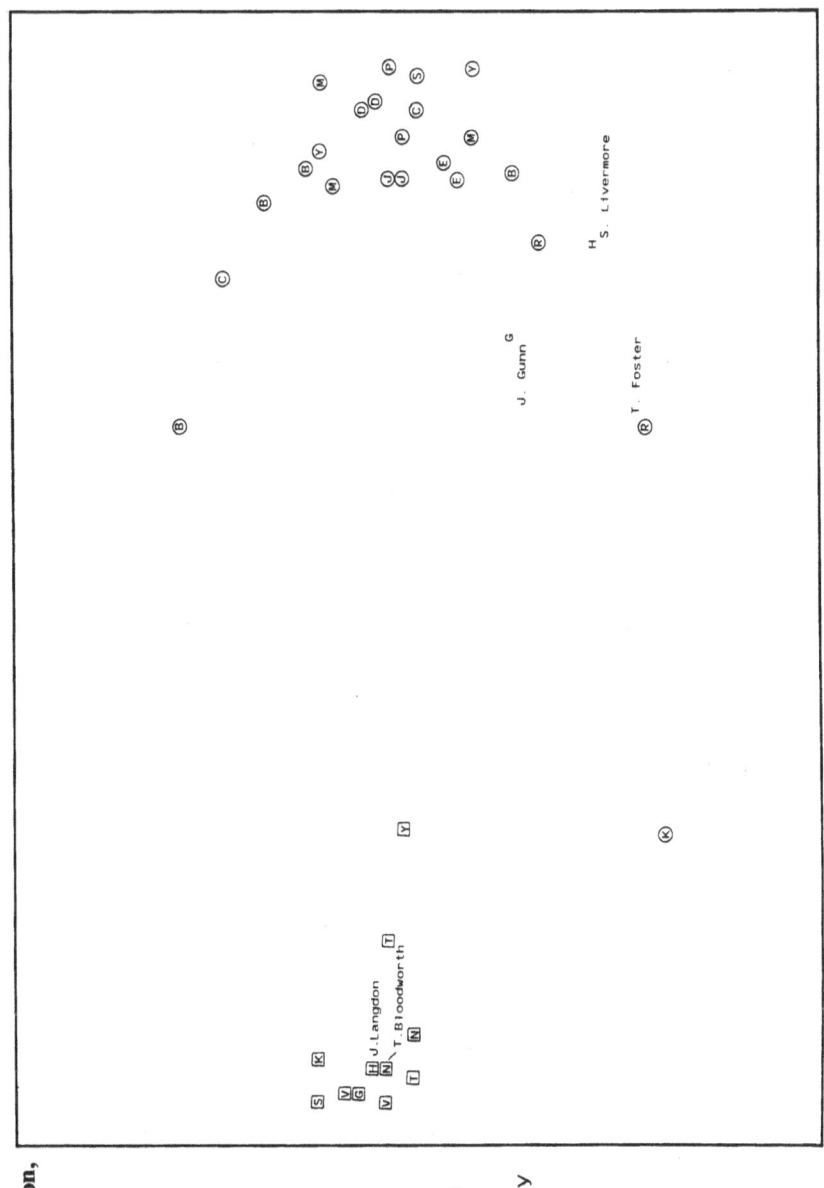

Fig. 36. Spatial Configuration, Sixth Congress, Senate, 1799-1801

KEY

B – Mass.   M – Md.
C – Conn.   N – N.C.
D – Del.   P – Penn.
E – Vt.   R – R.I.
G – Ga.   S – S.C.
H – N.H.   T – Tenn.
J – N.J.   V – Vir.
K – Ky.   Y – N.Y.

⊗ – Federalist
⊠ – Republican
X – No party/Unknown

Letter = state
Circle/square = party

France (DeConde, 1966). While no formal conflict ever took place, it was a time of difficult diplomatic maneuvers and extensive military preparation. Soon after inauguration, Adams called a special session of Congress to prepare for the upcoming negotiations with France. The agenda for this session included measures for creation of a navy to protect merchant vessels, for establishment of a provisional army to supplement the state militia, and for new revenue measures to support these defensive preparations (Bell, 1973; Dauer, 1953).

This agenda did not change greatly in the two regular sessions of the Fifth, although the context was altered by the intervention of events. In the early months of 1798, during the second session, dispatches arrived from Gerry, Marshall, and Pinckney, who had been sent to negotiate with France. Known later as the XYZ dispatches, these papers told of the French refusal to negotiate without payment of a substantial bribe. In April, the Congress passed a resolution requesting these dispatches from Adams. Upon their release and subsequent publication, opinion turned toward the Federalists and a strong policy against France. War was never declared, but a state of hostilities existed for several years (DeConde, 1966).

The XYZ affair set the stage for a new series of proposals for strengthening the American military establishment and providing an appropriate posture toward the French. These included new measures to enlarge the navy and create a standing army, as well as new revenue measures, and bills to permit limited actions against French ships and to withdraw from treaty obligations. The fact that France was at war with England meant that old fears about alliances with England were rekindled (Dauer, 1953; DeConde, 1966).

All of these defense and foreign policy proposals were products of the Federalist leadership, although it was itself internally divided. Hamilton, although holding no office, had remained active and was often more influential with the Cabinet than President Adams. There was much sentiment among the leaders for a formal declaration of war, but, in the end, the moderate course seemed preferable and was supported by Hamilton and Adams (Dauer, 1953).

The Republicans, who had always desired good relations with France, were eventually placed in a difficult position by the XYZ affair. Not only was public opinion aroused against France and, indirectly, the Republicans, but the resolve of the Republican leadership to resist Federalist programs was weakened. Jefferson and the others continued to speak out against preparations for war, but their case had been substantially hurt (Cunningham, 1957).

In the context of the partisan debate over foreign and military policy, several matters arose that in themselves demonstrated the strength of the partisan spirit marking the Fifth Congress. The first was an incident between two members, Lyon of Vermont and Griswold of Connecticut. Its importance would have been minimal, had it not arisen from the heat of partisan debate. Proposals to censure or expel these men occupied some time during the second session.

A more serious matter was the introduction of the Alien and Sedition Acts in April, 1798. These proposals "were a manifestation of the Federalist belief that they alone were fit to rule, and a resentment of all criticism of their policy" (Dauer, 1953, p. 153). In retrospect, they appear as a serious abridgment of basic civil liberties, but to the Federalists they were needed measures in a time of severe crisis.

It is clear that all important issues taken up during the Fifth Congress had a strong partisan component. It is equally clear from this overview of voting patterns that the divisions on most were sharply drawn between the parties. But there were exceptions, and these are noted in the comments that follow.

As indicated above, foreign policy was the dominant issue during the Fifth Congress, with nearly half of all votes taken in the House directly concerning some aspect of foreign policy. The level of partisanship was at least as great in this area as in other issue areas, with the party blocs united on most votes. It was rare for more than three or four members to vote with the opposing bloc on any roll call.

A contrasting position, however, has been taken by two historians, Bell (1973) and Dauer (1953). Dauer argues that the Federalist party experienced a serious split between the so-called High Federalists and the moderates. The former group included Hamilton and others who sided strongly with British interests. Bell, on the other hand, suggests that voting in the foreign policy arena was characterized by a more complex pattern of alliances: ten factions with distinct positions on the issues of the Fifth Congress.

Dauer finds evidence for a split within the Federalist camp from a variety of sources. The best indication comes from the actions of those known as High Federalists. In the presidential election, Hamilton and some allies had attempted to rig the election so that Adams would win only the second spot, making him vice-president once again. This plot backfired, but Hamilton retained an upper hand, since most of the Cabinet members were more loyal to him than to Adams. Additionally, a number of key Federalists in the House shared this perspective, being more closely allied to Hamilton than to Adams.

Differences between Adams and the extremists did not materialize on a regular basis, but the potential for disagreement was always present. One issue splitting the two groups was the call for releasing the XYZ dispatches, with the High Federalists supporting the position of the Republicans in asking Adams to release the papers.[5] Generally, the extremists supported a larger army and took a more belligerent stance toward France, and these positions were occasionally reflected in the roll calls.

It would be a mistake, however, to consider the High Federalists a major faction in the Fifth Congress. There is no evidence from the spatial analysis of any substantial division within the Federalist bloc. Nor does cluster analysis indicate any cluster that can be identified as the High Federalists (although Dauer never provides any list of members). Although this group probably did appear on several specific roll calls, they had no ongoing identity as a distinct voting bloc. It would appear that in most instances the differences within the party were resolved prior to the final decision in Congress, even though there were no formal party caucuses or leadership to initiate such resolutions of opposing points of view.

The factional structure identified by Bell, in contrast to the division shown by Dauer, is based only on roll call voting patterns and not on any self-conscious group identity. Bell selects twelve key votes during the first (special) session of the Fifth Congress taken on specific aspects of Adams's program for defensive preparations and new revenue sources. On the basis of these twelve roll calls, Bell finds ten distinct factions. He then traces the behavior of these factions during the two subsequent sessions of the Fifth Congress. It is odd to discover that nowhere among the ten factions can one find a group that can be labeled High Federalists. But, in fact, Bell (1973, pp. 170-71) is explicit on this point, noting that such a group is not evident in the roll call votes.

Neither multidimensional scaling nor cluster analysis of the votes for the entire Fifth Congress shows any evidence of a factional pattern like that described by Bell. Indeed, this fact is not even all that inconsistent with Bell's own discussion, for he himself demonstrates the shifting of coalitions among factions and the divisions within the factions. In effect, the ten factions were unique to the twelve roll calls in the first session for which they were identified. This conclusion then leaves us with the question of how useful it was even to designate these factions, for they appear to be nothing more than an artifact of a specific set of roll call votes.

Clearly, the dominant feature, then, of votes in the Fifth Congress—foreign policy or otherwise—was the opposition of the two major voting blocs. Yet, as we have seen, these blocs did not appear on each and every vote. It might be worthwhile to take note of several important votes where divisions did not fall along party (voting bloc) lines.[6]

Intensive examination of about thirty important votes on foreign policy again fails to reveal any consistent divisions within the two party blocs. There was indeed a lack of strict party cohesion, but this comes as no surprise. Certain individuals split from their parties more frequently than others, and they are evident in the spatial analysis (figure 33). It is also true that, in nearly every case where one party was divided, the other party was united. This supports the notion that we are seeing degrees of support, rather than the appearance of a new line of cleavage.

Three votes taken in the second session came closest to showing a regular split among the Federalists. These were a measure to authorize capture of French vessels (V108), and Republican moves to reduce the size of the navy (V71) and the army (V79). In each, about a dozen Federalists sided with the Republicans to defeat the Federalist position. Yet only five Federalists dissented on all three of these votes.

We can conclude from this analysis that there existed within the Federalist bloc a number of moderates who were unwilling to support certain Federalist proposals. This was not, however, a cohesive group in itself, as different moderates defected on different issues. A similar group seemed to exist among the Republicans, but there were fewer of them and they defected less frequently. Furthermore, the frequency of such defections from both parties was declining over time.

Economic policy in the Fifth Congress was closely linked to foreign policy, since the proposed revenue measures became necessary only with the increased spending for military preparations. Taxes were considered on retail liquor licenses, certificates of naturalization, stamps, salt, and the value of land and slaves.

In general, votes on economic matters were slightly less partisan than in any other issue area, but this was mostly due to a single series of votes on the proposed tax on land and slaves. Otherwise, votes on revenue measures involved a very limited number of defections, similar to the foreign policy measures.

The one exceptional issue, the tax on land and slaves, had its precedent in the Fourth Congress, when a similar proposal split directly across party lines. The votes taken in the Fifth Congress again split the parties. As such, it was a very atypical issue. Taxation of property holdings (slaves, of course, were regarded as property at that time) was an innovation that appeared threatening in a period when voting was still limited in some states to those with property. In a time of crisis, however, this tax provided a better means of financing defense spending. In a final vote (V106), this revenue measure received unanimous support from the Federalists. The Republicans, however, remained divided, presumably because they differed on the broader implications of this measure.

One additional roll call in the economic arena is worthy of attention. Outside of the revenue measures, very little time was being devoted to economic policy. The matter of the national and state debts had been generally resolved in the first years of the new government. But occasionally a new issue recalled those old debates. In the Fifth Congress, one such issue was whether states could credit expenditures for defensive fortifications toward their debts. Like the land tax, the vote on this issue (V118) cut across party lines. Here, however, a simple explanation lies in the advantage that accrued to certain states.

One of the strongest indications of the growing role played by the parties in the Fifth Congress was the existence of issues that arose directly from the partisan conflict. One such issue was the attempt to resolve a personal quarrel between Matthew Lyon, a Vermont Republican, and Roger Griswold, a Connecticut Federalist. The other important issue of partisan politics was the passage of the Alien and Sedition Acts.

The Lyon-Griswold affair was a direct result of the heated debates during the second session over foreign policy. Lyon, an ardent Republican, took offense at comments made by Griswold, one of the more extreme Federalists. Lyon spat in Griswold's face, an action beyond the realm of acceptable debate (even in those days). But when the Republicans failed to provide the needed two-thirds vote to expel Lyon, Griswold took matters into his own hands, attacking Lyon with a cane. Lyon defended himself with a pair of fire-tongs, but in the end neither was seriously injured (Dauer, 1953).

Naturally, this was a highly partisan issue, particularly in a closely divided House. Two votes where the issue was clearly posed came on the initial motion to expel Lyon (V54) and on a later motion to censure both men (V59). On the former vote, a united group of Federalists was joined by two Republicans, but this was substantially short of the two-thirds margin. In the latter case, the Federalists voted no, for they felt that only Lyon was deserving of punishment, while the Republicans favored the censure of both members. On this vote, no one broke party unity.

In a more serious vein, the Alien and Sedition Acts were proposed by

Federalists who believed that opposition to the administration brought unnecessary risks to the nation. The acts simultaneously demonstrated a clear awareness of party groups and an unwillingness to accept the consequences of their existence. In the absence of organized opposition, it would not seem necessary to take actions considered extreme even by their advocates. But the fact that people did not yet recognize that opposition had a legitimate role within a democracy is clear from the passage of these measures. It should be noted, however, that there was no move to outlaw the opposition completely, only to place constraints on its activities.

Two laws were passed during the second session of the Fifth Congress. The Alien Act was passed by the House on June 21, 1798, in a straight party-line vote (V100). This law, together with related measures, permitted deportation of "dangerous" aliens, required registration by aliens together with establishing a more difficult naturalization procedure, and made aliens from an enemy nation subject to apprehension or removal from the country. The Republicans, among whom were several naturalized citizens (including Gallatin, a party leader, and the infamous Lyon), opposed enactment on constitutional and other grounds, but were unable to block passage.

The Sedition Act was also passed by a cohesive group of Federalists, although two Federalists chose to vote against it (Bullock of Massachusetts and Matthews of Maryland). The vote (V117) came on July 10, near the end of the second session. The law made it a crime to take actions or publish writings that would oppose government acts, bring the government into disrepute, or aid and abet any enemy nation. In essence, it jeopardized First Amendment protections of freedoms of speech, assembly, and the press. Full discussion of the legislation is available elsewhere; suffice it to state here that this was clearly a partisan action by the Federalists in Congress to limit the activities of their Republican opponents (Dauer, 1953; Miller, 1951; Smith, 1956).

One prosecution under the Sedition Act is of special interest because it was directed at the Federalists' favorite enemy, Matthew Lyon. Between his Irish birth, his insult of Griswold, and his frequent outspoken attacks on them, the Federalists saw him as a prime target. He was indicted in October, 1798, in the midst of his campaign for reelection. In an atmosphere of heated partisan controversy, Lyon was convicted and given a fine and a jail sentence. Despite the fact that the election was held while he was in jail, he did win reelection. Upon his release, the Federalists attempted to expel him from Congress, but once again the loyalty of his fellow Republicans averted the necessary two-thirds majority.

In summary, we must continue to be wary of using the term *party* to describe the groups that were so much a part of the Fifth Congress, because questions remain about the existence of any real party organizations or the awareness of parties in the electorate. Yet, it is unmistakably clear that partisanship characterized the proceedings of the Fifth Congress. The ardor that produced the Alien and Sedition Acts, the emotional response to the presence of Lyon, and the consistency of divisions over the crucial measures connected with the French crisis were all clear signs of party politics. In fact, the members of the Fifth Congress were practicing partisanship with an enthusiasm that could not be matched in twentieth-century America, even though they still tried to deny or oppose the existence of parties.

Continuing Partisanship, 1799-1801

The selection of a new Congress in 1798 took place directly after the debates and passage of the Alien and Sedition Acts. Coming from such a display of partisanship, it would be remarkable if the elections could follow the norms of nonpartisanship that had persisted in most states since colonial days. Indeed, most observers seem to agree that the 1798 elections were contested on the basis of those issues debated in the Fifth Congress and that significant gains were made by the Federalists, especially in the South. Jefferson, Hindman (a Maryland Federalist), Sedgwick, and even Washington took notice of these trends in their letters (Cunningham, 1957; Dauer, 1953).

The Federalists made substantial gains in every southern state, electing between fifteen and twenty members of the House of Representatives from the region.[7] Still, the depth of this partisan transformation was somewhat illusory. The Federalists succeeded, apparently, in riding a wave of public opinion to victory, but they were less successful in establishing organizations. "Such an organization, however, had not even begun to be perfected at the close of the 1798 congressional campaigns. Instead, the Federalist style of politicking retained its traditional elitist orientation. Partisan leaders still presented themselves as reluctantly acquiescing to run for office only because of a popular draft or the backing of an influential patron . . . Because a permanent and effective party structure still was lacking, federalist strength in North Carolina in 1798 was built on a foundation of sand" (Rose, 1968, p. 179). Similar conclusions can be drawn about parties in the other southern states (Rose, 1968, ch. 5).

In New England, the Republicans had been weak and remained so. They held onto three congressional districts with Varnum and Bishop in Massachusetts and Lyon in Vermont. Although little evidence is available, it appears that party organizations in New England were little stronger than those in the South (Cunningham, 1957; Goodman, 1964).

It was in the Middle states, of course, that a fuller development of parties was already taking place. And it was here that the Republicans actually made some moderate gains in the 1798 elections. In Pennsylvania, the gain of an additional seat by the Republicans took place in a state where parties were becoming increasingly involved in electoral maneuvering. Evidence of this change comes in the regular use of committees to nominate congressional candidates and attempts, usually successful, to avoid splitting votes between two candidates representing the same party (Tinkcom, 1950, pp. 184-89).

Party development in Maryland's elections emerged slowly, due in part to the importance of local divisions. In addition, the independence of congressmen such as Dent and Smith was consistent with the pace of party growth, as either a cause or a result. In 1798, however, the congressional elections were hotly contested affairs, and choices were posed between alternatives from the two parties (Renzulli, 1972, pp. 203-8). While no statewide organizations provided leadership for the Maryland parties, there were rather sophisticated organizations at the local level in some parts of the state (Bohmer, 1978).

Although reliable evidence is lacking for most states, a strong case can therefore be made that the 1798 congressional elections came much closer to being partisan contests than preceding elections. At the least, voters were responding to candidates on the basis of issues. Since positions on the key issues coincided almost universally with party alignments (as evidenced by the votes cast during the Fifth Congress), there is at least circumstantial evidence that voters perceived choices in partisan terms. While party organizations were not yet commonplace, developments in several states showed that such organizations were beginning to play a greater role.

As we observed earlier, congressional voting was highly polarized in the Sixth Congress. Again, we can see this polarization in the MDS configurations for the House (figure 34) and the Senate (figure 36). Little more can be said about this overall picture of party cohesion. That we are generally justified in describing these blocs as party groups was established above, with the evidence in table 14. We can, however, reinforce this analysis with a look at the record of several individuals whose careers spanned several Congresses and who were not always loyal partisans.

One man whose career represents the development of partisanship in the South was William Barry Grove (N.C.). As suggested earlier, Grove was initially elected in 1791 and was always regarded in his home state as a Federalist, the only North Carolina Federalist to be elected until 1798. Yet in the Second, Third, and Fourth Congresses (see figures 25, 27, 29), his voting record was more in line with the Republican bloc and the rest of his state delegation (although not with the core group of Republicans). By the Fifth Congress, his votes placed him on the edge of the Federalist bloc (see figure 33); in the Sixth (and Seventh) Congress, he was a clearly partisan Federalist (see figures 34 and 37). Furthermore, he was joined in Congress by several other North Carolina Federalists in 1799. Grove's loyalty was accentuated by his votes in favor of such measures as the Alien and Sedition Acts.[8] His movement more generally demonstrated the change in the South that had taken place over this period. Prior to about 1796, identity as a Federalist in the South had little meaning on most national issues. But in the later years, the southern Federalists were in nearly complete agreement with their northern colleagues (Richards, 1966; Risjord, 1978; Rose, 1968).

Another southerner, Josiah Parker (Va.), also moved during the same period from an alliance with the southern (or Republican) bloc to the Federalist camp (see figures 17, 25, 27, 29, 33, and 34). He was initially elected to the First Congress as an Antifederalist opponent of the Constitution. While little has been written about his career, he apparently changed his loyalties at some time. In the Sixth Congress, he was clearly aligned with the Federalists, although he still was not willing to support the Alien and Sedition Acts (Risjord, 1978).

Another individual whose voting record did not fall neatly into party voting blocs was Samuel Smith (Md.). He was initially elected in 1792 in a contest based on personalities, but he was friendly with Hamilton and considered an ally of the administration. Once in Congress, he pursued an independent line. As a merchant shipper, he supported measures that he believed would be in the best interest of commerce. As a military officer, he supported an enlarged army and navy. He maintained this lack of alignment through the Fifth Congress. But with the abatement of the French crisis and the increasing dominance of parties, even Smith became a full-fledged Republican. Although his long career was marked by bursts of independence, he voted consistently with the Republicans in the Sixth (and Seventh) Congress. That such a man could become a party loyalist speaks strongly of the dominant force parties were becoming in the Congress (Cassell, 1971; Pancake, 1972; Renzulli, 1972).

Smith's fellow Marylander George Dent was another political maverick. Dent, Smith, and Parker followed such lines of independence during the Fifth Congress that they cannot be clustered with either party based on their roll call votes (see figure 33). About Dent, we know very little beyond his official voting record. He has been labeled a Federalist (Dauer, 1953), but it has been said that his victory in 1798 was "an accomplishment which party leaders accepted with a minimum of distaste" (Renzulli, 1972, p. 208). His support as a compromise candidate for Speaker was outlined in chapter 4. In any case, his record in four Congresses shows little consistent agreement with either party, and Risjord (1978, p. 511) describes his voting as "utterly random." By the Sixth Congress, he was allied most often with the Republicans, even on key tests of party loyalty like the Alien and Sedition Acts.

Through a look at these individual careers, we see more clearly the consistent movement toward the existence of cohesive parties. Prior to the Jay Treaty session, cohesion was not high, and people (like Grove) whose partisan and regional ties conflicted tended to remain loyal to their sectional partners. But even the three men who had not joined one of the voting coalitions in the Fifth Congress abandoned their independent paths in the Sixth.[9] From these general indications of the continuing growth of partisanship, we turn once again to a consideration of the issues.

Two events dominated the business of the Sixth Congress. One was the sending of a new delegation to France to negotiate a settlement of the quasi war. This had the effect of diffusing the hot debate over foreign policy that had dominated the last Congress. The other key event was the election of 1800, which occurred between the two sessions and brought Jefferson to the presidency. Campaign maneuvering was present throughout the first session, and the second was a true lame-duck session. As a result of these two events, there was little serious policy making; the agenda consisted mostly of a reconsideration of old issues and partisan division over relatively minor items (Bell, 1973; Cunningham, 1957; Dauer, 1953).

Furthermore, nearly every vote taken was highly partisan. There were few votes that did not divide the membership almost perfectly between the two clusters, shown in figure 34. Those votes that did cut substantially across party lines were mostly on minor bills or procedural matters.

In the foreign policy sphere, most of the small number of recorded votes were on a continuation of the suspension of trade with France and the size of the army and navy. But the likelihood of a settlement with France had turned public opinion around and had moved enough moderate Federalists, so that trade was eventually reinstated and moves were taken to reduce the armed forces. In the economic arena, there were again votes on a series of revenue measures. Once again, local interest dictated some deviation from party loyalty. The only new economic matter was a bill to establish a uniform system of bankruptcy, and this, too, was passed on a partisan vote. Several votes were taken on frontier matters. While party coalitions were slightly less cohesive here, partisanship was still the key factor.

Another old issue that resurfaced during the Sixth Congress was an attempt to repeal the Alien and Sedition Acts, an attempt that nearly succeeded in the first session. The Sedition Act, however, was scheduled to expire on the last day of the Sixth Congress. While the Federalists tried hard to extend the law, they were in the end unsuccessful. Motions to reject continuation and to approve continuation both failed, so the law expired of its own accord. (The difference between the votes on these two motions came from members who were absent on one vote or the other.) Throughout these considerations, three men voted against the Sedition Act, in spite of their general association with the Federalist party—Parker, whose position was noted above; and Huger and Nott of South Carolina. Otherwise, party loyalty was unbroken

The only really new issues on the congressional agenda of the Sixth Congress were either private bills or simply partisan disputes with little policy content.[10] Examples included debate over the case of a sailor who had been turned over to the British as a mutineer (Cunningham, 1957, p. 175) and the attempt to set up an electoral commission, the intent of which was supposedly to reject Republican electoral votes from Pennsylvania. But perhaps the most significant evidence of partisanship was an apparently trivial motion to thank the Speaker (Sedgwick) for his service at the end of the Sixth Congress. So great was the partisan temperament that even this vote split the two groups without exception.[11]

In fact, the most significant business of the Sixth Congress was a matter for which there was no full roll call vote. When the 1800 election ended in a tie between Jefferson and Burr, the House had the responsibility of determining the outcome. Votes in this case were cast by state and not by individual, but individual votes are known with but one exception. The partisanship that dominated this decision is shown below, after a brief look at the background of the election.

Crisis of Succession: The Election of 1800

Students of political development have suggested that we can view the problems of a new nation as a series of crises, such as legitimacy, integration, and participation (LaPalombara and Weiner, 1966). One particular crisis has often been cited as crucial in American political development—the crisis of succession (Grodzins, 1966). Could the reins of leadership be turned over peacefully from one person to another? To some, the key test was in 1796, when Washington voluntarily retired from office. The succession of Adams to the presidency without disruption of the union suggested that a degree of national stability had been achieved.

Three special factors made the 1796 crisis of succession a less severe test for the new nation. In the first place, the competition between Adams and Jefferson was limited that year. As noted earlier, Jefferson declined to wage an active campaign for office. This fact plus his old friendship with Adams certainly deterred Jefferson from cooperating in any possible attempt to overturn the results. Second, there was in fact substantial continuity between Adams and Washington. Adams had been Washington's vice-president. This linkage was further strengthened by his choice to retain the old Cabinet, although this decision was to give him difficulties before his term was over. Finally, the fact that partisanship had not reached its full strength certainly contributed to a peaceful succession. While the Republicans had been active in the Jay Treaty debates and the election campaign, they lacked the organization and unity of purpose that might have resulted in a challenge to the election results.

In 1800, however, the situation had changed in substantial ways. We have already noted the substantial growth of partisanship, both in Congress and in election campaigns. A party that was willing to use a Sedition Act to suppress opposition might well have been inclined to challenge an election that forced its removal from majority status. Furthermore, the restrained campaigning in 1796 could not have been expected to repeat itself in the political atmosphere of 1800.

The nature of the 1800 election has been the subject of much historical scholarship (Cassell, 1971; Chambers, 1963b; Cunningham, 1957; Dauer, 1953; Grodzins, 1966; Malone, 1962; McCormick, 1982; Miller, 1960; Rose, 1968; Welch, 1965), and the basic outcome of the election is well known. The ticket of Jefferson and Burr won seventy-three electoral votes, while Adams won sixty-five votes; the regional alignment is shown in table 17. The complicating factor was the constitutional system, which resulted in a tie between Jefferson and Burr. Having failed (or not wanted) to anticipate the appearance of parties so cohesive as to produce an equal vote for candidates for president and vice-president, the writers of the Constitution set up the potential for a major dilemma. The House of Representatives had the duty of resolving the tie.

But before discussing the way this tie was broken, let us look at the factors that contributed to the Republican victory. Special attention, of course, is given to the role of parties and evidence of partisan development in this election year.

Electoral procedures became very important during the 1800 campaign, as the two parties vied for additional votes in what they knew would be a close election. The party controlling the state legislature could enact provisions for choice of electors by the legislature, by district elections, or by general ticket elections. The choice was inevitably based on how they could maximize the number of votes for their candidate. Accordingly, elections for the state legislature became the first battleground for the parties. Often legislators were chosen solely on the basis of their preference for Adams or Jefferson, without regard to their positions on local issues.

Table 17. Regional Distribution of Electoral Votes, 1800

Region/State	Adams		Jefferson	
New England		39		0
Connecticut	9		0	
Massachusetts	16		0	
New Hampshire	6		0	
Rhode Island	4		0	
Vermont	4		0	
Middle States		22		25
Delaware	3		0	
Maryland	5		5	
New Jersey	7		0	
New York	0		12	
Pennsylvania	7		8	
South		4		48
Georgia	0		4	
Kentucky	0		4	
North Carolina	4		8	
South Carolina	0		8	
Tennessee	0		3	
Virginia	0		21	
Total Vote		65		73

Source: Dauer (1953, p. 257).

One of the most important developments in the election of 1800 was the appearance of significant party organizations in many states. The Republicans were the most active at creating organizations, but the Federalists followed their lead in many states. Cunningham (1957, pp. 147-61) has carefully documented the Republican party machinery arising in Virginia and New Jersey, as well as several other states. "The campaign of 1800 brought the most significant progress in the development of formal party organization that had yet been witnessed in the United States. . . . Although an informal party organization resting principally on political leadership still remained the basis of party management in most of the states until after 1800, considerable efforts were made during the campaign to introduce party machinery. The contest of 1800 served as a compelling stimulus for party organization" (Cunningham, 1957, pp. 147-48). The Federalists, as the party in power, were more able to rely on the use of federal patronage and thus had less need for formal organization. The drive to gain power, on the other hand, helped to inspire organizational efforts by the Republicans.

The parties, furthermore, were very active in the campaign effort. New York was a particularly significant battleground, for its twelve electoral votes were considered crucial to the outcome. In New York, the state legislature was selecting the electors, so the choice of legislators was the main event, coming early in 1800. Party efforts were intense, with Hamilton and Burr as the chief strategists for the two parties. Burr and the Republicans turned out to be more effective campaigners, and New York gave its votes to Jefferson. The success of the party appeal is demonstrated by strong evidence of straight party voting for the entire Republican ticket in some New York City wards (Cunningham, 1957, pp. 176-85).

The extent of the Republican effort is further illustrated by organized campaigning even in the Federalist strongholds of New England. While they made no breakthrough for electoral votes, their efforts undoubtedly paid off in congressional elections and in the general level of enthusiasm for the party (Cunningham, 1957, pp. 200-210).

Jefferson was still required by custom to be an inactive candidate for office, but his role was markedly different than in 1796. Previously, he was truly the reluctant candidate, but in 1800 he was simply being careful not to violate an important political tradition. In fact, he kept himself well informed through extensive correspondence with his friends.

In addition, Jefferson had put his election platform in writing early in 1799. Although never adopted by any official meeting, his statement of principles in a letter to Gerry was used around the country as an appeal to the voters. "The declarations made by recognized party spokesmen throughout the country testify to the fact that the Republican party in 1800 presented a definite platform to the voters; the well-measured statements of principle and objectives were available to all who were interested enough to read them" (Cunningham, 1957, p. 213). It is far from clear whether the choice made by voters was based on issues, but the possibility was there. This in itself was a step beyond the campaigns of earlier years.

To the extent that issues were a factor in the election outcome, the Republicans profited from a reaction to the excesses of past Federalist programs. Whereas the Federalists had gained votes in 1798 when national sentiment had moved away from France and toward a call for war preparations, the settlement of the quasi war had made the frenzy of the Federalists in 1798 seem excessive. In particular, the imposition of the land tax and other revenue measures, together with the Alien and Sedition Acts, had triggered a movement of popular opinion toward the Republican side.

Nor were the Federalists helped by the continuing split in their ranks. Relations between Adams and Hamilton were uneven at best. Some centrists had proposed that Adams and Jefferson should run together for president and vice-president. A more serious proposal, however, came from some extreme Federalists, who wanted to remove Adams from the presidency. Failing to find an acceptable alternative nominee for the top spot, they focused on a strategy to make Charles Cotesworth Pinckney, the vice-presidential candidate, emerge as the top vote-getter. The idea was that Pinckney would win the votes of some Republican electors in his home state of South Carolina and thus become president. The scheme failed when South Carolina voted for Jefferson and Burr, due largely to the efforts of Charles Pinckney, a cousin of the Federalist nominee.

Although South Carolina's votes ended the chances of both Adams and C. C. Pinckney, they did not make Jefferson president or end the maneuverings of the Federalist factions. Because the Republicans had not made adequate arrangements to drop one vote from Burr, the election had to be resolved by the House of Representatives. Furthermore, the decision was to be made by the lame-duck membership of the Sixth House, where the Republicans were in the minority. The Federalists were not about to make Jefferson president without a struggle.

In the House, the procedure outlined by the Constitution gave each state a single vote, with a majority of states needed for a decision. On the first ballot, Burr received six votes and Jefferson eight (two states were divided, casting no vote). Thus, Jefferson fell one short of the necessary nine states. What is notable about the vote is the strict partisanship revealed in the votes of individual members. While individual votes were not recorded by the House, they were reported in the press.[12] There was perfect correspondence between these votes and membership in the party voting blocs shown in figure 34, with all the Federalists voting for Burr and the Republicans for Jefferson. This cohesion, in conjunction with the high level of partisanship surrounding the election, helps to demonstrate that the voting blocs in Congress were in fact party groupings and not some kind of policy factions. This crucial result is the subject of further attention in chapter 9.

For thirty-five ballots, there was no change in the votes of the states. Finally, on February 17, 1801, several Federalists submitted blank ballots, so that Jefferson won with ten states. Historians have debated the role of various principals, including Jefferson, Burr, James Bayard (Del.), and Samuel Smith. But the general consensus is that Burr and Jefferson at least were innocent of making deals or otherwise interfering with the choice of the House. Apparently, the vote turned on misleading statements made by Smith to Bayard about Jefferson's intentions regarding Federalist officeholders (Cassell, 1971; Cunningham, 1957; Miller, 1960).

In any case, Jefferson was elected president with Burr as his vice-president. Less than a month after the House made its choice, Jefferson was inaugurated without further protest by the Federalists. The crisis of succession had been resolved without bloodshed or a breakup of the union. That the transition was accomplished without civil war is quite significant at a time that had seen a bitter partisan campaign and passage of repressive measures like the Sedition Act. Grodzins (1966) has suggested that the moderate course of Adams was crucial in the peaceful transition of power. As an opponent of the more extreme Federalists, as a longtime friend of Jefferson (although the friendship had been broken by the politics of those years), and as the advocate of a moderate course of action in foreign affairs, Adams muted the opposition of his party. Along with some other lesser factors, the Adams wing of the Federalist party checked the antidemocratic impulses of the extremists. Thus, the United States had passed a major milestone of national development and the emergent parties had achieved an increased level of sophistication.

While the Republicans prevailed by only a narrow margin in the presidential elections, success in the congressional elections proved that their fortunes were on the rise. The new Congress had a solid Republican majority in the House and the Senate.

In most states, House elections took place simultaneously with the presidential election. In New Jersey and Virginia, however, representatives were selected after it was known that the Federalists had been defeated, and a bandwagon effect increased the Republican success. The New Jersey situation was interesting, for the Federalists had switched to a general ticket system with the hope of electing the entire congressional delegation. The state's Republicans, who had shown little organized effort before 1800, were prepared to contest the Federalists. They called a statewide convention to approve their nominees and waged a tough campaign. The entire Republican slate won in a very close contest, with few voters splitting their tickets (Prince, 1967, pp. 61-81).

Republicans gained House seats in all regions of the country, as they swept convincingly into majority status. In the South, they regained most of the seats lost in the 1798 Federalist surge. In New England, the gains were not all that great in numbers, but that any real gains were made was highly significant. For the first time, there was a Republican presence in the region. Six Republicans were elected from Massachusetts, and the party also claimed both seats in Rhode Island.

In the Middle states, Republican gains culminated a transfer of power that had begun several years before. In contrast to the South, where the Republican interest had always been dominant, Republican progress in the Middle states had been slow. But by 1800, Republicans had gained control of congressional delegations in every state but Delaware. This partisan turnover coincided with the changes occurring on a national scale.

The Jefferson Era Begins, 1801-1803

Once the election of 1800 had been resolved and Jefferson had been sworn in as president, it remained to be seen how the transfer of power would affect the emerging parties. The Republicans had grown into a majority status, and the Federalists were beginning their journey into oblivion. The Seventh Congress, which convened in December, 1801, was the arena for a new engagement in the ongoing struggle for partisan advantage.

All available evidence suggests that the Seventh Congress was marked by an extremely high level of polarization along party lines. In both the House (figure 37) and the Senate (figure 38), the MDS analysis reveals very clearly the extent of polarization. (The partisan and regional distributions of the voting blocs are shown in table 18.) Stress for these two configurations (see table 1) is quite low, lower in fact than for any other Congress in this period. But we only need to look at the figures to see the extent to which the membership had polarized.

In the Senate, one member—John E. Colhoun (S.C.)—was not clustered with either voting bloc.[13] He was absent, however, on about three-fourths of the roll calls, and his position may have resulted in part from this fact. Otherwise, there was a high level of cohesion among the senators. While it is clear by now that these voting blocs represented the two competing parties, one anomaly exists. Theodore Foster (R.I.), identified as a Federalist and voting generally with that party since 1790, suddenly began to vote with the

166 Origins of American Political Parties

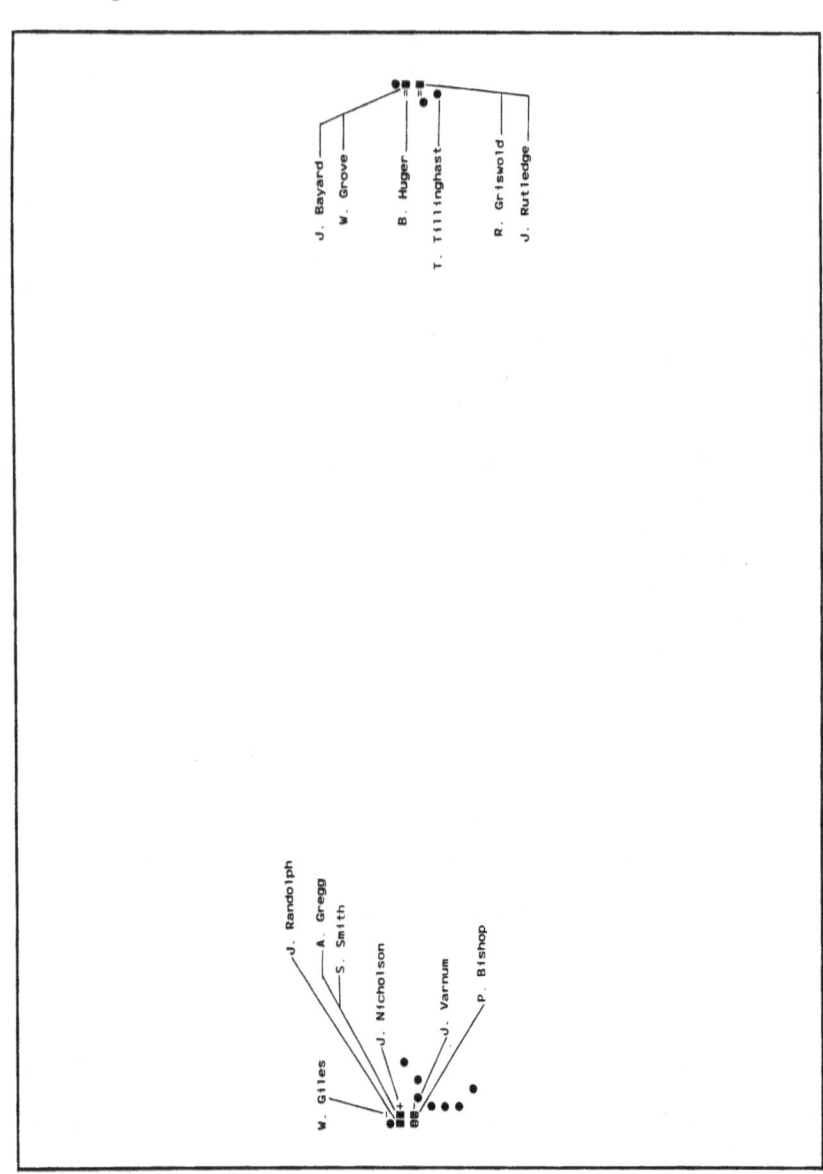

Fig. 37. Spatial Configuration, Seventh Congress, House, 1801–1803

KEY

Symbol	Number of Members
●	1
∣	2
∥	3
+	4
⦵	6
⊗	10
■	14–15

Each symbol represents the number of congressmen at a particular point in the space.

Partisan Competition in Congress 167

Fig. 38. Spatial Configuration, Seventh Congress, Senate, 1801-1803

KEY

B – Mass. M – Md.
C – Conn. N – N.C.
D – Del.   P – Penn.
E – Vt.   R – R.I.
G – Ga.   S – S.C.
H – N.H.   T – Tenn.
J – N.J.   V – Vir.
K – Ky.   Y – N.Y.

Ⓧ – Federalist
☒ – Republican
X – No party/Unknown

Letter = state
Circle/square = party

Table 18. Partisan and Regional Distribution of Voting Blocs, Seventh House (1801–1803)

MDS Bloc	Total	Party			Region			
		Fed.	Rep.	None	New Eng.	Middle	South	West
Federalist	38	37	1	0	20	10	8	0
Republican	62	3	59	0	8	26	25	3
Total	100	40	60	0	28	36	33	3

Note: Party codes are based on Dauer (1953); MDS blocs are based on the spatial configurations, figure 37.

Republicans. Unfortunately, no historical source can be found to provide any explanation of this change. We can note that he shared a boardinghouse with other Republicans during this Congress, but whether this was a cause of his change or simply another manifestation of it is unknown.

Polarization in the House of Representatives was, if anything, greater than in the Senate. Every member voted regularly with his fellow partisans. The smaller group of Federalists was somewhat more cohesive than the majority party. An average pair of Federalists was in agreement on 89.9% of all roll calls in the Seventh Congress, in contrast to an average agreement of 79.6% among Republicans.[14] Alternatively, we can see that the Federalists were unanimous on 61% of the votes, while the Republicans were totally united only about 28% of the time. This tendency toward disunity among the Republicans did not go unnoticed at the time. Roger Griswold wrote in a letter, "The ruling faction in the Legislature have [sic] not yet been able to understand each other. . . . There evidently appears much rivalry and jealousy among the leaders" (Griswold to John Rutledge, December 14, 1801, quoted in Cunningham, 1963, p. 74).

While the level of cohesion in the Republican party was high in historical terms, it is interesting that majority status hurt party unity. This, like the Federalist disunity in earlier sessions, illustrates the difficulty in working with a large majority. It also tends to foreshadow the increasing divisions within the party that appeared as the size of the competing Federalist bloc grew smaller.

The Seventh Congress was not marked by an overwhelming legislative output. The high priorities for the Republicans were undoing some of the more extreme Federalist measures and getting Republicans placed within the small federal bureaucracy. There were no major new legislative initiatives (Cunningham, 1963; Ellis, 1971; Smelser, 1968).

A top-priority item of business for the new Congress was to deal with the Judiciary Act passed at the end of the previous Congress. The principal objection to the bill was the manner in which it allowed Federalists to maintain a stronghold in the federal courts. The law was repealed in 1802 on a partisan vote (V41), but it apparently required the exercise of some party leadership to hold the majority in line (Ellis, 1971, pp. 45-51). Further legislation affecting the federal judiciary was passed later in the session, also with almost perfect party loyalty.

The legislative activity surrounding the judiciary is of particular importance for several reasons. First, the presence of Federalist judges was a major problem for the Republicans and a last strand of power for the Federalists. Many believed that these judges would block any administration initiatives. Second, the strong cohesion shown by the Republicans in repealing the Judiciary Act of 1801 demonstrated that the new majority was serious in its effort to gain full control of the reins of government. Finally, Republican unity required the exercise of discipline on members who were not happy with the repeal motion. Such dissent, even though not made public, did not bode well for a unified party in the future.

The other major action by the Republicans in reversing Federalist policy was the repeal of nearly all internal taxes on salt, sugar, coffee, domestic spirits, stamps, licenses, and various other commodities and services. These taxes had never brought in large sums and were greatly disliked by the citizenry. The resolution to abolish the taxes (V62) was passed without any break in Republican loyalty.

Another area of legislation where votes fell along party lines was the decision to admit Ohio into the union. This proposal, falling in the frontier issue domain, had obvious advantages for the Republicans, who were certain to add more votes to their majority from the new state. Not surprisingly, then, the decision was made on a straight party vote (V73).

During the second session, an issue arose that came to have major implications in coming years. The area known as Louisiana had passed from the control of Spain to France (from whom Jefferson arranged its purchase a few months later). The House (again on a partisan vote) called for an investigation of the territory's status. Soon it would become the cause of a special session of the Eighth Congress and the subject of a major constitutional debate.

Whereas foreign policy had been the major concern and chief partisan battleground in earlier Congresses, the Seventh Congress spent little of its time on such matters. Other than the investigation into Louisiana, business was generally limited to some final decisions on resolving the quasi war with France and several minor measures concerning the army and navy. Many Republicans would have been happy to eliminate the standing army and navy. Reductions, however, had been made previously, and it was thought dangerous to leave the nation without at least a defensive force. It is curious to note that most of the votes on foreign policy roll calls were *not* strictly cast along party lines, although most of them did not pose clear issue alternatives.

If this investigation were to look further into the Jeffersonian era, the appearance of new issues and the deterioration of Republican party loyalty would be major topics. But these trends mark a separate subject. What is important for the current effort is that the partisanship of the Adams years continued after the Republicans gained control. The highly emotional and intense partisan activity that had produced the Lyon-Griswold fight and the Sedition Act, however, had subsided. In its wake was an apparently well-developed party system in which Jefferson had some leverage to keep a unified legislative voting bloc. Furthermore, by 1803, partisanship was a regular factor in policy decisions in every significant issue domain.

Party Development: A Recapitulation

The political world of 1803 in the United States bore little resemblance to the world of 1789. When the First Congress convened, the only regularized opposition came from those Antifederalists who had fought the ratification of the Constitution. Madison and Jefferson still saw themselves as Federalists, Jefferson serving as Washington's secretary of state and Madison acting as a legislative leader for the administration in the House. But little time had passed before Madison withdrew his support and began to act the part of the opposition leader. The Republican interest then progressed from a disorganized opposition to Hamilton's fiscal policies to a better organized, although still unsuccessful, foe of the Jay Treaty. From there, the nation entered an era of intense partisanship culminating in the election of 1800 and the transfer of power that made the Republicans the majority party.

A review of the spatial configurations for the fourteen years of party growth has illustrated the dramatic appearance of polarized voting blocs. In this and the previous two chapters, the attempt has been to look at the election results that produced the seven Congresses and to consider the agenda of issues at each stage. It is difficult to speak with any great certainty about the degree of party competition in elections, since information is so scarce for these early contests. But it would be impossible not to conclude that parties were playing an increasing role in the electoral process across this period, coinciding with the rise of party voting in Congress.

Moreover, the study of the various issues before Congress also avoids simple answers. It is often difficult to compare the different issues that occupied Congress in any systematic way. The analysis in these chapters does make it clear that party voting took place in every issue area. While there were always individual roll calls that produced unusual coalitions, these were, by 1803, most likely to be on minor issues. In the final chapter, an attempt is made to draw together the analysis of the issue areas so as to uncover any systematic differences between domains and to determine whether the rise of party voting can in any way be attributed to the shifting agenda and the changing nature of issues.

9. Political Parties in Eighteenth-Century America

The loose patterns of association known as factionalism were present in nearly every colonial and national assembly predating the Constitution, and these patterns continued into the early years of Congress. For the First House, evidence of such patterns existed in the regional voting blocs. At least minimal patterns of association characteristic of factionalism can be detected for every Congress, with the exception of the unstructured voting of the First Senate. Indeed, it is difficult to imagine a legislative body without factions, particularly in a new nation with considerable geographic, economic, and cultural diversity.

While it seems certain that factions would arise, it was hardly inevitable that these factions should polarize. Yet there is no question that the empirical evidence shows such a movement. Examination of the chronological sequence of configurations, for either the House or the Senate, reveals a vivid picture of increasing polarization, culminating in the emergence of two highly cohesive voting blocs by 1797. These voting blocs were in fact more cohesive than twentieth century parties.

Two crucial questions can be raised with regard to this polarization of legislative voting. The first concerns the reasons why particular alignments developed, or in fact why any alignments appeared at all. The second is the fundamental question of whether these polarized voting blocs should be identified as parties.

Issues and the Emerging Alignments

Huntington (1968, p. 415) has argued that polarization is likely to be triggered by either "the cumulation of cleavages" or "the emergence of a single dominant issue which overshadows all others." In the American case he has suggested that the fiscal program presented by Hamilton to the First Congress met the latter criterion. The evidence presented here, however, does not support this claim, for the factions did not polarize for several years. This issue was merely a precursor of the new alignments, particularly in the leadership of Madison and his fellow Virginians. Numerous others (Bell, 1973; Charles, 1961; Cunningham, 1957) have suggested that the Jay Treaty provided the polarizing force. A more plausible case, however, can be made for the idea that polarization resulted from the cumulative effect of several issues, all of which came together in the Jay Treaty conflict.

Several cleavages were generally important in the early years of the new republic. One was the sectional division between North and South, which was manifested on issues such as the location of the capital for reasons of simple regional loyalty. A second significant cleavage was the conflict between commercial and agrarian interests (Beard, 1915). These economic differences were intensified by their convergence with the regional divisions. The northern economy was built upon commercial interests (shipping, fishing, trade, banking, and manufacturing), while the southern economy (with the exception of coastal South Carolina) was more agrarian, having an abundance of plantations dependent on slavery (Dauer, 1953). A third cleavage existed between coastal and interior regions. The former were naturally more concerned with trade and other commercial interests, while the latter, with agrarian economies, were concerned with internal improvements and protection of the frontier. A fourth cleavage set those wishing to maintain close relations with England against those more sympathetic to France. Against the background of the French Revolution, this division was a manifestation of a deeper philosophical disagreement over the form of democracy desired in this country, a dispute that provided the fifth major cleavage.

All five divisions were present in the political arena of 1795, and each tended to reinforce the emerging alignment of Federalists and Republicans. Federalists, coming most often from New England or the coastal regions of the Middle states and South Carolina, were generally representatives of commercial interests, sympathizers with the English, and supporters of a more aristocratic political system. Republicans, on the other hand, came generally from the interior or the South and were mostly allies of agrarian interests and believers in the direct democracy symbolized by the French Revolution.

The factions produced by these different cleavages were not always identical to each other or even as similar as they would become by the middle of the decade. This was most evident in the voting patterns of the First Congress. As illustrated by the comparison of certain key votes in table 8, there were at least three major distinct factions present in the House. But distinctive voting factions did not long persist as a principal feature of the Congress.

The different cleavages described above are closely related to the categorization of issues employed for the analysis in chapters 6, 7, and 8. This coincidence of groupings provides the opportunity to discuss the convergence of these different cleavages along with an overview of the changes in several issue domains.

The sectionalism that was so prominent in the political world of the late eighteenth century infused every issue domain, because the North and South were dissimilar in so many ways. In a later section, the argument that voting blocs are better characterized as regional than partisan is considered at greater length. The concern at this point is simply to identify those issues that may have provoked a more purely regional response.

The most obvious example was the controversy in the First Congress over locating the national capital. This issue in the end was complicated by the entry of strategic coalition formation and logrolling, but many of the early votes were clear cases of regional alliances. Another issue that should have produced a North-South cleavage was slavery, so strong sixty years later that it would split the country. But in the 1790s, slavery was the subject of an effective nondecision. So much did members of the political elite fear this issue that they effectively agreed not to debate it. When petitions on the subject were brought to Congress, they were dismissed with a near-unanimous vote.

In addition to these examples, there were other issues where sectionalism was a component of the decision. For example, there were a number of economic votes—taxes on a regional commodity like cotton and the collection of debts accumulated by certain states—on which the interests of various states and regions diverged. It should be noted, however, that in these cases sectionalism was not the central focus.

At this point, it seems fair to conclude that sectionalism was a pure factor motivating divisions only in the First Congress. Once a capital site had been determined, sectionalism did not reappear in such a blatant form. The subtle, but more long-lasting effects of sectionalism are the subject of further discussion later in the chapter.

Of obvious importance in the political debates of the early national period were the marked philosophical differences among the leadership of the new nation, differences that created a second major cleavage. Various issues had occupied time in the Constitutional Convention and other assemblies. These included the relative importance of federal and state governments and the amount of authority to be granted to the people. The Constitution, of course, was marked by a series of compromises on these crucial questions. But while compromise helped to diffuse these issues to some degree, they did persist in the deliberations of Congress.

The chief manifestation of these philosophical concerns came in the set of national authority votes taken during the First Congress. As was illustrated by the vector analysis of figure 21 and the comparisons in table 8, factions appeared on votes that were unlike the groups in opposition on other issues. But these were short-lived factions, since the national authority issue domain quickly declined as a major arena of conflict. This shifting of the agenda was primarily due to the fact that the legitimacy of the central government had been established by the ratification of the Constitution and the work of the First Congress. Broad philosophical questions were set aside while more mundane concerns came to the center.

It would be ideal if there were some more direct measures of the attitudes of congressional leaders toward popular government. Short of a comprehensive accumulation of evidence from writings and letters (or a posthumous opinion poll), such information is unavailable. There are those who have explored the philosophical bases of the emerging parties (Buel, 1972; Zvesper, 1977), and it is clear that these concerns were underneath many of the dominant issues. The imposition of taxes, alliance or opposition with France and England, and the establishment of a permanent army all were debated on deeper theoretical grounds as well as with the more immediate logic of partisan or regional advantage.

Nevertheless, it is clear that philosophical differences were not the immediate basis for the division into opposing parties. But it is equally evident that the parties had a substantial philosophical footing, just as they were solidly grounded in sectional biases.

Dating back at least to Beard (1915), the claim has been made that economic issues were crucial in explaining the alignments of the early Congresses. One can certainly not deny the importance of economic issues, especially in the First Congress. The debate in those sessions over Hamilton's fiscal programs was very intense, and it was this set of issues that pushed Madison and a few others into an opposition role. Furthermore, economic issues continued to play a substantial part in congressional proceedings throughout this period, although they made up a smaller proportion of all votes after 1795.

In spite of their importance, however, it appears that economic issues had a very mixed effect on alignments in Congress. Many of the roll call votes in this area involved something more than simply attitudes on economic policy. In the case of taxes and tariffs, the burden of taxation did not fall equally on all localities and groups in the country. Accordingly, these taxes drew a variety of opponents. Similarly, the ongoing attempts to settle the old debts of the states meant that one state or another would disproportionately benefit from the efforts of the federal government. Again, roll call votes often reveal these biases. Other votes in the area of domestic economics were as much based on responses to the administration as on basic questions of fiscal policy.

Economic interests did play a significant role in the eighteenth-century Congress. In some ways, those who argue for the prominence of economic concerns are vindicated by the influence of local economic interests on some of the revenue and debt settlement votes. But, in a more fundamental way, domestic economics appears relatively less central to the dominant alignments than some of the other key cleavages.

In the great tradition of the historian Frederick Jackson Turner, the impact of the frontier on the historical development of the United States can be viewed as a fourth issue domain relevant to the emerging congressional alignments. More specifically, there is the possibility of an alignment pitting those from the interior or frontier regions against the coastal interest.

Contrary to these expectations, however, the frontier never emerged as an important issue between 1789 and 1803. Even when the proportion of frontier votes reached 20% in the Third and Fourth Congresses, a majority of these involved the role of the army. While the army was primarily used for frontier protection at that time, debate on its role generated a broader set of concerns. Rarely did any issue clearly cause a split between the frontier representatives and others. Such a cleavage would have meant a quick defeat for frontier interests, given the distribution of population in the country.

In most cases, the Republicans were more sympathetic to frontier concerns, and self-interest suggests that western districts should have been represented by Republicans. It is true that the few members from districts across the mountains in Kentucky and Tennessee were all affiliated with the Republican side. But a broader look at the western districts in New York, Pennsylvania, Virginia, and North Carolina reveals little in the way of clear patterns. While these districts were probably more likely to elect Republicans than districts elsewhere in the nation, a number of Federalists were chosen from western districts.

In the end, the frontier cleavage, to the extent that it existed, was a minor one. Frontier protection never became a major item on the congressional agenda of this period. Still, the small role played by these issues was part of the set of factors that helped to shape the character of the emerging party system.

Questions of foreign policy were a major concern during the first decade of the new nation; thus, this fifth issue domain was the subject of considerable analysis in earlier chapters. During this entire period, the United States was being forced to deal with critical problems in its relations with France and England. Both countries took their turns at trying to intimidate their new rival into an inferior status. Different political interests in the United States had various motives for choosing alliances with one side or the other.

The first dramatic appearance of a foreign policy issue was the Jay Treaty debate in the Fourth Congress. At a time when the various blocs of interests were coalescing, controversy arose over ratification and implementation of the Jay Treaty. The treaty itself was the outcome of negotiations with Great Britain over a number of concerns, including British activity on the western frontier, British seizure of slaves during the war, American trade debts dating to before the war, the neutrality of American shipping in the war between Britain and France, and the general status of British-American trade. As the product of the Federalist administration, the treaty was opposed by the Republicans, who were particularly concerned about the favorable trade status granted to Britain at the expense of France and the failure to provide compensation for slaves seized by Britain (Chambers, 1963b; Charles, 1961; Varg, 1963).

As discussed in chapter 7, the Republicans mustered a substantial effort in their attempt to block the treaty. In the end, however, their followers were not united enough to bring victory. The Jay Treaty was significant because it represented in a single issue the cumulation of dominant cleavages in early American politics. The subsequent polarization of congressional voting and increased partisanship in electoral contests made this issue a crucial factor in the development of American political parties.

Nor was the Jay Treaty the only major component of foreign policy dealt with by Congress. Once the Jay Treaty went into effect, it stabilized relations with Great Britain for a time. But soon the focus turned to France, where the revolutionary government had taken an antagonistic view toward America's pro-England posture. The result was a state of undeclared war that the Republican leadership resisted. Much of the debate in the Fifth and Sixth Congresses was brought on by Republican attempts to block either hostile actions against France or extensive defensive preparations. Ultimately,

American policy was influenced more by the course of events than by political positions, but this fact did not cool the heated partisan tone of the debates.

No one can dispute the vital role of foreign policy issues in the emergence of partisanship during these early years. It is somewhat ironic, however, since foreign policy in later years has often been sheltered from the influence of party politics. But the crucial factor was undoubtedly the way in which divisions over foreign policy reinforced and heightened the conflicts over domestic policy.

Opposition Politics and the Policy Agenda

It is evident that the appearance of party voting was in no way limited to certain issue domains. Nevertheless, gradual changes in the agenda were related to the appearance of parties. The lessening importance of national authority issues and the failure of frontier protection to emerge as a big area of controversy prevented these items from providing competing lines of cleavage. Yet, in the end, even these issues generally divided the membership along the same lines as other issues.

If there was a clear common theme among the most partisan votes, it was the role of opposition to the government. The central issues all involved challenges by various leaders—eventually grouped in the Republican party—to the Federalist administrations of Washington and Adams. The economic policies of Hamilton were debated on their merits, but they also provoked direct criticism of Hamilton's role. Likewise, the Whiskey Rebellion of 1794 was a serious challenge to government legitimacy, but congressional debate centered mostly on the presidential condemnation of the "self-created societies." For the Jay Treaty, a key component of the debate was the administration's attempt to make policy without approval from the House of Representatives or its Republican group. During the Adams years, there was a continual process of move and countermove by the administration and opposition leaders in Congress, although it was further complicated by the lack of unity among the Federalists.

The theme of opposition to the administration is noteworthy for several reasons. First, the concept of opposition has been linked closely to the idea of party in theoretical literature (see chapter 1). Second, it is exceptional that a pattern of opposition politics would appear in an era when the legitimacy of opposition was generally questioned. People like Madison and Jefferson had feared the destructiveness of opposition, but they soon became the opposition. This paradoxical development is the subject of further discussion below.

The political opposition role being played by Republican leaders in Congress had even more direct implications for the party system. While the Republicans had implicitly resolved the contradictions between their beliefs about opposition and their practice of that role, the Federalists as the group in power saw the opportunity to act on their antiparty beliefs. By proposing the legislation known as the Alien and Sedition Acts, they attempted to protect themselves from serious opposition. As seen in the analysis in chapter 8, they were successful by means of their majority status at enacting this oppressive legislation, but they could not eliminate their opponents.

Nevertheless, the combined impact of regular opposition by the Republicans to administration proposals and the tough counterattack by the Federalists raised the heat of partisan acrimony while lowering the quality of debate, as illustrated by the Lyon-Griswold fight. Whether or not the participants would accept the name *party* for their groups, they were behaving much in the manner of partisan opponents.

All of these points lead directly back to that fundamental question: did parties exist by the beginning of the nineteenth century? In the pages that follow, a serious endeavor is made to address this question.

Sectional Influences and Political Parties

While there should be little question about the polarization of alignments in the early American Congresses, reasonable objections can be raised to the designation of polar voting blocs as parties. Formisano (1974), for example, has suggested that voting blocs may have formed not along party lines, but rather along lines related to such factors as regionalism and boardinghouse residences. Obviously, region and party were highly related during this period. But the multiplicity of cleavages would seem to deny a simply regional explanation. In fact, by the end of this era, the voting blocs had become less dominated by a single region. As long as the capital remained in New York or Philadelphia, boardinghouses were not a salient factor in congressional voting. Furthermore, when Congress did move to Washington in 1800, there is no evidence for distinct voting blocs corresponding to boardinghouse membership. Indeed, it is more likely that congressmen chose as messmates their established partisan allies. Thus, I argue that neither regionalism nor boardinghouses alone provide satisfactory explanations for the voting alliances.

A strong basis for geographical influences on political events already existed by 1789. The distinct origins of the colonies, the diverse cultural and economic bases in different areas, and the varying impact of the Revolution and other political issues all helped to create a variety of political cultures in the several states. In turn, this diversity produced different responses to the political cues of the new nation, in terms of acceptance of the idea of party and attachment to the positions of the two emerging groups.

The idea of regions is not simply a theoretical construct of later-day historians, geographers, and political scientists. It was evident from the writings of the day that people did invoke concepts of regionalism or sectionalism. A parochial New Englander such as Fisher Ames looked upon his colleagues from the South as if they came from a foreign land (Bernhard, 1965). And that keen observer Sen. William Maclay frequently made generalizations on a regional basis in his journal accounts (Maclay, 1927).

Sections were part of the American consciousness even before the ties with Britain were broken. New England, in fact, had a distinct regional identity as early as the seventeenth century. By the time of the Constitutional

Convention and the early Congresses, it was common to divide the states into sectional groups. This was true whether the reference was to one's legislative enemies or the administration of Indian affairs, the military or the courts. In 1793, a prominent American geographer described the American states as belonging to three divisions: North (New England), Middle (New York, New Jersey, Pennsylvania, Delaware), and South (Maryland, Virginia, Kentucky, North Carolina, South Carolina, Georgia). This seems to have been the standard categorization, with a single exception. Maryland is often grouped with the Middle states, its place being at best ambiguous (Mood, 1951).

For the purposes of the present study, three sections have been used, as described above, but with Maryland included among the Middle states. For some purposes, the West (Kentucky and Tennessee) has been distinguished from the South. While there are clear cultural and economic differences that call for this distinction, the region was not large enough by 1803 to be a very useful category for analysis. Placing Maryland with the Middle states is in part an arbitrary decision, since it has always been a "border" state. But there are enough factors that distinguish Maryland from the states below the Potomac to warrant excluding it from the South.

Political divisions began taking on a sectional character as soon as there was any sort of unified political action among the states. As the discussion in chapter 2 has elucidated, political differences between the sections were rooted in different forms of colonial government. But it was during the years under the Articles of Confederation that regional cleavages first became dominant, and these cleavages played a significant role in the Constitutional Convention. The New England states shared an economy based on trade, shipping, manufacturing, and other commercial interests, as well as an allegiance to the Congregationalist church. The South, on the other hand, had a generally agrarian economy, with an abundance of slaveholding plantations and a deferential political culture. The Middle states represented a mixture of the characteristics of the other regions, with economies built on both agriculture and commerce. In general, these states included the larger, more cosmopolitan cities and a more developed political system (Dauer, 1953).

That regionalism was a key factor in understanding early congressional voting patterns is readily apparent from an examination of the spatial configurations for the early Congresses. Some general observations should recall the more detailed commentary from earlier chapters. In either the House or Senate, voting patterns in the earliest Congresses (especially the First and Second) had a strong regional flavor. A high level of unity existed among the New England delegates and among those from the South. Only a few isolated individuals from those regions failed to align themselves with their geographical neighbors. Members from the Middle states were less united, however. In the First House, those from New York and part of New Jersey were aligned with New England, while a group from Pennsylvania, Delaware, and southern New Jersey formed an independent voting bloc. In other sessions, the Middle states were rarely represented by a distinct voting bloc, instead aligning themselves with one of the two dominant regional blocs.

As the 1790s progressed, the voting blocs were moving from a regional basis to a more partisan nature. Divisions within the delegations of the several

Table 19. Distribution of Congressmen in the MDS Space: An Analysis of Variance

House	State	Region	Party		
			Bell	Dauer	ICPSR
First	.704	.448	.154	——	.097
Second	.625	.393	.269	——	.263
Third	.544	.406	.541	——	.592
Fourth	.399	.374	.653	.684	.427
Fifth	.382	.358	.933	.932	.499
Sixth	.200	.181	.811	.811	.718
Seventh	.278	.174	——	.840	.760

Note: Entries are adjusted E^2.

Middle states became more clearly based on party lines, and a degree of partisan diversity began to emerge in the South and New England. Again, the specifics of this trend have already been discussed. But an overview can be presented by an analysis of the distribution of congressmen in the scaling space, using a technique analogous to classical analysis of variance.[1]

Direct comparisons between the impact of party and region on congressional voting are hindered by the variety of party variables (see Appendix A). But while the accuracy of these party variables differs, the trend in party voting is clear for any of them. In table 19, we see the adjusted E^2 for each variable in each Congress; this statistic represents the amount of variation in the MDS space accounted for by a particular variable, as adjusted for the number of cases (degrees of freedom).

The basic trends in table 19 are undeniable; party became increasingly related to the voting patterns, while sectional influences declined across this period. Regardless of which party variable is considered, the influence of party surpassed that of region beginning in the Third Congress. This is fully consistent with the observations made above. Regional and state influences were important in the earlier Congresses. In fact, sectionalism remained an important characteristic of congressional voting through the Fifth Congress, although its significance began to pale in comparison to that of party. But in the Sixth and Seventh Congresses, the role of sectionalism nearly disappeared. By that time, two-party competition had emerged in just about every state. What sectional influences remained were probably a result more of the dominance of one party in a particular state than of any truly regional voting patterns.

These results have shown that sectionalism had indeed declined during this decade as a determinant of congressional roll call voting. This finding, together with the absence of purely regional issues after the First Congress (as noted earlier), helps to strengthen the argument that congressional voting blocs were not best explained by sectionalism. It has been speculated that the decline of regional voting reflected an increasing partisan diversity within each part of the country. The discussion that follows traces the rise of two-party competition in the three major regions.

The cause of Federalism in the South can trace its roots to the debates over the federal Constitution. In each state there was a large group supporting ratification (large enough to win), and such groups were generally known as Federalists. The Federalist advantage, however, was narrow and might not have held up in a statewide popular count. Nevertheless, most of those who were sent to the First Congress from southern states were generally identified as Federalists (Paullin, 1904). Yet, there was a key distinction between these Federalists and those who claimed a Federalist affiliation in later years.

Voting patterns in the First and Second Congresses had a strong regional basis, as shown previously. In the first four years, the only southerners who voted in agreement with the New England Federalists were several members from South Carolina, who represented the coastal regions of that state. This small nucleus was the beginning of a true Federalist stronghold in the South. The important shipping and trading interests centered in Charleston were a key reason for this center of Federalist strength.

In North Carolina, the Antifederalists had been strong enough to delay ratification of the Constitution for one year. Yet there, too, the first congressional delegation was dominated by Federalists—four of five House members and both senators. On the basis of voting records, however, most of these people would be better described as Republicans. As observed by one historian, "even the nominal Federalists were not at this date suspected of entertaining the principles of loose constitutional construction and national centralization of powers for which the term 'Federalist' was soon to stand in the South" (Wagstaff, 1910, p. 24).

Still, there were times when even the Federalist label and an occasional vote in favor of Hamilton's programs were sufficient to endanger the political life of a North Carolina politician. Illustrative of these difficulties were the careers of Steele and Hawkins. Steele was elected to the House in 1789 and 1791 as a Federalist, but in the First Congress his voting record placed him in the middle of the southern bloc (see figure 17). By the Second Congress, his position was more central (see figure 25) but probably a little closer to the bloc of southern Republicans. Yet, as a candidate for the House in 1791 and later (in 1795) for the Senate, he was charged regularly with being a friend of Hamilton and a supporter of his policies. These charges apparently cost him a chance for the Senate. Hawkins was faced with a similar problem. While he retired voluntarily from the Senate in 1795, his reputation in the state was linked closely to Hamilton. Yet the votes he cast scarcely distinguished him from most of his southern colleagues (Gilpatrick, 1931; Wagstaff, 1910).

The situation in Virginia was similar to that in North Carolina but with one important difference. Many politicians followed the lead of Madison into a clear opposition role and thus were able to shed their Federalist labels. Of course, formal party labels never existed in this period; but it would appear that Madison's leadership role benefited some of his colleagues.

In general, there had been a core of "old" Federalists in each southern state, men whose political identities were primarily shaped by the issue of ratification. Some of these men moved into the opposition in response to Hamilton's economic proposals; others maintained a very weak loyalty to the emerging Federalist position on the new issues of the day. There were only a few southern members of Congress prior to 1797 who could be accurately identified with the new Federalist party, on the basis of their voting records. Most of these were from coastal South Carolina, but there was one Virginia Federalist. Richard Bland Lee served three terms in the House (1789-1795), but only in the Third Congress did his votes place him clearly with the northern Federalists, and he was rewarded for this record by a subsequent defeat (Cunningham, 1957, pp. 74-77).

While there was little southern Federalist representation in the Congress, there were beginnings of a new-style Federalist party in the southern states. "Policy, patronage, and simply the passage of time made of these southern proadministration interests of 1793 something far different from the old Federalist parties which existed there in 1787 and 1788" (Rose, 1968, p. 45). These new groups, which could hardly be called parties, provided at least a nucleus of support for the policies of the administration and a base on which stronger groups could be built.

This new Federalist strength finally appeared in the partisan era that followed the Jay Treaty session. The 1798 and 1800 elections, as seen in chapter 8, brought life into the southern Federalist group. Even then, however, they never succeeded in creating any substantial organizations. Had the Federalists not been so devastated nationally by the 1800 election, they might have been able to build on their southern beginnings. In any case, their short-lived success is evidence that they were more than a regional faction.[2]

Prior to the election of 1800, there was only a very small core of Republicans coming from the New England region. Domination by a single party was far greater there than in the South. Perhaps this was due to the general degree of homogeneity in the region. In any case, the Republican interest was chiefly represented by a set of individuals rather than by a unified bloc (Robinson, 1916).

The only New England state with a regular Republican presence was Vermont. It was the only state in the region without a coastline, and in many ways it had the characteristics of a frontier state. Given its differences from the other New England states, it is not surprising that Republicans made progress there. A steady delegation of Republicans represented Vermont in the Congress, including Lyon, whose exploits proved he was no marginal member of his party.

In the neighboring state of New Hampshire, John Langdon served for some years as a prominent Republican senator. But it is generally agreed that there was little organized party activity on either side. Many New Hampshire politicians were mavericks—men like Gilman and Livermore.

Outside of Vermont, the only significant Republican activity in New England was in Massachusetts. Active chapters of the Republican Society helped to breathe some life into the opposition party. As a result, several Republicans were sent to Congress from the state. But even here, much of the strength of the Republican party was due to local causes. The prominent role played by revolutionary leaders like Hancock, Gerry, and Sam Adams was crucial in developing a viable Republican party. But they often failed to agree among themselves or with the national leadership. The limited Republican strength in Massachusetts, like the Federalist groups in some southern states, was significant for its presence but still limited in its importance (Formisano, 1983; Goodman, 1964).

As discussed in chapter 8, the 1800 elections revealed fairly dramatic increases in Republican strength in New England, and the party's presence grew still further in subsequent years. Two-party politics was very slow to appear in New England, but it did eventually emerge. Like the rise of southern Federalism, this trend helps to support the thesis that the two competing voting blocs were not simply regional interest groups.

Finally, substantial attention was given to developments in the Middle states in previous sections of this work, and it would be repetitious to add much here. Additionally, historians have discussed in some detail the appearance of partisan politics in New York (Young, 1967), Pennsylvania (Tinkcom, 1950), New Jersey (Prince, 1967), and Maryland (Renzulli, 1972; Risjord, 1978). These rich treatments show clearly that a two-party system became a feature of politics in these states, although the timing and extent of developments varied from one state to the next. Only in Delaware, of all the Middle states, did one party (the Federalists) manage to maintain a near-perfect domination of political power.

The Boardinghouse and Voting Blocs

The boardinghouse theory of congressional voting was originally put forward by Young (1966), and Formisano (1974) has suggested that this theory might be a better explanation of early voting agreement than a theory of party politics. The role of the boardinghouse as a center of political activity was discussed in chapter 4, and it was seen that there were strong linkages between social structures in the community and political life.

But it is equally clear that the boardinghouses were not the central fact in political alliances, at least for the years from 1789 to 1803. During the years in New York and Philadelphia, members were scattered among a large number of residences (boardinghouses, hotels, and private homes), and many lived alone (or at least not with other members of Congress). A comparison of members' residences (Goldman and Young, 1973) with their alliances on roll call votes (from the configurations) fails to reveal, for this period, any substantial patterns supporting Young's thesis.

Because most members found boardinghouse partners among their colleagues from the same region, there was a substantial voting agreement among those living together. But it appears most accurate to regard such a correlation as spurious. Although it is ultimately impossible to assert statements of causality in this situation, it seems quite clear that the coincidence of residence and voting patterns occurred because members wanted compatible living situations. Life was more pleasant if one shared meals and evening entertainment with those on the same side of the day's political debates.

Some confirmation of these ideas comes from observing residence patterns for the first sessions in Washington. Directories are available for the two sessions of the Seventh Congress, although not for the second session of the Sixth, the first one in Washington (Goldman and Young, 1973). The proportion of members living in group residences and the number in each residence were greater than in Philadelphia. But there was no change in the tendency of each residence to house only members from a particular party or voting bloc. While this appears at first to support Young, more careful reflection suggests that other explanations work better. Since high levels of cohesion were present in the previous sessions in Philadelphia, I would argue that members upon arriving in Washington sought out colleagues from the same party in seeking a boardinghouse group. Thus, the agreement with boardinghouses was a direct *result* of the agreement within parties. This is further supported by the absence of any kind of clustering within the two party groups, to match the boardinghouse groups.

A more complete consideration of the boardinghouse theory should address various other concerns. One plausible hypothesis would be that new members were socialized into the legislative system and were led to strict agreement with their party by their boardinghouse associations. More generally, the boardinghouse might have served as a substitute for a system of party organization in Congress, as an informal whip system. One might also suggest that boardinghouse groups came to serve as an alternative source of agreement in later years, as the Federalist presence dwindled and the Republicans became divided. These interpretations might lend support to Young's thesis. But, because his empirical analysis commenced with the 1807 Congress, I cannot challenge his findings directly. Even so, Bogue and Marlaire (1975) have challenged Young's theory as it applied to the period from 1821 to 1842.

The important point here is that boardinghouse patterns were *not* a reasonable substitute for partisan politics as an explanation of voting cohesion, a conclusion also reached by Cunningham (1978*b*, pp. 282-87), who found support for the partisan basis of residence groups in the statements of members of Congress from the Jeffersonian years.

Partisan Voting Blocs and the Elements of Party

It appears evident that the high levels of voting cohesion by the start of the nineteenth century cannot be explained simply by factors such as sectionalism or the sharing of boardinghouse residences, nor by the appearance of issue-based factions. With the rejection of these alternative characterizations of voting blocs, we might conclude that we have isolated partisan voting blocs. Indeed, all the evidence presented thus far can reasonably be considered to support such a conclusion.

Nevertheless, there is more to the idea of party than simply the existence of congressional voting blocs. The several aspects of party identified in chapter 1 included common symbols or labels and groups of supporters in the electorate. Formisano (1974, p. 748) has pointed out, "Multivariate analysis of roll calls needs to be accompanied by evidence that men ran for Congress as openly identified members of a party. To show convincingly that the core factions of Federalist and Republican interests came to think of themselves in party terms, consideration must be given to legislators' self-images. ... " In the next few pages, we consider those elements of party other than cohesive voting by members of Congress. This brief review includes, first, evidence of the use of party labels in general discourse about politics, especially in the press. Second, it evaluates the degree to which public officials and candidates for office saw themselves and their contemporaries in partisan terms. Third, it looks at the actual involvement of party and partisan voting in elections, especially those for Congress. Finally, to complete the consideration of the elements of party, we review the evidence for the existence of party organizations. These comments finally allow us to draw conclusions about the existence of parties in the early national period.

Because the eighteenth-century parties had no legal status, we cannot look to some official document for a proper label or name for each group. We can, however, observe the use of labels in actual practice as one clue to the growing acceptance of parties. But such observations are difficult to make, because we must depend on the limited documentation surviving into the present.

Ideally, a comprehensive search should be made among the extant correspondence of members of Congress and other political leaders, together with the prominent newspapers of the day. Such a search could reveal not only the use of the Federalist and Republican labels, and other party designations, but also the incidence of references to the term *party*. The former information would aid in seeing whether voting blocs had taken on a true identity, while the latter might be a key to understanding how the idea of party eventually came to be accepted. A systematic search such as this requires resources far beyond those available to this project, but it might be quite revealing.[3] In the absence of such information, we must rely on the less systematic commentary of historians and a few selected writings of leaders of the period.

As we have seen, the earliest development of parties came in New York and Pennsylvania. But even here, the use of labels tended to trail the appearance of partisanship. In Young's (1967, p. 314) account of the rise of the Republican party in New York, he has noted Edward Livingston's use of the term *Republican* in a 1792 letter. A newspaper account later that same year stated that "there are two parties at present in the United States," and distinction was made between "Aristocrats ... endeavoring to lay the foundations of monarchical government ... [and Republicans] the real supporters of independence, friends to equal rights and warm advocates of a free elective government" (*N.-Y. Journal*, October 3, 1792, quoted in Young, 1967, p. 325). In spite of this evidence that party labels were gaining in acceptance, it is clear that it was not until at least 1796 or 1797 that the use of party labels was widespread in New York (Young, 1967, p. 576).

In Pennsylvania, Tinkcom (1950) has documented some early cases of the designation of party groups by name. In 1796, Bache, Republican editor of the *Aurora*, reported on election results in terms of parties. In one contest, he referred to a "majority for Republican Candidates," and in another to a majority "against [the] Republican Ticket" (quoted in Tinkcom, 1950, p. 161). The use of the Republican label (although not the word *Federalist*) was apparently the first such designation in a Pennsylvania newspaper. Fenno, of the Federalist-leaning *Gazette*, reversed the usage, referring to "Federalists" and "Anti-Federalists" (Tinkcom, 1950, pp. 161-62).

By the time of assembly elections in 1797, according to Tinkcom (1950, pp. 175-80), party labels were taking on "distinctive meanings." Since these elections followed the Jay Treaty debate and the Adams-Jefferson election in 1796, it should not be surprising that labels were more easily accepted by that time. "This is not to say that the practice of listing tickets under general labels suddenly became common or general: both Federalist and Republican editors still manifested a reluctance to concede formal recognition to the group they opposed by dignifying it with any inclusive identifying term that was not derogatory. Nevertheless, general party terms were beginning to creep into editorial phraseology" (Tinkcom, 1950, pp. 179-80). But at least in Pennsylvania and New York, party labels were gaining some acceptance.

It is clear that the use of party labels, not to mention agreement on appropriate labels, was slow to appear in the 1790s, especially in other states. The terms were at first more often used as epithets than as straight labels of identification. The newspapers were likely to be the first to publicize the names of parties, but most publishers were spokesmen for one of the parties and thus used their papers to advance those causes. Accordingly, they are not neutral sources for providing party labels.

The confusion over the variety of terms used to denote parties was stated in a letter published in the Northumberland *Gazette* in 1799: "I will not pretend to define or describe an Aristocrat, a Democrat, a Jacobin, a Sans-culot, a Frenchman, an Anarchist, a Revolutionist, a Leveller, a Disorganiser, a Regicide, a Liberticide, etc. etc. etc. or even a Federal, an Antifederal, or a Friend of Government; for I am utterly unable to fix their boundary lines, or trace their shades of difference; and I make perpetual blunders when I attempt to apply them to my neighbors" (Thomas Cooper, quoted in Tinkcom, 1950, p. 235). In a second letter, Cooper tried to sort out this confusion, concluding that the appropriate general terms were *Federalist* and *Republican*. Another attempt to deal with the plethora of labels came in a letter written by Jefferson:

> It is now well understood that two political Sects have arisen within the U.S. the one believing that the executive is the branch of our government which the most needs support; the other that like the analogous branch in the English Government, it is already too strong for the republican parts of the constitution; and therefore in equivocal cases they incline to the legislative powers: the former of these are called federalists, sometimes aristocrats or monocrats, and sometimes tories, after the corresponding sect in the English Government of exactly the same definition: the latter are stiled republicans, whigs, jacobins, anarchists, disorganizers etc. These terms are in familiar use with most persons . . . [Jefferson to John Wise, February 12, 1798, quoted in Cunningham, 1965, pp. 18-19].

These two sets of comments demonstrate that even toward the end of the century, no consensus existed on the identity of the two parties. At the same time, there was a general sense of understanding around different terms.

By the election of 1800, the confusion was quickly subsiding. That election, posed so clearly in partisan terms, helped to bring the terms *Federalist* and *Republican* into more common usage. As we shall see again below, the antiparty traditions continued to delay the open use of party labels. But most political observers and participants were fully aware of the dominant labels by the end of the century.

A concern closely related to the use of party labels is the development of partisan attitudes by political leaders. In order to speak convincingly about the emergence of parties, we need to know that we are not imposing a modern institutional structure onto the heads of eighteenth-century politicians. Even if we know reference is being made to group labels, that does not necessarily imply an acceptance of these as *party* labels.

This is a difficult concern to address for two reasons. First, as discussed in chapter 1, our modern concept of party does not match the concept in the 1790s. Even if we succeed in stripping the term of its more complex institutional meanings from modern usage, we must still face the value connotations of the word *party*. Politicians in the early national period might not have referred to political parties, because of the negative meaning connected to the concept.

Futhermore, even if this problem could be resolved, we are left with a lack of data on the subject of partisan self-images. A content analysis of private correspondence, similar to that described above for party labels, could be used to search for references to the party concept. But again, such an understanding would require a substantial allocation of resources and could not be attempted for this project. Once more we seek some evidence from secondary accounts.

The traditional attitude was illustrated by Ames, who as late as 1798 maintained his position that an opposition party would eventually be destructive to the government. As an avid Federalist, he saw the partisan struggle as one of good against evil. While he seemed most often to use the term *faction*, one suspects that he would have found the terms interchangeable, as Madison had used them in *The Federalist* (Bernhard, 1965).

It was this traditional view, held by many of the early political leaders, that probably deterred people from describing themselves as party members. Yet, even while they avoided the term or even condemned the parties, their actions and statements made it clear that they perceived themselves as part of the partisan battle. Cunningham (1978a, p. xxxvii), in introductory remarks for his compilation of circular letters from congressmen to their constituents, notes, "Not only were the comments on circular-letter writing unusually partisan during the Federalist years under Adams, but the letters themselves appear more partisan during these years than at any other time."

By 1800, nearly everyone could be classified as a Federalist or a Republican, based on voting records. But in addition, most regarded themselves as attached to the party with which they cast their votes. In 1801, Jefferson noted, "We [the Republicans] have a very commanding majority in the house" (letter, quoted in Cunningham, 1978b, p. 273). And an unsuccessful candidate for Congress wrote, in an open letter to his North Carolina district in 1800, about his partisan ties:

> To those of my Fellow-Citizens with whom I have not a personal Acquaintance, and who may not therefore be informed of my Political Principles, it may be necessary to state, that I am what the Phraseology of Politicians has denominated a FEDERALIST. But, although I am *the Friend of Order, of Government, and of the present Administration*, I will not pledge myself to support, in Consequence of a selfish, or a bigoted Policy, any Governmental Measure which I might think pernicious to the General Welfare of our Country, or the particular Interests of yourselves. [Samuel D. Purviance to the Freemen of Fayetteville District, July 1, 1800, quoted in Cunningham, 1965, p. 137].

Thus, Purviance was willing to identify himself as a Federalist, but he felt it necessary to qualify this designation.

While the evidence is very limited, it seems that this statement by a congressional candidate is representative of what others might have said had they felt it necessary to make a statement of their position. The concept of party was not an easy one to accept, given the historical and philosophical background of the period. Nevertheless, there was a clear trend toward an acceptance (not always articulated in public) of party terminology.

In chapter 1, we noted that a key element in defining the concept of party was the function of seeking power through the electoral process. This electoral connection was seen to be central in the movement of a party from the stage of polarization toward expansion and institutionalization. Nevertheless, the state of electoral traditions and institutions by the end of the eighteenth century placed a serious check on the role of the new parties (see chapter 3).

Before the congressional groups had polarized into two cohesive voting blocs (prior to 1796), elections rarely had any formal party involvement. Although certain exceptions were noted in chapters 6 and 7, these either came from the more developed party systems of New York and Pennsylvania or else were affected by specific local situations.

Even in New York and Pennsylvania, partisanship was muted up to 1796, as illustrated by this characterization of the 1795 elections in New York: "What gave the campaign a deceptive surface calm was an effort by each party to give the appearance of nonpartisanship. Both parties still avoided a label and clung to the customary usage in state politics of 'the supporters of Mr. Jay' or 'the friends of Mr. Yates' " (Young, 1967, p. 436). We saw above that it was only in 1796 that party terms were becoming accepted in Pennsylvania elections.

With the polarization of congressional voting sparked by the Jay Treaty debates and the other events of 1796, elections took on a more openly partisan tone. We saw evidence of this change in chapter 8. While parties were involved most actively in the Middle states, the other regions began to see a significant role being played by parties in the elections. "By the end of the decade of the nineties, the growth of political parties had wrought fundamental alterations in the political life of the country. The formation of parties was accompanied by a growth of campaigning; elections became more warmly contested, and even the most staid New England towns became infected with what their people had denounced as the 'vile practice of electioneering'" (Cunningham, 1957, pp. 251-52). Although traditional political norms still limited the display of partisanship, the new parties were gradually causing the erosion of the old norms.

An illustration of the degree of partisanship in elections was made possible by the data found in some old poll books in Maryland. Bohmer (1978) has used these data to demonstrate the patterns of individual attachment to party in a series of elections from 1796 to 1802, an effort made possible by the viva voce system of voting still in effect in Maryland until 1803 (see chapter 3 for a discussion of voting methods).

Bohmer shows first, with an aggregate analysis of county voting data, that when elections were contested by the two parties, voter turnout was generally high—over 50%. Furthermore, there was a strong persistence of the partisan distribution in each county over a series of elections. Thus, it appears that the parties were able to mobilize voters and to hold onto a broad and stable following in the electorate.

Bohmer further strengthens his findings about the importance of party voting, in moving to the analysis of individual votes from the poll books in two counties with competitive parties. He finds that the degree of party loyalty by the voters was very high. About 62% of the voters in one county and 80% in the other did not defect from their party's candidates in eight elections over a seven-year period, a record that would be hard to match in the modern era. This was true in spite of a variety of issues and candidates in elections for local, state, and national office. While the outcomes did not always favor the same party, this result was due to fluctuating turnout and not to voters switching parties from one election to the next.

This evidence, together with other signs of party involvement in elections, leads us still closer to the conclusion that late eighteenth-century groups can accurately be called parties. With appropriate adjustments for the old norms and traditions, this is a picture of party activity. While more research of the type done by Bohmer is needed, the direction of the evidence appears unmistakable. All that remains is a final look at the presence of party organizations.

The organizational element was probably the least developed segment of the early political parties. To form such a party unit would be too direct a confrontation of the traditional political norms of the era. Nevertheless, some informal organization did appear in the 1790s, both in Congress and in the states.

Evidence was presented in earlier chapters of the informal but often effective leadership provided by men such as Hamilton, Ames, Madison, and Gallatin. In addition, party caucuses are known to have been held, and they apparently had some impact on voting in the later years of this period. Many years passed before formal party structures appeared in Congress, but it is clear that the idea of organizing along party lines was not unimagined in the 1790s.

The appearance of organizational efforts in the elections of the several states began to occur in this period as well. Cunningham (1957) has built a strong case for the emergence of local organizations of the Republican party, and he argues that they were stimulated by the efforts of the congressional party group. Samples of these groups were given in the discussion of elections held from 1796 to 1800 (in chapter 8).

Once again, if eighteenth-century party organizations are to be judged by twentieth-century standards, they fall far short of the mark. But in the context of eighteenth-century norms and historical precedent, the efforts at party organizations were actually quite amazing.

The determination of whether parties existed in the 1790s has tended to become a game of definitions, where different conceptualizations have led to a variety of conclusions. It is certainly evident that this was a decade of party development—whether the word *party* is appropriate at any particular time should not be all that crucial.

In chapter 1, I set forth a view of party as a continuum from preparty politics to a highly institutionalized modern party system. The end of this continuum is one that has probably been attained at few points in history, and present-day American parties clearly fall short. Thus, it is not a startling conclusion to state that parties had not reached such a level of development by 1800. On the other hand, the groups competing for power in the 1800 election had certainly moved away from the least-developed end of the continuum.

American party politics took great strides during the decade of the 1790s, and the research here has helped to fill in the picture of a continually increasing prominence for parties in that era. In 1790, congressmen were voting together in regional and issue-based factions whose composition shifted considerably from one question to the next. By 1792, patterns of voting were beginning a clear transition from regional factions to an era of partisan politics, with conflict based on a variety of issues and evaluations of administration performance. By 1796, these voting patterns had polarized so much that two blocs of congressmen opposed each other on nearly every issue. The Jay Treaty debate that year was vital in leading to a coalescence of interests into the two competing party blocs. In just a few years, the political system had moved along the continuum from factionalism to polarization.

In the next several years, from 1797 to 1803, the parties continued to develop at an astounding pace. Whereas the earlier developments had nearly all taken place within the Congress, these later years saw the expansion of party politics into a broader arena. As the cohesiveness of party groups in Congress reached very high levels, party affiliations became a more significant factor in congressional elections. There were signs that party loyalties were reaching the general public and that rudimentary organizations were playing a greater role. These trends continued at least until 1803. Only thereafter, with the decline of the Federalists, did the nation experience a temporary hiatus in the process of party development.

Formisano (1974, 1981) has criticized the research on early party development for equating partisan voting blocs with fully developed parties and for referring to party systems at a time when many elements of party organization were not much in evidence. I would, however, return to the warning that we must not evaluate the eighteenth-century political world with twentieth-century concepts, unless we understand fully the eighteenth-century context.

It is in this context that the changes in the fourteen years from 1789 to 1803 were nothing short of remarkable. Parties had moved from factionalism through polarization into the expansion stage. A full and open involvement of the parties in the electoral process, as well as a degree of institutionalization, was not to take place until a number of years had passed. But the development of a permanent party system had begun to take place, to a degree that had not been foreseen a few years earlier.

Reflections: Parties in an Antiparty Age

When the new government was created by the Constituion, most political leaders shared a strong antiparty tradition.[4] Parties were perceived as agencies that would hinder the progress of good government, a view expressed forcefully by Madison in *The Federalist*, No. 10: "Among the numerous advantages promised by a well constructed Union, none deserves to be more accurately developed than its tendency to break and control the violence of faction" (Hamilton, Madison, Jay, 1961, p. 77). Yet, in spite of such sentiments, parties very quickly became a prominent feature of the political system. This antiparty stigma does, however, help to account for the fact that parties had not reached the highest stages of development during this period. The reluctance of candidates to run openly for office as members of a party and the failure of leaders to develop any substantial national organization were two factors that might be explained in part by this distrust of the idea of a party system.

One explanation for the anomaly of party development within the context of an antiparty tradition lies in the lack of any positive historical precedent. Nowhere in the eighteenth-century world did parties exist by any modern definition. There was considerable factionalism, both in Great Britain and in colonial America, but no clear development of parties beyond this stage (see chapter 2). Therefore, in their antiparty statements, American political thinkers were dealing with a concept of party that today would be characterized as faction. They simply did not recognize the possibility of a more constructive political party until some time after they had actually created such parties.

A second explanation for this anomaly lies in the emerging idea of legitimate opposition. Some of the philosophical objections to the idea of party were based on the belief that parties might hinder development of the unanimity considered essential for the stability of a state. People gradually realized that unanimity was impossible in a diverse society and that the right of opposition had to be recognized. Sartori (1976, p. 11) has suggested that "parties presuppose—for their acceptance and proper functioning—peace under a constitutional rule." The first set of elections for Congress (between

1788 and 1790) showed that the Constitution was quickly being accepted. In spite of large numbers opposing ratification in some states, most new congressmen were supporters of the Constitution. Furthermore, even an Antifederalist such as Elbridge Gerry could be found arguing in debate, "If this constitution, which is now ratified, be not supported, I despair of ever having a government for these United States" (Austin, 1829, p. 103).

When it became clear that the opposition was concerned only with specific policy alternatives within the existing constitutional system, it was far easier for such opposition to be tolerated. Once the legitimacy of opposition was established, the acceptance of parties followed. This was, of course, a slow process. The Sedition Act, passed by Federalist majorities in 1798, represented the old tradition. Nevertheless, the progress of party development was not seriously deterred by this act of a declining Federalist majority. Only two years later, the Republicans were victorious in both presidential and congressional elections. The peaceful transfer of power in 1801 reflected growing acceptance of the legitimacy of opposition and the idea of party.

In 1804, Thomas Jefferson wrote in a letter, "The party division in this country is certainly not among it's [sic] pleasant features. To a certain degree it will always exist" (Cunningham, 1965, p. 19). By this time, nearly everyone in Congress was clearly associated with one of the new parties. Acceptance of these parties, however, came reluctantly as their inevitability became more apparent. Whether recognized by those involved or still regarded as an undesirable development, the changing voting patterns exhibited by members of Congress between 1789 and 1803 and the subsequent development of popular and organizational elements provide strong evidence that a true party system had emerged.

APPENDIX A
Party Affiliation of Members of Congress

An important concern for the empirical analysis in this book is the correct identification of party affiliations for those who served in Congress between 1789 and 1803. Because many politicians did not readily and openly identify with any political party at this time, no definitive set of party labels exists for the congressmen who served in this period. Existing references, such as the *Biographical Directory of the American Congress*, have proved to be unreliable sources of information on party labels. In this appendix, I evaluate the available published sources for individual party affiliations and for the partisan breakdown of each Congress. Furthermore, I discuss and display my attempts to compile a definitive list of party affiliations for the individuals serving in Congress from 1789 to 1803, drawing from all available sources, including state histories, biographies, and contemporary newspapers and correspondence. The most recent and most comprehensive effort to publish a compilation of party affiliations is currently being undertaken by Kenneth Martis, in connection with his publication of *The Historical Atlas of United States Congressional Districts, 1789–1983* (Martis, 1982).

Individual Party Affiliations

In the modern Congress, the party affiliation of a member is a well-known fact, available in nearly any congressional publication and the basis for organizing committee and leadership positions, as well as staffing. But in the early years of Congress, this information was not so readily available: "Party affiliations of Representatives are identified for the first time in the official record of proceedings for the 28th Congress (1843); party affiliations of Senators for the first time in the *Congressional Globe* for the following Congress" (Young, 1966, p. 271n). Several attempts have been made since those early years to determine the party to which members of Congress belonged. One such attempt is the work of congressional staff members in compiling the *Biographical Directory of the American Congress*. Another effort began during the New Deal as a program to help unemployed academics, and a third culminated in the computer data archives of the ICPSR. In addition, several historians have compiled party affiliations for specific Congresses. These various sources can be evaluated in terms of their completeness and accuracy. Tables 24 and 25 display the most important listings of party affiliations.

The first official compilation of congressional biographies was published in 1859 by Charles Lanman. It did not, however, contain any information on party membership. There have been ten subsequent editions of this compilation, published under a

Table 20. Party Labels in the *Biographical Directory*

House	% with no party label
First	53.0
Second	48.6
Third	46.4
Fourth	40.0
Fifth	41.0
Sixth	28.9
Seventh	32.8

Source: U.S., Congress (1971).

variety of titles. The first one to include any party information was published in 1878 by Benjamin Poore.[1] The most recent edition is the *Biographical Directory of the American Congress 1774-1971*, which was published in 1971, again including party membership. The information in these biographical directories was compiled by congressional staff members, "from currently available biographical works, or revised in accordance with verified new information on earlier Members, generally made available by historical associations and individuals interested in family genealogy" (U.S., Congress, 1971, p. 9). It turns out that the 1971 edition differs little from the 1878 one in terms of party affiliation of early congressmen. While not every entry has been cross-checked, I found only one instance where the older book had better information: Abraham Baldwin of Georgia was listed in 1878 as a Republican, while more recent editions label him a Federalist. Accounts of his role in Congress, as well as his voting record, make it apparent that the former is more accurate in this case.

Although one might initially consider the *Biographical Directory* a good source because it has the official sanction of the U.S. Congress, its quality turns out to be questionable. The first problem is one of completeness, as many congressmen have no party listed (see table 20). Overall, only 58.1% of the 344 congressmen who served from 1789 to 1803 have party labels listed, thus limiting the usefulness of this source. But it is also true that the proportion with partisan affiliations was increasing during this period. While this may be an artifact of the incompleteness, it may also be an illustration of the growing acceptance of party labels as the party system developed.

The accuracy of the *Biographical Directory* is also open to question, however, Several individuals are listed as members of parties not existing in any form at that time. But we must defer an assessment of accuracy until other sources have been presented, thus allowing comparisons. One general difficulty lies in the fact that the *Biographical Directory* normally lists only a single party designation for a member's service in Congress. Thus, one who obtains a partisan affiliation only after several years in office is indistinguishable from one who is initially selected as a party identifier.

As part of the Works Progress Administration during the New Deal, numerous projects were undertaken to provide useful work for unemployed scholars, especially the preparation of inventories of historical government documents. One such project was the *Atlas of Congressional Roll Calls*, the work of the Historical Records Survey in New York City and New Jersey. Its goal was "the production of a complete series of maps portraying every one of approximately 54,000 Yea-and-Nay roll call votes

Table 21. Party Labels in the ICPSR File

House	% with no party label
First	33.3
Second	20.8
Third	26.4
Fourth	22.6
Fifth	19.7
Sixth	19.3
Seventh	31.9

Source: ICPSR data files.

taken in the Congress of the United States from 1789 to 1932" (Lord, 1941). Included within the plan for this enormous project was the designation of party affiliations for every member. The project itself was never completed. One volume was published (Lord, 1943), and the incomplete records were stored in the library of Columbia University.[2]

Unfortunately, no listing of members of Congress and their party affiliations was ever published by the Historical Records Survey. The nature of the task was described as follows: "The thorny problem of early party affiliations has been resolved where possible from authoritative works such as the *Dictionary of American Biography* and, with reservations, the *Biographical Directory of the American Congress*. Where such sources yielded inadequate information, the Editor has consulted with living biographers of the particular Congressmen" (Lord, 1941, p. 6). While this sounds like a very worthwhile effort, it is most unfortunate that its results are not available to us.

The next major project that included the compilation of party identification for members of Congress was undertaken by the Historical Archive of the Inter-University Consortium for Political and Social Research (ICPSR). This project included the collection of all roll call votes, as well as the compilation of popular election returns since 1824. It appears that the ICPSR project used the files of the WPA project, although I have found no statement to that effect. While the *Biographical Directory of the American Congress* was clearly one source for the ICPSR files, the two listings are not identical; evidently, further research was done.[3]

The ICPSR files are at least somewhat more complete for these early party affiliations than the *Biographical Directory*. In each Congress, there are more members with party labels listed in the former (by over 16 percentage points), as shown in table 21. Of course, this does not necessarily make the ICPSR files a better source. Some peculiar errors have been found in the ICPSR files: for example, one congressman is listed as a Whig, although that party did not exist until several decades later. Members of the Republican party are variously listed as Republicans, Democrats, Jefferson Republicans, Jefferson Democrats, Democrat-Republicans, or sometimes Antifederalists. Whether in fact this source is more accurate than the *Biographical Directory* is a judgment that must await more specific comparisons, later in this appendix.

Congressional Quarterly is one traditional source for congressional data, and its *Guide to Elections* (Diamond, 1975) would seem to be an ideal source. However, for the House of Representatives, nothing is recorded for those serving prior to 1824.[4] A second Congressional Quarterly publication, *Guide to Congress* (Diamond and O'Connor, 1976; Wormser, 1982), includes a listing with party affiliations for all members of Congress. However, its party labels have been taken exclusively from the *Biographical Directory*, so this publication is not an alternative source of information.[5]

In addition to these major collections of information on the party affiliations of congressmen, several historians have produced their own listings.[6] For the First Congress, Paullin (1904) has discussed both the mechanics and the results of the first federal elections (in 1789). In the process he has indicated whether each victorious candidate was a Federalist or an Antifederalist, that is, whether or not he supported the federal Constitution. This classification of those in the First Congress is thus a very useful one, for it provides an indication of the political stance of these individuals at the time of their election and as they began the business of the first session of Congress. As such, it is not comparable with the usual classifications presented in the sources described above. There people are classed as Federalist or Republican based on their records in Congress or their positions in later elections. Paullin's classification is far more useful as a measure of party prior to the casting of any roll call votes.

From Paullin's article, with the help of various other historical accounts of that first election, it is possible to produce a party identification for every member of that first Congress but one (Tucker of South Carolina, whose party preference was "in doubt" [Paullin, 1904, p. 18]). Its accuracy is easier to gauge than that of most party groupings, since opinions on the Constitution were well publicized and frequently discussed by historians.[7] While not every individual's position has been confirmed, there is enough evidence to vouch for the accuracy of Paullin's classification.

The second important contribution from an individual historian is *The Adams Federalists* (Dauer, 1953), which considers the state of party politics from 1795 to 1803. An appendix to Dauer's book includes complete listings of members of the House of Representatives for the Fourth through Seventh Congresses, along with a partisan identification. He states (p. 288) that the "party affiliation . . . is that claimed by the member at time of election. This is based on biographies, newspapers, and correspondence." These compilations, together with material on the congressional district boundaries, represent an enormous research output of great value to students of political history.

Dauer's research has produced party labels for nearly every congressman serving between 1795 and 1801, covering the Fourth, Fifth, and Sixth Congresses, and the first session of the Seventh. The exceptions are Crabb (Md.) and Strudwick (N.C.) in the Fourth, Skinner (Mass.) in the Fifth, Stewart (Pa.) in the Sixth, and eight members of the Seventh who served only partial terms (mostly in the second session). So, for the period covered, this listing is a very complete compilation of party labels.

Accuracy, of course, is always difficult to judge without some definitive source. Dauer's comments throughout the book imply that he has tried to define party attachment not on performance during a session of Congress, but on claims made at the time of election. The best available indications are that he was faithful to his aim, and these party labels are used as a baseline for comparisons with other sources and with voting records.

The third and last of the historians whose compilations of party labels are useful to the current effort is Bell (1973). He has provided, in an appendix to his book on early party development, a listing of party affiliations for all congressmen serving in the First through the Sixth Congresses. These listings are complete, with every single member listed as affiliated with one of the two major party groups: pro- or anti-administration in the first three Congresses, and Federalist or Republican in the later three. Unfortunately, this completeness is obtained at an expense. Bell (p. 184*n*) states:

196 Origins of American Political Parties

Table 22. Comparisons of Party Labels

Congress	Correct	Incomplete	Error	Unknown
Biographical Directory				
Fourth	52%	40%	6%	2%
Fifth	55	41	3	1
Sixth	65	29	4	2
Seventh	62	30	3	4
ICPSR				
Fourth	63	23	12	2
Fifth	68	20	11	1
Sixth	71	19	8	2
Seventh	63	29	3	4

Note: Correct and Error codes based on Dauer (1953).

All delegates for all years were assigned to one of two parties. Initially, assignments were made on the basis of available biographic materials, local studies, newspapers, and correspondence. There remained a substantial number of delegates whose party association was dubious or non-existent. In these instances voting records in the House were used to assign representatives to the bloc of "party" men with which they voted most frequently. This procedure created a bias towards maximizing the influence of party since the data to be tested, votes, were used to assure that the results would show party solidarity. . . . Universal inclusion of delegates maximizes the explanatory power of party (under either definition), a bias chosen because it is in the opposite direction from the conclusions reached in the present study.

Bell's method of determining party labels creates problems if the goal is to determine the extent of party voting, since it inflates the effect of partisanship. Furthermore, this procedure most heavily inflates the extent of party voting when party labels are most ambiguous, thus obscuring any movement toward increased cohesion.[8]

Tables 24 and 25 provide a summary listing of the party labels for members of the House and Senate, as included in the major sources discussed in this appendix. To assess the accuracy of these various sources, we should have some single definitive reference. But if we had such a source, there would be less need to evaluate the others. Thus, in the absence of any definitive compilation, we can assess accuracy through a comparison of the several available sources.

Various factors lead me to the conclusion that the compilation of party labels by Dauer is the best available listing. This is certainly true in terms of completeness, and it is probably true in terms of accuracy as well. The coincidence of these labels with the voting blocs in the Fifth, Sixth, and Seventh Congresses (see tables 14 and 18) is evidence for this conclusion.

On this basis, we can then compare Dauer's compilation with the principal alternatives. It is clear, first, that Bell has drawn his set of labels from Dauer's work for the overlapping years and so does not provide an independent source. Comparisons between Dauer's compilation and those provided in the *Biographical Directory* and by the ICPSR are shown in table 22. The information in this table reveals a substantial amount of conflict, as high as 12% of the membership in the Congress. If we accept

Dauer's labels as accurate, then there is an error rate for the ICPSR ranging from 3% to 12% of the total membership. The comparable figures for the *Biographical Directory* range from 3% to 6%. If we ignore those for whom no label is given, then the error rate would go as high as 16% for the ICPSR codes, and 10% for the *Biographical Directory*.

The clearest conclusion to be drawn from this analysis is that working with the historical record is risky in the case of party labels for the early American Congress. This is undoubtedly itself a reflection of the instability of party ties in this period. Nevertheless, Dauer's effort demonstrates that it is possible to compile a set of labels that are at least plausibly accurate.

An effort was made in the course of this research project to collect information on party labels from a variety of published sources, including individual biographies and state and regional histories, in addition to the references already discussed. One is initally struck by the vital need for such an effort. Based on the attempts made here, it is clear that published sources are generally insufficient for a relatively complete listing of party labels. For some states, substantial information is available; for other states, there is little or no information.

What is needed, however, is an extensive compilation from all available sources, published or unpublished. The Martis project, discussed earlier, is the biggest step in this direction, but it is not doing a complete search of historical materials. A lengthy search of surviving election documents, newspapers, and correspondence might provide a reasonably complete and accurate compilation of party labels.

Partisan Composition of Congress

If we had an accurate and complete listing of all members of Congress with their partisan affiliations, then it would be a simple matter of arithmetic to determine the partisan makeup of a particular Congress. But such a source does not exist. There are in fact two sources that have acquired a degree of acceptance with the passage of time, both of which have the official sanction of the United States government. One listing of party breakdowns is found in a publication of the U.S. Bureau of the Census (1975), while another is found in the "official" history of the House of Representatives (Galloway, 1961).

Galloway's book has the status of an official congressional document, but its information on party divisions was taken from an earlier unofficial history of the House of Representatives (Alexander, 1916, p. 411), which provides a listing but no source for this information. Young (1966, p. 271) says about this source, "one suspects that [the figures] are the subjective estimates made by contemporary officeholders on the basis of Senate and House votes which they considered to be 'tests' of party strength."

The other source for party divisions is *Historical Statistics of the United States* (U.S., Bureau of the Census, 1975, p. 1084), where listings are provided for both the House and the Senate. This book in turn cites as its source the following: "Library of Congress, Legislative Reference Service, 'Political Trends—Both Houses of Congress—1789-1944,' typewritten tabulation based on *Encyclopedia Americana*, 1936 edition, vol. 7, pp. 516-518." The relevant portions of this and Galloway's listings of party breakdowns in the House are provided in table 23. Clearly, there are substantial differences even between these two sources.

One could next turn to the various compilations of individual party affiliations discussed in the previous section. But, given the problems with those sources, it is a task with minimal reward. Alternatively, one might turn to reports made in the

198 Origins of American Political Parties

Table 23. Partisan Composition of Congress

Congress	Galloway's *History*			Historical Statistics	
	Federalist	Democratic	Not Listed	Federalist	Democrat-Republican
First	53	12	0	38	26
Second	55	14	0	37	33
Third	51	54	0	48	57
Fourth	46	50	9	54	52
Fifth	51	54	0	58	48
Sixth	57	48	0	64	42
Seventh	34	71	0	36	69

Note: First listing is based on Galloway (1961); second listing is based on U.S., Bureau of the Census (1975).

correspondence of political observers such as Jefferson, Madison, and King. In any case, we lack any definitive means of deciding which source might be the accurate one.

Conclusion

This search for a definitive list of party affiliations for members of the early Congress and even for accurate estimates of party strength has proven to be singularly troublesome. This raises a difficulty since this party information is necessary for consideration of voting patterns. The resolution of this difficulty is to use the several available listings in some parts of the analysis; in other situations, I use the best available information. In some cases, information from biographies and local histories has been used to update the standard sources.

As a final consideration, I should state again that the lack of party information is in itself a sign of the lack of full party development in this period. The fact that better information is available for the later years of the period can be seen as one further indicator of the growth of political parties.

Table 24. Party Affiliations of House Members, 1789-1803

House of Representatives, First Congress (1789-1791)

	BIOGDIR	ICPSR	PAULLIN	BELL	MDSBLOC
CONNECTICUT					
Benjamin Huntington	None	None	Fed	Pro-Adm	New Eng
Roger Sherman	None	None	Fed	Pro-Adm	New Eng
Jonathan Sturges	Fed	Fed	Fed	Pro-Adm	New Eng
Jonathan Trumbull	Fed	Fed	Fed	Pro-Adm	New Eng
Jeremiah Wadsworth	Fed	Fed	Fed	Pro-Adm	New Eng
DELAWARE					
John Vining	None	None	Fed	Pro-Adm	Middle
GEORGIA					
Abraham Baldwin	Fed	Fed	Fed	Anti-Adm	South
James Jackson	None	Rep	Fed	Anti-Adm	South
George Mathews	None	None	Fed	Anti-Adm	South
MARYLAND					
Daniel Carroll	Fed	Fed	Fed	Pro-Adm	Middle
Benjamin Contee	None	None	Fed	Pro-Adm	South
George Gale	None	None	Fed	Pro-Adm	Middle
Joshua Seney	None	None	Fed	Pro-Adm	Ind
William Smith	Fed	Fed	Fed	Pro-Adm	Ind
Michael J. Stone	None	None	Fed	Pro-Adm	South
MASSACHUSETTS					
Fisher Ames	Fed	Fed	Fed	Pro-Adm	New Eng
Elbridge Gerry	Antifed	Antifed	Antifed	Anti-Adm	New Eng
Benjamin Goodhue	None	Fed	Fed	Pro-Adm	New Eng
Jonathan Grout	Rep	Rep	Antifed	Anti-Adm	Ind
George Leonard	None	None	Fed	Pro-Adm	New Eng
George Partridge	None	None	Fed	Pro-Adm	New Eng
Theodore Sedgwick	Fed	Fed	Fed	Pro-Adm	New Eng
George Thacher	Fed	None	Fed	Pro-Adm	New Eng
NEW HAMPSHIRE					
Abiel Foster	None	Fed	Fed	Pro-Adm	New Eng
Nicholas Gilman	Fed	Fed	Fed	Pro-Adm	Middle
Samuel Livermore	None	None	Fed	Anti-Adm	Ind
NEW JERSEY					
Elias Boudinot	None	Whig	Fed	Pro-Adm	New Eng
Lambert Cadwalader	None	None	Fed	Pro-Adm	Middle
James Schureman	Fed	Fed	Fed	Pro-Adm	New Eng
Thomas Sinnickson	Fed	Fed	Fed	Pro-Adm	Middle
NEW YORK					
Egbert Benson	None	None	Fed	Pro-Adm	New Eng
William Floyd	None	None	Fed	Anti-Adm	Ind
John Hathorn	Fed	None	Antifed	Pro-Adm	Ind
John Laurance	None	Fed	Fed	Pro-Adm	New Eng
Peter Silvester	None	Fed	Fed	Pro-Adm	New Eng
Jeremiah Van Rensselaer	Rep	Rep	Antifed	Anti-Adm	Ind
NORTH CAROLINA					
John Ashe	Fed	Fed	Fed	Anti-Adm	South
Timothy Bloodworth	None	None	Antifed	Anti-Adm	South
John Sevier	Rep	Rep	Fed	Anti-Adm	Middle
John Steele	Fed	Fed	Fed	Pro-Adm	South
Hugh Williamson	Fed	Fed	Fed	Pro-Adm	South

Table 24. (continued)

House of Representatives, First Congress (1789-1791) (cont.)

	BIOGDIR	ICPSR	PAULLIN	BELL	MDSBLOC
PENNSYLVANIA					
George Clymer	Fed	Fed	Fed	Pro-Adm	Middle
Thomas Fitzsimons	Fed	Fed	Fed	Pro-Adm.	Middle
Thomas Hartley	None	Fed	Fed	Pro-Adm	Middle
Daniel Hiester	None	Antifed	Fed	Anti-Adm	Middle
Frederick Muhlenberg	None	Fed	Fed	Pro-Adm	(4)
John Peter Muhlenberg	Rep	Rep	Fed	Anti-Adm	Middle
Thomas Scott	None	None	Fed	Anti-Adm	Middle
Henry Wynkoop	None	None	Fed	Pro-Adm	Middle
RHODE ISLAND					
Benjamin Bourn	Fed	Fed	Fed	Pro-Adm	(1)
SOUTH CAROLINA					
Aedanus Burke	None	None	Antifed	Anti-Adm	Ind
Daniel Huger	None	Rep	Fed	Anti-Adm	Ind
William L. Smith	Fed	Fed	Fed	Pro-Adm	New Eng
Thomas Sumter	Rep	Rep	Antifed	Anti-Adm	South
Thomas T. Tucker	Fed	Fed	None	Anti-Adm	Ind
VIRGINIA					
Theodorick Bland	None	None	Antifed	Anti-Adm	(2)
John Brown	None	Rep	Fed	Anti-Adm	South
Isaac Coles	None	None	Antifed	Anti-Adm	South
William Branch Giles	Antifed	Antifed	Fed	Anti-Adm	(2)
Samuel Griffin	None	Rep	Fed	Anti-Adm	Middle
Richard Bland Lee	None	Fed	Fed	Pro-Adm	Middle
James Madison	Rep	Rep	Fed	Anti-Adm	South
Andrew Moore	None	Rep	Fed	Anti-Adm	South
John Page	Rep	Rep	Fed	Anti-Adm	South
Josiah Parker	None	Antifed	Antifed	Anti-Adm	South
Alexander White	Fed	Fed	Fed	Pro-Adm	South

House of Representatives, Second Congress (1791-1793)

	BIOGDIR	ICPSR	BELL	MDSBLOC
CONNECTICUT				
James Hillhouse	Fed	Fed	Pro-Adm	Fed
Amasa Learned	None	None	Pro-Adm	Fed
Jonathan Sturges	Fed	Fed	Pro-Adm	Fed
Jonathan Trumbull	Fed	Fed	Pro-Adm	(4)
Jeremiah Wadsworth	Fed	Fed	Pro-Adm	Fed
DELAWARE				
John Vining	None	None	Pro-Adm	Fed
GEORGIA				
Abraham Baldwin	Fed	Fed	Anti-Adm	Rep
John Milledge	None	Rep	Anti-Adm	(2)
Anthony Wayne	None	None	Anti-Adm	Rep
Francis Willis	None	None	Anti-Adm	Rep
KENTUCKY				
Christopher Greenup	None	Rep	Anti-Adm	(1)
Alexander D. Orr	None	None	Anti-Adm	(1)

Table 24. (continued)

House of Representatives, Second Congress (1791-1793) (cont.)

	BIOGDIR	ICPSR	BELL	MDSBLOC
MARYLAND				
William Hindman	None	Fed	Pro-Adm	(2)
Philip Key	None	Fed	Pro-Adm	Fed
John F. Mercer	Rep	Rep	Anti-Adm	Rep
William Vans Murray	Fed	Fed	Pro-Adm	Fed
William Pinkney	None	Fed	Pro-Adm	(2)
Joshua Seney	None	None	Pro-Adm	Rep
Upton Sheredine	Rep	Rep	Anti-Adm	Rep
Samuel Sterett	Antifed	Antifed	Anti-Adm	Fed
MASSACHUSETTS				
Fisher Ames	Fed	Fed	Pro-Adm	Fed
Shearjashab Bourne	None	None	Pro-Adm	Fed
Elbridge Gerry	Antifed	Antifed	Anti-Adm	Fed
Benjamin Goodhue	None	Fed	Pro-Adm	Fed
George Leonard	None	None	Pro-Adm	(3)
Theodore Sedgwick	Fed	Fed	Pro-Adm	Fed
George Thacher	Fed	Fed	Pro-Adm	Fed
Artemas Ward	Fed	Fed	Pro-Adm	Fed
NEW HAMPSHIRE				
Nicholas Gilman	Fed	Fed	Pro-Adm	Fed
Samuel Livermore	None	None	Anti-Adm	Fed
Jeremiah Smith	Fed	Fed	Pro-Adm	Ind
NEW JERSEY				
Elias Boudinot	None	Whig	Pro-Adm	Fed
Abraham Clark	None	None	Anti-Adm	Ind
Jonathan Dayton	Fed	Fed	Pro-Adm	Fed
Aaron Kitchell	Rep	Rep	Pro-Adm	Ind
NEW YORK				
Egbert Benson	None	None	Pro-Adm	Fed
James Gordon	Fed	Fed	Pro-Adm	Fed
John Laurance	None	Fed	Pro-Adm	Fed
Cornelius Schoonmaker	None	None	Anti-Adm	Ind
Peter Silvester	None	None	Pro-Adm	Fed
Thomas Tredwell	None	None	Anti-Adm	Ind
NORTH CAROLINA				
John Ashe	Fed	Fed	Anti-Adm	Rep
William Barry Grove	Fed	Fed	Pro-Adm	Rep
Nathaniel Macon	Rep	Rep	Anti-Adm	Rep
John Steele	Fed	Fed	Pro-Adm	Ind
Hugh Williamson	Fed	Fed	Pro-Adm	Rep
PENNSYLVANIA				
William Findley	Rep	Antifed	Anti-Adm	Rep
Thomas Fitzsimons	Fed	Fed	Pro-Adm	Fed
Andrew Gregg	None	Rep	Anti-Adm	Rep
Thomas Hartley	None	Fed	Pro-Adm	Fed
Daniel Hiester	None	Antifed	Anti-Adm	Rep
Israel Jacobs	None	None	Pro-Adm	Ind
John W. Kittera	Fed	Fed	Pro-Adm	Fed
Frederick Muhlenberg	None	Fed	Anti-Adm	Fed
RHODE ISLAND				
Benjamin Bourn	Fed	Fed	Pro-Adm	Fed
SOUTH CAROLINA				
Robert Barnwell	Fed	Fed	Pro-Adm	Fed
Daniel Huger	None	Rep	Anti-Adm	Fed
William L. Smith	Fed	Fed	Pro-Adm	Fed
Thomas Sumter	Rep	Rep	Anti-Adm	Rep
Thomas T. Tucker	Fed	Fed	Anti-Adm	Fed

Table 24. (continued)

House of Representatives, Second Congress (1791-1793) (cont.)

	BIOGDIR	ICPSR	BELL	MDSBLOC
VERMONT				
Nathaniel Niles	None	Rep	Anti-Adm	Ind
Israel Smith	Rep	Rep	Anti-Adm	Ind
VIRGINIA				
John Brown	None	Rep	Anti-Adm	Rep
William Branch Giles	Antifed	Antifed	Anti-Adm	Rep
Samuel Griffin	None	Rep	Anti-Adm	Rep
Richard Bland Lee	None	Fed	Pro-Adm	Rep
James Madison	Rep	Rep	Anti-Adm	Rep
Andrew Moore	None	Rep	Anti-Adm	Rep
John Page	Rep	Rep	Anti-Adm	Rep
Josiah Parker	None	Antifed	Pro-Adm	Rep
Abraham B. Venable	None	Rep	Anti-Adm	Rep
Alexander White	Fed	Fed	Pro-Adm	Rep

House of Representatives, Third Congress (1793-1795)

	BIOGDIR	ICPSR	BELL	MDSBLOC
CONNECTICUT				
Joshua Coit	Fed	Fed	Pro-Adm	Fed
James Hillhouse	Fed	Fed	Pro-Adm	Fed
Amasa Learned	None	None	Pro-Adm	Fed
Zephaniah Swift	Fed	Fed	Pro-Adm	Fed
Uriah Tracy	Fed	Fed	Pro-Adm	Fed
Jonathan Trumbull	Fed	Fed	Pro-Adm	Fed
Jeremiah Wadsworth	Fed	Fed	Pro-Adm	Fed
DELAWARE				
Henry Latimer	None	Fed	Pro-Adm	Fed
John Patten	None	Fed	Anti-Adm	(2)
GEORGIA				
Abraham Baldwin	Fed	Fed	Anti-Adm	Rep
Thomas P. Carnes	None	None	Anti-Adm	Rep
KENTUCKY				
Christopher Greenup	None	Rep	Anti-Adm	Rep
Alexander D. Orr	None	None	Anti-Adm	Rep
MARYLAND				
Gabriel Christie	None	None	Anti-Adm	Rep
George Dent	Rep	Rep	Pro-Adm	Rep
Gabriel Duvall	Rep	Rep	Anti-Adm	(2)
Benjamin Edwards	None	Fed	Pro-Adm	(2)
Uriah Forrest	Fed	Fed	Pro-Adm	(2)
William Hindman	None	Fed	Pro-Adm	Fed
John F. Mercer	Rep	Rep	Anti-Adm	(2)
William Vans Murray	Fed	Fed	Pro-Adm	Fed
Samuel Smith	Rep	Rep	Anti-Adm	Ind
Thomas Sprigg	None	None	Anti-Adm	Ind

Table 24. (continued)

House of Representatives, Third Congress (1793-1795) (cont.)

	BIOGDIR	ICPSR	BELL	MDSBLOC
MASSACHUSETTS				
Fisher Ames	Fed	Fed	Pro-Adm	Fed
Shearjashab Bourne	None	None	Pro-Adm	Fed
David Cobb	Fed	Fed	Pro-Adm	Fed
Peleg Coffin	None	None	Pro-Adm	Fed
Henry Dearborn	Rep	Rep	Anti-Adm	Ind
Samuel Dexter	Fed	Fed	Pro-Adm	Fed
Dwight Foster	Fed	Fed	Pro-Adm	Fed
Benjamin Goodhue	None	Fed	Pro-Adm	Fed
Samuel Holten	None	Antifed	Anti-Adm	Fed
William Lyman	Rep	Rep	Anti-Adm	Rep
Theodore Sedgwick	Fed	Fed	Pro-Adm	Fed
George Thacher	Fed	Fed	Pro-Adm	Fed
Peleg Wadsworth	None	None	Pro-Adm	Fed
Artemas Ward	Fed	Fed	Pro-Adm	Fed
NEW HAMPSHIRE				
Nicholas Gilman	Fed	Fed	Pro-Adm	Ind
John S. Sherburne	None	None	Anti-Adm	Ind
Jeremiah Smith	Fed	Fed	Pro-Adm	Fed
Paine Wingate	Fed	Fed	Pro-Adm	Ind
NEW JERSEY				
John Beatty	None	None	Pro-Adm	Ind
Elias Boudinot	None	Whig	Pro-Adm	Fed
Lambert Cadwalader	None	None	Pro-Adm	Fed
Abraham Clark	None	None	Anti-Adm	Ind
Jonathan Dayton	Fed	Fed	Pro-Adm	Ind
Aaron Kitchell	Rep	Rep	Pro-Adm	(2)
NEW YORK				
Theodorus Bailey	Rep	Rep	Anti-Adm	Rep
Ezekiel Gilbert	None	None	Pro-Adm	Fed
Henry Glen	None	None	Pro-Adm	Fed
James Gordon	Fed	Fed	Pro-Adm	Fed
Silas Talbot	Fed	Fed	Pro-Adm	Fed
Thomas Tredwell	None	None	Anti-Adm	Rep
John E. Van Alen	None	None	Pro-Adm	Fed
Philip Van Cortlandt	Rep	Rep	Anti-Adm	Rep
Peter Van Gaasbeck	Antifed	Antifed	Anti-Adm	Fed
John Watts	None	None	Pro-Adm	Fed
NORTH CAROLINA				
Thomas Blount	Rep	Rep	Anti-Adm	Rep
William J. Dawson	None	None	Anti-Adm	Rep
James Gillespie	None	None	Anti-Adm	Rep
William Barry Grove	Fed	Fed	Pro-Adm	Rep
Matthew Locke	Rep	Rep	Anti-Adm	Rep
Nathaniel Macon	Rep	Rep	Anti-Adm	Rep
Joseph McDowell	None	Rep	Anti-Adm	Rep
Alexander Mebane	None	None	Anti-Adm	Rep
Benjamin Williams	None	None	Anti-Adm	Rep
Joseph Winston	Rep	Rep	Anti-Adm	Rep
PENNSYLVANIA				
James Armstrong	Fed	Fed	Pro-Adm	Ind
William Findley	Rep	Rep	Anti-Adm	Rep
Thomas Fitzsimons	Fed	Fed	Pro-Adm	Fed
Andrew Gregg	None	Rep	Anti-Adm	Rep
Thomas Hartley	None	Fed	Pro-Adm	Fed
Daniel Hiester	None	Rep	Anti-Adm	Rep
William Irvine	None	None	Pro-Adm	Ind
John W. Kittera	Fed	Fed	Pro-Adm	Fed
William Montgomery	None	Rep	Anti-Adm	Rep
Frederick Muhlenberg	None	Fed	Anti-Adm	(4)
John Peter Muhlenberg	Rep	Rep	Anti-Adm	Rep
Thomas Scott	None	None	Anti-Adm	Ind
John Smilie	Rep	Rep	Anti-Adm	Rep

204 Origins of American Political Parties

Table 24. (continued)

House of Representatives, Third Congress (1793-1795). (cont.)

	BIOGDIR	ICPSR	BELL	MDSBLOC
RHODE ISLAND				
Benjamin Bourn	Fed	Fed	Pro-Adm	Fed
Francis Malbone	Fed	Fed	Pro-Adm	Fed
SOUTH CAROLINA				
Lemuel Benton	Rep	Rep	Anti-Adm	(3)
Alexander Gillon	None	None	Anti-Adm	(2)
Robert Goodloe Harper	Fed	Fed	Pro-Adm	(2)
John Hunter	Fed	Rep	Anti-Adm	Ind
Andrew Pickens	Rep	Rep	Anti-Adm	Ind
William L. Smith	Fed	Fed	Pro-Adm	Fed
Richard Winn	Rep	Rep	Anti-Adm	Ind
VERMONT				
Nathaniel Niles	None	Rep	Anti-Adm	Rep
Israel Smith	Rep	Rep	Anti-Adm	Rep
VIRGINIA				
Thomas Claiborne	None	Rep	Anti-Adm	Rep
Isaac Coles	None	None	Anti-Adm	Rep
William Branch Giles	Antifed	Antifed	Anti-Adm	Rep
Samuel Griffin	None	Rep	Anti-Adm	Ind
George Hancock	Rep	Rep	Pro-Adm	Rep
Carter B. Harrison	None	None	Anti-Adm	Rep
John Heath	Rep	Rep	Anti-Adm	Rep
Richard Bland Lee	None	Fed	Pro-Adm	Fed
James Madison	Rep	Rep	Anti-Adm	Rep
Andrew Moore	None	Rep	Anti-Adm	Rep
Joseph Neville	None	None	Anti-Adm	Rep
Anthony New	Rep	Rep	Anti-Adm	Rep
John Nicholas	Rep	Rep	Anti-Adm	Rep
John Page	Rep	Rep	Pro-Adm	Rep
Josiah Parker	None	Antifed	Pro-Adm	Rep
Francis Preston	None	Rep	Anti-Adm	Rep
Robert Rutherford	None	None	Pro-Adm	Rep
Abraham B. Venable	None	Fed	Anti-Adm	Rep
Francis Walker	None	None	Anti-Adm	Rep

House of Representatives, Fourth Congress (1795-1797)

	BIOGDIR	ICPSR	BELL	DAUER	MDSBLOC
CONNECTICUT					
Joshua Coit	Fed	Fed	Fed	Fed	Fed
Samuel W. Dana	Fed	Fed	Fed	Fed	(2)
James Davenport	None	Fed	Fed	Fed	Fed
Chauncey Goodrich	Fed	Fed	Fed	Fed	Fed
Roger Griswold	Fed	Fed	Fed	Fed	Fed
James Hillhouse	Fed	Fed	Fed	Fed	(2)
Nathaniel Smith	Fed	Fed	Fed	Fed	Fed
Zepharriah Swift	Fed	Fed	Fed	Fed	Fed
Uriah Tracy	Fed	Fed	Fed	Fed	(2)
DELAWARE					
John Patten	None	Fed	Rep	Rep	Rep
GEORGIA					
Abraham Baldwin	Fed	Fed	Rep	Rep	Rep
John Milledge	None	Rep	Rep	Rep	Rep
KENTUCKY					
Christopher Greenup	None	None	Rep	Rep	Rep
Alexander D. Orr	None	None	Rep	Rep	Rep

Table 24. (continued)

House of Representatives, Fourth Congress (1795-1797) (cont.)

	BIOGDIR	ICPSR	BELL	DAUER	MDSBLOC
MARYLAND					
Gabriel Christie	None	None	Rep	Rep	Rep
Jeremiah Crabb	Rep	Rep	Fed	None	(2)
William Craik	None	Rep	Fed	Fed	Fed
George Dent	Rep	Rep	Fed	Fed	Fed
Gabriel Duvall	Rep	Rep	Rep	Rep	(2)
William Hindman	None	Fed	Fed	Fed	Fed
William Vans Murray	Fed	Fed	Fed	Fed	Fed
Samuel Smith	Rep	Rep	Rep	Rep	Fed
Richard Sprigg	None	None	Rep	Rep	Rep
Thomas Sprigg	None	None	Rep	Rep	Rep
MASSACHUSETTS					
Fisher Ames	Fed	Fed	Fed	Fed	Fed
Theophilus Bradbury	Fed	Fed	Fed	Fed	Fed
Henry Dearborn	Rep	Rep	Rep	Rep	Rep
Dwight Foster	Fed	Fed	Fed	Fed	Fed
Nathaniel Freeman	None	Fed	Fed	Fed	Rep
Benjamin Goodhue	None	Fed	Fed	Fed	(2)
George Leonard	None	None	Fed	Fed	(3)
Samuel Lyman	None	None	Fed	Fed	Fed
William Lyman	Rep	Rep	Rep	Rep	Rep
John Reed	Fed	Fed	Fed	Fed	Fed
Theodore Sedgwick	Fed	Fed	Fed	Fed	(2)
Samuel Sewall	None	None	Fed	Fed	Fed
Thomas Skinner	Rep	Rep	Fed	Fed	(2)
George Thacher	Fed	Fed	Fed	Fed	Fed
Joseph B. Varnum	None	Antifed	Rep	Rep	Rep
Peleg Wadsworth	None	None	Fed	Fed	Fed
NEW HAMPSHIRE					
Abiel Foster	None	Fed	Fed	Fed	Fed
Nicholas Gilman	Fed	Fed	Fed	Fed	Fed
John S. Sherburne	None	None	Rep	Rep	Rep
Jeremiah Smith	Fed	Fed	Fed	Fed	Fed
NEW JERSEY					
Jonathan Dayton	Fed	Fed	Fed	Fed	(4)
Thomas Henderson	None	Fed	Fed	Fed	Fed
Aaron Kitchell	Rep	Rep	Fed	Fed	Rep
Isaac Smith	Fed	Fed	Fed	Fed	Rep
Mark Thomson	Fed	Fed	Fed	Fed	Fed
NEW YORK					
Theodorus Bailey	Rep	Rep	Rep	Rep	Rep
William Cooper	Fed	Fed	Fed	Fed	Fed
Ezekiel Gilbert	None	None	Fed	Fed	Fed
Henry Glen	None	None	Fed	Fed	Fed
John Hathorn	Fed	Fed	Rep	Rep	Rep
Jonathan N. Havens	Rep	Rep	Rep	Rep	Rep
Edward Livingston	Rep	Rep	Rep	Rep	Rep
John E. Van Alen	None	None	Fed	Fed	Fed
Philip Van Cortlandt	Rep	Rep	Rep	Rep	Rep
John Williams	None	None	Fed	Fed	Fed

Table 24. (continued)

House of Representatives, Fourth Congress (1795-1797) (cont.)

	BIOGDIR	ICPSR	BELL	DAUER	MDSBLOC
NORTH CAROLINA					
Thomas Blount	Rep	Rep	Rep	Rep	Rep
Nathan Bryan	None	None	Rep	Rep	Rep
Dempsey Burges	None	None	Rep	Rep	Rep
Jesse Franklin	Rep	Rep	Rep	Rep	Rep
James Gillespie	None	None	Rep	Rep	Rep
William Barry Grove	Fed	Fed	Fed	Fed	Rep
James Holland	Antifed	None	Rep	Rep	Rep
Matthew Locke	Rep	Rep	Rep	Rep	Rep
Nathaniel Macon	Rep	Rep	Rep	Rep	Rep
William F. Strudwick	Fed	Fed	Fed	None	Rep
Absalom Tatom	Rep	Rep	Rep	Rep	(2)
PENNSYLVANIA					
David Bard	None	None	Rep	Rep	Rep
George Ege	None	None	Fed	Fed	Fed
William Findley	Rep	Rep	Rep	Rep	Rep
Albert Gallatin	Rep	Rep	Rep	Rep	Rep
Andrew Gregg	None	Rep	Rep	Rep	Rep
Thomas Hartley	None	Fed	Fed	Fed	Fed
Daniel Hiester	None	Antifed	Rep	Rep	(2)
John W. Kittera	Fed	Fed	Fed	Fed	Fed
Samuel Maclay	None	Fed	Rep	Rep	Rep
Frederick Muhlenberg	None	Fed	Rep	Rep	Rep
John Richards	None	Fed	Rep	Rep	Rep
Samuel Sitgreaves	Fed	Fed	Fed	Fed	Fed
John Swanwick	Rep	Rep	Rep	Rep	Rep
Richard Thomas	Fed	Fed	Fed	Fed	Fed
RHODE ISLAND					
Benjamin Bourn	Fed	Fed	Fed	Fed	(2)
Francis Malbone	Fed	Fed	Fed	Fed	Fed
Elisha R. Potter	Fed	Fed	Fed	Fed	Fed
SOUTH CAROLINA					
Lemuel Benton	Rep	Rep	Rep	Rep	(3)
Samuel Earle	None	None	Rep	Rep	(3)
Wade Hampton	Rep	Rep	Rep	Rep	Rep
Robert Goodloe Harper	Fed	Fed	Fed	Fed	Fed
William L. Smith	Fed	Fed	Fed	Fed	Fed
Richard Winn	Rep	Rep	Rep	Rep	Rep
TENNESSEE					
Andrew Jackson	Rep	Rep	Rep	Rep	Rep
VERMONT					
Daniel Buck	Fed	Fed	Fed	Fed	Fed
Israel Smith	Rep	Rep	Rep	Rep	Rep
VIRGINIA					
Richard Brent	None	None	Rep	Rep	Rep
Samuel J. Cabell	Rep	Rep	Rep	Rep	Rep
Thomas Claiborne	None	Rep	Rep	Rep	Rep
John Clopton	Rep	Rep	Rep	Rep	Rep
Isaac Coles	None	None	Rep	Rep	Rep
William Branch Giles	Antifed	Antifed	Rep	Rep	Rep
George Hancock	Rep	Rep	Fed	Fed	Rep
Carter B. Harrison	None	None	Rep	Rep	Rep
John Heath	Rep	Rep	Rep	Rep	Rep
George Jackson	None	Rep	Rep	Rep	Rep
James Madison	Rep	Rep	Rep	Rep	Rep
Andrew Moore	None	Rep	Rep	Rep	Rep
Anthony New	Rep	Rep	Rep	Rep	Rep
John Nicholas	Rep	Rep	Rep	Rep	Rep
John Page	Rep	Rep	Fed	Fed	Rep
Josiah Parker	None	Antifed	Fed	Fed	Rep
Francis Preston	None	None	Rep	Rep	Rep
Robert Rutherford	None	None	Fed	Fed	Rep
Abraham B. Venable	None	Fed	Rep	Rep	Rep

Table 24. (continued)

House of Representatives, Fifth Congress (1797-1799)

	BIOGDIR	ICPSR	BELL	DAUER	MDSBLOC
CONNECTICUT					
John Allen	Fed	Fed	Fed	Fed	Fed
Jonathan Brace	Fed	Fed	Fed	Fed	(2)
Joshua Coit	Fed	Fed	Fed	Fed	Fed
Samuel W. Dana	Fed	Fed	Fed	Fed	Fed
James Davenport	None	Fed	Fed	Fed	(2)
William Edmond	Fed	Fed	Fed	Fed	Fed
Chauncey Goodrich	Fed	Fed	Fed	Fed	Fed
Roger Griswold	Fed	Fed	Fed	Fed	Fed
Nathaniel Smith	Fed	Fed	Fed	Fed	Fed
DELAWARE					
James Bayard	Fed	Fed	Fed	Fed	Fed
GEORGIA					
Abraham Baldwin	Fed	Fed	Rep	Rep	Rep
John Milledge	None	Rep	Rep	Rep	Rep
KENTUCKY					
Thomas T. Davis	None	None	Rep	Rep	Rep
John Fowler	None	Rep	Rep	Rep	Rep
MARYLAND					
George Baer	Fed	Fed	Fed	Fed	Fed
William Craik	None	Rep	Fed	Fed	Fed
John Dennis	Fed	Fed	Fed	Fed	Fed
George Dent	Rep	Rep	Fed	Fed	Ind
William Hindman	None	Fed	Fed	Fed	Fed
William Matthews	None	Fed	Fed	Fed	Fed
Samuel Smith	Rep	Rep	Rep	Rep	Ind
Richard Sprigg	None	None	Rep	Rep	Rep
MASSACHUSETTS					
Bailey Bartlett	Fed	Fed	Fed	Fed	Fed
Theophilus Bradbury	Fed	Fed	Fed	Fed	(2)
Stephen Bullock	Fed	Fed	Fed	Fed	Fed
Dwight Foster	Fed	Fed	Fed	Fed	Fed
Nathaniel Freeman	None	Fed	Rep	Rep	(3)
Samuel Lyman	None	None	Fed	Fed	Fed
Harrison G. Otis	Fed	Fed	Fed	Fed	Fed
Isaac Parker	None	Antifed	Fed	Fed	Fed
John Reed	Fed	Fed	Fed	Fed	Fed
Samuel Sewall	None	None	Fed	Fed	Fed
William Shepard	None	Fed	Fed	Fed	Fed
Thomas Skinner	Rep	Rep	Rep	None	Rep
George Thacher	Fed	Fed	Fed	Fed	Fed
Joseph B. Varnum	None	Antifed	Rep	Rep	Rep
Peleg Wadsworth	None	None	Fed	Fed	Fed
NEW HAMPSHIRE					
Abiel Foster	None	Fed	Fed	Fed	Fed
Jonathan Freeman	Fed	Fed	Fed	Fed	Fed
William Gordon	None	None	Fed	Fed	Fed
Jeremiah Smith	Fed	Fed	Fed	Fed	(2)
Peleg Sprague	None	None	Fed	Fed	Fed
NEW JERSEY					
Jonathan Dayton	Fed	Fed	Fed	Fed	(4)
James H. Imlay	None	None	Fed	Fed	Fed
James Schureman	Fed	Fed	Fed	Fed	Fed
Thomas Sinnickson	Fed	Fed	Fed	Fed	Fed
Mark Thomson	Fed	Fed	Fed	Fed	Fed

Table 24. (continued)

House of Representatives, Fifth Congress (1797-1799) (cont.)

	BIOGDIR	ICPSR	BELL	DAUER	MDSBLOC
NEW YORK					
David Brooks	None	Rep	Fed	Fed	Fed
James Cochran	None	Rep	Fed	Fed	Fed
Lucas C. Elmendorf	Rep	Rep	Rep	Rep	Rep
Henry Glen	None	None	Fed	Fed	Fed
Jonathan N. Havens	Rep	Rep	Rep	Rep	Rep
Hezekiah Hosmer	None	None	Fed	Fed	Fed
Edward Livingston	Rep	Rep	Rep	Rep	Rep
John E. Van Alen	None	None	Fed	Fed	Fed
Philip Van Cortlandt	Rep	Rep	Rep	Rep	Rep
John Williams	None	None	Fed	Fed	Fed
NORTH CAROLINA					
Thomas Blount	Rep	Rep	Rep	Rep	Rep
Nathan Bryan	None	None	Rep	Rep	Rep
Dempsey Burges	None	None	Rep	Rep	Rep
James Gillespie	None	None	Rep	Rep	Rep
William Barry Grove	Fed	Fed	Fed	Fed	Fed
Matthew Locke	Rep	Rep	Rep	Rep	Rep
Nathaniel Macon	Rep	Rep	Rep	Rep	Rep
Joseph McDowell	None	Rep	Rep	Rep	Rep
Richard D. Spaight	Rep	Rep	Fed	Fed	(2)
Richard Stanford	Rep	Rep	Rep	Rep	Rep
Robert Williams	None	None	Rep	Rep	Rep
PENNSYLVANIA					
David Bard	None	None	Rep	Rep	Rep
Robert Brown	Rep	Rep	Rep	Rep	(2)
John Chapman	Fed	Fed	Fed	Fed	Fed
George Ege	None	None	Fed	Fed	(2)
William Findley	Rep	Rep	Rep	Rep	Rep
Albert Gallatin	Rep	Rep	Rep	Rep	Rep
Andrew Gregg	None	Rep	Rep	Rep	Rep
John A. Hanna	Antifed	Antifed	Rep	Rep	Rep
Thomas Hartley	None	Fed	Fed	Fed	Fed
Joseph Hiester	Fed	Fed	Rep	Rep	Rep
John W. Kittera	Fed	Fed	Fed	Fed	Fed
Blair McClenachan	None	None	Rep	Rep	Rep
Samuel Sitgreaves	Fed	Fed	Fed	Fed	Fed
John Swanwick	Rep	Rep	Rep	Rep	(2)
Richard Thomas	Fed	Fed	Fed	Fed	Fed
Robert Waln	Fed	Fed	Fed	Fed	(2)
RHODE ISLAND					
Christopher Champlin	None	Fed	Fed	Fed	Fed
Elisha R. Potter	Fed	Fed	Fed	Fed	(2)
Thomas Tillinghast	None	Rep	Rep	Rep	Fed
SOUTH CAROLINA					
Lemuel Benton	Rep	Rep	Rep	Rep	(3)
Robert Goodloe Harper	Fed	Fed	Fed	Fed	Fed
Thomas Pinckney	Fed	Fed	Fed	Fed	(2)
John Rutledge	Fed	Fed	Fed	Fed	Fed
William Smith	None	Rep	Rep	Rep	Rep
William L. Smith	Fed	Fed	Fed	Fed	(2)
Thomas Sumter	Rep	Rep	Rep	Rep	Rep
TENNESSEE					
William Claiborne	Rep	Rep	Rep	Rep	Rep
VERMONT					
Matthew Lyon	Antifed	Antifed	Rep	Rep	Rep
Lewis R. Morris	Fed	Fed	Fed	Fed	Fed

Table 24. (continued)

House of Representatives, Fifth Congress (1797-1799) (cont.)

	BIOGDIR	ICPSR	BELL	DAUER	MDSBLOC
VIRGINIA					
Richard Brent	None	None	Rep	Rep	Rep
Samuel J. Cabell	Rep	Rep	Rep	Rep	Rep
Thomas Claiborne	None	Rep	Rep	Rep	Rep
Matthew Clay	Rep	Rep	Rep	Rep	Rep
John Clopton	Rep	Rep	Rep	Rep	Rep
John Dawson	Rep	Rep	Rep	Rep	Rep
Joseph Eggleston	Rep	Rep	Rep	Rep	(2)
Thomas Evans	None	None	Fed	Fed	Fed
William Branch Giles	Antifed	Antifed	Rep	Rep	(2)
Carter B. Harrison	None	None	Rep	Rep	Rep
David Holmes	None	Rep	Rep	Rep	Rep
Walter Jones	Rep	Rep	Rep	Rep	Rep
James Machir	None	None	Fed	Fed	Fed
Daniel Morgan	Fed	Fed	Fed	Fed	Fed
Anthony New	Rep	Rep	Rep	Rep	Rep
John Nicholas	Rep	Rep	Rep	Rep	Rep
Josiah Parker	None	Antifed	Fed	Fed	Ind
Abram Trigg	None	Fed	Rep	Rep	Rep
John J. Trigg	None	Fed	Rep	Rep	Rep
Abraham B. Venable	None	Fed	Rep	Rep	Rep

House of Representatives, Sixth Congress (1799-1801)

CONNECTICUT					
Jonathan Brace	Fed	Fed	Fed	Fed	Fed
Samuel W. Dana	Fed	Fed	Fed	Fed	Fed
John Davenport	Fed	Fed	Fed	Fed	Fed
William Edmond	Fed	Fed	Fed	Fed	Fed
Chauncey Goodrich	Fed	Fed	Fed	Fed	Fed
Elizur Goodrich	Fed	Fed	Fed	Fed	Fed
Roger Griswold	Fed	Fed	Fed	Fed	Fed
John C. Smith	Fed	Fed	Fed	Fed	(2)
DELAWARE					
James Bayard	Fed	Fed	Fed	Fed	Fed
GEORGIA					
James Jones	Rep	Rep	Fed	Fed	Rep
Benjamin Taliaferro	None	None	Fed	Fed	Rep
KENTUCKY					
Thomas T. Davis	None	None	Rep	Rep	Rep
John Fowler	None	Rep	Rep	Rep	Rep
MARYLAND					
George Baer	Fed	Fed	Fed	Fed	Fed
Gabriel Christie	None	None	Rep	Rep	Rep
William Craik	None	Rep	Fed	Fed	Fed
John Dennis	Fed	Fed	Fed	Fed	Fed
George Dent	Rep	Rep	Fed	Fed	Rep
Joseph H. Nicholson	Rep	Rep	Rep	Rep	Rep
Samuel Smith	Rep	Rep	Rep	Rep	Rep
John C. Thomas	Fed	Fed	Fed	Fed	Fed

Table 24. (continued)

House of Representatives, Sixth Congress (1799-1801) (cont.)

	BIOGDIR	ICPSR	BELL	DAUER	MDSBLOC
MASSACHUSETTS					
Bailey Bartlett	Fed	Fed	Fed	Fed	Fed
Phanuel Bishop	None	None	Rep	Rep	Rep
Dwight Foster	Fed	Fed	Fed	Fed	(2)
Silas Lee	Fed	Fed	Fed	Fed	Fed
Levi Lincoln	Rep	Rep	Rep	Rep	(2)
Samuel Lyman	None	None	Fed	Fed	(2)
Ebenezer Mattoon	Fed	Fed	Fed	Fed	(2)
Harrison G. Otis	Fed	Fed	Fed	Fed	Fed
Nathan Read	Fed	Fed	Fed	Fed	(2)
John Reed	Fed	Fed	Fed	Fed	Fed
Theodore Sedgwick	Fed	Fed	Fed	Fed	(4)
Samuel Sewall	None	None	Fed	Fed	Fed
William Shepard	None	None	Fed	Fed	Fed
George Thacher	Fed	Fed	Fed	Fed	Fed
Joseph B. Varnum	None	Antifed	Rep	Rep	Rep
Peleg Wadsworth	None	None	Fed	Fed	Fed
Lemuel Williams	None	None	Fed	Fed	Fed
NEW HAMPSHIRE					
Abiel Foster	None	Fed	Fed	Fed	Fed
Jonathan Freeman	Fed	Fed	Fed	Fed	Fed
William Gordon	None	None	Fed	Fed	(2)
James Sheafe	Fed	Fed	Fed	Fed	Fed
Samuel Tenney	None	None	Fed	Fed	(2)
NEW JERSEY					
John Condit	Rep	Rep	Rep	Rep	Rep
Franklin Davenport	None	None	Fed	Fed	Fed
James H. Imlay	None	None	Fed	Fed	Fed
Aaron Kitchell	Rep	Rep	Rep	Rep	Rep
James Linn	Rep	Rep	Rep	Rep	Rep
NEW YORK					
Theodorus Bailey	Rep	Rep	Rep	Rep	Rep
John Bird	Rep	Rep	Fed	Fed	Fed
William Cooper	Fed	Fed	Fed	Fed	Fed
Lucas C. Elmendorf	Rep	Rep	Rep	Rep	Rep
Henry Glen	None	None	Fed	Fed	Fed
Jonathan N. Havens	Rep	Rep	Rep	Rep	(2)
Edward Livingston	Rep	Rep	Rep	Rep	Rep
Jonas Platt	Fed	Fed	Fed	Fed	Fed
John Smith	Rep	Rep	Rep	Rep	Rep
John Thompson	Rep	Rep	Rep	Rep	Rep
Philip Van Cortlandt	Rep	Rep	Rep	Rep	Rep
NORTH CAROLINA					
Willis Alston	War Dem	War Dem	Fed	Fed	Rep
Joseph Dickson	Fed	None	Fed	Fed	Fed
William Barry Grove	Fed	Fed	Fed	Fed	Fed
Archibald Henderson	Fed	Fed	Fed	Fed	Fed
William H. Hill	Fed	Fed	Fed	Fed	Fed
Nathaniel Macon	Rep	Rep	Rep	Rep	Rep
Richard D. Spaight	Rep	Rep	Rep	Rep	Rep
Richard Stanford	Rep	Rep	Rep	Rep	Rep
David Stone	Rep	Rep	Rep	Rep	Rep
Robert Williams	None	None	Rep	Rep	Rep

Party Affiliation of Members of Congress 211

Table 24. (continued)

House of Representatives, Sixth Congress (1799-1801) (cont.)

	BIOGDIR	ICPSR	BELL	DAUER	MDSBLOC
PENNSYLVANIA					
Robert Brown	Rep	Rep	Rep	Rep	Rep
Albert Gallatin	Rep	Rep	Rep	Rep	Rep
Andrew Gregg	None	Rep	Rep	Rep	Rep
John A. Hanna	Antifed	Antifed	Rep	Rep	Rep
Thomas Hartley	None	Fed	Fed	Fed	(2)
Joseph Hiester	Fed	Fed	Rep	Rep	Rep
John W. Kittera	Fed	Fed	Fed	Fed	Fed
Michael Leib	Rep	Rep	Rep	Rep	Rep
John Peter Muhlenberg	Rep	Rep	Rep	Rep	Rep
John Smilie	Rep	Rep	Rep	Rep	Rep
John Stewart	Rep	Rep	Rep	None	(2)
Richard Thomas	Fed	Fed	Fed	Fed	Fed
Robert Waln	Fed	Fed	Fed	Fed	Fed
Henry Woods	None	None	Fed	Fed	Fed
RHODE ISLAND					
John Brown	Fed	Fed	Fed	Fed	Fed
Christopher Champlin	None	Fed	Fed	Fed	Fed
SOUTH CAROLINA					
Robert Goodloe Harper	Fed	Fed	Fed	Fed	Fed
Benjamin Huger	None	None	Fed	Fed	Fed
Abraham Nott	Fed	Fed	Fed	Fed	Fed
Thomas Pinckney	Fed	Fed	Fed	Fed	Fed
John Rutledge	Fed	Fed	Fed	Fed	Fed
Thomas Sumter	Rep	Rep	Rep	Rep	Rep
TENNESSEE					
William Claiborne	Rep	Rep	Rep	Rep	Rep
VERMONT					
Matthew Lyon	Antifed	Antifed	Rep	Rep	Rep
Lewis R. Morris	Fed	Fed	Fed	Fed	Fed
VIRGINIA					
Samuel J. Cabell	Rep	Rep	Rep	Rep	Rep
Matthew Clay	Rep	Rep	Rep	Rep	Rep
John Dawson	Rep	Rep	Rep	Rep	Rep
Joseph Eggleston	Rep	Rep	Rep	Rep	Rep
Thomas Evans	None	None	Fed	Fed	Fed
Samuel Goode	None	None	Fed	Fed	Rep
Edwin Gray	None	None	Fed	Fed	Rep
David Holmes	None	Rep	Rep	Rep	Rep
George Jackson	None	Rep	Rep	Rep	Rep
Henry Lee	Fed	Fed	Fed	Fed	Fed
John Marshall	None	Fed	Fed	Fed	(2)
Anthony New	Rep	Rep	Rep	Rep	Rep
John Nicholas	Rep	Rep	Rep	Rep	Rep
Robert Page	Fed	Fed	Fed	Fed	Fed
Josiah Parker	None	Antifed	Fed	Fed	Fed
Levin Powell	Fed	Fed	Fed	Fed	Fed
John Randolph	Rep	Rep	Rep	Rep	Rep
Littleton Tazewell	Rep	Rep	Rep	Rep	(2)
Abram Trigg	None	Fed	Rep	Rep	Rep
John J. Trigg	None	Fed	Rep	Rep	Rep

Table 24. (continued)

House of Representatives, Seventh Congress (1801-1803)

	BIOGDIR	ICPSR	DAUER	MDSBLOC
CONNECTICUT				
Samuel W. Dana	Fed	Fed	Fed	Fed
John Davenport	Fed	Fed	Fed	Fed
Calvin Goodard	Fed	Fed	Fed	Fed
Roger Griswold	Fed	Fed	Fed	Fed
Elias Perkins	Fed	Fed	Fed	Fed
John C. Smith	Fed	Fed	Fed	Fed
Benjamin Tallmadge	Fed	Fed	Fed	Fed
DELAWARE				
James Bayard	Fed	Fed	Fed	Fed
GEORGIA				
Peter Early	None	None	None	(2)
David Meriwether	Rep	Rep	None	(2)
John Milledge	None	None	Rep	Rep
Benjamin Taliaferro	None	None	None	(2)
KENTUCKY				
Thomas T. Davis	None	None	Rep	Rep
John Fowler	None	Rep	Rep	Rep
MARYLAND				
John Archer	Rep	Rep	Rep	Rep
Walter Bowie	Rep	Rep	Rep	(2)
John Campbell	Fed	Fed	Fed	Fed
John Dennis	Fed	Fed	Fed	Fed
Daniel Hiester	None	None	Rep	Rep
Joseph H. Nicholson	Rep	Rep	Rep	Rep
Thomas Plater	None	None	Fed	Fed
Samuel Smith	Rep	Rep	Rep	Rep
Richard Sprigg	None	None	Rep	(2)
MASSACHUSETTS				
John Bacon	Rep	Rep	Rep	Rep
Phanuel Bishop	None	None	Rep	Rep
Manasseh Cutler	Fed	Fed	Fed	Fed
Richard Cutts	Rep	Rep	Rep	Rep
William Eustis	Rep	Rep	Rep	Rep
Seth Hastings	Fed	Fed	Fed	Fed
Silas Lee	Fed	Fed	Fed	(2)
Levi Lincoln	Rep	Rep	Rep	(2)
Ebenezer Mattoon	Fed	Fed	Fed	Fed
Nathan Read	Fed	Fed	Fed	Fed
William Shepard	None	None	Fed	Fed
Josiah Smith	None	None	Rep	Rep
Samuel Thatcher	Rep	Rep	None	(2)
Joseph B. Varnum	None	None	Rep	Rep
Peleg Wadsworth	None	None	Fed	Fed
Lemuel Williams	None	None	Fed	Fed
NEW HAMPSHIRE				
Abiel Foster	None	Fed	Fed	Fed
Samuel Hunt	None	None	None	(2)
Joseph Peirce	None	None	Fed	Fed
Samuel Tenney	None	None	Fed	Fed
George B. Upham	None	None	Fed	Fed
NEW JERSEY				
John Condit	Rep	Rep	Rep	Rep
Ebenezer Elmer	Rep	Rep	Rep	Rep
William Helms	Rep	Rep	Rep	Rep
James Mott	Rep	Rep	Rep	Rep
Henry Southard	Rep	Rep	Rep	Rep

Table 24. (continued)

House of Representatives, Seventh Congress (1801-1803) (cont.)

	BIOGDIR	ICPSR	DAUER	MDSBLOC
NEW YORK				
Theodorus Bailey	Rep	Rep	Rep	Rep
John Bird	Rep	Rep	None	(2)
Lucas C. Elmendorf	Rep	Rep	Rep	Rep
Samuel L. Mitchill	Rep	Rep	Rep	Rep
Thomas Morris	None	None	Fed	Fed
John Smith	Rep	Rep	Rep	Rep
David Thomas	Rep	Rep	Rep	Rep
Thomas Tillotson	None	None	Rep	(2)
Philip Van Cortlandt	Rep	Rep	Rep	Rep
John P. Van Ness	Rep	Rep	Rep	Rep
Killian Van Rensselaer	Rep	Rep	Fed	Fed
Benjamin Walker	Rep	Rep	Fed	Fed
NORTH CAROLINA				
Willis Alston	War Dem	War Dem	Fed	Rep
William Barry Grove	Fed	Fed	Fed	Fed
Archibald Henderson	Fed	Fed	Fed	Fed
William H. Hill	Fed	Fed	Fed	Fed
James Holland	Antifed	None	Rep	Rep
Charles Johnson	None	None	Rep	(2)
Nathaniel Macon	Rep	Rep	Rep	(4)
Richard Stanford	Rep	Rep	Rep	Rep
John Stanly	None	None	Fed	Fed
Robert Williams	None	None	Rep	Rep
Thomas Wynns	Fed	Fed	None	(2)
PENNSYLVANIA				
Thomas Boude	Fed	Fed	Fed	Fed
Robert Brown	Rep	Rep	Rep	Rep
Andrew Gregg	None	Rep	Rep	Rep
John A. Hanna	Antifed	Antifed	Rep	Rep
Joseph Hemphill	Fed	Fed	Fed	Fed
Joseph Hiester	Fed	Fed	Rep	Rep
William Hoge	Fed	Fed	Fed	Rep
William Jones	Rep	Rep	Rep	Rep
Michael Leib	Rep	Rep	Rep	Rep
John Smilie	Rep	Rep	Rep	Rep
John Stewart	Rep	Rep	Rep	Rep
Isaac Van Horne	Rep	Rep	Rep	Rep
Henry Woods	None	None	Fed	Fed
RHODE ISLAND				
Joseph Stanton	Rep	Rep	Rep	Rep
Thomas Tillinghast	None	None	Rep	Fed
SOUTH CAROLINA				
William Butler	Antifed	Antifed	Rep	Rep
Benjamin Huger	None	None	Fed	Fed
Thomas Lowndes	Fed	Fed	Fed	Fed
Thomas Moore	None	None	Rep	Rep
John Rutledge	Fed	Fed	Fed	Fed
Thomas Sumter	Rep	Rep	Rep	(2)
Richard Winn	Rep	Rep	None	(2)
TENNESSEE				
William Dickson	None	None	Rep	Rep
VERMONT				
Lewis R. Morris	Fed	Fed	Fed	Fed
Israel Smith	Rep	Rep	Rep	Rep

214 Origins of American Political Parties

Table 24. (continued)

House of Representatives, Seventh Congress (1801-1803) (cont.)

VIRGINIA	BIOGDIR	ICPSR	DAUER	MDSBLOC
Richard Brent	None	None	Rep	Rep
Samuel J. Cabell	Rep	Rep	Rep	Rep
Thomas Claiborne	None	Rep	Rep	Rep
Matthew Clay	Rep	Rep	Rep	Rep
John Clopton	Rep	Rep	Rep	Rep
John Dawson	Rep	Rep	Rep	Rep
William Branch Giles	Rep	Rep	Rep	Rep
Edwin Gray	None	None	Fed	Rep
David Holmes	None	None	Rep	Rep
George Jackson	None	None	Rep	Rep
Anthony New	Rep	Rep	Rep	Rep
Thomas Newton	Rep	Rep	Rep	Rep
John Randolph	Rep	Rep	Rep	Rep
John Smith	Rep	None	Rep	Rep
John Stratton	None	None	Fed	Fed
John Taliaferro	Rep	Rep	Rep	Rep
Philip R. Thompson	Rep	Rep	Rep	Rep
Abram Trigg	None	None	Rep	Rep
John J. Trigg	None	None	Rep	Rep

Explanatory Notes

Note: Sources for Party Coding

    BELL = party codes from Bell (1973)
    BIOGDIR = party codes from U.S., Congress (1971)
    DAUER = party codes from Dauer (1953)
    ICPSR = party codes from ICPSR file codes
    MDSBLOC = party codes from spatial configurations
    PAULLIN = party codes from Paullin (1904)

Note: Explanations of Party Abbreviations
      (for BELL, BIOGDIR, DAUER, ICPSR, PAULLIN)

    Antifed = Antifederalist
    Anti-Adm = Anti-Administration
    Fed = Federalist
    None = No party listed or minor party
    Pro-Adm = Pro-Administration
    Rep = Republican
    War Dem = War Democrat
    Whig = Whig

Note: Explanations of Voting Bloc Abbreviations
      (for MDSBLOC)

    Fed = Federalist voting bloc
    Ind = No voting bloc
    Middle = Middle States voting bloc
    New Eng = New England voting bloc
    Rep = Republican voting bloc
    South = Southern voting bloc

    (1) State joined U.S. during session; insufficient votes
    (2) Served partial term; insufficient votes
    (3) Did not vote on a sufficient number of roll calls
    (4) Speaker does not vote on most roll calls

Table 25. Party Affiliations of Senators, 1789-1803

Senate, First Congress (1789-1791)

NAME	STATE	BIOGDIR	ICPSR	PAULLIN	MDSBLOC
Oliver Ellsworth	Connecticut	Fed	Fed	Fed	Ind
William S. Johnson	Connecticut	None	None	Fed	Ind
Richard Bassett	Delaware	Fed	Fed	Fed	Ind
George Read	Delaware	None	Fed	Fed	Ind
William Few	Georgia	Rep	Rep	Fed	Ind
James Gunn	Georgia	None	None	Fed	Ind
Charles Carroll	Maryland	Fed	Fed	Fed	Ind
John Henry	Maryland	Rep	Rep	Fed	Ind
Tristram Dalton	Massachusetts	None	None	Fed	Ind
Caleb Strong	Massachusetts	Fed	Fed	Fed	Ind
John Langdon	New Hampshire	Rep	Rep	Fed	Ind
Paine Wingate	New Hampshire	Fed	Fed	Fed	Ind
Philemon Dickinson	New Jersey	None	None	None	(2)
Jonathan Elmer	New Jersey	Fed	Fed	Fed	Ind
William Paterson	New Jersey	Fed	Fed	Fed	Ind
Rufus King	New York	Fed	Fed	Fed	Ind
Philip Schuyler	New York	Fed	Fed	Fed	Ind
Benjamin Hawkins	North Carolina	Fed	Fed	Fed	Ind
Samuel Johnston	North Carolina	Fed	Fed	Fed	Ind
William Maclay	Pennsylvania	Rep	Rep	Fed	Ind
Robert Morris	Pennsylvania	None	Fed	Fed	Ind
Theodore Foster	Rhode Island	None	None	Fed	Ind
Joseph Stanton, Jr.	Rhode Island	Rep	Rep	Fed	Ind
Pierce Butler	South Carolina	Rep	Rep	Fed	Ind
Ralph Izard	South Carolina	None	Fed	Fed	Ind
William Grayson	Virginia	None	Antifed	Antifed	(2)
Richard Henry Lee	Virginia	None	Rep	Antifed	Ind
James Monroe	Virginia	Rep	Antifed	Antifed	(2)
John Walker	Virginia	None	None	None	Ind

Senate, Second Congress (1791-1793)

NAME	STATE	BIOGDIR	ICPSR	MDSBLOC
Oliver Ellsworth	Connecticut	Fed	Fed	Fed-N
William S. Johnson	Connecticut	None	None	(2)
Roger Sherman	Connecticut	None	None	Rep-N
Richard Bassett	Delaware	Fed	Fed	Fed-N
George Read	Delaware	None	Fed	Fed-N
William Few	Georgia	Rep	Rep	Rep-S
James Gunn	Georgia	None	None	Rep-S
John Brown	Kentucky	None	Rep	(1)
John Edwards	Kentucky	None	Rep	(1)
Charles Carroll	Maryland	Fed	Fed	Fed-S
John Henry	Maryland	Rep	Rep	Fed-S
Richard Potts	Maryland	Fed	Fed	(2)
George Cabot	Massachusetts	Fed	Fed	Fed-N
Caleb Strong	Massachusetts	Fed	Fed	Rep-N
John Langdon	New Hampshire	Rep	Rep	Fed-N
Paine Wingate	New Hampshire	Fed	Fed	Rep-N
Philemon Dickinson	New Jersey	None	None	Fed-S
John Rutherfurd	New Jersey	Fed	Fed	Fed-N
Aaron Burr	New York	Rep	Rep	Ind
Rufus King	New York	Fed	Fed	Fed-N
Benjamin Hawkins	North Carolina	Fed	Fed	Rep-S
Samuel Johnston	North Carolina	Fed	Fed	Fed-S
Robert Morris	Pennsylvania	None	Fed	Fed-S
Theodore Foster	Rhode Island	None	None	Rep-N
Joseph Stanton, Jr.	Rhode Island	Rep	Rep	Rep-N
Pierce Butler	South Carolina	Rep	Rep	Rep-S
Ralph Izard	South Carolina	None	Fed	Fed-S

Table 25. (continued)

Senate, Second Congress (1791-1793) (cont.)

NAME	STATE	BIOGDIR	ICPSR	MDSBLOC
Stephen R. Bradley	Vermont	Rep	Rep	Rep-N
Moses Robinson	Vermont	Rep	Rep	Rep-N
Richard Henry Lee	Virginia	None	Antifed	Rep-S
James Monroe	Virginia	Rep	Antifed	Rep-S
John Taylor	Virginia	Rep	Rep	(2)

Senate, Third Congress (1793-1795)

NAME	STATE	BIOGDIR	ICPSR	MDSBLOC
Oliver Ellsworth	Connecticut	Fed	Fed	Fed
Stephen M. Mitchell	Connecticut	Fed	Fed	Fed
Roger Sherman	Connecticut	None	None	(2)
Henry Latimer	Delaware	None	None	(2)
George Read	Delaware	None	None	(2)
John Vining	Delaware	None	None	Fed
James Gunn	Georgia	None	None	Rep
James Jackson	Georgia	Rep	Rep	Rep
John Brown	Kentucky	None	None	Rep
John Edwards	Kentucky	None	None	Rep
John Henry	Maryland	Rep	Rep	Fed
Richard Potts	Maryland	Fed	Fed	Fed
George Cabot	Massachusetts	Fed	Fed	Fed
Caleb Strong	Massachusetts	Fed	Fed	Fed
John Langdon	New Hampshire	Rep	Rep	Rep
Samuel Livermore	New Hampshire	None	None	Fed
Frederick Frelinghuysen	New Jersey	Fed	Fed	Fed
John Rutherfurd	New Jersey	Fed	Fed	Fed
Aaron Burr	New York	Rep	Rep	Rep
Rufus King	New York	Fed	Fed	Fed
Benjamin Hawkins	North Carolina	Fed	Fed	Rep
Alexander Martin	North Carolina	None	None	Rep
Albert Gallatin	Pennsylvania	Rep	Rep	(2)
Robert Morris	Pennsylvania	None	None	Fed
James Ross	Pennsylvania	Fed	Fed	Ind
William Bradford	Rhode Island	None	None	Fed
Theodore Foster	Rhode Island	None	None	Fed
Pierce Butler	South Carolina	Rep	Rep	Rep
Ralph Izard	South Carolina	None	None	Fed
Stephen R. Bradley	Vermont	Rep	Rep	Rep
Moses Robinson	Vermont	Rep	Rep	Rep
Stevens T. Mason	Virginia	Rep	Rep	(2)
James Monroe	Virginia	Rep	None	Rep
John Taylor	Virginia	Rep	Rep	Rep
Henry Tazewell	Virginia	None	None	(2)

Senate, Fourth Congress (1795-1797)

NAME	STATE	BIOGDIR	ICPSR	MDSBLOC
Oliver Ellsworth	Connecticut	Fed	Fed	Fed
James Hillhouse	Connecticut	Fed	Fed	(2)
Uriah Tracy	Connecticut	Fed	Fed	(2)
Jonathan Trumbull	Connecticut	Fed	Fed	Fed
Henry Latimer	Delaware	None	Fed	Fed
John Vining	Delaware	None	None	Fed
James Gunn	Georgia	None	None	Fed
James Jackson	Georgia	Rep	Rep	(2)
Josiah Tattnall	Georgia	None	None	Rep
George Walton	Georgia	None	None	(2)

Party Affiliation of Members of Congress 217

Table 25. (continued)

Senate, Fourth Congress (1795-1797) (cont.)

NAME	STATE	BIOGDIR	ICPSR	MDSBLOC
John Brown	Kentucky	None	Rep	Rep
Humphrey Marshall	Kentucky	Fed	Fed	Ind
John Henry	Maryland	Rep	Rep	Ind
John E. Howard	Maryland	Fed	Fed	(2)
Richard Potts	Maryland	Fed	Fed	Fed
George Cabot	Massachusetts	Fed	Fed	Fed
Benjamin Goodhue	Massachusetts	None	None	(2)
Theodore Sedgwick	Massachusetts	Fed	Fed	(2)
Caleb Strong	Massachusetts	Fed	Fed	Fed
John Langdon	New Hampshire	Rep	Rep	Rep
Samuel Livermore	New Hampshire	None	None	Fed
Frederick Frelinghuysen	New Jersey	Fed	Fed	Fed
John Rutherfurd	New Jersey	Fed	Fed	Fed
Richard Stockton	New Jersey	Fed	Fed	(2)
Aaron Burr	New York	Rep	Rep	Rep
Rufus King	New York	Fed	Fed	Fed
John Laurance	New York	None	None	(2)
Timothy Bloodworth	North Carolina	None	Rep	Rep
Alexander Martin	North Carolina	None	Rep	Rep
William Bingham	Pennsylvania	None	Fed	Fed
James Ross	Pennsylvania	Fed	Fed	Fed
William Bradford	Rhode Island	None	None	Fed
Theodore Foster	Rhode Island	None	None	Fed
Pierce Butler	South Carolina	Rep	Rep	Rep
John Hunter	South Carolina	Fed	None	(2)
Jacob Read	South Carolina	Fed	Fed	Fed
William Blount	Tennessee	None	None	(1)
William Cocke	Tennessee	None	None	(1)
Elijah Paine	Vermont	Fed	Fed	Fed
Moses Robinson	Vermont	Rep	Rep	Rep
Isaac Tichenor	Vermont	Fed	Fed	(2)
Stevens T. Mason	Virginia	Rep	Rep	Rep
Henry Tazewell	Virginia	None	Rep	Rep

Senate, Fifth Congress (1797-1799)

NAME	STATE	BIOGDIR	ICPSR	MDSBLOC
James Hillhouse	Connecticut	Fed	Fed	Fed
Uriah Tracy	Connecticut	Fed	Fed	Fed
Joshua Clayton	Delaware	None	None	Fed
Henry Latimer	Delaware	None	Fed	Fed
John Vining	Delaware	None	None	(2)
William H. Wells	Delaware	None	None	(2)
James Gunn	Georgia	None	None	Ind
Josiah Tattnall	Georgia	None	None	Rep
John Brown	Kentucky	None	Rep	Rep
Humphrey Marshall	Kentucky	Fed	Fed	Ind
John Henry	Maryland	Rep	Rep	(2)
John E. Howard	Maryland	Fed	Fed	Fed
James Lloyd	Maryland	Rep	Rep	Rep
Benjamin Goodhue	Massachusetts	None	Fed	Fed
Theodore Sedgwick	Massachusetts	Fed	Fed	Fed
John Langdon	New Hampshire	Rep	Rep	Rep
Samuel Livermore	New Hampshire	None	None	Fed
Franklin Davenport	New Jersey	None	None	(2)
John Rutherfurd	New Jersey	Fed	Fed	Fed
Richard Stockton	New Jersey	Fed	Fed	Fed
John Hobart	New York	None	None	(2)
John Laurance	New York	None	Fed	Fed
William North	New York	Fed	Fed	Fed
Philip Schuyler	New York	Fed	Fed	(2)
James Watson	New York	Rep	Rep	(2)

Table 25. (continued)

Senate, Fifth Congress (1797-1799) (cont.)

NAME	STATE	BIOGDIR	ICPSR	MDSBLOC
Timothy Bloodworth	North Carolina	None	Rep	Rep
Alexander Martin	North Carolina	None	Rep	Rep
William Bingham	Pennsylvania	None	Fed	Fed
James Ross	Pennsylvania	Fed	Fed	Fed
William Bradford	Rhode Island	None	None	(2)
Theodore Foster	Rhode Island	None	None	Fed
Ray Greene	Rhode Island	Fed	None	Fed
John Hunter	South Carolina	Fed	None	Ind
Charles Pinckney	South Carolina	Rep	Rep	(2)
Jacob Read	South Carolina	Fed	Fed	Fed
Joseph Anderson	Tennessee	None	None	Rep
William Blount	Tennessee	None	None	(2)
William Cocke	Tennessee	None	None	(2)
Andrew Jackson	Tennessee	Rep	Rep	(2)
Daniel Smith	Tennessee	Rep	Rep	(2)
Nathaniel Chipman	Vermont	None	Fed	Fed
Elijah Paine	Vermont	Fed	Fed	Fed
Isaac Tichenor	Vermont	Fed	Fed	(2)
Stevens T. Mason	Virginia	Rep	Rep	Rep
Henry Tazewell	Virginia	None	Rep	Rep

Senate, Sixth Congress (1799-1801)

NAME	STATE	BIOGDIR	ICPSR	MDSBLOC
James Hillhouse	Connecticut	Fed	Fed	Fed
Uriah Tracy	Connecticut	Fed	Fed	Fed
Henry Latimer	Delaware	None	Fed	Fed
William H. Wells	Delaware	None	None	Fed
Samuel White	Delaware	Fed	Fed	(2)
Abraham Baldwin	Georgia	Fed	Fed	Rep
James Gunn	Georgia	None	None	Fed
John Brown	Kentucky	None	Rep	Rep
Humphrey Marshall	Kentucky	Fed	Fed	Ind
William Hindman	Maryland	None	Fed	Fed
John E. Howard	Maryland	Fed	Fed	Fed
James Lloyd	Maryland	Rep	Rep	Rep
Samuel Dexter	Massachusetts	Fed	Fed	Fed
Dwight Foster	Massachusetts	Fed	Fed	Fed
Benjamin Goodhue	Massachusetts	None	Fed	Fed
Jonathan Mason	Massachusetts	Fed	Fed	Fed
John Langdon	New Hampshire	Rep	Rep	Rep
Samuel Livermore	New Hampshire	None	None	Fed
Jonathan Dayton	New Jersey	Fed	Fed	Fed
Aaron Ogden	New Jersey	Fed	Fed	(2)
James Schureman	New Jersey	Fed	Fed	Fed
John Armstrong	New York	Rep	Rep	Rep
John Laurance	New York	None	Fed	Fed
Gouverneur Morris	New York	Fed	Fed	Fed
James Watson	New York	Rep	Rep	(2)
Timothy Bloodworth	North Carolina	None	Rep	Rep
Jesse Franklin	North Carolina	Rep	Rep	Rep
William Bingham	Pennsylvania	None	Fed	Fed
James Ross	Pennsylvania	Fed	Fed	Fed
Theodore Foster	Rhode Island	None	Fed	Fed
Ray Greene	Rhode Island	Fed	None	Fed
Charles Pinckney	South Carolina	Rep	Rep	Rep
Jacob Read	South Carolina	Fed	Fed	Fed
Joseph Anderson	Tennessee	None	None	Rep
William Cocke	Tennessee	None	None	Rep
Nathaniel Chipman	Vermont	Fed	Fed	Fed
Elijah Paine	Vermont	Fed	Fed	Fed
Stevens T. Mason	Virginia	Rep	Rep	Rep
Wilson C. Nicholas	Virginia	Rep	Rep	Rep

Table 25. (continued)

Senate, Seventh Congress (1801-1803)

NAME	STATE	BIOGDIR	ICPSR	MDSBLOC
James Hillhouse	Connecticut	Fed	Fed	Fed
Uriah Tracy	Connecticut	Fed	Fed	Fed
William H. Wells	Delaware	None	None	Fed
Samuel White	Delaware	Fed	Fed	Fed
Abraham Baldwin	Georgia	Fed	Fed	Rep
James Jackson	Georgia	Rep	Rep	Rep
John Breckenridge	Kentucky	Rep	Rep	Rep
John Brown	Kentucky	None	Rep	Rep
William Hindman	Maryland	None	Fed	(2)
John E. Howard	Maryland	Fed	Fed	Fed
Robert Wright	Maryland	Rep	Rep	Rep
Dwight Foster	Massachusetts	Fed	Fed	Fed
Jonathan Mason	Massachusetts	Fed	Fed	Fed
Samuel Livermore	New Hampshire	None	None	(2)
Simeon Olcott	New Hampshire	Fed	Fed	Fed
William Plumer	New Hampshire	Fed	Fed	Fed
James Sheafe	New Hampshire	Fed	Fed	(2)
Jonathan Dayton	New Jersey	Fed	Fed	Fed
Aaron Ogden	New Jersey	Fed	Fed	Fed
John Armstrong	New York	None	Rep	(2)
DeWitt Clinton	New York	Rep	Rep	Rep
Gouverneur Morris	New York	Fed	Fed	Fed
Jesse Franklin	North Carolina	Rep	Rep	Rep
David Stone	North Carolina	Rep	Rep	Rep
George Logan	Pennsylvania	Rep	Rep	Rep
John Peter Muhlenberg	Pennsylvania	Rep	Rep	(2)
James Ross	Pennsylvania	Fed	Fed	Fed
Christopher Ellery	Rhode Island	Rep	Rep	Rep
Theodore Foster	Rhode Island	None	None	Rep
Ray Greene	Rhode Island	Fed	None	(2)
John E. Colhoun	South Carolina	Rep	Rep	Rep
Charles Pinckney	South Carolina	Rep	Rep	(2)
Thomas Sumter	South Carolina	Rep	Rep	Rep
Joseph Anderson	Tennessee	None	None	Rep
William Cocke	Tennessee	None	None	Rep
Stephen R. Bradley	Vermont	Rep	Rep	Rep
Nathaniel Chipman	Vermont	None	Fed	Fed
Elijah Paine	Vermont	Fed	Fed	(2)
Stevens T. Mason	Virginia	Rep	Rep	Rep
Wilson C. Nicholas	Virginia	Rep	Rep	Rep

Explanatory Notes

Note: For Sources for Party Coding (BIOGDIR, ICPSR, MDSBLOC, PAULLIN) and Explanations of Party Abbreviations (for BIOGDIR, ICPSR, PAULLIN), see page 214.

Note: Explanations of Voting Bloc Abbreviations
(for MDSBLOC)

    Fed   = Federalist voting bloc
    Fed-N = Federalist-North voting bloc
    Fed-S = Federalist-South voting bloc
    Ind   = No voting bloc
    Rep   = Republican voting bloc
    Rep-N = Republican-North voting bloc
    Rep-S = Republican-South voting bloc

    (1) State joined U.S. during session; insufficient votes
    (2) Served partial term; insufficient votes

APPENDIX B

Representing Individual Roll Calls in Spatial Configurations

After deriving configurations that represent the patterns of voting over all roll calls in a particular Congress, it is helpful to examine certain individual roll calls so as to highlight various aspects of the configurations, particularly for the earlier years of the period being studied. Taken over time, the relative positions of various roll calls help to show how emerging partisanship is related to issues. Finally, it is possible to learn whether there are roll calls or issue areas that do not fit the basic spatial patterns, thus providing a further indication of the extent to which spatial configurations provide an accurate representation of voting patterns.

The general model of legislative voting used here is one where a roll call is represented by a line of cleavage in a space of legislators, separating those voting yes from those voting no. Unfortunately, no existing procedure accurately reproduces these cleavage lines (without restrictive distributional assumptions), although it may ultimately be possible to derive such a procedure.

There are several methods that make it possible to obtain an approximation of the cleavage line: multiple regression analysis, multiple optimal regression (MORALS), discriminant analysis, and "visual" analysis.[1] The latter procedure has no mathematical properties, but it is subject to the limitations of the human eye (or the searching capabilities of the computer). Multiple regression and discriminant analysis both require distributional assumptions that often cannot be met, while the MORALS procedure is new and relatively untested. Nevertheless, with a few leaps of faith and some triangulation of methods, an exploratory analysis can proceed.

It is important, however, to treat this analysis in a exploratory manner. The main interest is in a general indication of the direction for roll calls in a particular issue area. If several roll calls in the same issue area can be represented in similar ways, then our confidence in this representation grows. Further, if the methods of analysis seem to produce similar results, then again greater confidence is possible. This brings us, then, to a consideration of the available methods.

Several Analytical Methods

Multiple regression can in general be used to embed a vector, representing some external trait, in a configuration space.[2] This technique can thus be used to locate a vector representing an individual roll call. The roll call (where yes is coded 1 and no is coded 0, or vice versa) is entered as the dependent variable, while the two dimensions of the configuration are independent variables.[3] From the results of the regression analysis, the position of the vector can be determined by a line segment connecting the (arbitrary) center of the space and the point ($b1$, $b2$), where $b1$ and $b2$ are the (unstandardized) regression coefficients corresponding to the two dimensions. The vector determined by this line segment indicates the directions of yes and no votes (see figure 39). More precisely, if points for legislators are projected onto this vector, those voting yes should cluster at one end, with those voting no at the other end (depending on the amount of error).

Next, it is possible to draw an appropriate line of cleavage as a line that is orthogonal to this vector. One obvious point for constructing the line of cleavage is that point where the predicted value of the dependent variable is equal to 0.50.[4] This point is equidistant from the predicted values of 1 and 0, and thus it is a logical dividing point. Given this or any other line of cleavage, it is then simple to determine the proportion of correct predictions—a statistic that may prove to be a better measure of fit than R^2 for this type of analysis (see figure 39).

There are some good features in the use of regression analysis. First, its general suitability has been well demonstrated, and it clearly provides the general type of information desired. Second, it is an accepted technique for which computer programs are easily available.

There are well-known difficulties in using regression analysis with a dichotomous dependent variable.[5] First, the assumption of a normally distributed error term is violated, since the dependent variable takes on only two values. Because of this, the standard ordinary least-squares (OLS) procedure for estimating regression coefficients is inappropriate. Its use would lead to residuals that are correlated with the independent variables and whose variance is not constant across the values of the independent variables (Aldrich and Cnudde, 1975, pp. 577-79).

A second problem with the use of dichotomous dependent variables comes in the predicted values resulting from the regression equation. These values are not restricted to the two values of the dependent variable (0 and 1), but range continuously (see figure 40). Even if these values are given a probability interpretation (i.e., the predicted value is the probability of the event coded 1), these values are unsatisfactory, because their range includes values greater than 1 and less than 0. Furthermore, the usual measure of fit (R^2) is calculated from the residuals, or the deviations between the actual values (0 or 1) and the estimates. Thus, when the predicted value is, say, 0.7 and the actual value is 1, there is a substantial error term, even though the simple dichotomous prediction is correct.[6] Thus, R^2 is not a very satisfactory measure of fit for the present situation.

One significant variation in the use of regression analysis is the multiple optimal regression by alternating least squares (MORALS) technique, which draws upon the methodology of multidimensional scaling analysis (Young, deLeeuw, Takane, 1976). In general, this method is an extension of multiple regression "to the situation where the variables may be measured at a variety of levels . . . , and where they may be either continous or discrete" (p. 105). Basically, it rescales the observations on each variable, subject to the appropriate measurement restrictions, so as to maximize the multiple correlation. It is an iterative technique, alternating between an optimal rescaling of the data and a multiple regression on the rescaled data.

In the present case, the two independent variables are measured at the interval level and so are not affected by this analysis. Technically, any dichotomous variable can be regarded as being measured at the interval level (since there is only one interval), the ordinal level, or the nominal level. For various reasons, it turns out best to regard the dichotomous dependent variable as an ordinal variable. The MORALS procedure has two ways of treating a noncontinuous variable where ties exist (i.e., where several cases share the same value). Under one option, known as the discrete process (secondary method), it is assumed that ties are meaningful and that observa-

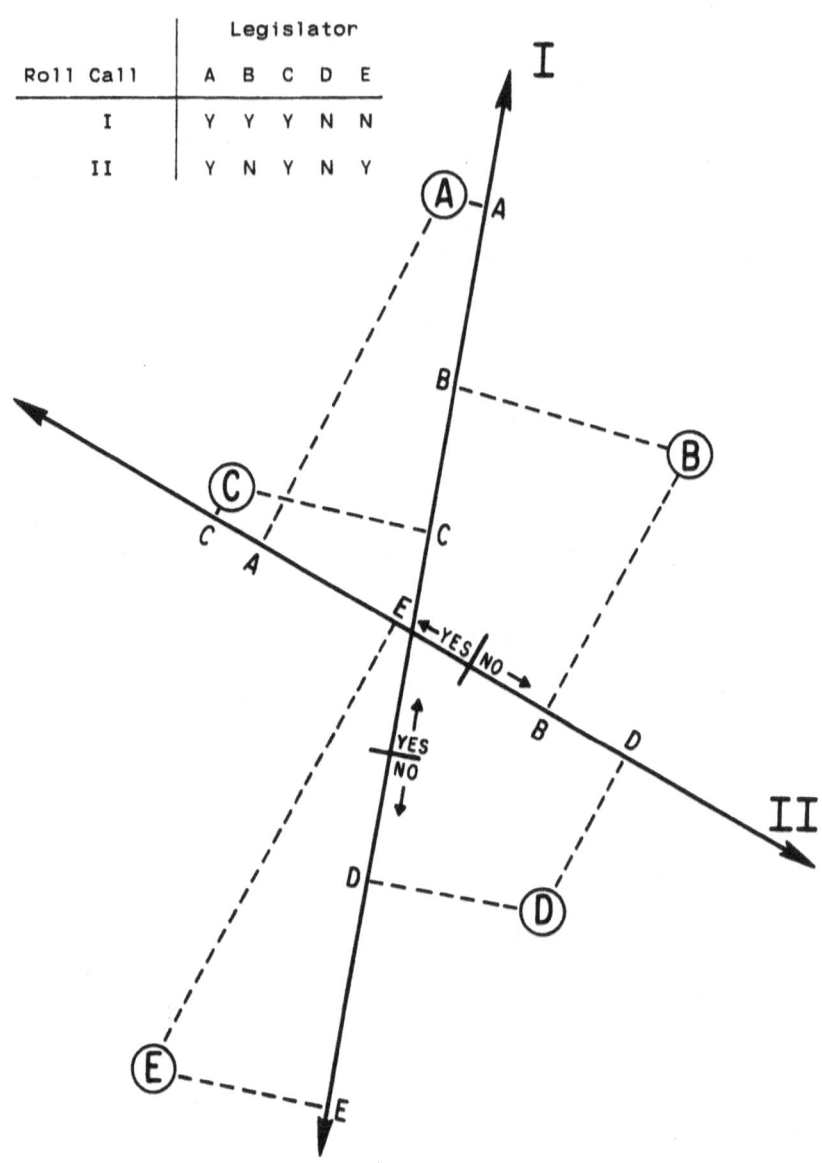

Source: Rabinowitz (1975, fig. 12).

Fig 39. Vectors in a Multidimensional Scaling Space

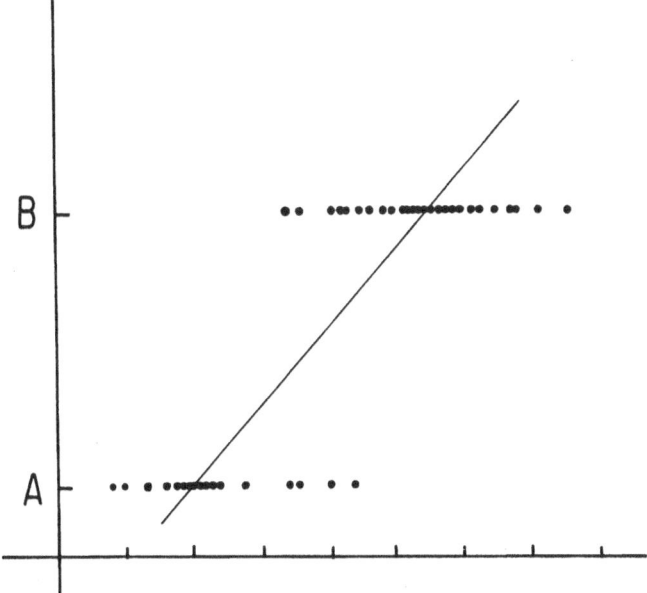

Fig. 40. Regression with a Dichotomous Dependent Variable

tions should remain tied. In this case, MORALS simply assigns new values to the yes and no votes, and the actual regression coefficients change, but not the position of the resulting vector. Nor should the value of R^2 or the percentage of classification errors change.

Under the alternative option, known as the continous process (primary method), the results are far more interesting. Here the cases in a particular category of the dependent variable are not constrained to be all assigned the same value; the only constraint is that the values for the two categories cannot overlap. For the present situation of a roll call with two alternatives, the procedure has the following effect: the transformed dependent variable is first set equal to the predicted value from the regression equation; where an overlap exists between observations in the two categories, the transformed value for a group of observations is set equal to the mean of the predicted values for that group, the smallest such group that eliminates the overlap (see figure 41). This is done in such a way as to minimize the sum of squared differences betwen the predicted values and the transformed values. This rescaling (known as the least-squares monotonic transformation) then provides the dependent variable for the new regression analysis. The yes and no votes are thus rescaled, so that different legislators in effect have different "degrees" of yes and no.

The two processes (regression and rescaling) are then iterated in an alternating manner until the results converge. In practice (with the dichotomous dependent variable), there should be little improvement beyond the single rescaling just described. The promise of this procedure is to avoid some problems of using a dichotomous dependent variable, since (under the continuous option) it removes the dichotomy. No longer are predicted values outside the (0, 1) interval a problem. Still, it is not clear whether the results of this technique are useful, or even whether meaningful solutions are generated.

Discriminant analysis is a technique that shares the goals and assumptions of

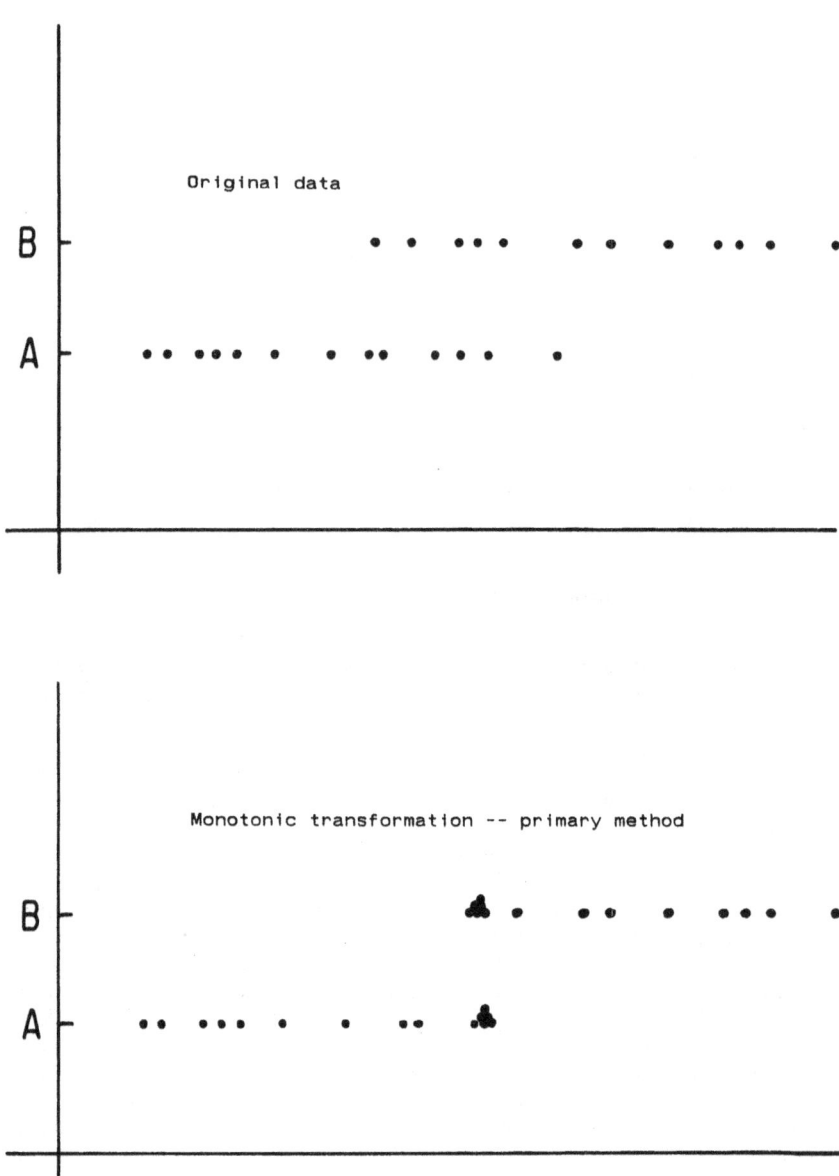

Fig. 41. Primary Method for Ties

regression analysis, but where the dependent variable is measured at the nominal level and where a key aim is the classification of cases into groups defined by this nominal variable. With a dichotomous dependent variable, discriminant analysis involves finding the best discrimination between cases in the two groups of the dichotomy.[7]

On the surface, it appears that discriminant analysis is well suited to the task at hand. As before, the dependent variable is an individual roll call vote (or a party variable), and the independent variables are the dimensions of the space. A discriminant function is then derived, being that linear combination of the independent variables that best discriminates between the two groups.[8] This discriminant function is similar in form to the regression function, but estimation procedures are different. The (unstandardized) coefficients can be used to position a vector representing the roll call, in the same way as the regression weights.

Once the discriminant function has been determined, the remaining task is to classify the cases. This requires determination of a constant that demarcates the cases of one group from the other group. Under the assumption that both groups are normally distributed on the independent variables with equal variance-covariance matrices, it is possible to compute the probability that a particular case came from one group or the other. A case can then be classified into the group with which it has a greater probability, and the two groups are demarcated accordingly.

Several factors affect this process of classification. One is the selection of prior probabilities. The simplest assumption is that all cases have an equal probability of belonging to each group. An alternative assumption is to set the prior probabilities equal to the proportions of cases in each group. Different priors correspond to different lines of cleavage drawn parallel to each other (see figure 42).

An additional factor affecting the classification of cases is the variance-covariance matrices of the two groups. The procedures described thus far make the assumption of equal covariance matrices. With this assumption, a pooled covariance matrix is used, and the constant can be determined as described above. Should this assumption not be met, this simple designation of the line of cleavage is not correct. In some cases, a curved line may yield the best prediction (see figure 43). In fact, the entire analysis becomes more complex, for the estimation of the discriminant function coefficients is also affected, and interpretation becomes more difficult. It is possible to test this assumption, and the results of such a test are reported below.

Two statistics are available that can measure the degree of fit for a particular discriminant analysis. The most appealing measure is the percentage of cases that are correctly classified. This is a direct measure of how well the analysis has succeeded in the classification task. An alternative statistic is the Mahalanobis D^2, a generalized measure of the distance between the two groups. It tests whether the two groups are effectively distinguished by the discriminant function.

The advantage of discriminant analysis for the representation of individual roll calls in a multidimensional scaling space is that it is designed for precisely that sort of task. It avoids the problems associated with using a dichotomous dependent variable in regression analysis, for it aims at discriminating between groups or classifying into groups, rather than estimating values along a continuum.

The principal disadvantage, however, lies in the normality assumption imposed on the distributions of the two groups on the independent variables. Such an assumption is rather obviously not met by most roll call groupings. Aldrich and Cnudde (1975, p. 588) point out, "With this [normality] assumption it is possible to estimate the probability of each observation being in any one of the classes of [the dependent variable]." While computation of the actual discriminant function is unaffected by distributional assumptions, the usual probabilistic means of making classifications does require the normality assumption. Without this assumption, one

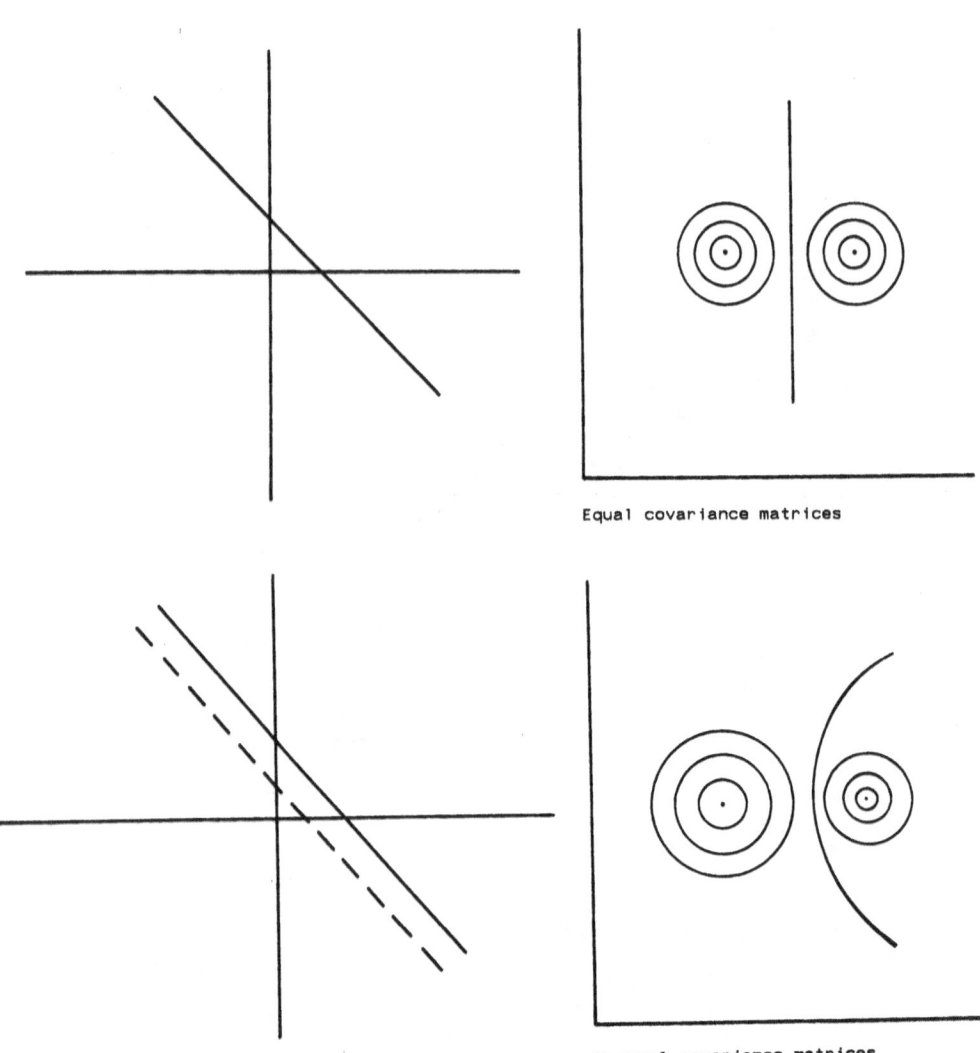

Fig. 42. Discriminant Analysis with Different Priors

Fig. 43. Discriminant Analysis with Equal and Unequal Covariance Matrices

Representing Individual Roll Calls 227

can still designate a cutting point for the values of the discriminant function, so as to make classifications. But there is then no systematic means of choosing that cutting point.

Therefore, without making a normality assumption, we seem to be little better off than with regression analysis. In fact, it turns out that there is an equivalence between the two methods. It has been proved (Cramer, 1967; Kort, 1973) that the regression coefficients are proportional to the coefficients for the discriminant function. The equal ratio between the coefficients means that, for our model, the same vector is drawn. Since neither method provides an adequate means of finding a cutting point along this vector, they are equally useful for our purposes.[9] While the discriminant function is generated under more pleasing assumptions, the results are equivalent.

The final method, glorified by the name *visual analysis*, is motivated by a very simple goal: to find the line of cleavage that minimizes the number of incorrect classifications, without regard to any assumptions concerning distributions, variance matrices, or anything else. As it stands now, there is no systematic way to search for such a line. Particularly in the absence of a smooth distribution of cases, it is possible for very different lines to produce very similar numbers of errors.

Therefore, the technique for locating the best line is strictly a visual one. A plot of points is produced and labeled according to group membership, and a physical search is made, perhaps with the help of the computer. The quality of a line is measured simply by the percentage of classification errors. The advantage of this method is that it tends to locate the best line in terms of classification. But this search may be difficult or at least slow. Furthermore, minimizing the number of errors takes no account of the magnitude of the errors. Thus, a line producing three large errors is chosen over one producing six very small errors. Whether this criterion is satisfactory is not at all clear.

A variation on this method of analysis is to search only among those lines that are orthogonal to the regression (or discriminant) vector. Such an approach proves to be useful and is considered later.

Some Empirical Examples

In order to show how these methods of representing roll calls in a spatial configuration actually work in practice, several extended examples are presented here. The idea is to demonstrate the use of the methods, to learn something about their suitability, and to reach a conclusion concerning what approach should be used for the analysis of congressional issues.

Three examples form the basis for the following section, all concerning the House of Representatives of the First Congress— for which a two-dimensional configuration provides an adequate representation (stress = .337). One variable considered is a party variable, where congressmen are labeled as Federalist (52 members), Antifederalist (9), or unknown (1).[10] The other two variables are roll call votes on two of the chief components of Hamilton's economic plans for the new government: assumption of state debts (32 yes, 29 no, 1 not voting) and creation of a national bank (34 yes, 21 no, 7 not voting). These three variables provide different classifications of the sixty-two active members of the First House. In the analyses that follow, only the two major categories are considered: that is, those unknown or not voting are excluded from the analysis.

The first method presented here is multiple regression analysis.[11] The basic results are presented in table 26. Each variable, on the basis of the ratio between the two coefficients, is then represented as a vector in the configuration. Figures 44, 45,

Table 26. Results of Regression Analysis

	N	R^2	a	b1	b2	Ratio	% errors
Party	61	.353	.156	.001	.452	651.6	9.8
Assumption	61	.456	.528	.328	−.360	−1.099	21.3
Bank	55	.596	.595	.357	−.445	−1.248	14.6

and 46 demonstrate this representation. As later discussion makes clearer, these vectors are generally oriented in reasonable directions. The party vector runs nearly from the bottom to the top of the configuration, and one can see that the small group of Antifederalists are mostly at the top of the plot. On the two economic votes, oriented in nearly the same way, one end includes some of Hamilton's chief lieutenants in the House, such as Ames and Sedgwick. Toward the other end are the southern opponents of Hamilton, such as Virginia's Madison and Georgia's Jackson. Using the R^2 measure of fit, it would appear that the representations of these variables are moderately good, with an "explained variance" from 35% to 60%.

Classification of the individual members is accomplished by drawing a cutting line where the predicted value is 0.5. These lines are represented in the accompanying figures, and those cases that are incorrectly classified are determined. In the worst one of the three, the assumption vote, 21% of the congressmen are erroneously classified. Most of these classification errors are clustered around the cutting line. Furthermore, the three largest errors involve two members from South Carolina, one of the two states with the largest debts to be assumed (Rogers, 1962, p. 195), and White (whose Virginia district was along the Potomac), who voted in favor of assumption as part of a deal to win the placement of the permanent seat of government along the Potomac (Cunningham, 1957, p. 5). On the bank vote, the two most serious misclassifications represent members whose votes over a series of four bank votes were not consistent. For the party variable, all Federalists are correctly classified, while only three out of nine Antifederalists were placed in the right group (although the errors are not very large).

These comments allow us to conclude that this general representation of these variables by vectors and lines of cleavage is meaningful. The specific placement of the line of cleavage, however, may not be the best possible one, and the measures of fit do not seem to measure adequately the quality of the representation.

The application of discriminant analysis to our three variables should bring few surprises, given the theoretical equivalence between it and regression analysis. We know already that the discriminant function yields the same vectors as the regression function, and that the classification criteria are dependent upon a normality assumption that is not met. Nevertheless, the results of this discriminant analysis are presented in table 27.[12] Within the limits of rounding error, the ratio between the two coefficients is indeed the same for both regression and discriminant analysis. The actual values of the coefficients are not important, for simple transformations can make the necessary adjustments.

Since the classification criteria are based on distributional assumptions, these results are only discussed for comparative purposes. Two assumptions concerning prior probabilities produce different cutting lines, as shown in figures 44, 45, and 46. For the three variables being considered here, both cutting lines yield the same number of errors, but it turns out that, for the party variable and the bank bill, the errors

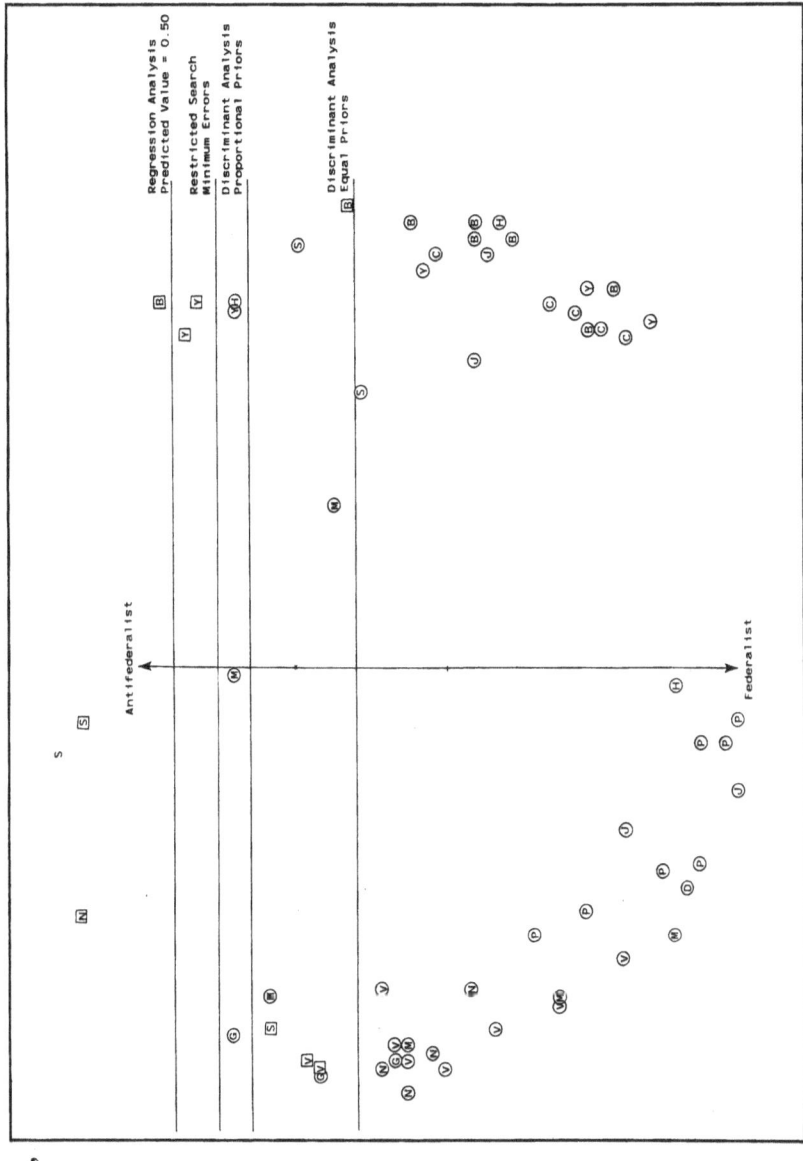

Fig. 44. Spatial Configuration, First Congress, House, 1789-1791—Party Variable

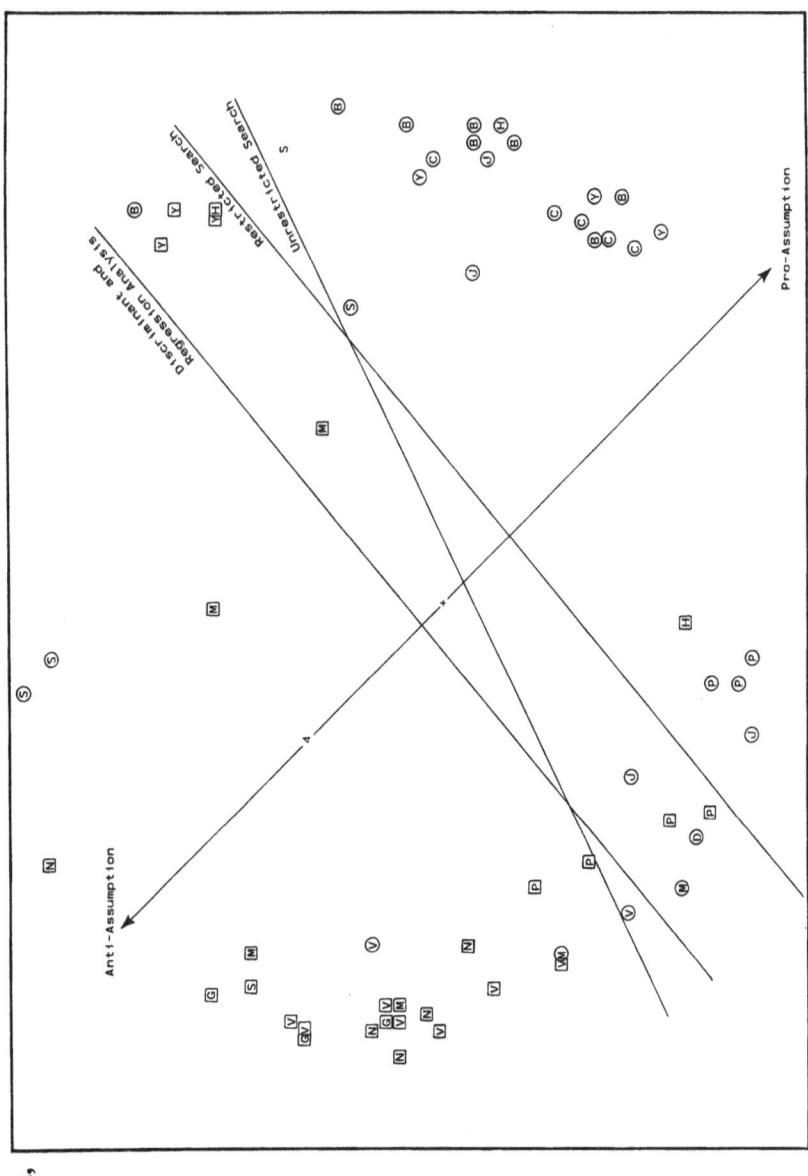

Fig. 45. Spatial Configuration, First Congress, House, 1789-1791—Assumption Roll Call

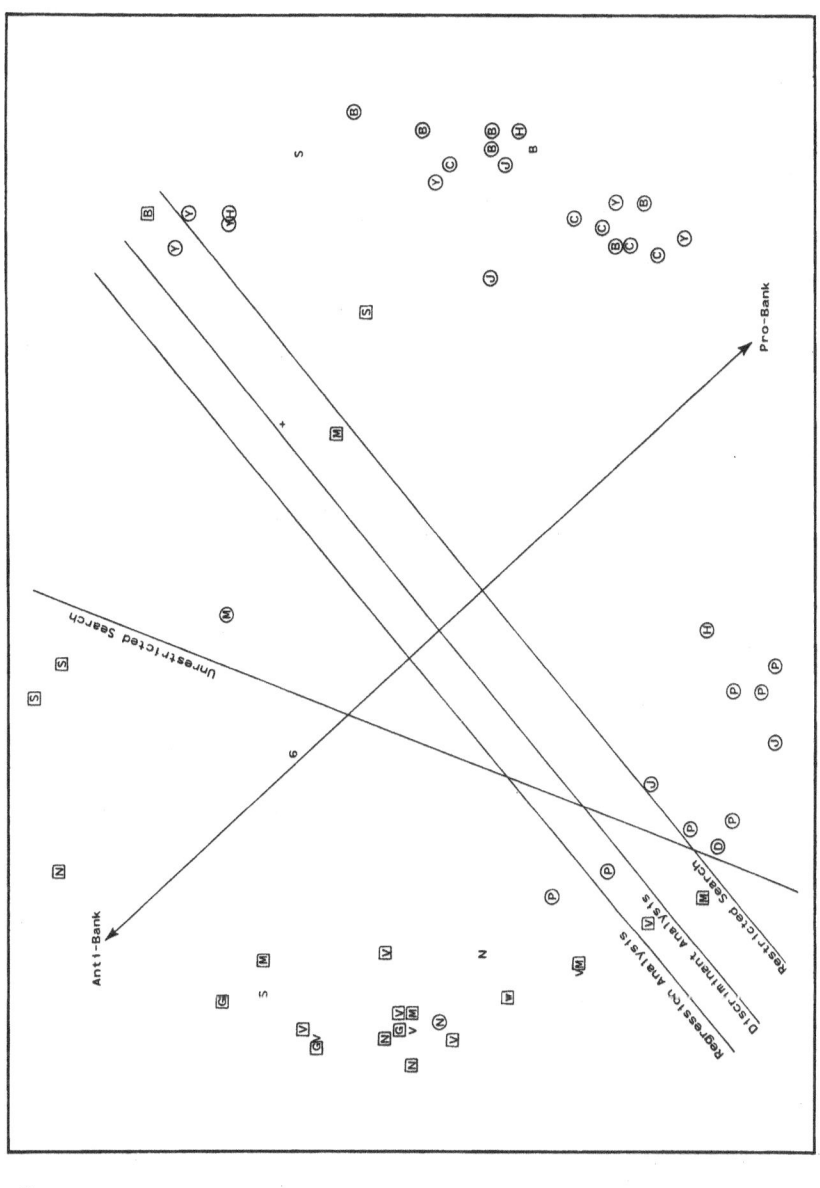

Fig. 46. Spatial Configuration, First Congress, House, 1789-1791—National Bank Roll Call

KEY

B – Mass. M – Md.
C – Conn. N – N.C.
D – Del.   P – Penn.
E – Vt.   R – R.I.
G – Ga.   S – S.C.
H – N.H.   T – Tenn.
J – N.J.   V – Vir.
K – Ky.   Y – N.Y.

○ – Yes vote
☒ – No vote
X – Not voting

Letter = state
Circle/square = vote

Table 27. Results of Discriminant Analysis

	N	a	b1	b2	Ratio	% errors*
Party	61	.039	.003	2.127	652.5	13.1
Assumption	61	.011	.964	−1.059	−1.099	21.3
Bank	55	.061	−.943	1.177	−1.248	14.6

*Both equal priors and proportional priors.

involved are not the same ones. There are also some differences between these classifications and those based on the regression function. For the party variable, regression finds a better classification. This fact tends to confirm the difficulties resulting from the violation of assumptions, since discriminant analysis should otherwise produce at least as good a classification.[13]

The only conclusion one can draw from this experience with discriminant analysis is that it provides no advantage over regression for the present task, other than a more viable assumption about the form of the dependent variable. Without the needed normality assumption, the classification problem remains. It is worth noting, however, that discriminant analysis is a promising method for a situation where the groups are normally distributed.

Because neither regression analysis nor discriminant analysis has adequate means of determining a cutting point along the vector representation of a dichotomous variable, some form of search strategy is probably desirable to find a cutting point. One plausible strategy is simply to search along the vector for that cutting point that produces the minimum number of errors. Such a search is not difficult with the help of the computer, and the results are listed in table 28 (where this search is designated the restricted search, since it is limited to a search of all lines orthogonal to the regression vector). For each of the sample variables, a search strategy produced a better line of cleavage—in the sense of having fewer errors. In each case, too, there is a unique line drawn (or at least a unique range, since it can fall anywhere between the two appropriate projections); however, there is nothing about the procedure that guarantees this uniqueness.

The apparent success of this search strategy leads one to ask whether an unrestricted search might produce even better results. Of course, an unrestricted search is difficult even with the computer. For the present, a visual search has been made. As reported in the above table, a "better" cleavage line has been found for one of the three variables. Additionally, for the bank variable, a second line was found with equally good prediction (but with different errors). The various prediction lines are shown in figures 44, 45, and 46.

Before concluding, we must consider results from the optimal regression program, MORALS. It turns out that the MORALS procedure, for the case of interval independent variables and a dichotomous dependent variable, is not very helpful. As described earlier, the solution essentially converges after only one iteration. The results, not reported in detail, are slightly different regression coefficients and a vastly higher R^2. The nature of the monotonic transformation is such that one large error causes many observations to be rescaled to a single value, producing an analysis that is not very meaningful. Small shifts in the regression coefficients appear to produce a less satisfactory vector, one where the errors are, if anything, greater in size and number. The size of R^2 seems to be inversely proportional to the width of the overlapping region of the two groups. Thus, it is apparent that the MORALS

Table 28. Comparisons among Analytic Methods
(Number of Errors)

	Regression	Discriminant	Restricted Search	Unrestricted Search
Party	6	8	4	4
Assumption	13	13	10	8
Bank	8	8	6	6

procedure does not help this analysis at all. Its results are a less satisfactory vector and a large (probably inflated) measure of fit.

Selecting a Method

On the basis of these findings, there is no totally satisfactory method of drawing a line of cleavage to represent a roll call vote. Each method has both advantages and disadvantages. We can conclude that the vector produced by regression or discriminant analysis is a reasonable representation of the direction of a vote. Using the logic of discriminant analysis, this vector represents the combination of the two dimensions that minimizes the distance between the group means relative to within-group variances. While these means and variances can behave in peculiar ways for a distribution that is not smooth or symmetric, it should tend to be a reasonable representation of the particular dichotomy. But there is no obvious way to produce the best cutting line orthogonal to this vector.

Ultimately, it might be feasible to devise a technique for drawing the cutting line that would minimize the total magnitude of the errors. If we were interested in finding very precise representations of individual roll calls or in testing carefully some closely drawn hypotheses, we would need to proceed with a more careful and more theoretically based derivation of a suitable method. But since the purpose of representing roll calls is to make some general descriptions of how different issues affect voting patterns and to assist in labeling directions in the various configurations, the approach described here should be acceptable.

One remaining problem is to measure the quality of fit for the final representation of a roll call. In applying regression analysis to a dichotomous dependent variable, the R^2 statistic tends to be a very low estimate of the fit—because the estimated values (being on a continuous scale) never match the values of the dichotomy. The percentage of correct classifications has been discussed above, but it depends on the existence of a cutting line and has the disadvantage of counting all errors equally, regardless of magnitude. This application of the MORALS procedure suggests possible ways of deriving an improved measure of fit, by using the deviations between the values predicted by the regression equation and that monotonic transformation of the original values closest to the regression estimates. The measure of fit would then be the squared correlation between the regression estimates and the transformed observations.[14] While the R^2 measure produced by ordinary least-squares regression clearly falls short of being an ideal measure, it is easily calculated and interpretable in familiar ways.

Further research should seek better methods for representing individual roll calls in a multidimensional space of legislators. Until such a method is available, I shall use ordinary regression, keeping in mind its flaws. Throughout the analysis in chapters 6 and 7, I have tried to proceed cautiously with this technique, using it as a general guide to the interpretation of the spatial configurations. While this appendix has shown the drawbacks of the method, it should be clear that the discrepancies should not in general be too great.

Notes

Chapter 1. The Concept of Party

1. See Sartori (1976, pp. 3-5) for a fuller explanation.
2. The references are taken from *The Federalist* No. 10 (Hamilton, Madison, and Jay, 1961, p. 77) and No. 50 (p. 320). Elsewhere Madison clearly shows that he equates the two words, referring to "the most numerous party, or in other words, the most powerful faction" (No. 10, p. 80). See Bell (1973), however, for an alternative interpretation of Madison's use of these words.
3. Major sources for this section are Hofstadter (1969, pp. 9-39) and Sartori (1976, pp. 3-13).
4. These traditions identified by Hofstadter are also featured by Sartori (1976).
5. See chapter 2 for an evaluation of the state of British parties in 1770.
6. Ironically, Sartori gives no consideration to what I call the structural definitions.
7. It seems that a number of theoretical treatments of party grew from the American model. Chambers (1963*a*) and Huntington (1968) are examples of scholars who have seen party development in this way.
8. While the American and British parties (other than the Labour party) are the usual examples, there have been others, such as the parties in the first two French republics (Duverger, 1959, pp. xxiv-xxv).
9. Huntington's terminology (1968, pp. 412-20) is used here, but the actual meaning of the stages has been modified to take into account the ideas of others, particularly Duverger (1959). It should also be noted that these theories distinguish between parties with internal (parliamentary) origins and parties with external (e.g., labor union) origins. In the American setting, only the internal processes were relevant, at least for the parties of this early period.

Chapter 2. The Historical Tradition

1. Prior to 1789, there had been some primitive party developments in both Italy and Poland. But the main exception was a party system in Sweden during the eighteenth century. The Swedish parliamentary system was, however, abolished in 1772 (Stjernquist in Dahl, 1966, pp. 119-20).
2. The words *Whig* and *Tory* were first applied to political groups late in the seventeenth century, having been "terms of abuse subsequently appropriated with defiant pride by those who were abused." (Blake, 1970, p. 8). *Tory* had referred to a set of lawless Irish bog-trotters, Catholic outlaws, and was applied to supporters of the Catholic heir to the throne. *Whig* (or Whiggamore) had meant a Scottish horse thief

and was used to designate Presbyterian rebels in Scotland and eventually all those opposed to a Catholic king (Blake, 1970, p. 8; Mackenzie, 1951, p. 109).

3. Loewenstein (1967, pp. 79-80) refers to these elections as the first that "led to a change of ministers along party lines."

4. Some historians do not acknowledge the existence of parties in the modern sense, even after the 1832 Reform Act. "Parties of the mid-nineteenth century, as compared to those of the mid-twentieth, were parliamentary groupings rather than national organizations, and even in Parliament, they were rudimentary in structure, undisciplined, loosely organized and controlled, and frequently unable to provide the support needed for a firm government" (Aydelotte, 1966, p. 102). "Nineteenth-century parliamentary historians now seem agreed in deferring the full emergence of the modern party till after the Second Reform Bill: what preceded it were intermediary forms which should not be treated anachronistically in terms of a later age" (Namier, 1955, p. 35).

5. These data were obtained from McDonald (1958, p. 96).

Chapter 4. Party Institutions in Congress

1. The principal sources for the office of Speaker are Follett (1897), Fuller (1909), and Lientz (1978). Apparently, no other sources have considered these early contests at length. Material on individual speakers has been useful where cited below.

2. The only source for this fact is a letter written by Rep. Henry Wynkoop (Pa.) on April 2, 1789 (Beatty, 1914, pp. 50-51).

3. Although individual votes were not recorded, we do know who was in attendance on the day of the vote (*Annals*, 6th Cong., 1st sess., p. 186). Using the best available party labels, the distribution that day was forty-seven Federalists and thirty-nine Republicans.

4. More on Sedgwick's speakership is presented in a later discussion of issues in the Sixth Congress.

5. See *Annals*, (5th Cong., 1st sess., p. 52) and Lientz (1978).

6. In the Sixth Congress (1st session) 14.3% of House members lived alone, compared to 3.1% in 1807 (Young, 1966, p. 99).

7. See, for example, biographies of James Madison (Brant, 1950, pp. 245-6, 324, 335), William L. Smith (Rogers, 1962, pp. 169n, 198-99), Theodore Sedgwick (Welch, 1965, pp. 70, 104, 138), and Fisher Ames (Bernhard, 1965, pp. 75, 162-63, 185-86).

8. According to his votes, Henry had already moved toward a position of moderation prior to this time. His resignation early in the Fifth Congress makes it difficult to see the effect of his fellow lodgers. He was generally associated with the moderate wing of the Federalist party (Renzulli, 1972).

9. See Bogue and Marlaire (1975) for a further critique of Young's thesis—for the period from 1821 to 1842. My conclusions and the implied criticisms of Young's study are fully consistent with the conclusions of Bogue and Marlaire.

10. The lowest proportion of new members in this period was 46% for the Sixth Congress. All members were, of course, new in the First Congress. Otherwise, the high was 62% in the Third Congress; however, that year the size of the House was enlarged. The next highest proportion was 54% in the Seventh. Of the 344 members in Congress between 1789 and 1803, about 43% (147) served only a single term in this period (although some continued to serve after 1803). Only 45 of the 344 served 4 or more of the 7 possible terms.

Chapter 5. Spatial Analysis of Party Development

1. Some limitations of roll call analysis are immediately obvious. Roll call votes may not always be accurate records of either the scope of activity in Congress or the true positions of members. Also, for a variety of reasons, roll calls are not taken on every issue before the legislature. Furthermore, when votes are recorded, members may sometimes misrepresent their positions, for reasons such as friendship or future reelection. Roll calls nevertheless do provide an official record of positions taken on a variety of issues and thus may be more important than a legislator's own preferences in cases where they differ.

2. A more detailed presentation and justification of the methodology used here is found in Hoadley (1979, 1981). A good general discussion of multidimensional scaling is provided by Rabinowitz (1975) and Kruskal and Wish (1978).

3. The percentage of agreement between each pair of legislators was calculated using the CORREL program in the OSIRIS III package of statistical programs. The inclusion in the analysis of all roll calls with equal weight may possibly introduce a bias into the analysis, although the degree and nature of this bias is unknown. Because any scheme of exclusion or weighting would be difficult to justify, all votes have been included here. Given the nonmetric assumptions of MDS and the strength of the results, it seems unlikely that any resulting bias has affected the conclusions.

4. In general, a member of Congress was excluded from the analysis if he was absent on more than three-fourths of all roll calls.

5. The multidimensional scaling was performed using the KYST program, developed by Kruskal and Young. A frequent concern in the use of MDS is reaching a local minimum, that is, a solution that results from a failure by the search algorithm to find the lowest possible stress. To combat such a possibility, some of the data matrices were reanalyzed with different programs (including MDSCAL, ALSCAL, and KYST-2), and most configurations were run under different program options. In particular, each configuration was reentered as an initial configuration, a procedure that is often used to avoid local minima. The changes made by these procedures were nearly always of a marginal nature, and confidence in the results appears to be justified.

6. Traditional guidelines suggest that a level of stress below 0.20 is considered to be a "good" fit (Rabinowitz, 1975). Furthermore, it has been shown that, for a given quality solution, stress increases as the number of points increases (Young, 1970). Thus, with relatively large numbers of points being scaled, these configurations are definitely good fits to the data.

7. For further discussion of the limitations of cluster analysis, see MacRae (1970, pp. 208-26). For a defense of this method, see Willetts (1972).

8. The hierarchical clustering is the maximum (or diameter) method proposed first by Johnson (1967). The traditional cluster analysis was performed using the CLUSTER program in the OSIRIS III package.

9. The ratio statistic is provided in the OSIRIS III package and explained briefly in the manual for that package.

10. This calculation is based on the binomial distribution. Given the expected probability of agreement of an average roll call and the number of roll calls, Willetts (1972) calculates the probability of any specific number of agreements.

11. Most tables of the binomial distribution include probabilities only for n (here, number of roll calls) ≤ 20. Thus, exact probabilities cannot be determined with precision. Willetts (1972, p. 574) provides a table for various values of n when $p = .5$, and the normal approximation to the binomial distribution provides some help. Values for the cutoff vary slightly from one Congress to the next. Nevertheless, the approximate cutoffs cited in the text should be adequate guidelines for this analysis.

12. The one exception is a large cluster in the Third House, comprising nearly 40% of the members that year. The unusually cohesive group, mostly made up of Federalists, is considered in chapter 7.

13. Rice's index of cohesion is the absolute difference between the percentage yes votes and percentage no votes for a particular group. His index of difference is the absolute difference between the percentage yes for any two groups. A party vote, according to Lowell, is any vote where more than 90% of one party opposed more than 90% of the other. MacRae (1970, pp. 177-84) provides a fuller discussion of the use of these indices. See Appendix A for a discussion of the party codes used in this analysis.

14. The averages for the Congresses of the twentieth century were computed from tables in Turner and Schneier (1970, pp. 17, 21, 45), Shannon (1968, p. 11), and Cooper, Brady, and Hurley (1977).

Chapter 6. Factionalism in the Early Years, 1789-1793

1. Clausen's method for identifying a scalable set of roll calls is based on the idea that Yule's Q is a measure of the scalability of two roll calls. Thus, Clausen performs a cluster analysis, setting a minimum Q of 0.6, as well as a requirement that the average value of Q should stay above 0.7. All roll calls falling into such a cluster are defined to be a scale. The chief drawback of this method is that the relatively low levels of Q used as thresholds in the cluster analysis permit a substantial amount of error. In addition, Clausen's method of scoring legislators on a scale fails to use the cumulative quality of the scale.

2. The most useful source in identifying key votes was Bell (1973), because his analysis is directed most specifically at those issues where roll calls were taken. Other useful sources are indicated in the sections dealing with the individual Congresses.

3. See Appendix B for the graphical representation of this party variable.

4. See the brief descriptions of these key votes in table 6.

5. Two votes—V92 and V93—have been excluded from the representation in figure 20 because of extremely low fit (as measured by R^2).

6. One warning is in order here before proceeding. The location of these vectors in a space not evenly filled with individuals may be very sensitive to small shifts in the votes of subgroups of congressmen. However, the common position of vectors for several issues where votes are not fully identical should increase our confidence in this procedure.

7. See Appendix B, where the first vote on assumption is used to illustrate the methodology. The imperfect fit for this vote is probably explainable by the special situations for the South Carolina delegation and those involved in the deal over the capital site.

8. The exception—V96, the duty on salt—was taken in the second session. It produced the poorest fit of this set of votes, and its direction is least like the others. One possible reason for this difference might be the regressive nature of a tax on an important commodity like salt.

9. An examination of cohesion and party difference indices for all roll calls (not presented here) helps to demonstrate this statement.

10. See the congressional vote by county in Young (1967, p. 590).

11. The idea of "friends and neighbors" voting patterns is from Key (1949, pp. 37-41).

12. Grove and Williamson (North Carolina); Richard Bland Lee, White, and Parker (Virginia); and Wayne (Georgia).

Notes to Pages 116–138   239

13. Furthermore, on one vote—V64—aid to fisheries was included with defense of the frontiers, in another case of congressional logrolling.

Chapter 7. Polarization and Party Politics, 1793-1797

1. Nathaniel Freeman was not elected as a Republican, although his votes place him closer to the Republican bloc than to the Federalist bloc.
2. These problems should not be considered as evidence for the abandonment of the approach, for the vectors are accurate when interpreted in the proper fashion. It should be recalled that we are concerned with projections onto the vectors. Thus, in figure 32, the two blocs are projected onto the end of any of several different vectors, including those drawn on the figure for the Jay Treaty, military establishment, and naval construction (but not the land tax vector). The differences lie in the votes of those who are not in the core clusters; in fact, this is why they do not fall in these core clusters.
3. The results of cross-tabular analysis of the key votes are not displayed here for the reasons of limited space.
4. Curiously, the vote on whether to seat Latimer, which was a highly partisan issue in content, appears not to have generated a partisan vote in Congress (see #6 in figure 31).
5. The angle of the party axis is not significant in itself. The orientation of the plots is not strictly comparable across Congresses, although the general direction is comparable.
6. Finally, we see the limitations of depending upon vector representations of roll calls. That the vector for V22 does not point directly at the Republican bloc does not denote a lesser degree of cohesion by that bloc; rather, the behavior of the intermediate bloc of congressmen can shift the vector for a vote considerably, even while the two party blocs remain cohesive and opposed. Still, the supplementary use of cross-tabular analysis is adequate to discover the correct interpretation of these vectors.
7. For the role of one member of this intermediate bloc on foreign policy matters, consider the accounts of the activity of Samuel Smith of Baltimore (Cassell, 1971, pp. 47-61).
8. Madison's role as an opposition leader on this issue has been open to debate. It has been suggested that he was pleased that a tough debate took place, but also that the treaty was approved. Correspondingly, it has been charged that his strategy was intended to lose in the end (see Kurtz [1957] and Combs [1970]).
9. Bailey and Van Cortlandt (New York); Kitchell (New Jersey); Gregg, F. Muhlenberg, and Richards (Pennsylvania); Christie, S. Smith, and T. Sprigg (Maryland); T. Claiborne, Hancock, J. Parker, and Heath (Virginia); Bryan and Grove (North Carolina).
10. Young (1967, pp. 464-67) and Combs (1970, p. 185) find this important for the defections of the two New York Republicans. Contemporaries such as John Beckley, John Adams, and even Washington believed that public petitions were of prime importance (Charles, 1961, p. 112; Young, 1967).
11. Further discussions of the motives of these ten individuals can be found in Bell (1973, pp. 147-49), Charles (1961, pp. 103-22), Combs (1970, pp. 183-87), Renzulli (1972, pp. 173-77), Wallace (1950, pp. 285-87), and Young (1967, pp. 464-67). The unique circumstances surrounding this vote are aptly illustrated by the case of Frederick Muhlenberg of Pennsylvania, a former Speaker. The marriage of his son was made conditional on his vote by the prospective bride's father (a Federalist),

who stated, "If you do not give us your vote, your son shall not have my Polly." But after casting a vote in favor of the treaty and thus ensuring his son's marriage, Muhlenberg was stabbed by a brother-in-law, who was described as "a rabid Republican" (Combs, 1970, p. 184; Renzulli, 1972, pp. 176-77; Wallace, 1950, pp. 285-87).

Chapter 8. Partisan Competition in Congress, 1797-1803

1. The votes in table 13 are only for the presidential selections (in effect, the "first" vote of each elector), although one Maryland elector voted for both Adams and Jefferson. Most of the "second" votes went to Thomas Pinckney (the Federalist) and Burr (the Republican). There was, however, considerable scattering of the "second" votes on each side.

2. Compare with the behavior of factions in southern politics between 1910 and 1950 (Key, 1949, ch. 14).

3. In technical terms, this amounts to a severe case of heteroscedasticity—or unequal variance at different values of the independent variables.

4. The higher level of dissent among the Federalists is partially attributable to the format of data presentation. Because they were larger by anywhere from about five to twelve men, and because table 16 is not expressed in percentage form, the difference between the parties is exaggerated.

5. Sewall, Bartlett, Wadsworth (Mass.); Allen (Conn.); Bayard (Del.); Pinckney, Rutledge, Harper (S.C.); Brooks, Hosmer (N.Y.).

6. In spite of my critique of certain of their findings, discussions by Bell (1973) and Dauer (1953) were still quite valuable in identifying important votes and issues in the Fifth Congress. Also useful were Cunningham (1957), DeConde (1966), and Kurtz (1957). Because I am not presenting a vector analysis, there is no listing of specific key votes.

7. Several men were thought to be Federalist, but their loyalty was questionable. There were, for example, three Virginians Jefferson thought would "not go with them [Federalists] on questions of importance" (quoted in Cunningham, 1957, p. 134).

8. In 1796, he was among those voting for the Jay Treaty but opposing the administration on earlier votes.

9. Table 14 shows a total of six Federalists voting with the Republican coalition—Jones and Taliaferro of Georgia, Dent of Maryland, Alston of North Carolina, Goode and Gray of Virginia. Dent's status has been considered, but little is known about the other five, all from the South. To call them Federalists in an electoral system where party labels were not used is probably questionable in any case. It would appear that these men were opponents of Republican candidates, but that the contests were chiefly based on local issues (Gilpatrick, 1931; Rose, 1968). While these cases reinforce the slowness of party development, the presence of fourteen men from the South who did vote with the Federalists shows that bipartisan politics was progressing.

10. The slavery question, which might have cut across party lines, was raised on two votes. In each case, serious disputes were avoided and nearly unanimous votes were the result.

11. Three votes on rulings by the Speaker earlier in the session had also divided the House along party lines, with only minor exceptions. See chapter 4 for additional discussions of the speakership.

12. Votes were reported in the *Gazette of the United States*, February 20, 1801,

and were later included in the *Annals* (6th Cong., 2nd sess., p. 1032). These votes were reprinted in Dauer (1953, pp. 322-25).

13. John E. Colhoun was a cousin of the well-known John C. Calhoun, although the spelling of the name was different. He has been called "a moderate Republican who had commercial connections in Charleston" (Ellis, 1971, p. 47).

14. Compare these figures to those for the Fifth and Sixth Congresses earlier in this chapter.

Chapter 9. Political Parties in Eighteenth-Century America

1. In the classic ANOVA model, the total sum of squared deviations from the overall mean is partitioned into two parts: the sum of squares within categories of a particular classification and the sum of squares between categories (Blalock, 1960, pp. 242-53).

$$TSS = WSS + BSS$$
$$\Sigma \Sigma (X_{i,j} - \bar{X})^2 = \Sigma \Sigma (X_{ij} - \bar{X}_j)^2 + \Sigma \Sigma (X_j - \bar{X})^2$$

where X_{ij} is the value of the dependent variable for observation i in category j.

From this partition, we can derive an F-statistic:

$$F = (BSS / k - 1)/(WSS / N - k),$$

where k is the number of categories and N is the total number of observations. We can also derive E^2, the coefficient of multiple determination:

$$E^2 = BSS/TSS.$$

Furthermore, E^2 should be adjusted to account for degrees of freedom:

$$E^{2*} = [(1 - k) / (N - k)] + [(N - 1) / (N - k)] E^2.$$

For the current analysis, the dependent variable is actually the position in a multidimensional space, as represented by the coordinates on a set of axes. The necessary adaptation can be made by substituting squared distance for the squared deviations in the above formulas. Thus,

$$d^2 (X_{ij} - \bar{X}) = (x_{ij} - \bar{x})^2 + (y_{ij} - \bar{y})^2,$$

where $X_{ij} = (x_{ij}, y_{ij})$ and $\bar{X} = (\bar{x}, \bar{y})$, and the partition becomes:

$$\Sigma \Sigma d^2 (X_{ij} - \bar{X}) = \Sigma \Sigma d^2 (X_{ij} - \bar{X}_j) + \Sigma \Sigma d^2 (X_j - \bar{X})$$

where X_{ij} is the location of observation i in category j.

From this partition, F, E^2, and E^{2*} can be calculated precisely as indicated above.

2. For additional discussions of southern Federalism, see Broussard (1978), Risjord (1978), and Rose (1968).

3. A model for the described search can be found in Merritt (1966). His content analysis of newspapers addresses the question of when a national identity emerged in the United States, by looking at the use of specific terms for the period from 1735 to

1775. He concludes from this analysis that after about 1763, the newspapers had begun to make reference to Americans as a single group, and not as residents of separate colonies or as members of the British community.

4. It is ironic to note the publication of a book with the title *Parties and Elections in an Anti-Party Age* (Fischel, 1978), a collection of articles about the contemporary state of political parties. In some ways, the weakness of our modern parties helps to accentuate the strength of the parties of 1800.

Appendix A

1. The first of the volumes that preceded the *Biographical Directory* was that published by Lanman (1859). Later editions were published by Lanman in 1869, 1876, and 1887. A competing volume was published by Poore (1878). The first to have official status was the *Biographical Directory* published by Wold in 1928 (U.S., Congress, 1928). Additional volumes were published in 1950, 1961, and 1971.

2. The one published volume deals only with the roll call votes of the Continental Congress (1774-1789), and thus it is not of direct relevance to this project.

3. The erroneous labeling of Baldwin (Ga.) which appears first in the *Biographical Directory*, also appears in the ICPSR files.

4. Party labels are provided for senators in the *Guide to Elections* (Diamond, 1975).

5. Several discrepancies do exist between the labels provided by Congressional Quarterly (Diamond and O'Connor, 1976; Wormser, 1982) and those in the *Biographical Directory* (U.S., Congress, 1971).

6. Excluded in this regard are several historians, such as Libby (1913), Cunningham (1957), and Henderson (1973), whose listings of party attachment are derived solely from roll call voting records.

7. In the near future, original source material will be available for those first federal elections, thus allowing further examination of party affiliations for the members of the First Congress. This project, taking place at the University of Wisconsin, has now published two of four volumes (Jensen and Becker, 1976; Den Boer, 1984).

8. One reference book (Parsons, Beach, and Hermann, 1978) draws heavily on the work of Bell and Dauer for its party labels. The book is valuable for its maps of congressional districts but provides no new information on party labels.

Appendix B

1. Other available methods include probit analysis (Aldrich and Cnudde, 1975; McKelvey and Zavoina, 1975) and tobit analysis (Jackson, 1970).

2. Sources for this use of regression include Rabinowitz (1975, pp. 374-78), Cliff and Young (1968), and Carroll (1972).

3. Note that the coding of the dichotomous independent variables does not affect the results in any meaningful way. Without loss of generality, I shall assume that configurations have two dimensions. Any orthogonal set of axes can be used for this analysis, for only the relative positions are important.

4. Another possibility is the midpoint between the projections of the two group means. Alternatively, one might search along the set of all orthogonal lines for the one that minimizes the number of errors in prediction. The latter approach is discussed below.

5. A good discussion of these problems can be found in Aldrich and Cnudde (1975).

6. Alternatives here include probit analysis, which directly predicts the probability of the event occurring; or the development of a modified regression procedure that computes residuals only for those cases where the dichotomous prediction is incorrect.

7. The principal sources consulted for this discussion are Aldrich and Cnudde (1975), Klecka (1980), and Kort (1973). An earlier application to roll call analysis is found in Heyck and Klecka (1973).

8. Best discrimination is achieved when the ratio of the squared distance between group means to the pooled within-group variance is maximized.

9. In addition, it turns out that there exists an equivalence between the Mahalanobis D^2 and R^2 for a dichotomous dependent variable (Namboodiri, 1974).

10. This classification was mostly compiled from material by Paullin (1904) and was confirmed by a variety of other sources. It represents a reasonably accurate account of the attitudes of these congressmen on the questions of federal authority raised at the Constitutional Convention and on the Constitution itself. As such, it is a measure not derived from the voting records expressed during the First Congress.

11. Two different regression programs were used, one from SPSS and one from SAS. Fortunately, the results from both programs were identical

12. Two discriminant analysis programs were used here, one from SPSS and one from SAS. They are not totally comparable, since different information is included in the output from each. For instance, SAS does not print the basic discriminant function. Nevertheless, the equivalence of the two programs can be seen in the classification results, where classification probabilities are identical in both.

13. Ironically, for the party variable, discriminant analysis produced the best possible classification (fewest errors) when one congressman was coded incorrectly. Tucker, whose party was unknown, was erroneously coded as a Federalist during one run. Although his position turns out to be high on the Antifederalist direction, his inclusion as a Federalist led to an improvement in prediction, reducing the number of errors from six to four.

14. An alternative measure can be defined in a similar manner. It deals with the deviations between the regression estimates and a different monotonic transformation of the observations. For a particular cutting point along the regression vector (I use the one determined by the restricted search), the monotonic transformation is defined as the regression estimates for values predicted correctly and as the cutting point for erroneous predictions. Thus, nonzero deviations exist only for misclassified observations—with a magnitude corresponding to the distance away from being classified correctly. The actual measure, then, is the squared correlation between regression estimates and this special transformation of the observations.

Bibliography

Albright, Spencer D. 1942. *The American Ballot.* Washington, D.C.: American Council on Public Affairs.
Aldrich, John, and Charles F. Cnudde. 1975. "Probing the Bounds of Conventional Wisdom: A Comparison of Regression, Probit, and Discriminant Analysis." *American Journal of Political Science* 19: 571-608.
Alexander, DeAlva Stanwood. 1916. *History and Procedure of the House of Representatives.* Boston: Houghton Mifflin.
Ammon, Harry. 1953. "The Formation of the Republican Party in Virginia, 1789-1796." *Journal of Southern History* 19: 283-310.
Annals of the Congress of the United States. 1834-1851. First Congress to Seventh Congress. Washington, D.C.: Gales and Seaton.
Austin, James T. 1829. *The Life of Elbridge Gerry.* 2 vols. Vol. 2. Boston: Wells and Lilly.
Aydelotte, William O. 1966. "Parties and Issues in Early Victorian England." *Journal of British Studies* 5: 95-114.
Bailyn, Bernard. 1968. *The Origins of American Politics.* New York: Alfred A. Knopf.
Beard, Charles A. 1913. *An Economic Interpretation of the Constitution of the United States.* New York: Macmillan.
_____. 1915. *Economic Origins of Jeffersonian Democracy.* New York: Macmillan.
Beatty, Joseph M., ed. 1914. "The Letters of Judge Henry Wynkoop." *Pennsylvania Magazine of History and Biography* 38: 39-64, 183-205.
Beeman, Richard R. 1972. *The Old Dominion and the New Nation, 1788-1801.* Lexington: Univ. Press of Kentucky.
Beer, Samuel H. 1969. *British Politics in the Collectivist Age.* New York: Vintage Books.
Bell, Rudolph M. 1973. *Party and Faction in American Politics: The House of Representatives, 1789-1801.* Westport, Conn.: Greenwood Press.
Bemis, Samuel Flagg. 1962. *Jay's Treaty: A Study in Commerce and Diplomacy.* Rev. ed. New Haven: Yale Univ. Press.
Bernhard, Winfred E.A. 1965. *Fisher Ames: Federalist and Statesman, 1758-1808.* Chapel Hill: Univ. of North Carolina Press.
Binkley, Wilfred E. 1966. *American Political Parties: Their Natural History.* New York: Alfred A. Knopf
Blake, Robert, 1970. *The Conservative Party from Peel to Churchill.* London: Eyre and Spottiswoode.
Blalock, Hubert M., Jr. 1960. *Social Statistics.* New York: McGraw-Hill.
Bogue, Allan G., and Mark Paul Marlaire. 1975. "Of Mess and Men: The Boardinghouse and Congressional Voting, 1821-1842." *American Journal of Political Science* 19: 207-30.
Bohmer, David A. 1978. "The Maryland Electorate and the Concept of a Party System in the Early National Period." In J. Silbey et al., eds., *The History of American Electoral Behavior*, pp. 146-73. Princeton: Princeton Univ. Press.

Brant, Irving. 1950. *James Madison, Father of the Constitution, 1787-1800.* Vol. 3 of *James Madison*, 6 vols. Indianapolis: Bobbs-Merrill.
Broussard, James H. 1978. *The Southern Federalists, 1800-1816.* Baton Rouge: Louisiana State Univ. Press.
Buel, Richard, Jr. 1972. *Securing the Revolution: Ideology in American Politics.* Ithaca: Cornell Univ. Press.
Carroll, J. Douglas, 1972. "Individual Differences and Multidimensional Scaling." In Roger N. Shepard, A. Kimball Romney, and Sara Beth Nerlove, eds., *Multidimensional Scaling: Theory and Applications in the Behavioral Sciences*, 2 vols. Vol. 1, pp. 105-55. New York: Seminar Press.
Cassell, Frank A. 1971. *Merchant Congressman in the Young Republic: Samuel Smith of Maryland, 1752-1839.* Madison: Univ. of Wisconsin Press.
Chambers, William Nisbet. 1963a. "Party Development and Party Action: the American Origins." *History and Theory* 3: 91-120.
_____. 1963b. *Political Parties in a New Nation: The American Experience, 1776-1809.* New York: Oxford Univ. Press.
_____. 1966. "Parties and Nation-Building in America." In Joseph LaPalombara and Myron Weiner, eds., *Political Parties and Political Development*, pp. 79-106. Princeton: Princeton Univ. Press.
_____. 1967. "Party Development and the American Mainstream." In William Nisbet Chambers and Walter Dean Burnham, eds., *The American Party Systems: Stages of Political Development*, pp. 3-32. New York: Oxford Univ. Press.
Charles, Joseph. 1961. *The Origins of the American Party System: Three Essays.* New York: Harper Torchbook.
Clausen, Aage R. 1973. *How Congressmen Decide.* New York: St. Martin's Press.
Clausen, Aage R., and Richard B. Cheney. 1970. "A Comparative Analysis of Senate-House Voting on Economic and Welfare Policy: 1953-1964." *American Political Science Review* 64: 138-52.
Cliff, Norman, and Forrest W. Young. 1968. "On the Relation between Unidimensional Judgments and Multidimensional Scaling." *Organizational Behavior and Human Performance* 3: 269-85.
Combs, Jerald A. 1970. *The Jay Treaty: Political Battleground of the Founding Fathers.* Berkeley: Univ. of California Press.
Commager, Henry Steele. 1950. "The American Political Party." *American Scholar* 19: 309-16.
Cooper, Joseph. 1970. *The Origins of the Standing Committee and the Development of the Modern House.* Rice University Studies, vol. 56, no. 3.
Cooper, Joseph, David W. Brady, and Patricia A. Hurley. 1977. "The Electoral Basis of Party Voting: Patterns and Trends in the U.S. House of Representatives, 1887-1969." In L. Maisel and J. Cooper, eds., *The Impact of the Electoral Process*, pp. 133-65. Beverly Hills: Sage Publications.
Cramer, Elliot M. 1967. "Equivalence of Two Methods of Computing Discriminant Function Coefficients." *Biometrics* 23: 153.
Cunningham, Noble E., Jr. 1956. "John Beckley: An Early American Party Manager." *William and Mary Quarterly* (3rd Series) 13: 40-52.
_____. 1957. *The Jeffersonian Republicans: The Formation of Party Organization, 1789-1801.* Chapel Hill: Univ. of North Carolina Press.
_____. 1963. *The Jeffersonian Republicans in Power: Party Operations, 1801-1809.* Chapel Hill: Univ. of North Carolina Press.
_____, ed. 1965. *The Making of the American Party System: 1789 to 1809.* Englewood Cliffs: Prentice-Hall.

―――. 1978a. *Circular Letters of Congressmen to Their Constituents, 1789-1829.* 3 vols. Vol. 1. Chapel Hill: Univ. of North Carolina Press.
―――. 1978b. *The Process of Government under Jefferson.* Princeton: Princeton Univ. Press.
Dahl, Robert A., ed. 1966. *Political Oppositions in Western Democracies.* New Haven: Yale Univ. Press.
Dallinger, Frederick W. 1897. *Nominations for Elective Office in the United States.* Cambridge: Harvard Univ. Press.
Dauer, Manning J. 1953. *The Adams Federalists.* Baltimore: Johns Hopkins Press.
DeConde, Alexander. 1958. *Entangling Alliances: Politics and Diplomacy under George Washington.* Durham: Duke Univ. Press.
―――. 1966. *The Quasi-War: The Politics and Diplomacy of the Undeclared War with France, 1797-1801.* New York: Scribner.
Den Boer, Gordon, ed. 1984. *The Documentary History of the First Federal Elections, 1788-1790*, vol. 2. Madison: Univ. of Wisconsin Press.
Diamond, Robert A., ed. 1975. *Guide to Elections.* Washington, D.C.: Congressional Quarterly.
Diamond, Robert A., and Patricia Ann O'Connor, eds. 1976. *Guide to Congress.* 2nd ed. Washington, D.C.: Congressional Quarterly.
Dinkin, Robert J. 1982. *Voting in Revolutionary America.* Westport, Conn.: Greenwood Press.
Duverger, Maurice. 1959. *Political Parties.* Rev. ed. Translated by Barbara and Robert North. New York: John Wiley and Sons.
Ellis, Richard E. 1971. *The Jeffersonian Crisis: Courts and Politics in the Young Republic.* New York: Oxford Univ. Press.
Epstein, Leon D. 1967. *Political Parties in Western Democracies.* New York: Praeger.
Fay, Bernard. 1936. "Early Party Machinery in the United States: Pennsylvania in the Election of 1796." *Pennsylvania Magazine of History and Biography* 60: 375-90.
Ferguson, E. James. 1961. *The Power of the Purse.* Chapel Hill: Univ. of North Carolina Press.
Fishel, Jeff, ed. 1978. *Parties and Elections in an Anti-Party Age.* Bloomington: Indiana Univ. Press.
Follett, Mary P. 1896. *The Speaker of the House of Representatives.* New York: Longmans, Green.
Formisano, Ronald P. 1974. "Deferential-Participant Politics: The Early Republic's Political Culture, 1789-1840." *American Political Science Review* 68: 473-87.
―――. 1981. "Federalists and Republicans: Parties, Yes—System, No." In Paul Kleppner et al., eds., *The Evolution of American Electoral Systems*, pp. 33-76. Westport, Conn.: Greenwood Press.
―――. 1983. *The Transformation of Political Culture: Massachusetts Parties, 1790s-1840s.* New York: Oxford Univ. Press.
Fuller, Hubert B. 1909. *The Speakers of the House.* Boston: Little, Brown.
Galloway, George B. 1961. *History of the House of Representatives.* New York: Thomas Y. Crowell.
Gilpatrick, Delbert H. 1931. *Jeffersonian Democracy in North Carolina.* New York: Columbia Univ. Press.
Goldman, Perry M., and James S. Young. 1973. *The United States Congressional Directories, 1789-1840.* New York: Columbia Univ. Press.
Goodman, Paul. 1964. *The Democratic-Republicans of Massachusetts: Politics in a Young Republic.* Cambridge: Harvard Univ. Press.
Grodzins, Morton. 1966. "Political Parties and the Crisis of Succession in the United

States: The Case of 1800." In Joseph LaPalombara and Myron Weiner, eds., *Political Parties and Political Development*, pp. 302-27. Princeton: Princeton Univ. Press.
Hall, Van Beck. 1972. *Politics without Parties: Massachusetts, 1780-1791*. Pittsburgh: Univ. of Pittsburgh Press.
Hamilton, Alexander; James Madison; and John Jay. 1961. *The Federalist Papers*. With an introduction by Clinton Rossiter. New York: New American Library.
Harlow, Ralph V. 1917. *The History of Legislative Methods in the Period before 1825*. New Haven: Yale Univ. Press.
Harris, Joseph P. 1934. *Election Administration in the United States*. Washington, D.C.: Brookings Institution.
Henderson, H. James, 1973. "Quantitative Approaches to Party Formation in the United States Congress: A Comment; With a Reply by Mary P. Ryan." *William and Mary Quarterly* (3rd Series) 30: 307-24.
_____. 1974. *Party Politics in the Continental Congress*. New York: McGraw-Hill.
Heyck, T.W., and William R. Klecka. 1973. "British Radical M.P.'s, 1874-1895: New Evidence from Discriminant Analysis." *Journal of Interdisciplinary History* 4: 161-84.
Hill, B.W. 1976. *The Growth of Parliamentary Parties, 1689-1742*. Hamden, Conn.: Archon Books.
Hoadley, John F. 1979. "The Development of American Political Parties: A Spatial Analysis of Congressional Voting." Ph.D. dissertation, University of North Carolina.
_____. 1981. "The Multidimensional Scaling of Roll Call Votes." Unpublished manuscript.
Hofstadter, Richard. 1969. *The Idea of a Party System: The Rise of Legitimate Opposition in the United States, 1780-1840*. Berkeley: Univ. of California Press.
Huntington, Samuel P. 1968. *Political Order in Changing Societies*. New Haven: Yale Univ. Press.
Ionescu, Ghita, and Isabel de Madariaga. 1968. *Opposition: Past and Present of a Political Institution*. Harmondsworth, Middlesex, England: Penguin Books.
Jackson, John E. 1970. "Ordinal Data, Ordinary Least Squares, and Senate Voting." Paper presented at the Conference on Structural Equation Models, Madison, Wisconsin.
Jennings, William Ivor. 1961. *Party Politics*, Vol. 2 of *The Growth of Parties*. Cambridge: Cambridge Univ. Press.
Jensen, Merrill, and Robert A. Becker, eds. 1976. *The Documentary History of the First Federal Elections, 1788-1790*. Vol. 1. Madison: Univ. of Wisconsin Press.
Jillson, Calvin C. 1981. "Constitution-Making: Alignment and Realignment in the Federal Convention of 1787." *American Political Science Review* 75: 598-612.
Jillson, Calvin C., and Cecil L. Eubanks. 1984. "The Political Structure of Constitution Making: The Federal Convention of 1787." *American Journal of Political Science* 28: 435-58.
Johnson, Stephen C. 1967. "Hierarchical Clustering Schemes." *Psychometrika* 32: 241-54.
Key, V.O., Jr. 1949. *Southern Politics in State and Nation*. New York: Vintage Books.
_____. 1964. *Politics, Parties, and Pressure Groups*. 5th ed. New York: Thomas Y. Crowell.
Klecka, William R. 1980. *Discriminant Analysis*. Sage University Paper Series on Quantitative Applications in the Social Sciences, 07-019. Beverly Hills: Sage Publications.

Kort, Fred. 1973. "Regression Analysis and Discriminant Analysis: an Application of R.A. Fisher's Theorem to Data in Political Science." *American Political Science Review* 66: 555-59.

Kruskal, Joseph B., and Myron Wish. 1978. *Multidimensional Scaling*. Sage University Paper Series on Quantitative Applications in the Social Sciences, 07-011. Beverly Hills: Sage Publications.

Kurtz, Stephen G. 1957. *The Presidency of John Adams: The Collapse of Federalism, 1795-1800*. Philadelphia: Univ. of Pennsylvania Press.

Lanman, Charles. 1859. *Dictionary of the United States Congress*. Philadelphia: J.B. Lippincott.

LaPalombara, Joseph and Myron Weiner. 1966. "The Origin and Development of Political Parties." In LaPalombara and Weiner, eds., *Political Parties and Political Development*, pp. 3-42. Princeton: Princeton Univ. Press.

Libby, Orin G. 1912. "A Sketch of the Early Political Parties in the United States." *Quarterly Journal of the University of North Dakota* 2: 205-42.

———. 1913. "Political Factions in Washington's Administration." *Quarterly Journal of the University of North Dakota* 3: 293-318.

Lientz, Gerald R. 1978. "House Speaker Elections and Congressional Parties, 1789-1860." *Capitol Studies* 6: 63-89.

Link, Eugene P. 1942. *Democratic-Republican Societies, 1790-1800*. New York: Columbia Univ. Press.

Loewenstein, Karl. 1967. *British Cabinet Government*. New York: Oxford Univ. Press.

Lord, Clifford, ed. 1941. *A Description of the Atlas of Congressional Roll Calls: An Analysis of Yea-Nay Votes*. Newark: New Jersey Historical Records Survey Program.

———. 1943. *Atlas of Congressional Roll Calls*, vol. 1. Cooperstown: New York State Historical Association.

Luetscher, George D. 1903. *Early Political Machinery in the United States*. Philadelphia: n.p.

MacIver, R.M. 1964. *The Modern State*. London: Oxford Univ. Press.

Mackenzie, Kenneth R. 1951. *The English Parliament*. Harmondsworth, Middlesex, England: Penguin Books.

Maclay, William. 1927. *The Journal of William Maclay*. New York: Albert and Charles Boni.

MacRae, Duncan, Jr. 1970. *Issues and Parties in Legislative Voting*. New York: Harper and Row.

Main, Jackson Turner. 1961. *The Antifederalists: Critics of the Constitution, 1781-1788*. Chapel Hill: Univ. of North Carolina Press.

———. 1973. *Political Parties before the Constitution*. Chapel Hill: Univ. of North Carolina Press.

Malone, Dumas. 1962. *Jefferson and the Ordeal of Liberty*. Vol. 3 of *Jefferson and His Times*, 6 vols. Boston: Little, Brown.

Martis, Kenneth C. 1982. *The Historical Atlas of United States Congressional Districts, 1789-1983*. New York: Free Press.

Mayo, Langdon Shaw. 1937. *John Langdon of New Hampshire*. Concord, N.H.: Rumford Press

McCormick, Richard P. 1953. *The History of Voting in New Jersey: A Study of the Development of Electoral Machinery 1664-1911*. New Brunswick: Rutgers Univ. Press.

Bibliography 249

———. 1966. *The Second American Party System: Party Formation in the Jacksonian Era*. Chapel Hill: Univ. of North Carolina Press.
———. 1973. "New Jersey's First Congressional Election, 1789: A Case Study in Political Skulduggery." In Winfred E.A. Bernhard, ed., *Political Parties in American History*. 3 vols. Vol. 1, pp. 65-78. New York: G.P. Putnam's Sons.
———. 1982. *The Presidential Game: The Origins of American Presidential Politics*. New York: Oxford Univ. Press.
McDonald, Forrest. 1958. *We the People: The Economic Origins of the Constitution*. Chicago: Univ. of Chicago Press.
———. 1965. *E Pluribus Unum: The Formation of the American Republic 1776-1790*. Boston: Houghton Mifflin.
McKelvey, Richard D., and William Zavoina. 1975. "A Statistical Model for the Analysis of Ordinal Dependent Variables." *Journal of Mathematical Sociology* 4: 103-20.
Merritt, Richard L. 1966. *Symbols of American Community, 1735-1775*. New Haven: Yale Univ. Press.
Miller, John C. 1951. *Crisis in Freedom: The Alien and Sedition Acts*. Boston: Little, Brown.
———. 1960. *The Federalist Era, 1789-1801*. New York: Harper and Row.
Miller, William. 1938. "The Democratic Societies and the Whiskey Insurrection." *Pennsylvania Magazine of History and Biography* 62: 324-47.
———. 1939. "First Fruits of Republican Organization: Political Aspects of the Congressional Election of 1794." *Pennsylvania Magazine of History and Biography* 63: 118-43.
Mood, Fulmer. 1951. "The Origin, Evolution, and Application of the Sectional Concept, 1750-1900." In Merrill Jensen, ed., *Regionalism in America*, pp. 5-98. Madison: Univ. of Wisconsin Press.
Munroe, John A. 1954. *Federalist Delaware 1775-1815*. New Brunswick: Rutgers Univ. Press.
Namboodiri, N. Krishnan. 1974. "Which Couples at Given Parities Expect to Have Additional Births? An Exercise in Discriminant Analysis." *Demography* 11: 45-56.
Namier, Lewis B. 1955. "Monarchy and the Party System." In *Personalities and Powers*, pp. 13-38. New York: Macmillan.
———. 1957. *The Structure of Politics at the Accession of George III*. 2nd ed. New York: St. Martin's Press.
Nichols, Roy F. 1967. *The Invention of the American Political Parties*. New York: Macmillan.
North Carolina Chronicle or Fayetteville Gazette. February 7, 1791.
Olson, Alison Gilbert. 1973. *Anglo-American Politics 1660-1775*. New York: Oxford Univ. Press.
Pancake, John S. 1972. *Samuel Smith and the Politics of Business: 1752-1839*. University: Univ. of Alabama Press.
Parsons, Stanley, William W. Beach, and Dan Hermann. 1978. *United States Congressional Districts, 1788-1841*. Westport, Conn.: Greenwood Press.
Paullin, Charles O. 1904. "The First Elections under the Constitution." *Iowa Journal of History and Politics* 2: 3-33.
Phillips, Ulrich B., ed. 1909. "South Carolina Federalist Correspondence." *American Historical Review* 14: 776-90.
Pole, J.R. 1972. "Deference Politics in Virginia." In William N. Chambers, ed., *The First Party System: Federalists and Republicans*, pp. 30-38. New York: John Wiley and Sons.

Polsby, Nelson W. 1968. "The Institutionalization of the U.S. House of Representatives." *American Political Science Review* 62: 144-68.
Poore, Benjamin P., comp. 1878. *The Political Register and Congressional Directory, 1776-1878*. Boston: Houghton, Osgood.
Porter, Kirk H. 1918. *A History of Suffrage in the United States*. Chicago: Univ. of Chicago Press.
Prince, Carl E. 1967. *New Jersey's Jeffersonian Republicans: The Genesis of an Early Party Machine, 1789-1817*. Chapel Hill: Univ. of North Carolina Press.
Rabinowitz, George B. 1975. "An Introduction to Nonmetric Multidimensional Scaling." *American Journal of Political Science* 19: 343-90.
Ranney, Austin, and Willmore Kendall. 1956. *Democracy and the American Party System*. New York: Harcourt, Brace.
Renzulli, L. Marx, Jr. 1972. *Maryland: The Federalist Years*. Rutherford, N.J.: Fairleigh Dickinson Univ. Press.
Richards, Leonard L. 1966. "John Adams and the Moderate Federalists: The Cape Fear Valley as a Test Case." *North Carolina Historical Review* 43: 14-30.
Risjord, Norman K. 1973. "The Virginia Federalists." In Winfred E.A. Bernhard, ed., *Political Parties in American History*, vol. 1, pp. 109-39. New York: G.P. Putnam's Sons.
———. 1978. *Chesapeake Politics, 1781-1800*. New York: Columbia Univ. Press.
Robinson, William A. 1916. *Jeffersonian Democracy in New England*. New Haven: Yale Univ. Press.
Rogers, George C., Jr. 1962. *Evolution of a Federalist: William Loughton Smith of Charleston (1758-1812)*. Columbia: Univ. of South Carolina Press.
Rose, Lisle A. 1968. *Prologue to Democracy: The Federalists in the South, 1789-1800*. Lexington: Univ. of Kentucky Press.
Ryan, Mary P. 1971. "Party Formation in the United States Congress, 1789 to 1796: A Quantitative Analysis." *William and Mary Quarterly* (3rd Series) 28: 523-42.
Sartori, Giovanni. 1976. *Parties and Party Systems: A Framework for Analysis*, vol. 1. Cambridge: Cambridge Univ. Press.
Schattschneider, E.E. 1941. *Party Government*. New York: Holt, Rinehart and Winston.
Schumpeter, Joseph A. 1950. *Capitalism, Socialism, and Democracy*. 3rd ed. New York: Harper and Row.
Shannon, W. Wayne, 1968. *Party, Constituency and Congressional Voting*. Baton Rouge: Louisana State Univ. Press.
Smelser, Marshall. 1968. *The Democratic Republic, 1801-1815*. New York: Harper and Row.
Smith, James Morton. 1956. *Freedom's Fetters: The Alien and Sedition Laws and American Civil Liberties*. Ithaca: Cornell Univ. Press.
Sorauf, Frank J. 1964. *Political Parties in the American System*. Boston: Little, Brown.
———. 1967. "Political Parties and Political Analysis." In William Nisbet Chambers and Walter Dean Burnham, eds., *The American Party Systems: Stages of Political Development*, pp. 33-55. New York: Oxford Univ. Press.
———. 1968. *Party Politics in America*. Boston: Little, Brown.
Sydnor, Charles S. 1952. *American Revolutionaries in the Making: Political Practices in Washington's Virginia*. New York: Free Press.
Thorpe, Francis N., ed. 1898. "A Letter of Jefferson on the Political Parties." *American Historical Review* 3: 488-89.
Tinkcom, Harry M. 1950. *The Republicans and Federalists in Pennsylvania, 1790-1801*, Harrisburg: Pennsylvania Historical and Museum Commission.

Trevelyan, George M. 1949. "The Two-Party System in English Political History." In *An Autobiography and Other Essays*, pp. 183-99. London: Longmans, Green.
Truman, David B. 1959. *The Congressional Party*. New York: Wiley.
Turner, Julius, and Edward V. Schneier, Jr. 1970. *Party and Constituency: Pressures on Congress*. Rev. ed. Baltimore: Johns Hopkins Press.
Ulmer, S. Sidney. 1966. "Subgroup Formation in the Constitutional Convention." *Midwest Journal of Political Science* 10: 288-303.
U.S., Bureau of the Census. 1975. *Historical Statistics of the United States: Colonial Times to 1970*. Bicentennial ed., part 2. Washington, D.C.: U.S. Government Printing Office.
U.S., Congress. 1928. *Biographical Directory of the American Congress. 1774-1927*. Washington, D.C: G.P.O.
―――. 1950. *Biographical Directory of the American Congress, 1774-1949*. Washington, D.C.: G.P.O.
―――. 1961. *Biographical Directory of the American Congress, 1774-1961*. Washington, D.C.: G.P.O.
―――. 1971. *Biographical Directory of the American Congress, 1774-1971*. Washington, D.C.: G.P.O.
Varg, Paul A. 1963. *Foreign Policies of the Founding Fathers*. Baltimore: Penguin Books.
Wagstaff, Henry M. 1910. "Federalism in North Carolina." *James Sprunt Historical Publications* 9, no. 2: 11-44.
Wallace, David L. 1968. "Clustering." In *International Encyclopedia of the Social Sciences*, vol. 2, 519-24. New York: Macmillan and Free Press.
Wallace, Paul A. 1950. *The Muhlenbergs of Pennsylvania*. Philadelphia: Univ. of Pennsylvania Press.
Walters, Raymond, Jr. 1957. *Albert Gallatin: Jeffersonian and Diplomat*. New York: Macmillan.
Webster's Seventh New Collegiate Dictionary. 1967. Springfield, Mass.: G. and C. Merriam.
Welch, Richard E., Jr. 1965. *Theodore Sedgwick, Federalist: A Political Portrait*. Middletown, Conn.: Wesleyan Univ. Press.
Willetts, Peter, 1972. "Cluster-Bloc Analysis and Statistical Inference." *American Political Science Review* 66: 569-82.
Williamson, Chilton. 1960. *American Suffrage from Property to Democracy, 1760-1860*. Princeton: Princeton Univ. Press.
Wormser, Michael D., ed. 1982. *Congressional Quarterly's Guide to Congress*. 3rd ed. Washington, D.C.: Congressional Quarterly.
Young, Alfred F. 1967. *The Democratic Republicans of New York: The Origins, 1763-1797*. Chapel Hill: Univ. of North Carolina Press.
Young, Forrest W. 1970. "Nonmetric Multidimensional Scaling: Recovery of Metric Information." *Psychometrika* 35: 455-73.
―――. 1972. "A Model for Polynomial Conjoint Analysis Algorithms."In Roger N. Shepard, A. Kimball Romney, and Sara Beth Nerlove, eds., *Multidimensional Scaling: Theory and Applications in the Behavioral Sciences*. 2 vols. Vol. 1, pp. 69-104. New York: Seminar Press.
Young, Forrest W., Jan deLeeuw, and Yoshio Takane. 1976. "Regression with Qualitative and Quantitative Variables: An Alternating Least Squares Method with Optimal Scaling Features." *Psychometrika* 41: 505-29.
Young, James Sterling. 1966. *The Washington Community, 1800-1828*. New York: Harcourt, Brace and World.
Zvesper, John. 1977. *Political Philosophy and Rhetoric: A Study of the Origins of American Party Politics*. Cambridge: Cambridge Univ. Press.

Index

Adams, John: as president, 4, 51-53, 141, 152-54, 160-61, 176; as vice-president, 54; as presidential candidate, 54, 141-43
Adams, Samuel, 91, 181
Alexander, DeAlva Stanwood, 50
Alien and Sedition Acts, 4, 148, 152, 155-56, 157-60, 161, 163, 176-77, 191
Ames, Fisher, 11, 51, 56, 91, 101, 113, 117, 124, 138, 140, 177, 186
Antifederalists: in colonial America, 28, 29-31; in elections, 89, 91; in First Congress, 91-96, 99, 105-7
antiparty tradition, 5, 9-12, 19, 186-87, 190-91
Articles of Confederation, 27, 178
assumption of state debts, 101-3, 105, 227-33
at large elections. *See* general ticket system
authority of national government. *See* national authority issues

Bache, Benjamin Franklin, 184
ballot, Australian (secret), 43
Bayard, James, 49, 164
Beard, Charles A., 3, 14, 28, 174
Beckley, John, 41, 43, 50, 142
Bell, Rudolph M., 4, 87, 101, 148, 153-54, 195-96
Binkley, Wilfred E., 14
Biographical Directory of the American Congress, 192-97
Bloodworth, Timothy, 108
boardinghouses, 56-58, 168, 177, 182-83
Bogue, Allan G., 56, 183
Bolingbroke, Henry St. John, 9-10
Burke, Edmund, 9-12, 14-15, 40
Burr, Aaron, 54, 108-9, 160-61, 163-64

capital, location of the, 103-5, 106, 173
Chambers, William Nisbet, 4, 16-17

Charles, Joseph, 4
Clausen, Aage R., 88, 238n.1
clerk of the House, 50
Clinton, George, 54
cluster analysis, 3, 60; method explained, 79-83
Colhoun, John E., 165
configuration, spatial. *See* multidimensional scaling
Congress, 47, 50, 58. *See also* House of Representatives; Senate; *individual congresses*
Congress, First: voting patterns, 3-4, 76, 77, 91-107, 171-74, 178-80, 227-33; speaker, 48; leadership, 51-52, 55; elections, 89-93; part labels, 195
Congress, Second: speaker, 48; elections, 107-8; voting patterns, 108-17, 178-80
Congress, Third: speaker, 48; elections, 118-24; voting patterns, 125-34, 138, 181
Congress, Fourth: speaker, 48-49; voting patterns, 77, 125-39, 175-76; elections, 118-24
Congress, Fifth: speaker, 49; cluster analysis, 81, 144-45; elections, 143-44; voting patterns, 144-57, 175-76
Congress, Sixth: speaker, 49; elections, 157-58; voting patterns, 158-60, 175-76
Congress, Seventh: speaker, 49; leadership, 52-53; elections, 164-65; voting patterns, 165-70, 182-83
congressional caucus. *See* party caucus
Constitution, 5, 31, 33, 45, 47, 53, 161, 164, 173; ratification of, 29-31, 89, 91; Bill of Rights, 99-101
Constitutional Convention, 9, 27-29, 32-33, 101, 178
Continental Congress, 26-27, 27-28
Cooper, Joseph, 50
Cooper, Thomas, 185

Cunningham, Noble E., Jr., 4, 41, 183, 186, 189

Dahl, Robert A., 5, 12
Dauer, Manning J., 4, 145, 153, 195-97
Dayton, Jonathan, 49
Declaration of Independence, 26
Delaware, 45, 119-24
democracy, 5
Democratic societies, 40-42, 119, 124, 134
Democrats, Jacksonian, 3
Democrats, Jeffersonian. *See* Republicans
Dent, George, 49, 143, 144, 159
dimensionality, in multidimensional scaling, 61, 76, 79
Dinkin, Robert J., 35
discriminant analysis, 220, 223-27, 228-33
districting, 35-37, 46
domestic economics. *See* economic issues
Duverger, Maurice, 17

economic issues, 26-27, 28-31, 171-72, 174; in First Congress, 99-103, 106-7, 227-33; in Second Congress, 116; in Third Congress, 138-40; in Fourth Congress, 138-40; in Fifth Congress, 154-55; in Sixth Congress, 160
electioneering, 19, 38-42, 142
election of 1792, presidential, 54
election of 1796, presidential, 40, 41-42, 43, 54, 141-43, 161
election of 1800, presidential, 54, 160-64
elections, disputed, 45, 116-17, 119-24
elections of 1788-89, congressional, 89, 91; Maryland, 36; New Jersey, 36; Pennsylvania, 36, 38; Virginia, 37, 39, 91; Massachusetts, 91
elections of 1790-91, congressional, 107-8; Maryland, 36, 107; Pennsylvania, 36, 38, 108; New York, 108; North Carolina, 108; Georgia, 108
elections of 1792-93, congressional, 118-25; Pennsylvania, 38
elections of 1794-95, congressional, 118-25; New York, 41; Pennsylvania, 41
elections of 1796-97, congressional, 141, 143-44
elections of 1798-99, congressional, 157-58; New Jersey, 36; Maryland, 40
elections of 1800-1801, congressional, 164-65; New Jersey, 36, 165
Electoral College, 31, 53

electoral procedures, 18, 42-45, 46, 161, 188
electorate, size of, 33-35
Epstein, Leon D., 15
Eubanks, Cecil L., 29
expansion, as stage of party development, 18, 187, 190

faction, definition of, 8-12, 13-14
factionalism: as stage of party development, 17, 171-73, 189-90; in colonial America, 25-31; in First Congress, 105-7; in Fifth Congress, 153-54
Federalist, The, 9, 13, 101; Number 10, 11, 190, 235n.2
Federalists: origins of, 4, 77, 170, 172, 176-77, 180-82, 183-87, 191; leaders, 11, 48-49, 51-55; in colonial America, 28, 29-31; in elections, 89, 91, 124, 143-44, 157, 162-65; in First Congress, 91-96, 99-101, 105-7; in Second Congress, 109, 113, 116-17; in Third Congress, 126-34, 138-40; in Fourth Congress, 126-40; in Fifth Congress, 144-57; High Federalists, 153-54; in Sixth Congress, 158-60; in Seventh Congress, 165-70
Fenno, John, 184-85
Fitzsimons, Thomas, 41
foreign policy issues, 172, 175-76; in Second Congress, 116; in Fourth Congress, 135-40; in Fifth Congress, 148-54; in Sixth Congress, 159-60; in Seventh Congress, 169. *See also* Jay Treaty
Formisano, Ronald P., 4, 16, 177, 182, 183-84, 189-90
Foster, Theodore, 165
France: party development in, 20; foreign policy with, 116, 135-36, 148-52, 159-60, 169, 175
Francis' Hotel, 57
Freneau, Philip, 117
frontier protection issues, 115-16, 134, 139, 172, 174-75

Gallatin, Albert, 52-53, 55, 57, 127, 139, 156
general ticket system, 35-36, 46, 119, 165
Georgia, 45, 116-17
Gerry, Elbridge, 36, 91, 113, 117, 152, 163, 181, 191
gerrymandering, 36-37
Giles, William Branch, 52, 113, 127
Great Britain: party development in, 12-13,

20-25, 190; foreign policy with, 135-38, 148-49, 175
Griswold, Roger, 152, 155-56, 168
Grodzins, Morton, 164
Grout, Jonathan, 91
Grove, William Barry, 108, 113, 117, 127, 144, 158

Hamilton, Alexander: as secretary of the treasury, 3, 101, 171, 174, 176, 227-28; philosophical views, 11; as Federalist leader, 51-53, 54-55, 107, 116-17, 127, 135, 153, 163
Harper, Robert Goodloe, 12, 52
Hawkins, Benjamin, 125, 180
Henderson, H. James, 3, 27, 29
Henry, John, 57, 236n.8
Henry, Patrick, 36-37, 39, 91
Hindman, William, 157
Hofstadter, Richard, 4, 9-12
House of Representatives, 47, 137, 161, 164, 197. *See also* Congress; *individual congresses*
Hume, David, 9-11
Huntington, Samuel P., 17-18, 171, 235n.9

institutionalization, as stage of party development, 18, 187, 190
Inter-University Consortium for Political and Social Research, 192, 194, 196
issues, and congressional voting, 87-89, 96-99, 127-34, 171-76

Jackson, James, 45, 108, 116-17
Jay, John, 136
Jay Treaty, 4, 51-52, 55, 135-40, 141-43, 148, 161, 172, 175, 176
Jefferson, Thomas: as presidential candidate, 40, 41-42, 54, 141-43, 159-64; as secretary of state, 52-53, 103, 117; as vice-president, 57; as Republican leader, 127, 135, 140, 152, 157, 176, 185; as president, 165, 169, 191
Jillson, Calvin C., 29
Johnson, Samuel, 8, 13
Johnston, Samuel, 93, 125
judiciary, 168-69

Kendall, Willmore, 15
Key, V. O., Jr., 15-16
Kitchell, Aaron, 109

Langdon, John, 125, 181
Latimer, Henry, 45, 124
Lee, Richard Bland, 126, 181
Libby, Orin G., 4
Livingston, Edward, 41, 119, 184
Lyon, Matthew, 152, 155-56, 181

McCormick, Richard P., 4
McDonald, Forrest, 28-29
MacIver, R. M., 15
Maclay, William, 51, 55, 93, 107, 177
Macon, Nathaniel, 49, 52, 57
MacRae, Duncan, Jr., 83
Madison, James: *The Federalist,* 9, 11, 13, 190, 235n.2; philosophical views, 11-12, 13, 31; and Constitutional Convention, 28; election of 1788, 37, 39, 91; as Federalist leader, 51, 101; as Republican leader, 53, 55, 103, 113, 117, 135, 140, 174, 176, 180, 239n.8
Main, Jackson Turner, 26-27, 29-30
Marache's boardinghouse, 54, 57
Marlaire, Mark Paul, 56, 183
Marshall, John, 37, 152
Martis, Kenneth C., 192, 197
Maryland: districting, 36; nominating process, 37-38; Second Congress, 107; Sixth Congress, 157-58; electoral procedures, 188
Massachusetts, 91, 181-82; electoral procedures, 44-45
Middle states, 109, 118-24, 143, 157-58, 182. *See also individual states*
Miller, William, 41
Monroe, James, 37, 39, 91
Muhlenberg, Frederick A. C., 48, 49, 239-40n.11
multidimensional scaling: of Constitutional Convention, 29; method explained, 60-61, 76-79, 237n.5; comparison of results, 80, 83, 84; representation of roll calls, 89, 96-99, 144, 220-34, 239nn.2, 6

Namier, Lewis B., 24
national authority issues, 27-28, 139, 173-74; First Congress, 99-101, 105; Second Congress, 115
New England, 25, 124, 143, 157, 181-82. *See also individual states*
New Hampshire, 181
New Jersey, 109; districting, 36; nominating process, 38; electoral procedures, 43, 44
newspapers, 39, 117, 184-85

256 Origins of American Political Parties

New York (city), 56, 103, 182
New York (state), 25; election of 1794, 41; electoral procedures, 44; Second Congress, 108-9; Third Congress, 119; Fourth Congress, 119; presidential election of 1800, 162-63; party labels, 184
Nicholas, John, 52, 57
Nichols, Roy F., 4
Nicholson, Joseph H., 52
nominating process, 19; congressional, 37-38; presidential, 53-55
nonvoting, 35, 188
North Carolina, 108, 125, 180

opposition: concept of, 12-13, 20-21; politics of, 176-77, 190

Page, John, 40
Parker, Josiah, 127, 144, 158
Parliament, British, 12-13, 20-25, 26
party: origins of, 3-5, 84-85, 107, 113, 117, 119, 124-25, 126-27, 134, 139-40, 141, 145-48, 153-54, 156-57, 161-63, 168-70, 171, 183-91; definition of, 8-12, 13-17, 18-19, 186-87; philosophical views of, 9-12, 190-91; historical precedents, 20, 24-25; in colonial America, 25-31; and regionalism, 177-82; and boardinghouses, 182-83. *See also* party development; party labels; party leadership; party organization
party affiliations. *See* party labels
party caucus, 19, 53-55, 107, 188
party development, 17-18, 19, 45, 170, 171-72, 187-90; in First Congress, 60, 77, 80-81, 83-85, 105-7; in Second Congress, 113-15, 117; in Third Congress, 125-27, 139-40; in Fourth Congress, 125-27, 137-40; in Fifth Congress, 144-49, 156-57; in Sixth Congress, 158-59; in Seventh Congress, 165-68
party labels, 77, 119, 134, 143, 145, 184-87, 192-98
party leadership, 188-89; formal, 47-50; informal, 51-53
party organization, 18, 40-42, 58-59, 156-57, 158, 162, 187-89
party voting, indices of, 4, 60, 83-84, 238n.13
Patten, John, 45, 119-24
Paullin, Charles O., 195
Pennsylvania: districting, 36; nominating process, 38; congressional election of 1794, 41; presidential election of 1796, 41-42, 43;
Second Congress, 108; Third Congress, 119; Fourth Congress, 119; Sixth Congress, 157; party labels, 184-85
Philadelphia, 56-58, 103-6, 182-83
philosophical issues, 172-74
Pinckney, Charles, 163
Pinckney, Charles C., 54, 152, 163
Pinckney, Thomas, 54, 240n.1
polarization, as stage of party development, 17-18, 171-72, 187, 189-90; evidence of, 77, 81, 84-85, 118, 125-27, 139-40, 149, 158, 165, 168
polling places, 43-44
Polsby, Nelson W., 59
Purviance, Samuel D., 187

quasi war, 149, 159, 163, 169

Randolph, John, 52, 57
Ranney, Austin, 15
regionalism: in colonial America, 27, 28-31; and congressional voting, 86, 172-75, 177-82; in First Congress, 93, 96; in Second Congress, 108-9, 113, 117; in Third Congress, 125-26; in Fourth Congress, 125-26; in Fifth Congress, 145, 148; in Sixth Congress, 159
regression: multiple, 220-21, 227-32, 233-34; multiple optimal, 220-23, 232-33
Republicans: origins of, 4, 41, 77, 107, 170, 172, 174-75, 176-77, 180-82, 183-87, 189, 191; leaders, 11, 48-49, 52-55, 57; in Second Congress, 109-13, 117; in elections, 124, 141-44, 157, 161-65; in Third Congress, 126-34, 138-40; in Fourth Congress, 126-40; in Fifth Congress, 144-57; in Sixth Congress, 158-60; in Seventh Congress, 165-70
Risjord, Norman K., 3, 159
roll call voting, 61, 87-88, 96-99, 149, 237n.1
runoff elections, 44
Ryan, Mary P., 3

Sartori, Giovanni, 13-14, 15, 190
Schattschneider, E. E., 15
Schumpeter, Joseph A., 15
sectionalism. *See regionalism*
Sedgwick, Theodore, 39, 48-49, 51-52, 56, 113, 157, 160
Sedition Act. *See* Alien and Sedition Acts
Senate, 47, 137. *See also* Congress; *individual congresses*

Shays's Rebellion, 27
slavery issue, 28, 136, 138, 140, 154-55, 173, 240n.10
Smith, Samuel, 40, 143, 144, 158-59, 164, 239n.7
Smith, William L., 51-52, 57
Sorauf, Frank J., 16
South, 113, 124, 144, 157, 180-81. *See also individual states*
South Carolina, 96, 180
spatial analysis. *See* multidimensional scaling
Speaker of the House, 47-50, 58, 159, 160
Steele, John, 180
stress statistic, 61, 76, 77-79, 118, 144, 165, 237n.6
succession, crisis of, 160-64
suffrage laws, 33-35, 45
Swanwick, John, 41, 119

Tillinghast, Thomas, 145
Tinkcom, Harry M., 184-85
Tories (Great Britain), 21-25, 235-36n.2
Trumbull, Jonathan, 48

Ulmer, S. Sidney, 29

Vermont, 181
Virginia, 29, 91-93, 180-81; suffrage laws, 34-35; nominating process, 37; electioneering, 39; electoral procedures, 42-44
voice voting, 19, 42-43, 45

Washington, George, 41, 52, 54, 77, 135, 141, 157, 160-61, 176
Washington (city), 56-58, 103-6, 182-83
Watts, John, 41
Wayne, Anthony, 45, 108, 113, 116-17
Whigs (Great Britain), 21-25, 235-36n.2
Whigs (United States), 3, 4
Whiskey Rebellion, 41, 134-35, 176
Willetts, Peter, 83
Williams, John, 119

XYZ affair, 152-53

Young, Alfred F., 119, 184
Young, James Sterling, 50, 51-53, 55, 56-58, 182-83

www.ingramcontent.com/pod-product-compliance
Lightning Source LLC
Chambersburg PA
CBHW021837220426
43663CB00005B/284